ELECTRIFICATION
BY GE

BULLETIN 116

CENTRAL ELECTRIC RAILFANS' ASSOCIATION.

CERA Bulletins are technical, educational references prepared as historical projects by members of Central Electric Railfans' Association, working without salary in the interest of the subject as a hobby. This Bulletin is consistent with the stated purpose of the corporation: To foster the study of the history, equipment and operation of electric railways.

CERA wishes to express its appreciation to General Electric Co. for granting us permission to reprint this material on mainline and suburban electrifications. Many of these articles had a very limited printing and have been out-of-print for many years. We wish to thank G.E. for granting us the opportunity to give wider circulation to these most interesting technical and historical publications.

CONTENTS

The
ELECTRIC DIVISIONS
of the
CHICAGO MILWAUKEE & ST. PAUL
RAILWAY

GENERAL ELECTRIC COMPANY
SCHENECTADY, N. Y.

NOVEMBER, 1927

BULLETIN GEA-150A

The "Olympian" in the Cascades

*"   .   .   .   .   .   . No grinding,
no jerking, no puffing, no pulling, no straining,
no disturbed slumbers—just a keen sense of
moving swiftly, of being propelled by power
vastly in excess of requirements. You ride
with ease—you are at ease—it is the very last
word in transportation."* —Edison

The Electric Divisions of the Chicago, Milwaukee & St. Paul Railway

THE progress in electrification accomplished by the Chicago, Milwaukee & St. Paul Railway is the greatest single step made in this field in any part of the world. In many ways, this work has been unique in the history of the application of electricity to the haulage of main-line trains. With the exception of the Butte, Anaconda & Pacific Railway, no other heavy traffic road has turned to electricity solely for the purpose of reducing operating costs and for expediting traffic over its lines. In earlier projects such as the Baltimore & Ohio Belt line electrification, the Cascade Tunnel on the Great Northern Railway, the New York, New Haven & Hartford and the New York Central lines entering New York City, the Hoosac Tunnel section of the Boston & Maine Railroad, and others, electrification was undertaken as a necessity because of tunnel and terminal operation which made the use of steam locomotives extremely objectionable, if not impossible.

On no other steam road are electric locomotives used over more than one division. The full economies of electrical operation, therefore, have not previously been demonstrated because of the necessary duplication of steam and electric equipments.

The initial electrification of the Chicago, Milwaukee & St. Paul Railway included the conversion of four steam engine divisions extending from Harlowton, Montana, to Avery, Idaho, a distance of 438 miles. This distance is approximately equal to that from New York to Buffalo and is more than six times as great as any trunk line now operating electric locomotives. Electric service was started during the month of December, 1915, and was gradually extended over the entire Rocky Mountain and Missoula divisions, steam engines being entirely superseded about a year later. At this time there were 42 main-line freight and passenger locomotives in operation and two switching locomotives, these machines replacing 112 steam locomotives of various types used just prior to the beginning of electrification. Because of conditions arising from the war and the closing of the Panama Canal, the traffic over this section of main-line transcontinental road was immensely increased, and much more motive power was required during initial electrical operation than during the previous year.

The Electrified Divisions

In traversing the Rocky Mountain district, the tracks of this system include many long grades and short-radius curves. In crossing the three mountain ranges, there are several grades of one per cent or more, the most difficult of which is the 21-mile, two per cent grade between Piedmont and Donald and the longest, the 49-mile, one per cent grade ascending the west slope of the Belt Mountains. The maximum curvature is 10 degrees and there are many sections where this maximum is reached. There are also numerous tunnels in the electric zone, 36 in all, the longest being the St. Paul Pass Tunnel, over 1½ miles in length, piercing the ridge of the Bitter Root Mountains. In the winter, the heavy snows in the Bitter Root Mountains make the problem of train movement most difficult, and winter temperatures as low as minus 40 deg. F. caused serious delays under steam operation through engine failure or inability to make steam.

FREIGHT TRAIN ASCENDING TWO PER CENT GRADE IN THE ROCKIES

Coast and Columbia Divisions

Electrical operation began during the fall of 1919 on the Coast and Columbia Divisions of the Chicago, Milwaukee & St. Paul Railway, extending from Othello, Washington, to the Pacific Coast, and a ten-mile line between Black River and Seattle was placed in operation in 1927, making a total of 218 miles. Pusher service was first inaugurated with freight locomotives on the heavy grades and passenger service was started in March, 1920. In general, the same type of equipment was used as on the original electrification with the exception of the passenger locomotives, which are of the gearless type instead of the geared units as used on the initial electrification. The profile of this division includes many severe grades and a number of tunnels crossing the Cascade Ranges. Westbound, there is an 18-mile, 2.2 per cent grade extending from Beverly Junction to Boylston, and, eastbound, a 20-mile, 1.74 per cent grade from Cedar Falls to the summit of the Cascades.

Experience with electrical operation through the Bitter Root Mountains convinced the Railway Company that electrification of the tracks over the Cascade Range would greatly reduce the delays which in winter running were caused by cold weather and lack of sufficient motive power to drive through the deep snows. On these divisions, fuel oil was used for all locomotives and the conservation of this fuel by the use of hydroelectric power is of national importance.

Passenger and Freight Traffic

The passenger service over this system is provided by two all-steel, finely equipped transcontinental trains in each direction, the Olympian and Columbian, operating from Chicago to the Pacific Coast. Local passenger trains were also operated between Deer Lodge and Harlowton during the early part of the electrical operation.

Freight traffic comprises from four to six trains daily in each direction. The larger part of this traffic is through freight, trains being made up of an assortment of foreign cars, including box and flat cars, coal and ore hoppers, stock cars, refrigerators, etc., varying in weight from 11 to 25 tons empty and weighing as much as 70 tons loaded. Since these cars are owned by many different railway systems, they are equipped with air brakes adjusted for different conditions of operation and in accordance with different standards as to braking power and type of equipment. This makes the problem of holding the long trains on down grades by use of air brakes a most difficult one.

Direct-current Power Supply

The choice of 3000-volt direct current for the overhead power supply was the result of an exhaustive study of all possible systems with special reference to the requirements of the Chicago, Milwaukee & St. Paul Railway.

The unqualified success of this system is attested by M. Maudit, secretary of an important French Railway Commission which spent three months visiting the various electrified railways in this country.

With regard to the choice of systems M. Maudit makes the following statement:

"On account of the remarkable results obtained by the Chicago, Milwaukee & St. Paul Railway with 3000 volts direct current, the writer does not hesitate to formally conclude in favor of the adoption of this system, and he believes it to be actually the only system suitable for the electrification of heavy traction lines."

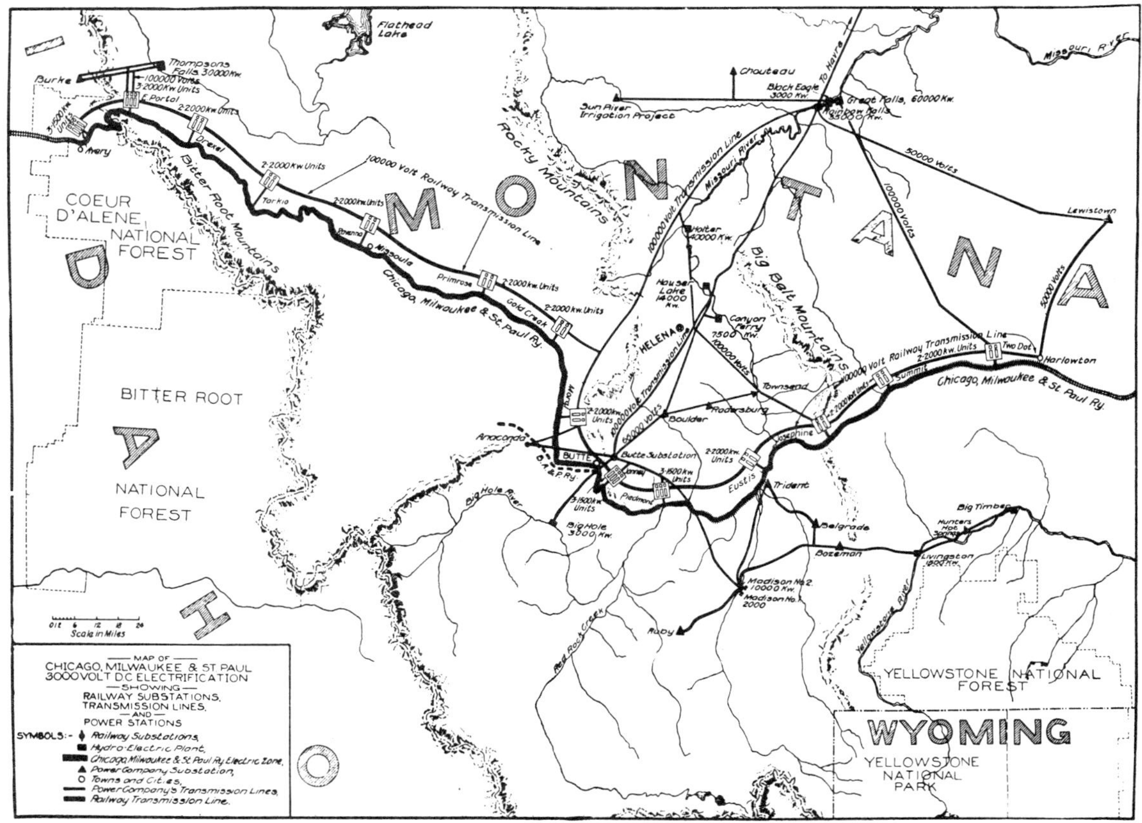

MAP OF ORIGINAL 438-MILE ELECTRIC ZONE

CLE ELUM SUBSTATION—COAST DIVISION

Electrical Operation

Eight years of electrical operation with both passenger and freight trains between Harlowton and Avery has produced operating results fully equal to the expectations of the advocates of the electrification project. The capabilities of the electric locomotive for heavy-grade service have been amply demonstrated, and the two per cent, twenty-mile grade over the Rocky Mountains no longer limits the capacity of the road. Congestion of freight traffic has been eliminated by increasing the weight of trains and also the speed of trains hauled over this section. Freight trains of 3000 tons trailing are now handled eastward over a 1.66 per cent grade and 2800 tons westward over a two per cent grade, a helper being used in both cases on the heavy grade.

The new passenger locomotives are designed to handle 12-car trains weighing 960 tons trailing and they have been able to run on schedule much more easily than the steam engines. During the early part of the electrical operation, a local train in each direction was operated daily between Harlowton and Deer Lodge. As a matter of economy, this train was taken off during the war period, and the transcontinental passenger trains have since been required to make local stops, the running time being slightly increased to allow for the larger number of stops.

During the winter period, the electric locomotives have shown themselves especially serviceable, delays due to low temperatures being eliminated; and in the Bitter Root and Cascades, where the deep snows cause much trouble, electrical operation has proven much more reliable than steam. Under the present system of operation, freight locomotives are changed at the junction points with the steam lines and at a point midway between the ends of the electric zone at Deer Lodge. Each locomotive, therefore, makes a 220-mile run, changing crews midway. Passenger trains in most cases make the 438-mile run without change of engines.

During the first few months of operation, the late Mr. C. A. Goodnow, Vice President of the Chicago, Milwaukee & St. Paul Ry., in charge of the electrification, said:

"Our electrification has been tested by the worst winter in the memory of modern railroaders. There were times when every steam locomotive in the Rocky Mountain district was frozen, but the electric locomotive went right along. Electrification has in every way exceeded our expectations. This is so as respects not only tonnage handled and mileage made, but also the regularity of operation."

Regeneration

Regeneration, or the recovery of energy on the descending grades by reversing the function of the electric motors, reduces the cost of operation and furnishes a ready solution of the difficult braking problem. On the long sustained grades encountered in crossing the several mountain ranges, great skill is required to handle either the heavy and varied freight or the high speed passenger trains with the usual air brakes. The entire energy of the descending train must be dissipated by the friction of the brake shoes on the wheels. This energy approximates 3500 kw. or 4700 h.p. for a 2500-ton train running at 17 miles per hour down a 2 per cent grade. This explains why brake shoes frequently become red hot, and other serious damage is done.

With regenerative braking, the motors become generators which absorb the energy of the descending train and convert it into electricity, thus restricting the train to a safe speed down the grade and at the same time returning electric power to the trolley for use by other trains. The strain on draw-bars and couplings is minimized, since the entire train is bunched behind the locomotive and held to a uniform speed. The electric-braking mechanism automatically controls the speed by regulating the amount of energy fed back to the line. This smooth and easy descent is in marked contrast to the periodical slowing down and speeding up of a train controlled by air brakes.

The usual speed of the electrically hauled freight train is 15 miles per hour ascending and 17 miles per hour descending the maximum grade, but half these speeds can easily be maintained with series connections of the motors should conditions require it.

In case there are no other trains between the substations to absorb the power generated by a descending train, this power passes through the substation machinery, is converted from direct to alternating current, and fed into the distribution system connecting all substations. The power company's lines are so extensive and the load is of such a diversified character that any surplus power returned by regenerating locomotives can readily be absorbed by the system. Credit is given for all energy returned.

The advantages of regenerative braking are summarized as follows:

Elimination of difficulties incident to the use of air brakes on heavy freight trains when descending mountain grades.

Elimination of brake shoe and wheel wear with resultant reduction in maintenance.

Reduced wear on tracks, especially on severe curves.

A saving of approximately 15 per cent in the total power consumption.

Maximum safety in operation assured by a duplicate braking system relieving the air brakes.

The entire absence of grinding of the brakes, which is especially disagreeable on a heavy passenger train.

Increased comfort to passengers and reduced wear and tear on freight equipment, owing to uniform speed on grades.

WASHINGTON WATER POWER DEVELOPMENT AT LITTLE FALLS, SPOKANE, WASH.

Electric Equipment

The Chicago, Milwaukee & St. Paul electrification is operated from hydroelectric power generated at the several plants of the Montana Power Company in Montana and at the Washington Water Power and the Puget Sound Power & Light Companies in Washington. Energy is transmitted from the point of purchase over the Railway Company's transmission lines at 100,000 volts, 3-phase, 60 cycles to the several substations and converted to 3000 volts direct current for distribution over a catenary trolley system.

Motive Power

The main line locomotives furnished for the initial 440-mile electrification in Montana were of uniform design, except that 30 units were geared for freight and 12 for passenger speeds. The passenger units were also equipped with oil-fired steam boilers for train heating. This type of engine, however, was distinctly a freight design and all have now been changed over for freight service. To replace the original passenger engines and to handle passenger trains on the Cascade electrification, 15 new passenger locomotives were purchased, making the complete motive power for the electric zone as follows. Additional data are included in the data section. (Pages 36, 37, and 39.)

ELECTRIC LOCOMOTIVES

Type	WEIGHT TONS		No.	Date Put in Service	Manufacturer
	Total	on Drivers			
Main line freight............	288	225	42	1916-17	G. E. Co.
Main line passenger.........	260	229	5	1920	G. E. Co.
Main line passenger.........	300	189 .	10	1920	W. E. & M. Co.
Switchers.................	70	70	2	1917-18	G. E. Co.
Switchers.................	70	70	2	1919-20	G. E. Co.

ONE OF THE FIVE 260-TON GEARLESS LOCOMOTIVES WHICH HANDLE ALL PASSENGER TRAINS
ON THE COAST AND COLUMBIA DIVISIONS

Electric Freight Locomotives

The main-line freight locomotives are constructed in two units, permanently coupled together, the halves being duplicates, each capable of independent operation.

The railway company has taken advantage of this feature, and a few of these units have been separated into half units supplied with suitable draw-bars and couplers for use in light freight service, on construction trains, and on snow-plows. The main-line electric locomotive in freight service has a total weight of 288 tons, a running tractive force of 85,000 pounds, and a starting tractive force of 136,000 pounds. These figures are con-

TYPE OF OIL-BURNING MALLET LOCOMOTIVE FORMERLY USED ON THE WESTERN DIVISIONS

GE-253-A 1500/3000-VOLT MOTOR

trasted with the capacity of the heavy Mallet steam locomotive weighing 278 tons with tender, which has a maximum tractive force at starting of 76,200 pounds. There are 30 main-line freight locomotives on the Montana Divisions and 12 similar units on the Coast Divisions. The latter were originally equipped with passenger gear ratios and handled the main line trains until replaced by new passenger engines. These locomotives were the first to be operated at a potential as high as 3000 volts and the first to use direct-current regeneration. The freight locomotives haul a 2500-ton trailing train at a speed of approximately 16 m.p.h. on all grades up to and including one per cent. On two per cent grades the trailing load was originally limited to 1250 tons, although this figure has been increased to 1400 tons in actual operation.

Motors and Control

The freight locomotives are equipped with eight Type GE-253-A 1500-volt motors insulated for 3000 volts to the ground. Each motor has a one-hour rating of 430 h.p. and a continuous rating of 375 h.p., making a normal rating for the locomotive of 3440 h.p. and a continuous rating of 3000 h.p.

Each motor is twin-geared to its driving axle in the same manner as on the Butte, Anaconda & Pacific, Detroit River Tunnel, and Baltimore & Ohio locomotives, a pinion being mounted on each end of the armature shaft. Ample flexibility is obtained by the use of a spring gear and a spring nose suspension which minimize the effect of all shocks and also reduce gear wear to the minimum. The motor is of the commutating pole type with longitudinal ventilating ducts in the armature for forced ventilation from a blower in the cab.

Control Equipment

The control equipment is the well-known Sprague General Electric Type "M" arranged for multiple unit operation. The

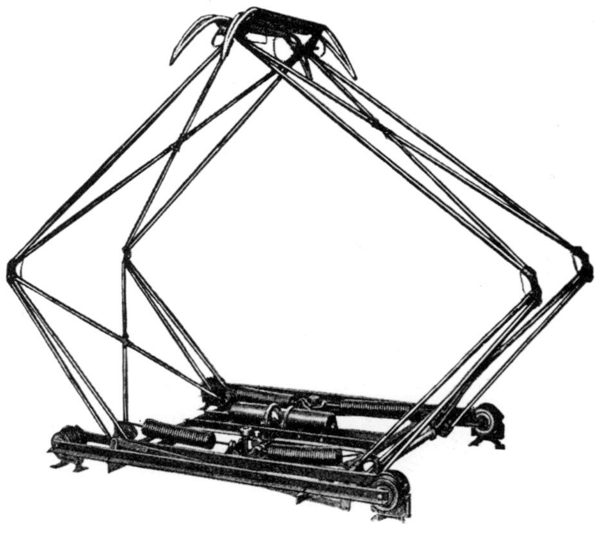

SLIDING PANTOGRAPH TROLLEY

main 3000-volt control switches are mounted in steel compartments in the center of each locomotive cab with convenient aisles for inspection and repair. These switches are actuated from the master controller by a 125-volt control circuit furnished by the motor-generator set. One of these sets is located in each half of the locomotive and consists of a double-commutator, 3000-volt d-c. motor, a small control generator, and a double-commutator, 250-volt generator which is used for regenerative braking. This generator is also utilized when hauling passenger trains for charging the train-lighting storage batteries. Two slip rings are also provided on the control generator for supplying alternating current at low voltage for operation of the headlights. On the end of the motor-generator shaft is a blower which supplies forced ventilation to the four traction motors on each half unit. Current is taken from the trolley wire by a pantograph collector, one of which

INTERIOR OF FREIGHT LOCOMOTIVE CAB

is mounted on each half of the locomotive. This collector is of the double-pan type with a working range of from 17 to 25 ft. above the rail. The contact elements are of the same metal as the trolley wire so that current passes from copper to copper. Under normal operation, only one pantograph is used, the second collector being held as a spare part. The trolley pan is lubricated in order to reduce wear on the trolley wire.

The air brake equipment is practically the same as that on steam locomotives, except that motor-driven air compressors are used to furnish compressed air. One of these air compressor sets is located in each half unit and has a capacity of 100 cubic feet of free air per minute. Beside the air brakes, compressed air is used for signals, whistles, bell ringers, sanders, flange oilers, pantograph collectors, part of the control equipment, and, on the passenger locomotives, for the oil-fired steam boilers.

Switching Locomotives

The switching locomotives, four of which are now in operation, are of the swivel-truck, steeple-cab type, each weighing 70 tons,

3000-VOLT D-C. SWITCHING LOCOMOTIVE

TRANSCONTINENTAL PASSENGER TRAIN "OLYMPIAN" ASCENDING WESTERN SLOPE OF THE CASCADE RANGE

equipped with four geared motors. A single pantograph, similar in construction to that used on the main-line locomotives, is mounted on the cab and many of the locomotive parts are interchangeable with those of the main-line locomotives, notably the air compressors, small switches, headlights, and cab heaters. The motors are the GE-255, box frame, commutating pole type designed for 1500 volts with an insulation of 3000 volts to permit operation of two in series.

High-speed Passenger Locomotives

The twin-geared locomotives used on the Rocky Mountain electrification were primarily designed for freight service, and the twelve passenger locomotives originally operated on these divisions have therefore been utilized by changing the gear ratio for freight service on the Coast Divisions.

For passenger service on the Coast Divisions, a new gearless locomotive has been designed, embracing the principal features of the New York Central gearless engines. These locomotives are equipped with twelve driving axles and a guiding axle at each end. The armature is mounted directly upon each axle and the fields are carried upon the truck springs, so that there is full freedom for vertical play of the armature between them. The locomotives are guaranteed to haul a twelve-car train weighing 960 tons up a two per cent grade at a speed of 25 m.p.h. The total weight of the locomotive is 521,000 pounds with 457,800 pounds on the driving axles.

The control equipment is in most respects similar to that used on the freight locomotives except that the motor-generator set for regeneration is eliminated and four of the traction motors are utilized to furnish the necessary excitation while regenerating on the down grades. A storage battery is also provided for furnishing lights and auxiliary circuits.

The cab arrangement is somewhat novel, the operator's position being near the center of the locomotive and the control apparatus located under a rounded hood at each end. A center cab is provided between the two operating positions, in which the train heating apparatus is located. Double pan type collectors, similar to those used on the original units, are installed over each of the operating cabs.

EAST PORTAL SUBSTATION AND OPERATORS' BUNGALOWS. THIS TYPE OF ROOF CONSTRUCTION IS
NECESSARY BECAUSE OF HEAVY SNOW FALLS

Substations

On the original electrification, there are fourteen substations, each equipped with 100,000-volt/2300-volt transformers and either two or three synchronous motor-generator sets transforming to 3000 volts direct current. These stations are distributed along the route at average intervals of 32 miles. The synchronous motors operate at 2300 volts, driving two 1500-volt, direct-current generators, connected permanently in series. The fields of both the synchronous motors and the direct-current generators are separately excited by small direct-current generators mounted at either end of the set.

The substations on the Missoula and Rocky Mountain Divisions have been in operation since 1915, and have given unqualified satisfaction. In specifying equipment for the Cascade electrification, the original installation was recommended throughout, with the exception of a few minor details mentioned below.

Some of the important features of this equipment are:

1. Design of motor-generator sets for heavy overloads, both for direct and reverse operation.
2. Compounding of motor exciters so as to furnish the most efficient excitation over a wide variation of load.
3. Forced ventilation of the direct-current generators.

All of these features worked out with the greatest success on the original electrification, and the principal features have been included in the equipment for the new electric zone. The table on page 15 shows the location and equipment of the original stations.

THREE 1500-KW. SYNCHRONOUS MOTOR-GENERATOR SETS IN PIEDMONT SUBSTATION. THESE SETS CONVERT ALTERNATING CURRENT TO 3000 VOLTS DIRECT CURRENT

EUSTIS SUBSTATION AND OPERATORS' BUNGALOWS

LOCATION AND EQUIPMENT OF THE FOURTEEN ORIGINAL SUBSTATIONS

Station	Miles from Harlowton	No. and Size of Units in Kilowatts	Substation Capacity in Kilowatts
Two Dot	12	2–2000	4000
Summit	45.6	2–2000	4000
Josephine	75.8	2–2000	4000
Eustis	105.8	2–2000	4000
Piedmont	148.5	3–1500	4500
Janney	175.9	3–1500	4500
Morel	209.3	2–2000	4000
Gold Creek	244.9	2–2000	4000
Ravenna	277.6	2–2000	4000
Primrose	315.4	2–2000	4000
Tarkio	352	2–2000	4000
Drexel	390.1	2–2000	4000
East Portal	413.9	3–2000	6000
Avery	437.6	3–1500	4500
TOTALS	. . . . . .	32	59,500

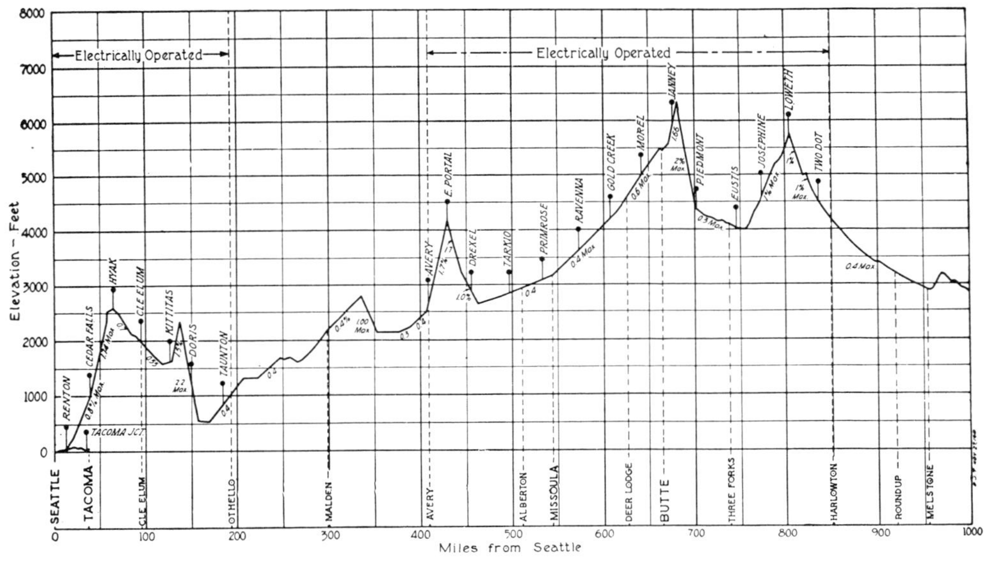

PROFILE, C., M. & ST. P. RY., HARLOWTON, MONT., TO SEATTLE AND TACOMA, WASH.

LOCATION AND EQUIPMENT OF THE EIGHT NEW SUBSTATIONS

Station	No. of 2000-kw. Units Installed	Installed Capacity Kw.	Ultimate Capacity Kw.	Miles from Tacoma	Manufacturer of Equipment
Tacoma	2	4000	4000	0	G. E. Co.
Renton	1	2000	4000	30.5	G. E. Co.
Cedar Falls	2	4000	6000	57.7	G. E. Co.
Hyak	2	4000	6000	79.4	G. E. Co.
Cle Elum	1	2000	4000	108.4	G. E. Co.
Kittitas	2	4000	6000	140.0	W. E. & M. Co.
Doris	2	4000	6000	163.0	W. E. & M. Co.
Taunton	2	4000	4000	197.9	W. E. & M. Co.
TOTALS	14	28000	40000	. . . . . .	. . . .

3000-VOLT, DIRECT-CURRENT SWITCHBOARD—PIEDMONT SUBSTATION

2000-KW., 3000-VOLT, DIRECT-CURRENT SYNCHRONOUS MOTOR-GENERATOR SET—CLE ELUM SUBSTATION

100,000/2300-VOLT TRANSFORMERS AND OIL CIRCUIT BREAKERS—MOREL SUBSTATION

Coast and Columbia Divisions

Eight substations are required to supply 3000 volts direct current to the 208-mile section between Othello and the Pacific Coast. These are located as shown on the profile, page 34. This diagram also shows the present and ultimate capacity of each of these substations, the size of feeders, and the weight of freight trains upon which the feeder sizes were determined. The arrangement of equipment in the substations is practically the same as that used in the original installation on the Montana Division, except that the starting and running oil circuit breakers for the synchronous motors are installed in the basement instead of in the dividing wall between the machine and transformer rooms. This re-arrangement affords greater space in the motor-generator room and gives greater reliability. Another improvement is in the installation of the direct-current feeder disconnecting switches on a framework outside the building instead of behind the switchboard. Practical operation on the original electrification indicated that it was very desirable that these switches should be installed outdoors and that they should be of such design as to open under load if emergency required it. Their operating mechanisms are so arranged that they may be controlled from within the building, and they have been thoroughly tested under conditions which will be met in actual operation. These requirements include the successful opening of a current of from 7000 to 8000 amperes.

CEDAR FALLS SUBSTATION—COAST DIVISION

Equipment

The substation apparatus for the Cle Elum, Hyak, Cedar Falls, Renton, and Tacoma substations was furnished entirely by the General Electric Company and is in all essentials a duplicate of that supplied for the original electrification. On the new divisions, one high-speed circuit breaker is used for each motor-generator set instead of one per station— an arrangement which somewhat simplifies the wiring connections. The breakers are of a more simple design than those originally furnished and are interchangeable with those used on the new electric locomotives.

There is a total of eight motor-generator sets furnished by the General Electric Company, each set of 2000-kw. capacity. These units consist of two 1000-kw., compound-wound, 1500-volt, direct-current generators operating in series for 3000 volts. The generators are driven by a 2500-kv-a., 2300-volt, 3-phase, 60-cycle synchronous motor. Two direct-connected exciters, one of 12-kw. capacity and the other of 30-kw. capacity, supply 125-volt current for exciting the fields of the two generators and the fields of the synchronous motor. The synchronous motor exciter (30 kw.) is compounded by the line current of the direct-current generators in order to provide the most economical excitation for the synchronous motor over the wide variation in the load. This compounding also assists in the regulation of the alternating-current line voltage by operating at a lagging power-factor on light loads and at a leading power-factor on heavy loads.

The main motor-generator sets are cooled by external automatic blower equipments which are not started until the load reaches a value sufficient to produce a pre-determined heating. The blowers are again shut down as soon as the load is reduced to an amount sufficient to lower the temperature below this value. This arrangement greatly increases the all-day efficiency, as the average load will probably be slightly below that necessary to operate the blower equipments.

These sets are designed to operate under 300 per cent load for 5 minutes either as straight synchronous motor-generator sets or operating inverted under regenerated current.

The transformers are of 2500-kv-a. capacity, each oil insulated, self-cooled, wound for 102,000-volt Y primary and 2400-volt delta secondary with one-half voltage starting taps. They are of the circular disk core type with the windings mounted on three vertical

TRANSCONTINENTAL PASSENGER TRAIN "OLYMPIAN" IN THE ROCKIES BEFORE ELECTRIFICATION

VIEW OF TRACK FROM CAB OF PASSENGER LOCOMOTIVE

members of the core. The high-tension winding is divided into 44 sections per leg, insuring a low voltage between sections and thorough ventilation of the coil stack. Taps on the low-tension winding give the desired range of voltage in the high-tension winding from 92,400 volts Y to 102,000 volts.

The external tube construction for circulation of cooling oil is used for the transformer tanks, this construction being identical with that used on the transformers previously supplied. The high-tension bushings are of the oil-filled type and the low-tension bushings of the solid type. Both bushings have their ground sleeves extended from the cover beneath the oil level to obtain an electrically neutral atmosphere in the chamber above the oil. This construction prevents the possibility of an explosion due to static discharge, which might otherwise occur.

The main circuit breakers have combined series and shunt blowout coils with a large magnetic circuit suitably proportioned and an improved narrow arc chute which insures the circuit being opened under all conditions of operation. At the same time, a gradual reduction of the current is effected so as to keep the potential strains of the various parts at a comparatively low value. The design of the breaker is most liberal and great care was exercised in proportioning the various parts in order to insure obtaining the desired operating characteristics.

Protection from lightning and surges on the transmission line is provided by one aluminum cell lightning arrester of the latest type, per substation, connected to the high-tension bus with choke coils installed in the high-tension leads of each transformer. The horn gaps, in the case of the flat roof substations which are used where there is very little snow, are installed on the roof and, in the case of the gable-roof stations used in the snow belts, are installed inside the station. The protection afforded by the arresters in operation for the past four years has been remarkable, very little trouble having been experienced from lightning.

High-speed Circuit Breaker Protection for Substations and Passenger Locomotives

TYPE JR 3000-VOLT HIGH-SPEED
CIRCUIT BREAKER

A notable improvement made in the electrification equipment supplied for the Cascade Division of the Chicago, Milwaukee & St. Paul Railway is the circuit breaker protection provided for both the substation machinery and the new gearless type passenger locomotive. High-speed circuit breakers were installed in the original substations on the Rocky Mountain and Missoula divisions, but these were tripped electro-mechanically and operated through a train of latches and triggers which necessarily so increased the size and weight as to preclude the possibility of installation on a locomotive. These original breakers have operated very successfully in the fourteen substations in Montana. The new breaker has been developed to operate on entirely different principles as regards method of tripping and the arrangement of blow-out. These improved features allow a reduction in size, weight, and cost over the original type. The Type JR breaker is tripped electromagnetically and the size of spring necessary to operate the device is, therefore, comparatively small.

In order to protect the substation and locomotive equipment from injury due to flashing under short-circuit conditions, it is necessary to make use of a circuit breaker operating at a much higher rate of speed than the standard switchboard type. Exhaustive experiments conducted by the General Electric Company's Railway Testing Department have indicated that to prevent flashover, a circuit breaker should operate, stop the current rise, and reduce it below the flashing value in somewhat less than the time required for a commutator bar to pass from one brush-holder to the next. On a 60-cycle generator this means a speed of approximately eight one-thousandths of a second. As the standard circuit breaker operates in about eight to fifteen one-hundredths of a second, it has less than one tenth the required speed. On the Type JR breaker all mechanical latches and triggers have been eliminated. The magnetic blow-out has been improved and has a combination of two powerful magnetic fields and a narrow arc chute which increases the speed of blow-out and reduces the arcing space required.

One of the breakers is installed in series with each of the eight 3000-volt, 2000-kw. motor-generator sets supplying power for the Coast Divisions. A similar breaker is also installed on each of the gearless

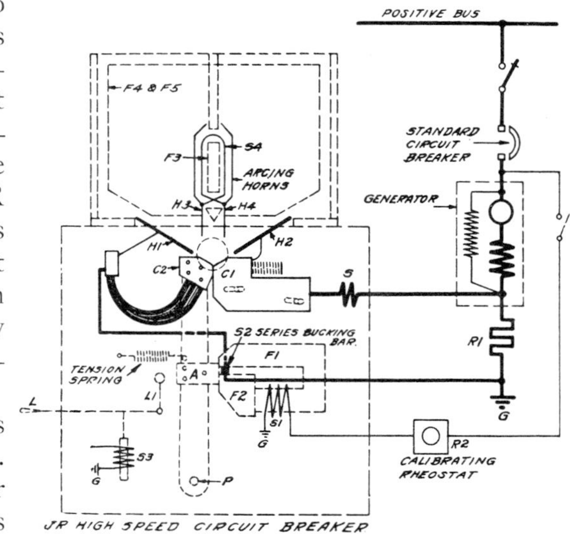

DIAGRAM OF CONNECTIONS

passenger locomotives. In the substations the breaker is so connected that it inserts a resistance between the direct-current generator and the ground, thus limiting the current rise until the standard circuit breaker on the switchboard can open and clear the line. On the locomotives the circuit breaker opens the line current without the aid of resistance. One of the novel features of this breaker is the method of adjusting the setting for various overload trips. The illustration shows a calibration curve for one of these breakers, from which it will be noted that for zero line current, 0.17 amp. in the holding coil is necessary to close the breaker. If it is desired to have the breaker trip at 2000 amperes, it is necessary only to adjust the holding current to 0.7 amperes by means of a rheostat in the auxiliary circuit.

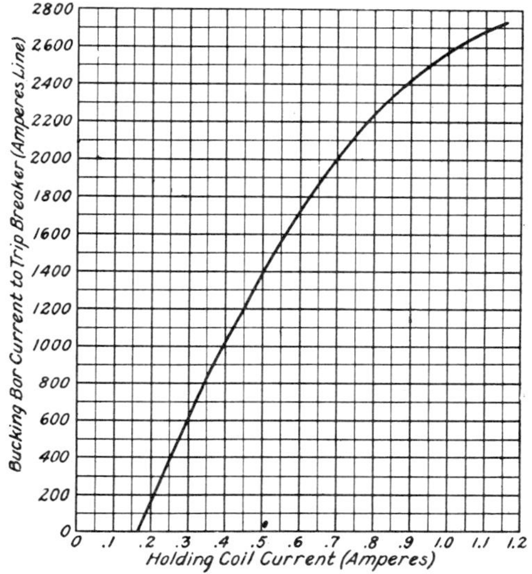

CALIBRATION CURVE FOR 1500-AMPERE 3000-VOLT HIGH-SPEED CIRCUIT BREAKER

A series of extensive tests was made before shipment in order to determine the operation of this breaker under every conceivable condition. The acceptance test alone required approximately 65 successive short circuits of various degrees of magnitude. Five dead short circuits were thrown on the set within ten consecutive minutes, at the conclusion of the acceptance tests, without flashovers. The accompanying cut shows the comparative magnitude of short-circuit current with and without the high-speed breaker. The areas enclosed by the two curves indicate the relative effects of the two short circuits. The curve A shows the line current with a high-speed circuit breaker in operation on a 2000-kw. generator. Curve B is the theoretical line current with the standard circuit breaker in operation.

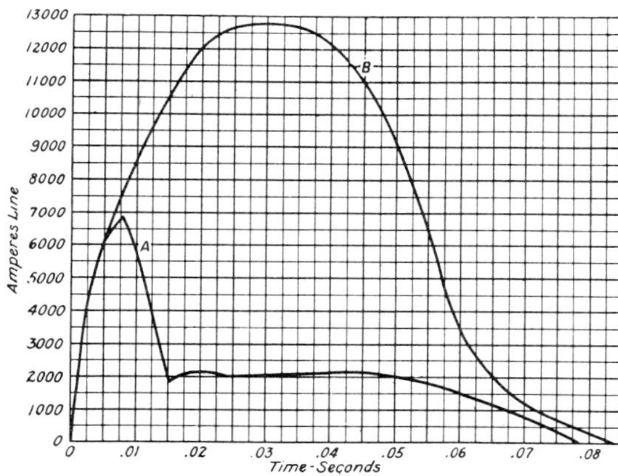

COMPARATIVE LINE CURRENTS WITH AND WITHOUT HIGH-SPEED BREAKER

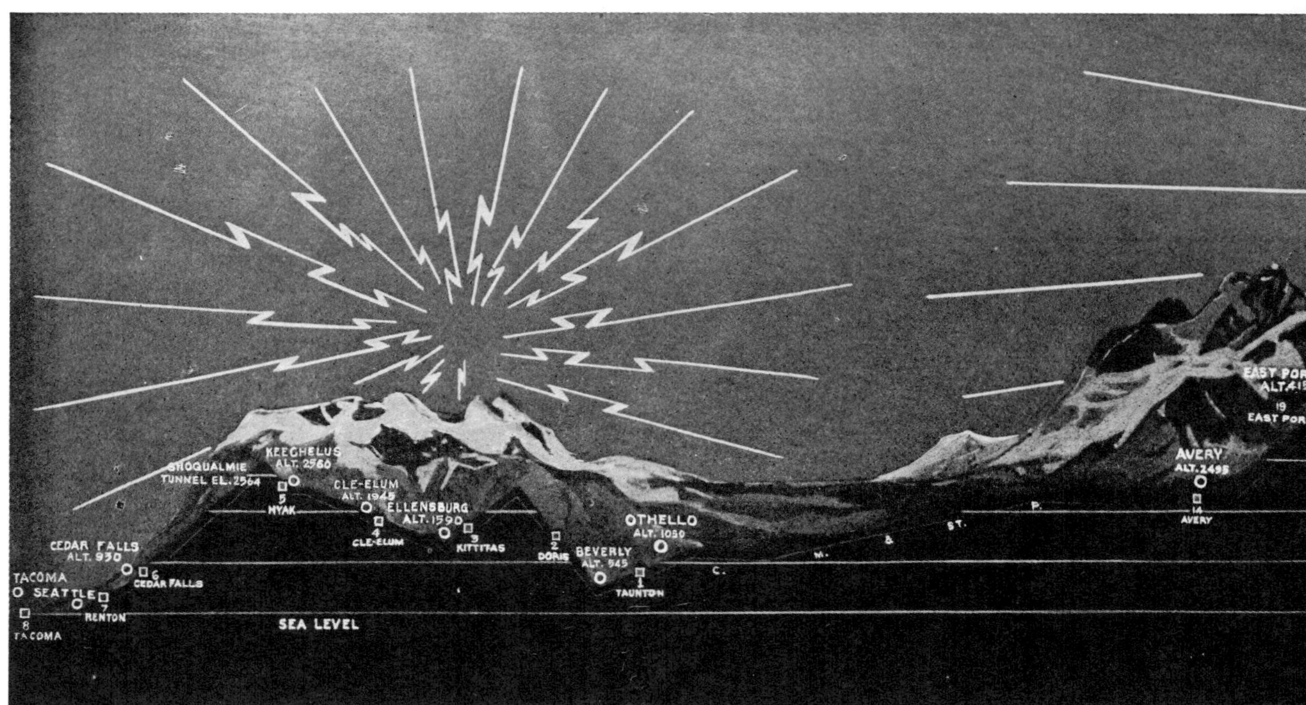

HYDROELECTRIC DEVELOPMENT OF THE MONTANA POWER COMPANY AT GREAT FALLS
ON THE MISSOURI RIVER

ROCKY MOUNTAINS

INTERIOR OF GREAT FALLS POWER STATION SHOWING SIX 10,000-KV-A.,
6600-VOLT GENERATORS

ELECTRIC TRAINS AT THE ENTRANCE TO SILVER BOW CANYON ON THE CHICAGO, MILWAUKEE & ST. PAUL AND THE BUTTE, ANACONDA & PACIFIC RAILWAYS OPERATING AT 3000 VOLTS AND 2400 VOLTS DIRECT CURRENT

Power-limiting and Indicating System

One of the most important auxiliary features developed in connection with the Chicago, Milwaukee & St. Paul electrification is the power-limiting and indicating system. The equipment performs the important duties of limiting the total peak load to a predetermined maximum, limiting the individual peak on any substation, metering the purchased power on a permanent record, as a basis of monthly bills, and indicating at all times to the dispatcher in charge the gross amount of power being consumed by the locomotives. The last-named feature is especially important as it enables the train dispatcher to check very closely the movement of the trains under his direction.

The duties of train dispatcher at the Deer Lodge office include the control of the electric power supply drawn from fourteen substations located east and west of the dispatcher's main office. For convenience in handling

INDICATING KILOWATT TOTALIZER
DISPATCHER'S OFFICE

and in order to keep separate records on the two divisions, the section from Deer Lodge east to Harlowton is operated as one unit and the section from Deer Lodge west to Avery as another.

The apparatus required for the performance of these duties consists of:

(a) Pilot wire circuit of two No. 8 wires extending the length of each division, connecting in series the seven substations and the train dispatcher's office.

(b) Contact-making wattmeter with rheostats at feeding-in points and contact-making ammeters and voltage-regulating rheostats in each substation.

(c) A 2-kw., 1200-volt, d-c. motor-generator set with switchboard and instruments in dispatcher's office for energizing the pilot circuit, the rheostats, instruments, etc., in each substation.

The first equipment was installed in 1917 on the 220-mile Rocky Mountain Division operating between Deer Lodge and Harlowton, Montana. This section was chosen for the initial try-out on account of the difficulties existing with regenerative braking on heavy grades, and because of the fact that the high-tension power is fed in at five different points. The equipment as first installed was arranged for metering the power at five points (Two Dot, Josephine,

POWER-LIMITING AND INDICATING EQUIPMENT IN
DISPATCHER'S OFFICE AT DEER LODGE

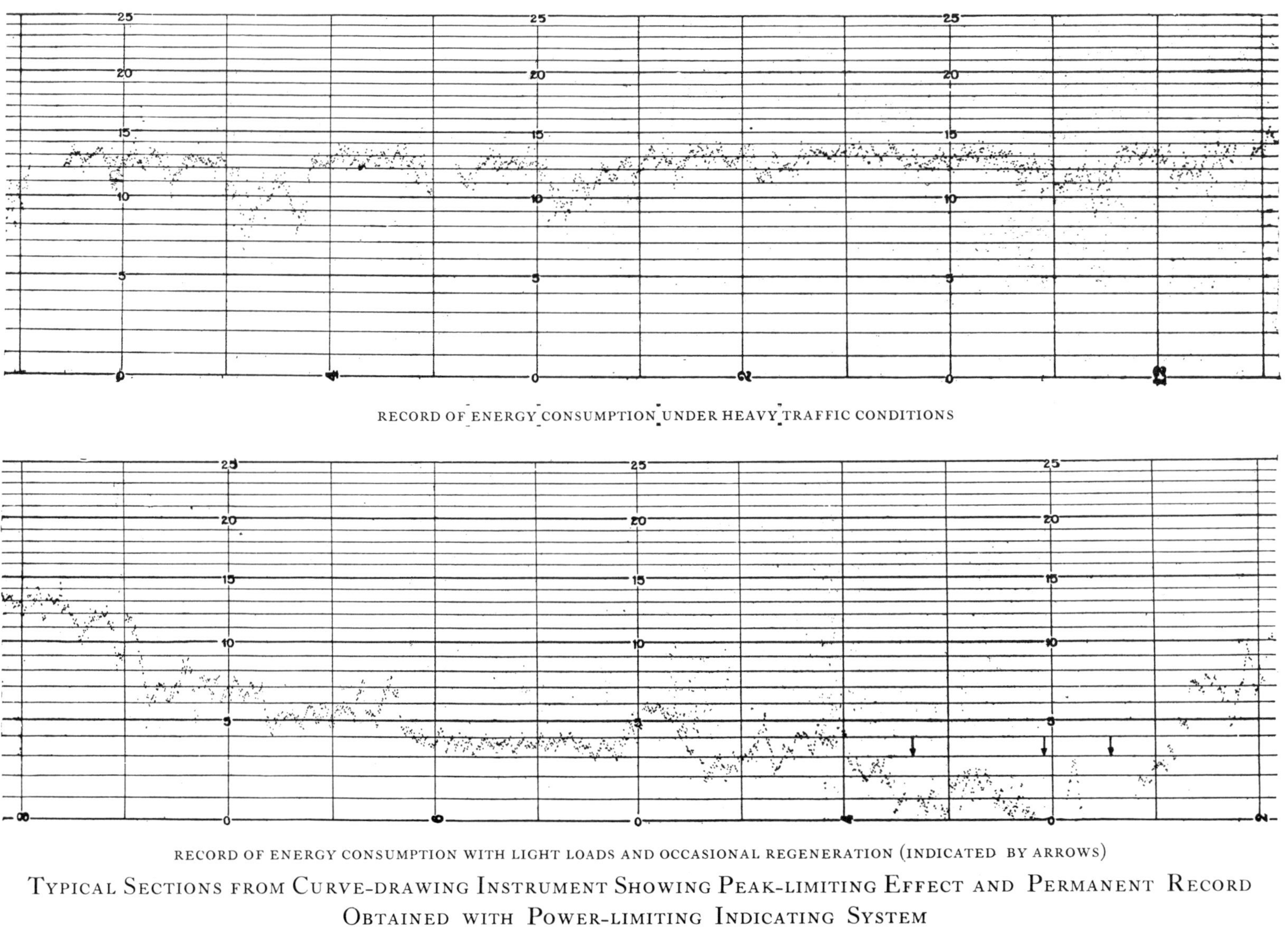

RECORD OF ENERGY CONSUMPTION UNDER HEAVY TRAFFIC CONDITIONS

RECORD OF ENERGY CONSUMPTION WITH LIGHT LOADS AND OCCASIONAL REGENERATION (INDICATED BY ARROWS)

TYPICAL SECTIONS FROM CURVE-DRAWING INSTRUMENT SHOWING PEAK-LIMITING EFFECT AND PERMANENT RECORD OBTAINED WITH POWER-LIMITING INDICATING SYSTEM

Piedmont, Janney, and Morel Substations) on the high-tension side of the system. After the installation, however, arrangements were made to change the meter lines to the low-tension side of the transformer with watt-meters in each substation in order to make use of the railway company's high tension line for emergency switching or line troubles. The Missoula division has only two feeding-in points and it is, therefore, feasible to meter the incoming power on the high-tension lines.

The system is essentially an ohmmeter on a large scale by means of which the resistance of a pilot wire circuit extending the entire length of the division is measured by a constant-voltage direct current, and the resistance indicated on instruments calibrated to read in kilowatts. The total length of the pilot wire circuit on the Rocky Mountain Division is 434 miles with a total resistance, at 75 deg. F., of approximately 1450 ohms. The operation of the regulating rheostats, which form a part of the pilot wire circuit in the substations, is effected by contact-making ammeters which actuate motor-operated rheostats connected into the field circuits of

POWER-LIMITING AND INDICATING EQUIPMENT INSTALLED IN SUBSTATION

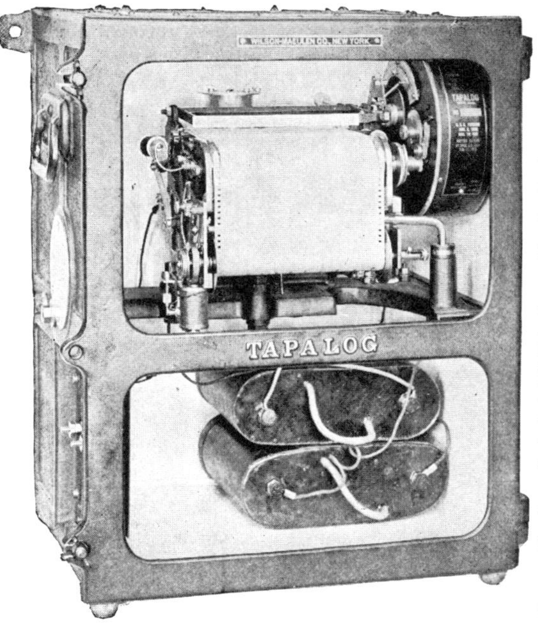

CURVE-DRAWING KILOWATT-TOTALIZING WATT-METER, DISPATCHER'S OFFICE

the direct-current generators. The indicating and limiting feature is obtained by inserting or removing certain sections of resistance for a definite change in the kilowatt demand as indicated by the current flowing in the pilot wire circuit.

In order to record power regenerated as well as normal consumption, a zero-center instrument is provided which necessitates having the resistance for regeneration in the line permanently, while the resistance for power input is used only at each wattmeter. This arrangement gives very accurate indications under normal load conditions. The rheostats used are desgined on the basis of 15 kw. for each ohm resistance and 125 kw. for each step on the wattmeter rheostats. This gives a resistance per step of $8\frac{1}{3}$ ohms, at the power kilowatt setting. The operating

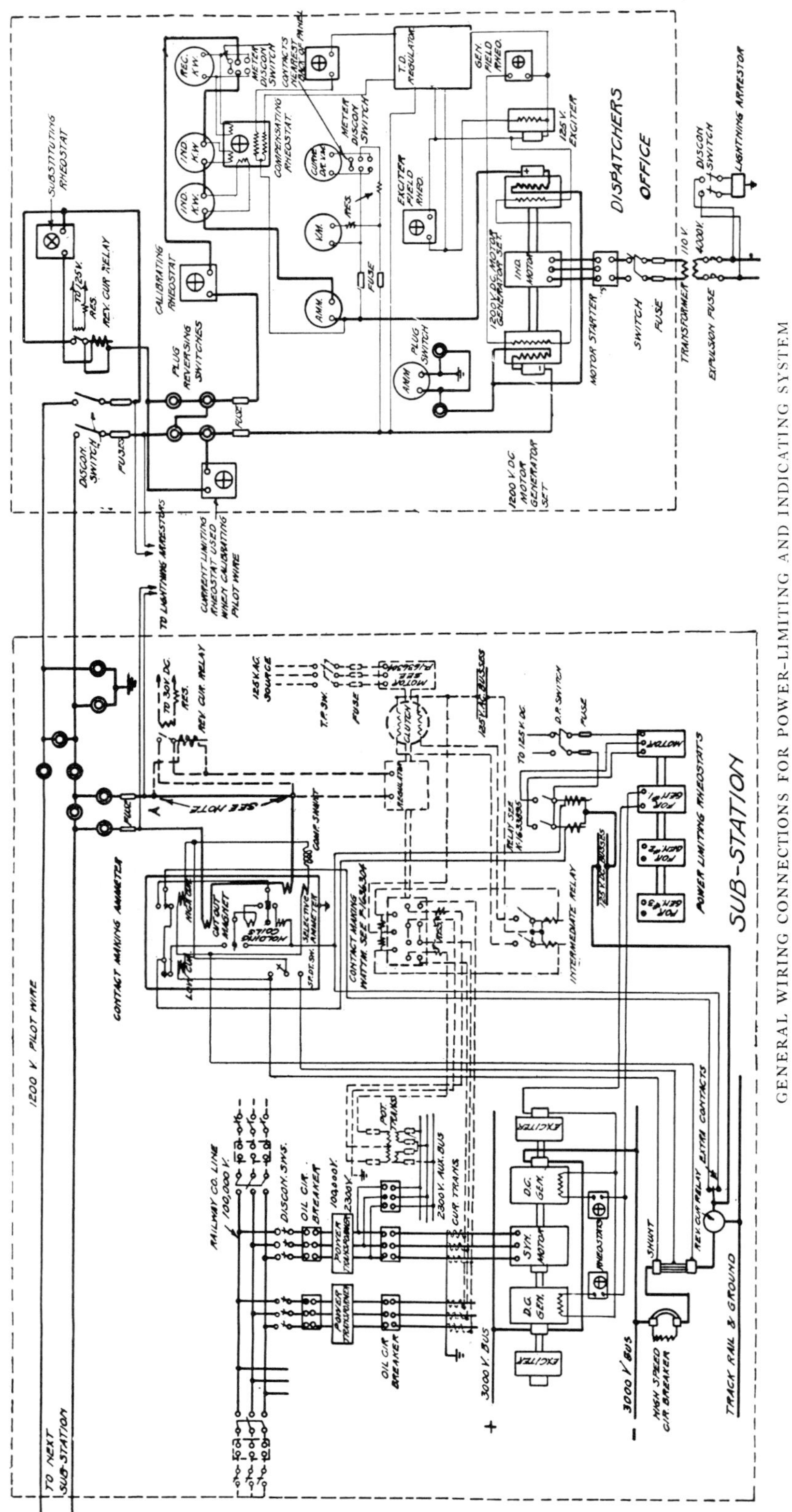

GENERAL WIRING CONNECTIONS FOR POWER-LIMITING AND INDICATING SYSTEM current flowing in the pilot wire is 0.237 amperes, at which point the load on the system corresponds to the peak-load setting.

The kilowatt peak-load setting of the system is directly dependent upon the voltage held across the pilot wire by the motor-generator set in the dispatcher's office. This voltage setting varies from 1200 at the 25,000-kw. peak down to 964 for the 10,000-kw. peak. The currents flowing in the pilot wire circuit for various peak-load settings and for the different loads on the system are indicated in the accompanying table.

CURRENT IN PILOT WIRE CORRESPONDING TO VARIOUS POWER LIMITS

KILOWATT SCALE

Kilowatt Peak Limit	Volts Across Pilot Wire	0	2000	4000	6000	8000	10000	12000	14000	16000	18000	20000	22000	24000	25000
		Milliamperes													
25,000	1200	353.0	339.5	327.2	315.8	305.1	295.0	285.5	277.0	268.5	261.0	253.5	246.5	240.0	**237.0**
24,000	1184	348.5	335.0	323.0	311.6	301.0	291.0	282.0	273.3	265.0	257.5	250.0	243.0	**237.0**	233.7
22,000	1152.5	339.0	326.5	314.5	303.5	293.0	283.5	274.5	266.0	258.0	250.5	243.5	**237.0**	230.5	227.5
20,000	1121	330.0	317.5	206.0	295.0	285.0	275.6	267.0	259.0	251.0	244.0	**237.0**	230.5	224.0	221.0
18,000	1089.5	320.5	308.5	297.0	287.0	277.0	268.0	259.5	251.5	244.0	**237.0**	230.5	224.0	218.0	215.0
16,000	1058.5	311.0	299.5	288.5	278.5	269.5	260.0	252.0	244.0	**237.0**	230.0	224.0	218.0	212.0	209.0
14,000	1027	302.0	290.5	280.0	270.0	261.0	252.0	244.5	**237.0**	230.0	223.0	217.0	212.0	205.5	203.0
12,000	995.5	293.0	281.5	271.0	262.0	253.0	244.7	**237.0**	230.0	223.0	216.0	210.5	205.5	199.0	196.5
10,000	964	285.5	272.5	263.0	253.5	245.0	**237.0**	230.0	222.5	216.0	209.5	204.0	198.0	193.0	190.5
Resistance (Ohms)		3400	3533	3667	3800	3933	4067	4200	4333	4467	4600	4733	4867	5000	5067

For example:

Assume the peak load setting is 14,000 kw. This means that 1027 volts are being held across the pilot wire circuit and that at a load of 14,000 kilowatts, the current is reduced to 0.237 amperes, which operates the contact-making ammeters. It will be noted that the current in the pilot wire varies inversely as the load on the system. When the load, for example, is 10,000 kw., with the 14,000-kw. peak setting, the current in the pilot wire will be 0.252 amperes.

In order to make the instruments indicate the correct load for all settings, the several rheostats are geared to a common handwheel, so that any change in the voltage setting changes the resistance constants of the meters, thus compensating for the change in voltage. The figure 0.237 amperes, therefore, can be made to represent 10,000 kw., 12,000 kw., etc., up to 25,000 kw. by simply turning the rheostat wheel and changing the generator voltage. Arrangements have been made with the power company to base charges upon the monthly peak load, so that one month the peak load paid for may be 18,000 kw. and the next month 14,000 kw., depending upon the amount of traffic handled.

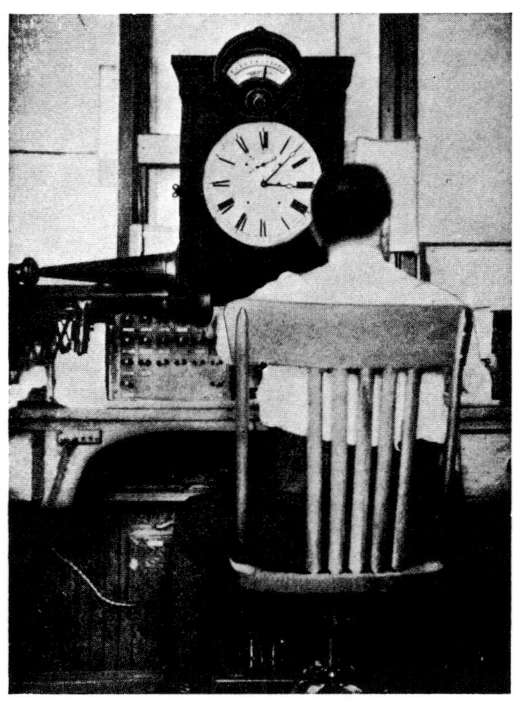

INDICATING KILOWATT TOTALIZER IN THE
DISPATCHER'S OFFICE

Protective Relays

An overload and an underload relay are installed in each substation. The underload relay is calibrated to operate at about one-half load on the station, so that the effect of the load-limiting equipment is confined to the heavily loaded substation while the lightly loaded substations are not affected. The overload relay is adjusted to take control of the motor-operated rheostats at three times normal load and prevents the load on the station from exceeding this amount by lowering the generator voltage independently of the power limiting equipment in other stations.

A secondary current coil forming a part of the contact-making ammeter in each station is energized by the current from a shunt in the negative side of the substation. This coil has the effect of decreasing the voltage on the heavily loaded substations slightly ahead of those with lighter loads.

In case a locomotive is regenerating through a substation, and the power demand on the system is greater than the peak limit, the station operating inverted is protected by a reverse-current relay which opens one of the control circuits so that the rheostats normally operating to reduce the station voltage will become inoperative. With this device the potential is held constant during regeneration.

Measuring Instruments

With the ordinary metering equipment it would be necessary to take the records from the several incoming power lines and add them, in order to determine the peak load on the system. This would be a difficult matter, since it would be necessary to synchronize the records in order to determine the peak load accurately. The instrument used for recording power consumption is a curve-drawing ammeter, calibrated in kilowatts, installed in the dispatcher's office. The equipment also includes indicating instruments and a curve-drawing voltmeter which gives a permanent record of the voltage across the pilot wire. The curve-drawing totalizing wattmeter is of the Tapalogue type, in which a tapping bar, actuated by clockwork and dry batteries, taps the meter needle at intervals of five seconds, making a small dot on the paper at the point where the needle happens to be at that time. This instrument operates between limits of 0.19 and 0.353 amperes and is calibrated for correct kilowatts.

The contact-making wattmeter is built along standard lines with the indicating pointer contacts moving between two stationary terminals. The spiral spring of the pointer is connected to the shaft of the pilot wire rheostat, located immediately above the wattmeter. This shaft is rotated by the clutch mechanisms geared to the driving motor. When contact is made on one of these terminals through an increase in the amount of incoming power, the clutch engages the rheostat gearing and inserts a certain amount of resistance in the pilot wire. At the same time, the wattmeter spring is wound up, through the movement of the shaft. This action continues until the torque of the wattmeter is balanced by the torque of the spring, causing the rheostat to come to a stop. The rheostats forming a part of this unit have the same number of contact points with 8⅓ ohms resistance between points. The complete motor-operated unit, including wattmeter and resistance, is assembled in a closed case for installation.

As a matter of convenience to the dispatchers, two indicating kilowatt meters are installed for each division, one on the switchboard and the other over the train dispatcher's desk. With the assistance of this instrument, the track dispatcher can read at any moment the exact amount of power being consumed on his division and can also note the change in power demand resulting from orders issued to the train crew.

Motor-generator Set

The motor-generator set consists of two 1-kilowatt, 600-volt, direct-current generators, connected in series for 1200 volts and direct-connected to a 3-h.p., 110-volt, 60-cycle induction motor and a ⅓-kilowatt, 125-volt exciter. Power is supplied by a 3-kilowatt, 2300/110-volt transformer connected to the local power circuit. Separate excitation at 125 volts is used in connection with a voltage regulator to insure accurate direct-current voltage. This regulator is of special design in order to take care of the wide voltage limits (964 to 1200 volts) required for the specified range of peak loads.

MAXIMUM KILOWATT CAPACITY FOR INCOMING POWER AND REGENERATION
AT EACH SUBSTATION

Substations	Maximum Incoming Power	Maximum Regeneration
Morel	10,000 kw.	2,000 kw.
Janney	10,000 kw.	6,000 kw.
Piedmont	10,000 kw.	6,000 kw.
Eustis	10,000 kw.	1,000 kw.
Josephine	10,000 kw.	3,000 kw.
Summit	10,000 kw.	3,000 kw.
Two Dot	10,000 kw.	1,000 kw.

SUMMARY OF PERFORMANCE OF POWER-LIMITING AND INDICATING SYSTEMS FOR SIX MONTHS
ROCKY MOUNTAIN DIVISION

Date 1919	Time Peak Limit Hours	Per Cent Peak Time of Actual Running Time	Load Factor
April	43.6	6.4	59.3
May	32.6	4.6	56.1
June	6.1	1.6	56.5
July	4.6	.77	55.6
August	26.7	4.1	54.7
September	65.8	9.5	58.8

Average Load Factor....................56.8

Missoula Division

The equipment for the Missoula Division is the same as for the Rocky Mountain Division except that wattmeters are supplied only at the feeding-in points. This arrangement is possible because of the location of the instruments in the high-tension lines, previously explained.

Summary of Functions on the System

A brief summary of the duties performed by the power-limiting and indicating system as installed on the Rocky Mountain and Missoula Divisions of the Chicago, Milwaukee & St. Paul Railway follows:

1. Indicates total net amount of energy being delivered at all times and makes a permanent record for future study and for a power bill basis.
2. Automatically deducts regenerated power, if returned to the company's lines, or power transferred from one line to another over the railway company's transmission line.
3. Automatically limits the amount of power supplied to the division by lowering the trolley voltage and slowing down the trains, thus limiting the maximum peak load on the system to a predetermined amount.
4. If desired, the equipment can be adjusted so that the lightly loaded substations will not be affected while the heaviest-loaded substations will have their voltage reduced slightly in advance of the other stations, thereby equalizing to some extent the load on all substations.
5. If an excessive demand for power occurs near any one substation, the voltage is automatically reduced on this station, without affecting the regulation of stations on either side. A portion of the load is thus shared by the other stations.

The average load factor per month for a period of 6 months is shown in the table on page 31, which indicates an average of 56.8 per cent for the period. This figure is so near the 60 per cent specified by the power company that the increase above the minimum rate is very small. Tests have shown that should the power-limiting feature be removed, peaks as great as 21,000 to 22,000 kw. would result.

FREIGHT TRAIN AT DONALD, THE SUMMIT OF THE CONTINENTAL DIVIDE

Power Supply

The system of the Montana Power Company supplies an unusually reliable source of power for operating the original 438-mile electric zone. This company operates a network of lines covering a large part of Montana, fed from the main plant at Great Falls, and a number of other widely separated stations of adequate capacity at all seasons of the year.

The system operated by this company is one of the most extensive in the country and supplies an unusually diversified load. Extensive smelting operations constitute the heaviest portion, with a connected load of 95,419 horse power. Electrified railroads take second place with 71,000 horse power; and mines third with 69,000 horse power. This entire system operates at 60 cycles and the industrial power, lighting, and railway loads are fed from the same network. It has been stated that energy is supplied by the Montana Power Company at the lowest rate per kilowatt-hour offered by any company doing a similar business. The

ANGLE TOWER ON 100,000-VOLT
TRANSMISSION LINE

company claims the highest energy consumption per capita. The hydroelectric plants are located at widely separated points and are supplied from such dependable reservoirs that the system operates without any steam reserve. The average power-factor of the Montana power system exceeds 90 per cent.

At several places the 100,000-volt transmission lines of the railway company connect the same points as those reached by the Montana Power Company's lines. It is, therefore, mutually arranged that these lines are to be used for the transfer of large blocks of power under emergency conditions, thus assisting to maintain the continuity of service of all types of load.

The 100,000-volt railway transmission paralleling the Columbia and Coast Divisions is supplied by the Intermountain Power Company, which in turn purchases energy from the Puget Sound Power & Light Company and the Washington Water Power Company. The tabulation on pages 40 and 42 lists the several power plants of the two operating companies from which energy is derived for the operation of the Chicago, Milwaukee & St. Paul Railway.

STANDARD WOODEN POLE CONSTRUCTION FOR
100,000-VOLT TRANSMISSION

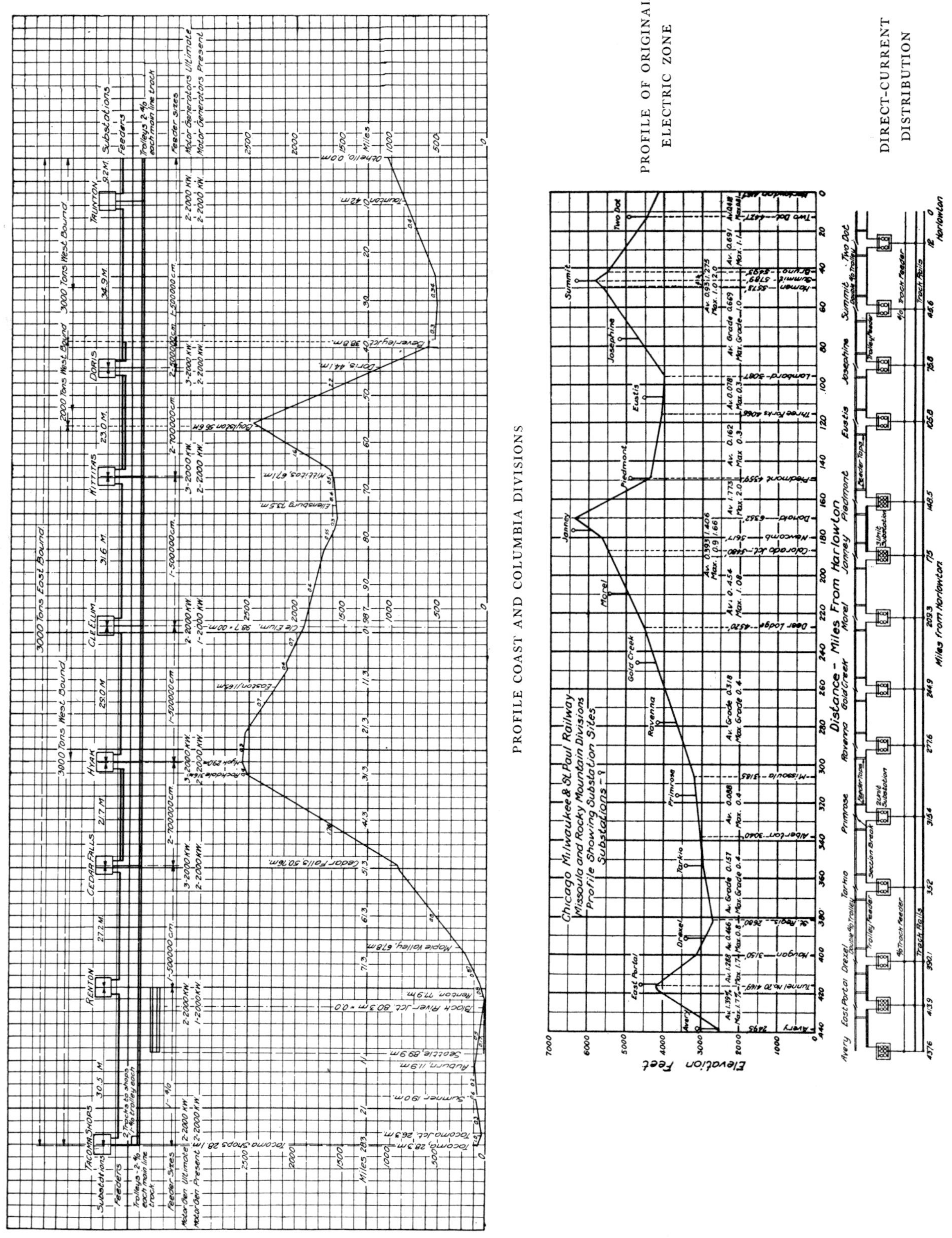

PROFILE COAST AND COLUMBIA DIVISIONS
PROFILE OF ORIGINAL. ELECTRIC ZONE
DIRECT-CURRENT DISTRIBUTION
Chicago Milwaukee & St Paul Railway
Missoula and Rocky Mountain Divisions
Profile Showing Substation Sites
Substations - 9
Distance - Miles From Harlowton
Miles from Harlowton
Elevation Feet

Connected to the Southern system of the Puget Sound Company, which supplies the railway load, are two steam plants with a combined rating of 26,500 kw. These plants are used chiefly to compensate for deficiencies in water flow and stand ready to take on an emergency load at any time. The generating capacity of the Washington Water Power Company is ample for the load supplied and no steam stations are provided.

Overhead Construction

The overhead construction is of the modified flexible catenary type designed by the General Electric Company and installed under the direction of the railway company's engineers. This overhead is known as the twin catenary type and comprises two 4/0 copper wires flexibly suspended, side by side from the same steel messenger, by independent loop hangers alternately connected to each contact wire. Bracket construction is used wherever the track alignment will permit, and cross-span construction is used in switching yards and in double-track work. The trolley wire is normally located at a height of 24 feet above the rail but tunnel clearances require, under some conditions, a minimum height of 16 feet above the track. All of the overhead construction is supported on 40-foot wooden poles suitably guyed and spaced. With this novel construction, through the four contacts secured by the double-pan collector and the twin trolley wire, current is collected in both high-speed passenger service and heavy freight service without visible sparking.

A 4/0 solid copper wire is used the entire length of the electrification as a negative feeder, being connected to the track at suitable points to avoid interference with the signal system. A 500,000-cir. mil positive feeder is also installed the entire length of the main line, except on limiting grades, where the feeder copper is increased to insure proper voltage under heavy train service. The track rails (85 and 90 lb. per yard) are bonded with a single 500,000-cir. mil bond on sections up to one per cent grade, while on the heavier grades these rails are double bonded to reduce voltage drop.

MAIN LINE, SHOWING OVERHEAD CONSTRUCTION LOOKING
EAST FROM CEDAR FALLS SUBSTATION

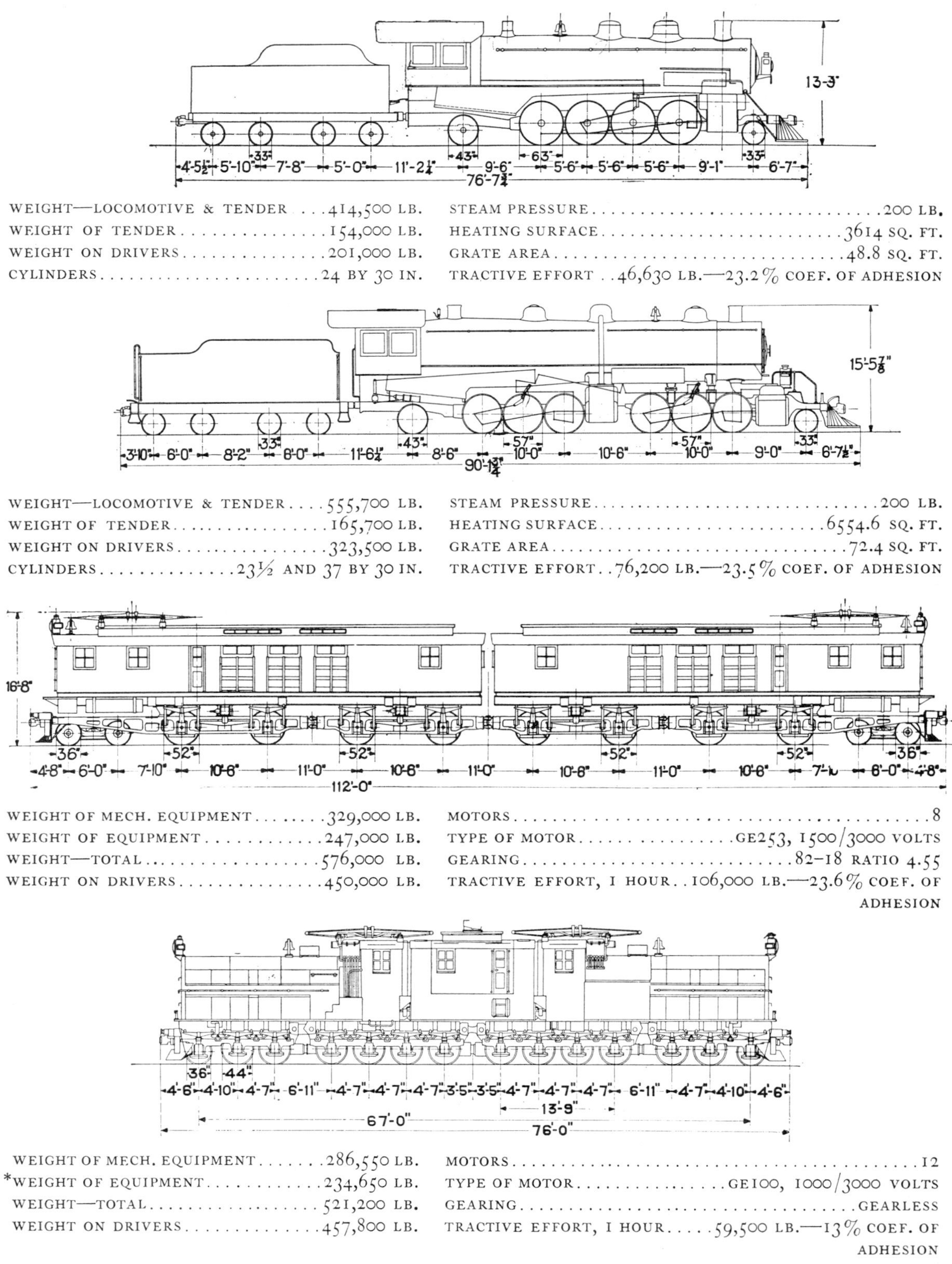

WEIGHT—LOCOMOTIVE & TENDER . . . 414,500 LB.
WEIGHT OF TENDER . . . . 154,000 LB.
WEIGHT ON DRIVERS . . . . 201,000 LB.
CYLINDERS . . . . 24 BY 30 IN.

STEAM PRESSURE . . . . 200 LB.
HEATING SURFACE . . . . 3614 SQ. FT.
GRATE AREA . . . . 48.8 SQ. FT.
TRACTIVE EFFORT . . 46,630 LB.—23.2% COEF. OF ADHESION

WEIGHT—LOCOMOTIVE & TENDER . . . . 555,700 LB.
WEIGHT OF TENDER . . . . 165,700 LB.
WEIGHT ON DRIVERS . . . . 323,500 LB.
CYLINDERS . . . . 23½ AND 37 BY 30 IN.

STEAM PRESSURE . . . . 200 LB.
HEATING SURFACE . . . . 6554.6 SQ. FT.
GRATE AREA . . . . 72.4 SQ. FT.
TRACTIVE EFFORT . . 76,200 LB.—23.5% COEF. OF ADHESION

WEIGHT OF MECH. EQUIPMENT . . . . 329,000 LB.
WEIGHT OF EQUIPMENT . . . . 247,000 LB.
WEIGHT—TOTAL . . . . 576,000 LB.
WEIGHT ON DRIVERS . . . . 450,000 LB.

MOTORS 8
TYPE OF MOTOR . . . . GE253, 1500/3000 VOLTS
GEARING . . . . 82-18 RATIO 4.55
TRACTIVE EFFORT, I HOUR . . 106,000 LB.—23.6% COEF. OF
ADHESION

WEIGHT OF MECH. EQUIPMENT . . . . . . 286,550 LB.
*WEIGHT OF EQUIPMENT . . . . 234,650 LB.
WEIGHT—TOTAL . . . . 521,200 LB.
WEIGHT ON DRIVERS . . . . 457,800 LB.

MOTORS 12
TYPE OF MOTOR . . . . GE100, 1000/3000 VOLTS
GEARING . . . . GEARLESS
TRACTIVE EFFORT, I HOUR . . . . . 59,500 LB.—13% COEF. OF
ADHESION

TYPES OF STEAM AND ELECTRIC LOCOMOTIVES ON THE CHICAGO, MILWAUKEE & ST. PAUL RAILWAY

* Includes steam heating equipment

GEARLESS PASSENGER LOCOMOTIVES

Type of locomotive	High-speed, gearless
Length over all	76 ft.
Total wheel base	67 ft.
Rigid wheel base	13 ft. 9 in.
Total weight	521,200 lb.
Weight on drivers	457,800 lb.
Weight per driving axle	38,150 lb.
Weight per guiding axle	31,700 lb.
Diameter of driving wheel	44 in.
Diameter of guiding wheel	36 in.
Number of driving motors	12
Total output (continuous rating)	3180 h.p.
Total output (1 hour rating)	4020 h.p.
Tractive effort (continuous rating)	42,300 lb.
Per cent of weight on drivers (trac. coef. continuous rating)	9.24%
Speed at this tractive effort at 3000 volts	28.2 m.p.h.
Tractive effort (1 hour rating)	59,500 lb.
Per cent of weight upon drivers (trac. coef. 1 hour rating)	13%
Speed at this tractive effort at 3000 volts	25.3 m.p.h.
Tractive effort available for starting 30% coef.	137,340 lb.

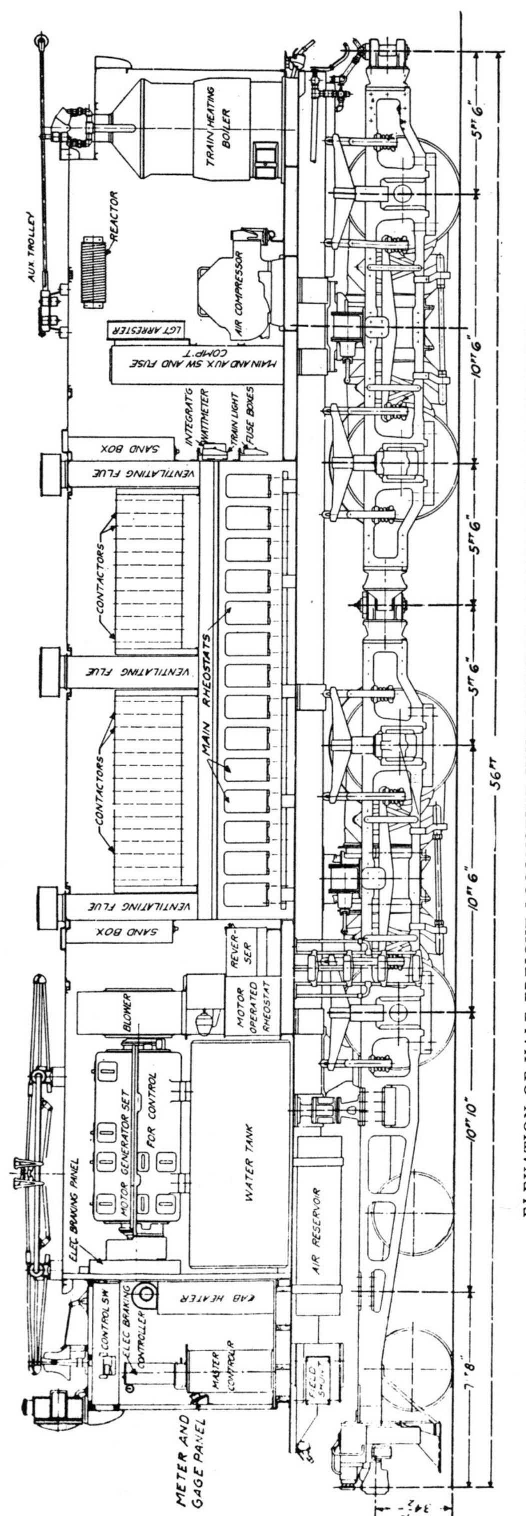

ELEVATION OF HALF FREIGHT LOCOMOTIVE UNIT SHOWING ARRANGEMENT OF APPARATUS

PLAN OF HALF FREIGHT LOCOMOTIVE UNIT SHOWING ARRANGEMENT OF APPARATUS

Main Line Freight Locomotives

Type of locomotive... 3000 volts d-c.
Length over-all.. 112 ft.
Total wheel base.. 102 ft. 8 in.
Rigid wheel base... 10 ft. 6 in.
Total weight.. 576,000 lb.
Weight on drivers.. 450,000 lb.
Weight per driving axle...................................... 56,250 lb.
Weight per guiding axle...................................... 31,500 lb.
Diameter of driving wheel.................................... 52 in.
Diameter of guiding wheel.................................... 36 in.
Number of driving motors..................................... 8
Total output (continuous rating)............................. 3000 h.p.
Total output (1 hour rating)................................. 3440 h.p.
Tractive effort (continuous rating).......................... 80,800 lb.
Per cent of weight on drivers (trac. coef.).................. 18.0
Speed at this tractive effort at 3000 volts.................. 15.5 m.p.h.
Tractive effort (1 hour rating).............................. 106,000 lb.
Per cent of weight on drivers (trac. coef.).................. 23.6
Speed at this tractive effort at 3000 volts.................. 14.5 m.p.h.
Tractive effort available for starting 30% coef.............. 135,000 lb.

Switching Locomotives

Length inside knuckles.. 41 ft. 5 in.
Height over cab... 14 ft. 3 in.
Height—trolley down.. 16 ft. 8 in.
Width over-all... 10 ft. 1 in.
Total wheel base... 30 ft. 4 in.
Rigid wheel base... 8 ft.
Diameter of wheels... 40 in.
Weight—locomotive complete.................................. 143,000 lb.
Weight per driving axle...................................... 35,750 lb.
One hour rating of locomotive................................ 726 h.p.
Tractive effort at one hour rating........................... 24,800 lb.
Speed at this rating... 11.0 m.p.h.
Continuous tractive effort................................... 15,200 lb.
Speed at continuous rating................................... 12.6 m.p.h.
Tractive effort 30%.. 42,000 lb.

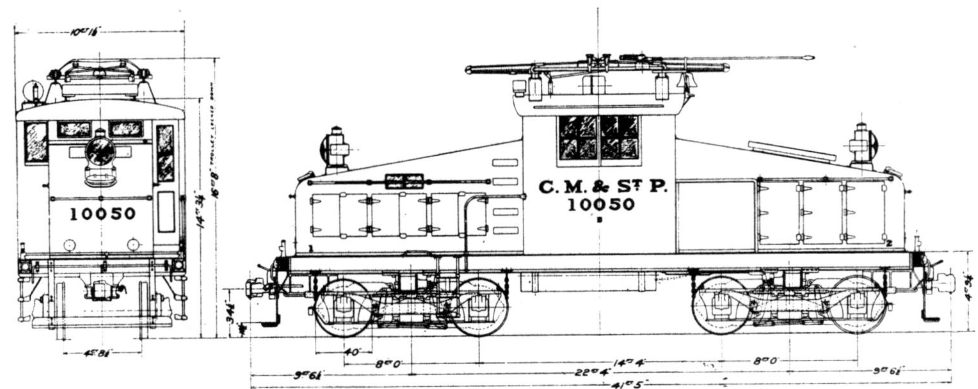

DIMENSION OUTLINE OF 70-TON SWITCHING LOCOMOTIVE

Electric Power Plants of the Montana Power Co.

COMPLETED HYDROELECTRIC PLANTS

	INSTALLED CAPACITY KW.
IN OPERATION	
Great Falls, on Missouri River, completed 1916	60,000
Holter, on Missouri River, near Helena, completed 1918	50,000
Thompson Falls, on Clarks Fork of Columbia River, completed 1917	35,000
Rainbow Falls, on Missouri River, near Great Falls, completed 1910, enlarged 1916	35,000
Hauser lake, on Missouri River, N. E. of Helena, completed 1911	18,000
Canyon Ferry, on Missouri River, northeast of Helena, completed in 1898, enlarged 1901	7,500
Madison No. 2, on Madison River, 60 miles southeast of Butte, completed 1906	9,000
Mystic Lake, 45 miles southwest of Columbus on the West Rosebud, completed 1925	12,500
	227,000

PLANTS IN RESERVE READY FOR OPERATION	
Big Hole on Big Hole River, 22 miles southwest of Butte, completed in 1908	3,000
Black Eagle Falls, on Missouri River, near Great Falls, reconstructed 1913	3,000
Livingston, on Yellowstone River, completed 1906, enlarged 1908	1,500
Lewistown No. 1, on Spring Creek	350
	7,850
Total Completed Hydroelectric Plants	234,850

HYDROELECTRIC POWER SITES UNDEVELOPED

Site "C" at Great Falls, on Missouri River, between Rainbow and Great Falls	28,500
Below Great Falls, on Missouri River (Sheep Creek)	28,500
Clarks Fork of Columbia River, about 30 miles northwest of Missoula	13,500
Madison No. 3, on Madison River	18,500
Black Eagle Plant, reconstruction	10,000
Snake River Falls, on Henry's Fork of Snake River, 20 miles north of St. Anthony, Idaho	22,500
Total	121,500

These water-power plants are so located at widely separated points that there is little probability of an interruption of the supply.

Available capacity of storage reservoirs in service is 589,150 acre feet, of which the largest, the Hebgen Reservoir, on the Madison River, contributes 346,000 acre feet

Data on Transmission Lines

100,000-VOLT LINES:

	MILES
Great Falls to Morel and Anaconda	142
Branch to Gold Creek	15
Great Falls to Two Dot and Harlowton	115
Rainbow to Butte via East Helena (two lines, 130)	260
Butte to Anaconda	20
East Helena to Josephine	55
Madison to Butte	61
Thompson Falls to East Portal and Coeur d'Alene (two lines 30.3)	61
Holter to East Helena	31
Branches, etc	15
	775
65,000-volt lines	313
50,000-volt lines	1,017
22,000-volt lines and less	118
Total	2,223

THE "OLYMPIAN" LEAVING SEATTLE

Power Supply for Coast Divisions

Power for the operation of the Coast and Columbia Divisions is supplied by the Washington Water Power Company and the Puget Sound Power and Light Company. The transmission circuits to the railway substations include the 11,000-volt lines of the Intermountain Power Company. The generating stations of these two companies and their capacity are listed below, together with the mileage of the transmission lines.

HYDROELECTRIC PLANTS OF THE PUGET SOUND POWER AND LIGHT COMPANY

	KV-A.
Snoqualmie Falls, Nos. 1 and 2 (1898 and 1910)	22,250
White River (1911 and 1925)	72,600
Electron (1903)	14,000
Baker River (1925)	39,000
Wenatchee	3,000
Georgetown Steam Plant	23,500
	174,350

WASHINGTON WATER POWER COMPANY

	KV-A.
Spokane, Spokane River	16,250
Post Falls, Spokane River	11,250
Little Falls, Spokane River (1910)	23,000
Long Lake on Long Lake (1915)	55,600
Oroville	4,000
	110,100

TRANSMISSION LINES ABOVE 50,000 VOLTS

	MILES
Intermountain Power Co., 100,000 Volts	167
Washington Water Power Co., 100,000 Volts	261
Washington Water Power Co., 60,000 Volts	745
Puget Sound Power and Light Co., 100,000 Volts	71
Puget Sound Power and Light Co., 55,000 Volts	566
	1,810

Comparative Cost of Electric and Steam Operation

The comments of various consulting engineers and members of foreign commissions who have inspected and studied the operation of the Chicago, Milwaukee & St. Paul electrification have been uniformly complimentary. In view of the great extent of this electric division, the weight of trains handled, and the fact that it was the first 3000-volt, direct-current electrification in this country, the question has frequently been raised as to the relative cost of steam and electrical operation.

Detailed figures comparing operating costs with steam and electric locomotives have not been made public except in two other cases; that of the Butte, Anaconda & Pacific Railway, electrified in 1913, and the Paulista Railway in Brazil, electrified in 1920. The Butte, Anaconda & Pacific Railway is an ore-hauling road with a heavy percentage of switching service. The Paulista Railway, on account of its location, encounters conditions, especially with respect to fuel, which are not comparable with those in this country. Students of railroad electrification are, therefore, especially interested in the report issued by President Byram, of the Chicago, Milwaukee & St. Paul Railway, in February, 1925, detailing the costs of electrical and steam operation over the two electrified sections of the St. Paul. These costs have been adjusted to the figures obtaining in 1923.

It is significant that, in spite of the fact that the tonnage hauled over the Coast Division during the year for which figures were selected for electrical operation was very low in comparison with the tonnage during the steam period, the net savings are very considerable and the study of the figures by the officers of the railroad company indicate possibilities of much greater saving with increased passenger and freight business.

The table below which forms a part of this report shows the net savings from electrical operation, using steam costs for the last 12 months of such operation adjusted to the cost obtaining in 1923, and for electrical operation the actual costs determined for the year 1923. The net additional investment for electrification, amounting to $15,625,739, and the net savings, amounting to $12,400,000, are arrived at after deducting charges for interest and depreciation on this new investment. A detailed summary of the data contained in the railroad company's report is included in reprint GEA-33.

Years	HARLOWTON TO AVERY ELECTRICAL OPERATION BEGAN APRIL AND NOV., 1916		OTHELLO TO TACOMA ELECTRICAL OPERATION BEGAN MARCH, 1920		ALL ELECTRIFIED SECTIONS	
	Volume of Traffic—Gross Ton Miles Frt. and Pass.	Net Savings by Electrification	Volume of Traffic—Gross Ton Miles Frt. and Pass.	Net Savings by Electrification	Volume of Traffic—Gross Ton Miles Frt. and Pass.	Net Savings by Electrification
1916	†1,639,054,000	†$ 1,098,166			1,639,054,000	$ 1,098,166
1917	2,677,097,000	1,641,369			2,677,097,000	1,641,369
1918	2,759,178,000	1,734,687			2,759,178,000	1,734,687
1919	2,894,063,000	1,888,037			2,894,063,000	1,888,037
1920	2,710,745,000	1,679,623	*691,674,000	*$249,003	3,402,419,000	1,928,626
1921	1,812,714,000	658,651	664,238,000	12,363	2,476,952,000	671,014
1922	2,109,868,000	996,485	734,121,000	103,301	2,843,989,000	1,099,786
1923	2,247,102,000	1,152,508	746,405,000	119,285	2,993,507,000	1,271,793
1924	2,129,426,000	1,018,721	691,476,000	47,808	2,820,902,000	1,066,529
Total		$11,868,247		$531,760		$12,400,007

†Tonnage and savings for 6½ months.
*Tonnage and savings for 9 months.

Electrification
of the
Butte, Anaconda & Pacific Railway

GENERAL ELECTRIC COMPANY

GEA-828

THE
ELECTRIFICATION OF THE BUTTE, ANACONDA & PACIFIC

Fig. 1. Standard Electric Passenger Train on Main-line Between Butte and Anaconda

THE Butte, Anaconda & Pacific Railway is, in many ways, a remarkable example of steam-road electrification. Besides being the first 2400-volt, direct-current road in the United States, it is also the first steam road, operating both freight and passenger schedules, to electrify its lines purely for reasons of economy. A number of steam railway electrifications have been made because of peremptory factors, such as terminal or tunnel operation or rapid inter-urban service. This road, however, cannot be classed as an "enforced electrification," since no such special limitations have been the determining factors.

The first locomotives were put into service May 28, 1913, hauling ore between the East Anaconda yards and the smelter. The entire freight traffic was gradually taken over, and since November, 1913, all trains have been handled by electric locomotives. During the first year of operation, the electric locomotives made approximately 430,000 miles and hauled about 4,500,000 tons of ore.

The trains now being hauled by electricity are much heavier than those formerly hauled by steam, and the speed at which they are handled is approximately twice as great as with steam locomotives. The freight movement on the Butte, Anaconda & Pacific Railway handled by electric locomotives is one of the heaviest in the world. Because of the increased weight of trains and the faster scheduled speed, night work is minimized, and a larger tonnage is being hauled than was ever possible with steam.

The Butte, Anaconda & Pacific is essentially an ore-hauling road, the freight traffic from this source originating at the copper mines located near the top of Butte Hill. From the mines, the trains are lowered down the mountain a distance of $4\frac{1}{2}$ miles to the Rocker yards, located a few miles west of the city of Butte. At this point, new main-line trains are made up for transportation to Anaconda. The main-line division extends through a rough, mountainous country, a distance of about 20 miles, with grades as high as 0.3 per cent against the loaded trains and 1 per cent against the trains of empty cars. In addition to the 32 miles of main-line electrified road, there are also numerous sidings, yards, and smelter tracks equipped with overhead trolley, which make a total of 123 miles on a single-track basis.

At East Anaconda, the main-line trains are broken up and hauled up Smelter Hill to the stock bins where each car is run over the scales and weighed. The shifting of cars in connection with weighing and delivery to the concentrators is done by single locomotives.

The Electrification of the Butte, Anaconda & Pacific Railway

Fig. 2. 80-ton Electric Locomotive

The east-bound traffic consists of the return of empty cars to the mines and the transportation of copper ingots to the Butte yards for shipment to refineries over other roads.

Between the cities of Butte and Anaconda, which are located at the ends of the electrified portion of the system, there is considerable local traffic, both freight and passenger. The city of Butte and vicinity has a population of about 65,000, and Anaconda about 10,000. At Butte, the Butte, Anaconda & Pacific connects with the Great Northern, the Northern Pacific, and the Chicago, Milwaukee and St. Paul; and at Silver Bow, about six miles from the city, with the Oregon Short Line.

Train Service

The freight traffic consists largely of copper ore and, at times, has exceeded 5,000,000 tons a year. This material is handled in steel ore cars weighing about 18 tons and having a capacity of 54 tons each. Trains of 30 to 40 loaded cars, weighing 2000 to 3000 tons, are made up at the Butte Hill yards and hauled by two-unit locomotives to the Rocker yards, where 4000- to 5000-ton trains are made up for the main line. At the East Anaconda yards, the trains are again broken up and 1900-ton trains are sent up Smelter Hill to the ore bins.

Four passenger trains per day are operated between Butte and Anaconda, two in each direction. The main-line passenger trains were first hauled by electric locomotives on October 1, 1913, and promptly demonstrated their ability to make better time than was possible with steam locomotives.

Power Supply

Energy for the operation of electric trains is purchased from the Montana Power Company. The generating plant is located at Great Falls, Montana, on the Missouri River, and has for some time been supplying electric power for the operation of the mines and smelters at Butte and Anaconda. Six hydroelectric units are installed, having a nominal rated capacity of 21,000 kw. The power is stepped up to 102,000 volts for transmission to the transformer substation at Butte, a distance of 130 miles, over two, separate, parallel lines constructed on the same right of way. An extension of the system transmits power at 102,000 volts to a second transformer station at Anaconda, 26 miles beyond.

TABLE 1

CONDENSED INFORMATION ON FREIGHT MOVEMENT

	WEST BOUND			EAST BOUND		
	Butte Hi l Line	Main Line	Smel- ter Hill	Smel- ter Hill	Main Line	Butte Hill Line
Trailing load in tons	3900	5000	1900	1000	1ʼ00	810
Number of cars	55	68	26	55	90	45
Number of 80-ton locomotives per train	2	2	2	2	2	2
Approximate grade against load—per cent	—2.5	0.3	1.1	—1.1	1	2.5
Approximate speed on level tangent track, miles per hour		21			25	
Approximate speed on maximum grade	12	16	16	20	16	16
Average trolley voltage	2200	2200	2200	2200	2200	2200
Length of run in miles	4.6	20.1	7	7	20.1	4.6

The Butte station forms the center of the extensive power system operated by the Montana Power Company. In addition to the Great Falls 102,000-volt transmission lines, there are several 60,000-volt transmissions terminating at this point, which form a part of the Montana Power Company's system, bringing power to the Butte substation. At Butte and Anaconda this power is stepped down to 2400 volts, three-phase, and all of these lines are tied in on the 2400-volt, alternating-current bus. Ample protection is, therefore, afforded against interruption of service.

It is an interesting fact that the railway load was taken on without any increase in the high-tension transmission facilities. It is estimated that the additional load from this source is approximately .20 per cent of the railway, industrial, and lighting load furnished by the street railways, mines, and smelters at Butte and Anaconda.

Railway Substations

The two substations already built at Butte and Anaconda were used to house the 2400-volt motor-generator sets, no additional buildings being constructed for this purpose. There are four 1000-kw., three-unit sets at Anaconda and three at Butte, which receive power from the 2400-volt a-c. buses. These stations operate continuously to supply the necessary current for train operation. Each set consists of a 3-phase, 60-cycle, 1450-kv-a., 720-r.p.m. synchronous motor direct connected to two 500-kw., 1200-volt generators insulated to operate in series at 2400 volts. The generators are operating shunt wound and have both commutating poles and compensating pole face windings. These fields are connected on the grounded side of the armature, and the main fields are separately excited from 125-volt exciters.

The 1200-volt generators are provided with heat-proof insulation and, owing to their unusually good commutating characteristics, will carry three times normal load for periods of five minutes, as well as the usual 50 per cent overload for two hours. The value of this feature will be appreciated when it is noted that each electric locomotive unit has a continuous rating of approximately 900 kw., which is almost equal to that of a single motor-generator set.

Fig. 3.   Generator Room in the Rainbow Station of the Great Falls Power Company

The Electrification of the Butte, Anaconda & Pacific Railway

Fig. 4.   2400-volt Switchboard and Motor-generator Set in Butte Substation

The motors are protected from overload by inverse time-limit relays which are set to open at four times normal load. These relays have been adjusted to open under sustained overload in about two seconds. Upon short circuit, their action is practically instantaneous.

Exciters

Excitation for the generating units is obtained from induction motor-driven sets, rated 50 kw. each at 125 volts. There are two of these exciters in each substation. One is used to supply current to the field of the synchronous motor and is controlled by the automatic voltage regulator. The second unit supplies current to the separately excited fields of the direct-current generators.

Switchboards

The 2400-volt switchboards for controlling these sets are the first direct-current boards to be constructed for this high voltage. In general, they are similar to the standard 1200-volt types with increased insulation and special provision for interrupting the 2400-volt current. The circuit breakers and switches are also arranged for remote control, and all apparatus on the panels is provided with ample insulation to insure safety to the operators.

The 2400-volt circuit breakers and switches are installed on separate panels above and back of the main panels and are operated by connecting rods from handles mounted on the front of the main switchboard. These handles

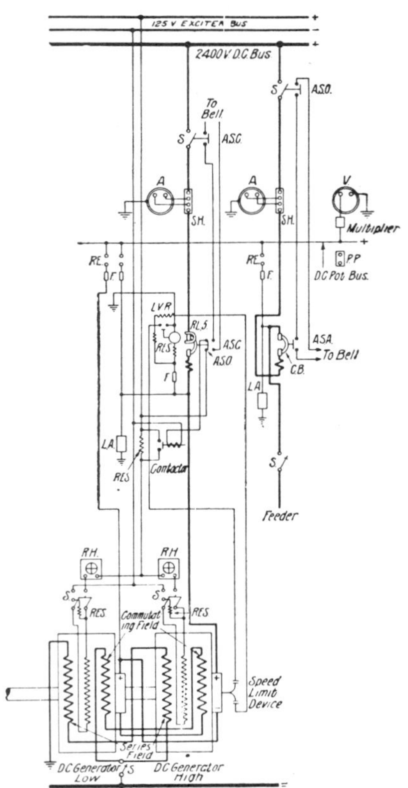

Fig. 5.   Wiring Diagram of 2400-volt Substation

Fig. 6. Overhead Construction on Single-track Curve

verted. The breakers are equipped with special magnetic blowouts and arc chutes. Provision is also made for automatically inserting a high resistance in the generator fields (as shown in the diagram) at the instant the main circuit breaker opens, thus reducing the generator voltage.

Overhead Construction

The overhead construction for this system was especially designed to give maximum flexibility for the pantograph trolleys used on the locomotives. The 4/0 grooved copper trolley wire used over all tracks is supported by an eleven-point catenary suspension from a stranded steel messenger cable. Both side-bracket and cross-span construction are used as required by the local conditions. There is a large amount of special work on account of the many yards and sidings, and in one case, fifteen tracks are spanned. The cross-span construction used at this point is supported by additional poles between the fourth and fifth and between the twelfth and thirteenth tracks. The hanger used on tangent construction is looped over the messenger wire and closed at the ear. The wire is clamped in place by a single bolt. Special pull-offs are used to increase the

are similar in appearance; therefore, to avoid confusion, the circuit breaker handles are in-

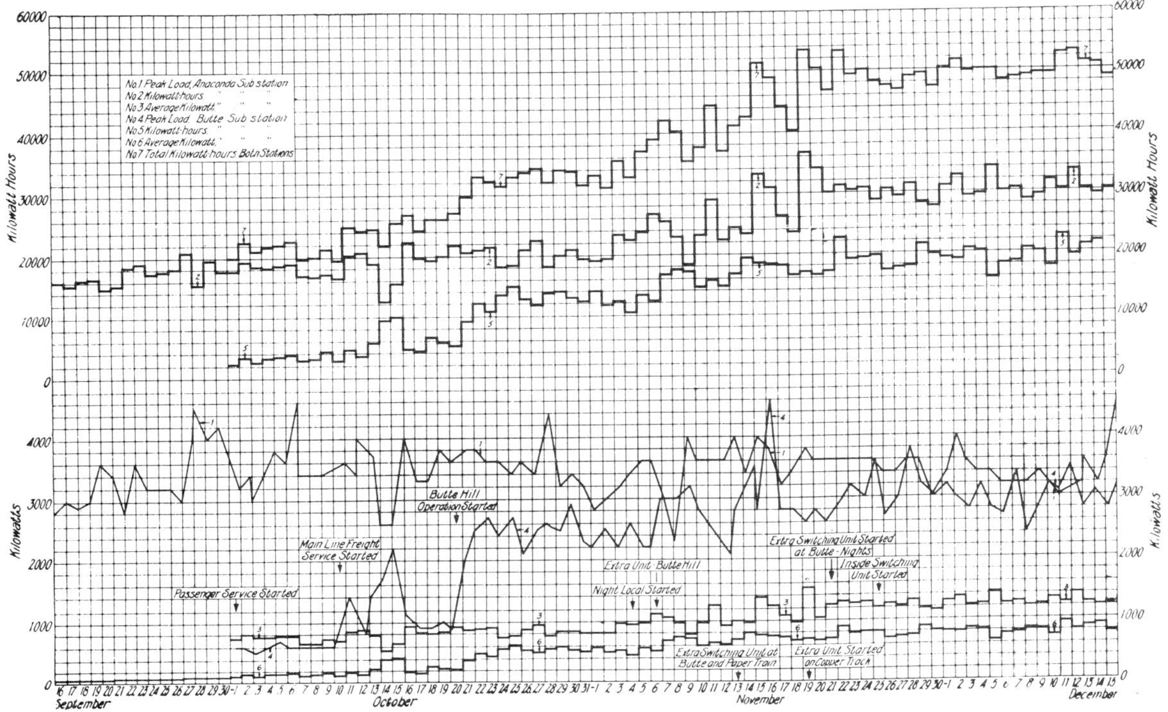

Fig. 7. Diagram of Substation Load

The Electrification of the Butte, Anaconda & Pacific Railway

Fig. 8. Pantograph in Operation on Single Trolley Wire

flexibility of the suspension. Recently a number of these parts were replaced by lighter devices to lighten the whole construction.

The section breakers were designed for the 2400-volt service, and at six points insulated crossings are necessary where the 2400-volt trolley and the 600-volt trolley of the city system intersect. On the main line, the air section insulator is used. This consists of paralleling the two trolley wires from the ends of each section at a suitable distance for insulation so that the pantograph bridges the two circuits for a short distance and thus prevents interruption of the power supply to the locomotive. The construction in the yards and sidings is simplified by paralleling the trolley from the side tracks for a short distance along the main line. This obviates the use of switch plates or similar devices. At some of these junction points the pantograph engages as many as six trolley wires.

The uniformly successful operation of this overhead work is largely due to its very simple and flexible construction and to the absence of frogs at meeting points.

Feeders

The 4/0 trolley is reinforced between the substations with two 500,000-cir. mil bare copper cables tapped to the trolley at intervals of 1000 feet. A 4/0 negative return wire is also installed between Rocker and East Anaconda. This wire is carried on the trolley poles and is connected to the cross bonds at intervals of 1000 feet. The rails are connected by 4/0 bonds at every joint. The substations are normally connected together by these feeders, allowing an interchange of current. In emergency, either station can supply current to the entire system.

Locomotives

The locomotive equipment consists of twenty-eight units, weighing 82.25 tons each, twenty-seven for freight and one for passenger service, and three 40-ton tractor trucks. The freight locomotives are geared for low speed and are operated in pairs for the main-line service. The maximum free-running speed is 35 miles per hour.

The passenger locomotive is of the same construction as the freight units, but is geared for a maximum free-running speed of 55 miles per hour. A speed of 45 miles per hour is made with three passenger coaches on tangent level track.

The continuous tractive effort of a single freight locomotive is 25,000 lb. at 15 miles per hour. The maximum tractive effort for a period of five minutes is 48,000 lb. based on a tractive coefficient of 30 per cent. In the Butte yards, the three 40-ton tractor trucks are used with the locomotives for heavy duty. A locomotive and a tractor truck form a 120-ton, six-axle locomotive which is capable of handling much heavier trains but at a slightly lower speed. The tractor truck motors are controlled from the cab through the regular control equipment.

These locomotives are of the articulated double-truck type with all the weight on the drivers. The cab contains an engineer's compartment at each end and a control compartment for control apparatus. This cab is of the box type, extending the entire length of the locomotive, and is provided with both end and side doors. The entire weight of the locomotive is carried on semi-elliptic springs suitably equalized.

The central channels forming a part of the underframe, are enclosed and are utilized as a distributing air duct for the forced ventilation of the motors. The air is conducted through the center plates, which are hollow, into the

Fig. 9. Pantograph Engaging Six Trolley Wires

truck transoms and thence to the motors. The engineer's compartment at each end of the cab contains the operator's seat, controller, air brake valves, bell and whistle ropes, ammeter, air gauges, sanders, and other control apparatus—all within immediate reach of the engineer.

The contactors, reverser, and rheostats, which are located in the central portion of the cab, are mounted in two banks running lengthwise of the compartment and are conveniently arranged for cleaning, inspection, and repair. All apparatus and circuits carrying 2400 volts are thoroughly protected from accidental contact.

The motors are of the GE-229-A commutating-pole type, wound for 1200 and insulated for 2400 volts. These motors were designed for locomotive service and are provided with forced ventilation. Ventilation of the motors is provided by an auxiliary blower mounted on an extension of the dynamotor shaft. The gear reduction on the freight locomotive is 4.84 and on the passenger locomotive 3.2. The double-unit, 160-ton locomotive is capable of giving a continuous sustained output of 2100 horsepower. The motors are connected to the driving wheels by twin gears similar to those used on the Detroit River Tunnel, Baltimore & Ohio, and the Great Northern locomotives.

The control equipment is Sprague-General Electric Type M, multiple-unit, operating the four motors in series and in series-parallel. Two 1200-volt motors are permanently connected in series. The controller provides ten steps in series and nine in series-parallel. The transition between series and series-parallel is effected without opening the motor circuit and there is no appreciable reduction in tractive effort during the change. The transfer of circuits at this point is made by a special change-over switch, which is operated electro-pneumatically.

The 2400-volt contactors are operated from the 600-volt control circuit and are specially constructed to separate the 2400-volt parts from the coils and interlocks which carry the 600-volt current.

Current is collected by roller pantographs, pneumatically operated and controlled from the engineer's compartment by an air valve. A 2400-volt insulated bus runs along the center of the cab roof. These buses are connected together by couplers between the two freight units, so that current may be obtained from either one of two collectors. The air brakes are of the combined straight and automatic type; and the compressor is of the 600-volt, CP-26 type,

Fig. 10.   DB-254-A 2400-volt Contactor

having a piston displacement of 100 cu. ft. of air per minute when pumping against a tank pressure of 135 pounds. Radiating pipes are provided on the roof of the cab for reducing the temperature of the compressed air before it reaches the high-pressure cylinder.

For operating the control equipment and air compressor and for lighting the locomotive and cars, 600-volt current is supplied from the 2400/600-volt dynamotor installed on each locomotive. This machine is similar in construction to the 1200/600-volt dynamotor, having two distinct sets of armature coils wound on the same core and brought out to a commutator at each end. One of these windings is designed for 1800 volts and the other for 600 volts, the two commutators being connected in series across the 2400-volt circuit. The load current is taken from the 600-volt commutator.

The mechanical load furnished by the direct-connected blower supplies sufficient current in the series field windings to provide for the necessary excitation, so that no shunt windings are required. The blower which supplies ventilating air to the motors consists of a multi-vane fan mounted on an extension of the dynamotor shaft. It has a capacity of 7200 cu. ft. per minute at 4 inches water pressure.

The Electrification of the Butte, Anaconda & Pacific Railway

LOCOMOTIVE DATA

The principal data and dimensions applying to the locomotives are as follows:

Length inside of knuckles............37 ft. 4 in.
Length over cab......................31 ft.
Height over cab......................12 ft. 10 in.
Height with trolley down.............16 ft. 6 in.
Width over all.......................10 ft.
Total wheel base.....................26 ft.
Rigid wheel base.....................8 ft. 8 in.
Track gauge..........................4 ft. 8½ in.
Total weight.........................164,500 lb.
Weight per axle......................41,125 lb.
Wheels, steel tired..................46 in.
Journals.............................6 in. by 13 in.
Gears, forged rims, freight locomotives..87 teeth
Gears, forged rims, passenger locomotive..80 teeth
Pinions, forged, freight locomotives...18 teeth
Pinions, forged, passenger locomotive..25 teeth
Tractive effort at 30 per cent coefficient .48,000 lb.
Tractive effort at one hour rating......30,000 lb.
Tractive effort at continuous rating....25,000 lb.

Costs of electrification of the Butte, Anaconda & Pacific Railway classified in accordance with Interstate Commerce regulations.

Engineering and superintendence (including preliminary report).........	$10,937.15
Roadway tools (used for construction).	3,851.74
Crossings, fences, guards, and signs....	234.08
Interlocking and signal apparatus, new system required because of electrification....................	22,367.62
Poles and fixtures (approx. 91 miles track)............................	135,263.98
Distribution system (approx. 91 miles track wired)......................	357,009.45
Substation building (existing building used)..............................	191.15
Electric equipment, 5 1000-kw. motor-generator sets and 17 locomotive units	671,764.78
Interest................................	9,975.80
Total.........................	$1,211,595.75

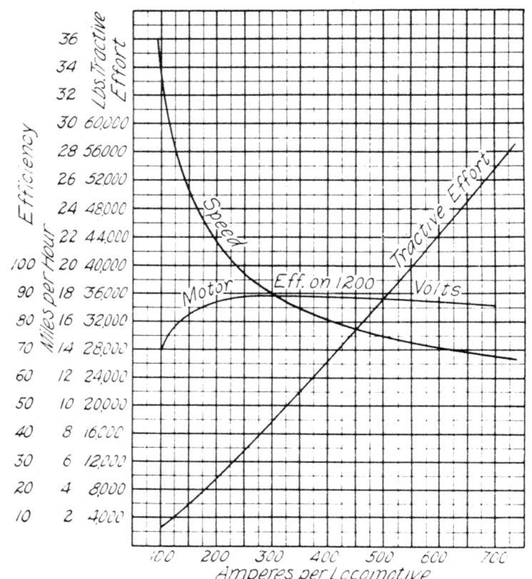

Fig. 11. Characteristic Curves of Freight Locomotive

Operation

Work on the electrification began in the spring of 1912, and the first electric locomotive was run in Anaconda on May 14, 1913, about a year later.

On the 27th of May, two ore trains were hauled up Smelter Hill with electric locomotives; and on the following day, a double-unit electric locomotive took over the regular day service of hauling the ore from the East Anaconda yards to the concentrator yards, a distance of about seven miles. The ruling gradient is 1.1 per cent and is compensated.

The total weight of the steam locomotives replaced averaged 108 tons, 83 tons of which were on the drivers. The weight of the loaded

TABLE 2

ELECTRIC LOCOMOTIVE MAINTENANCE,

Butte, Anaconda

	Fiscal Years			Calendar Years			
	1914	1915	1916	1916	1917	1918	1919
Maintenance of Electric Locomotives:							
Repairs in Dollars.	27,811	35,253	35,790	49,811	55,846	60,295	36,748
Depreciation in Dollars	26,829		29,143	24,143	36,695	38,132	38,009
Electric Locomotive Mileage:							
Freight Revenue Miles	321,946	317,595	480,979	506,162	412,509	438,033	240,185
Passenger Revenue Miles	65,428	87,625	88,608	100,290	94,659	80,020	90,970
Switching Revenue Miles	136,892	161,871	317,405	404,356	367,690	414,158	234,485
Mixed and Special Revenue Miles				616	456		
Total Revenue Miles	524,266	567,091	886,992	1,011,424	875,314	932,211	565,640
Non-revenue Miles		5,507	4,447	2,477	10,796	3,072	1,337
Total Locomotive Miles	524,266	572,598	891,439	1,013,901	886,110	935,283	566,997
Maintenance per Locomotive Mile in cents (not including retirements and depreciation)	5.3	6.16	4.01	4.91	6.30	6.45	6.48
Maintenance prorated to 100 tons on Locomotive Drivers	6.44	7.44	4.87	5.97	7.65	7.84	7.88

Fig. 12. GE-229 1200-volt Motor Showing Opening for Ventilating Pipe

tender was approximately 55 tons, making the total weight of engine and tender about 163 tons, which approximated the weight of the superseding double-unit electric locomotive.

The steam locomotives ordinarily made six round trips per shift, hauling 16 loaded cars per trip or 96 cars per shift. The average time of the trip from East Anaconda to the concentrator yards was about 45 minutes. Each electric locomotive now hauls a train of 25 loaded cars, requiring about 25 minutes for the trip, and delivering 200 cars per shift—an increase of 108 per cent over the number delivered by the steam locomotive with the same crew. The loaded cars weigh about 70 tons each, making the trailing load for the 25-car train approximately 1750 tons.

Early in October, 1913, the main-line passenger and freight service was taken over by the electric locomotives. Here again a great saving in time and an increase in capacity were

realized. A comparison of freight train movement and tonnage is shown in Table 3.

The principal savings resulting from electrification are shown in Table 4. The saving from the partial substitution of electric power for coal is the chief item, being at the rate of $150,727.04 per year. This is remarkable when it is considered that more than 39 per cent of the total combined costs for fuel and power for the period considered was for coal and was charged against electrical operation. In this instance, the saving in this item alone would undoubtedly justify the expenditure covering the entire cost of electrification. It is to be noted that with a single exception, that for depreciation of equipment, every item of expenditure in the locomotive performance sheets Table 5 shows a substantial percentage of decrease in favor of electrical operation.

The total saving from locomotive performance alone, as indicated by Table 5, is at the rate of $237,581.82 per year, to which should be added the credit of handling an increase of traffic at the rate of 13,938,136 ton-miles per year, or 8.77 per cent more than was handled

Fig. 13. Electric Locomotive Delivering Ore Train to Concentrator Bins

28 LOCOMOTIVES AND 3 TRACTOR TRUCKS

	Calendar Years						
	1920	1921	1922	1923	1924	1925	1926
Maintenance of Electric Locomotives:							
Repairs in dollars	46,610	19,235	36,372	44,491	48,414	52,508	50,220
Depreciation in dollars	36,488	38,015	38,015	38,015	38,015	38,015	38,015
Electric Locomotive Mileage:							
Freight Revenue Miles	321,677	128,798	259,442	308,834	313,868	317,560	298,981
Passenger Revenue Miles	83,524	80,968	79,330	72,364	39,767	40,746	39,208
Switching Revenue Miles	283,951	95,899	236,320	302,775	326,657	322,848	311,025
Mixed and Special Revenue Miles	108		104	120			
Total Revenue Miles	689,260	305,665	575,196	684,093	680,201	681,154	649,214
Non-revenue Miles	3,544	732	2,050	2,007	1,962	748	209
Total Locomotive Miles	692,804	306,397	577,246	686,100	682,163	681,902	649,423
Maintenance per Locomotive Mile in cents (not including retirements and depreciation)	6.73	6.28	6.30	6.55	7.10	7.70	7.73
Maintenance prorated to 100 tons on Locomotive Drivers	8.18	7.63	7.65	7.96	8.63	9.39	9.63

The Electrification of the Butte, Anaconda & Pacific Railway

Fig. 14.   Locomotive and Tractor Truck, the Equivalent of a 120-ton Locomotive

by the steam locomotives during the period compared. To this saving from locomotive performance should be added the saving from trainmen's wages, which is at the rate of $31,146.30 per year, or a decrease of approximately 21 per cent. This is due largely to the elimination of overtime, making the total saving from these two items $268,728.12 per year. From this should be deducted $10,839.12 for maintenance of the distribution system, leaving $257,889 as the net operating saving per year resulting from electrical operation.

If a correction were made for the item of depreciation, charging the regular monthly amount of $2711.13, begun in March, for each of the six months, the total would be $16,266.78. The total saving per year from locomotive performance would be reduced to $221,991.94, making the total net saving $242,299.12, which

is equal to 20.02 per cent of the entire cost of electrification.

The estimate upon which the electrification was made placed the annual net saving at 17.5 per cent, which is practically 2.5 per cent less than the saving actually realized. This, in addition to the increased capacity of the lines, the decrease in traffic delays and overtime, and the improved service, has more than demonstrated the benefits from this electrification.

The total cost of the electrification, including a change of signal system on Smelter Hill, interest during construction, and all incidentals due in any way to the electrification, was, in round numbers, $1,211,000.00. This does not include the step-down transformers, which are the property of the power company, nor does it include any deduction for the salvage of 20 steam locomotives.

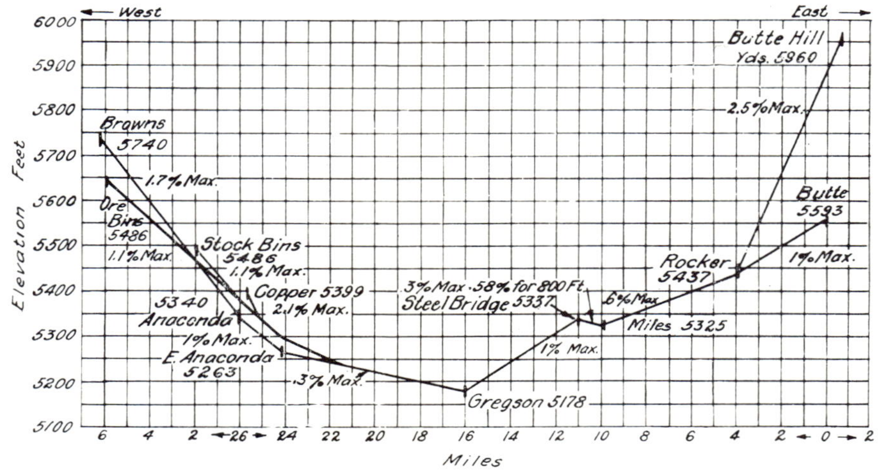

Fig. 15.   Profile of Butte, Anaconda & Pacific Railway

The Electrification of the Butte, Anaconda & Pacific Railway

Electric Locomotive Maintenance

No electrical shop has been provided for the maintenance of electric locomotives, all of the work being carried on in an old steam shop with the addition of a few special tools for handling the electric apparatus. Three electricians are required, to comply with the rulings of the Interstate Commerce Commission. Prior to this ruling two men performed all inspections, made replacements, and attended to other duties. Locomotives are inspected summer and winter over a cinder pit which is open on one side, making it comparatively easy to get access to the bottoms of all motors. Inspections that are made on short notice are usually made by two men.

Mechanical inspections are made simultaneously with electrical inspections. The shop work, which is done when engines are in for change of wheels or motor, consists of turning or

Fig. 16.   Steam Engine Superseded by Electric Locomotive

TABLE 3

BUTTE, ANACONDA & PACIFIC RAILWAY

Comparison of Freight Train Movements Between Rocker and Anaconda—Steam Operation for Month of June, 1913, with Electrical Operation for Same Month, 1914

Date June 1 to June 30	1923 STEAM				1924 ELECTRIC			
	East Bound		West Bound		East Bound		West Bound	
	No. Trains	Total Tons	No. Trains	Total Tons	No. Trains	Total Tons	No. Trains	Total Tons
Total	193	163,130	182	497,124	141	167,796	138	495,697
Average	6.4	845	6.1	2,731	4.7	1,190	4.6	3,592

Grand Average—12.5 trains per day, 1761 tons per train.—9.3 trains per day, 2378 tons per train.
Results—25.6 per cent less trains.   35.0 per cent greater tonnage per train.

TABLE 4

SAVINGS FROM LOCOMOTIVE PERFORMANCE

Item of Operating Expense	Steam 1913	Electric 1914	Decrease 1914	Per Cent Decrease
Fuel and power	$315,235.74	$164,508.70	$150,727.04	47.81
Repairs	124,787.90	92,278.08	32,509.82	26.05
Enginemen's wages	104,461.18	71,225.28	33,235.30	31.81
Engine-house expenses	29,907.80	18,638.38	11,269.42	37.68
Water	4,953.66	1,193.70	3,759.96	75.90
Lubricants	9,751.44	4,942.32	4,809.12	49.30
Other supplies	5,823.52	4,552.36	1,271.16	21.83
Total locomotive performance	$594,921.24	$357,339.42	$237,581.82	39.93
Trainmen's wages	147,632.30	116,486.00	31,146.30	21.10
Grand total	$742,553.54	$473,825.12	$268,728.12	36.19
Ton-miles hauled	158,917,720	172,855,856	13,938,136	8.77*

*Increase.

The Electrification of the Butte, Anaconda & Pacific Railway

TABLE 5

BUTTE, ANACONDA

**EXPENDITURES IN DETAIL AND PERFORMANCE OF LOCOMOTIVE, COMPARING
WITH SIX MONTHS' ELECTRICAL OPERATION,**

	LOCOMOTIVE MILES					MAINTENANCE OF EQUIPMENT EXPENSES			
	Freight	Passenger	Switching	Non-Revenue and Special	Total	Repairs	Depreciation	Supervision	Total
Total 6 month–steam	148943	42485	153499	35454	380381	$51,162.97	$ 8,082.83	$ 3,148.15	$62,393.95
Cost per locomotive mile—cents						13.45	2.12	0.83	16.40
Cost per ton mile—cents						0.0644	0.0102	0.0039	0.0785
Total 6 mos.—steam	16309	420	53063	16217	86009	$15,299.04	$ 3,729.41	$ 1,372.47	$20,400.92
electric	210404	43170	88804	2250	344628	15,822.47	8,471.84	1,443.81	25,738.12
Total	226713	43590	141867	18467	430637	$31,121.51	$12,201.25	$ 2,816.28	$46,139.04
Cost per locomotive mile, steam—cents						17.79	4.34	1.59	23.72
Cost per locomotive mile, electric—cents						4.59	2.46	.42	7.47
Average cost per locomotive mile, combined steam and electric—cents						7.23	2.83	0.65	10.71
Average costs per mile, combined steam and electric—cents						0.0360	0.0141	0.0033	0.0534
Decrease shown in favor of electrical operation	77770*	1105*	11632	16987	50256*	$20,041.46	$ 4,118.42*	$ 331.87	$16,254.91
Savings resulting per year on the above basis (decreased operating expenses)						$40,082.92	$ 8,236.84*	$ 663.74	$32,509.82
Percentage of saving of electrical account operation (decreased operating expenses)						39.17	50.95*	10.54	26.05

*Increase.

renewing tires, renewing gears or pinions, replacing hub-liners, or repairs to pantographs. Motor pinions have an average life of 90,000 miles, and the gears are making as high as 300,000 miles.

The inspection of motors, contactors, etc., is made at periods of 30 days in compliance with Interstate Commerce Commission rulings. This work can all be comfortably taken care of by two electricians in addition to other necessary electrical work.

Fig. 17. Hoist and Storage Bins on Butte Hill

Auxiliary apparatus is cleaned, inspected, and repaired, when necessary, once a year. The electrolytic lightning arresters are placed on each unit as soon as winter conditions permit and removed in the fall after the danger from lightning is passed.

The locomotives have made a total of approximately ten million miles to date at an average cost per unit which is unusually low over the entire period.

A comparison of electrical and mechanical expense shows that mechanical labor is approximately 80 per cent of the total; and materials for mechanical repairs, about 86 per cent of the total.

It is reported by the Electrical Superintendent that the electric locomotives are ready for use practically 355 days of the year.

Maintenance of the Catenary System

The maintenance crew for the overhead line equipment is stationed at Anaconda and normally consists of three men. A tower-car, driven by a four-cylinder, 75-hp. gasoline engine and equipped with suitable platform and auxiliary

& PACIFIC RAILWAY

SIX MONTHS' STEAM OPERATION, DECEMBER, 1912, TO MAY, 1913, INCLUSIVE

DECEMBER, 1913, TO MAY, 1914, INCLUSIVE

TRANSPORTATION EXPENSES							Grand Total	Tons Coal	Kw-hr.	Ton Miles
Wages of Enginemen	Eng'h'se Expenses	Fuel and Power	Water	Lubrication	Other Supplies	Total				
$ 52,230.59	$14,953.90	$157,617.87	$ 2,476.83	$ 4,875.72	$ 2,911.76	$235,066.67	$297,460.62	37,400	39,748	79,458,860
13.73	3.93	41.43	0.65	1.28	0.77	61.79	78.19	10.17 locomotive-miles per ton of coal.		
0.0657	0.0188	0.1984	0.0031	0.0061	0.0037	0.2958	0.3743	2125 ton-miles per ton of coal.		
$ 12,875.02 22,737.92	$ 3,187.94 6,131.25	$ 32,488.41 49,765.94	$ 596.85	$ 1,235.05 1,236.11	$ 1.071.28 1,204.90	$ 51,454.55 81,076.12	$ 71,855.47 106,814.24	8361	9,062,918	
$ 35,612.94	$ 9,319.19	$ 82,254.35	$ 596.85	$ 2,471.16	$ 2,276.18	$132,530.67	$178,669.71	8361	9,062,918	86,427.928
14.97	3.71	37.78	0.69	1.44	1.24	59.83	83.55	10.29 locomotive-miles per ton of coal.		
6.60	1.78	14.44	0.00	0.36	0.35	23.53	31.00	26.30 kw-hr. per locomotive-mile		
8.27	2.16	19.10	0.14	0.57	0.53	30.77	41.48			
0.0412	0.0108	0.0952	0.0007	0.0028	0.0026	0.1633	0.2067			
$16,617.65	$ 5,634.71	$ 75,363.52	$ 1,879.98	$ 2,404.56	$ 635.58	$102,536.00	$118,790.91	29039	9,023,170*	6,969,068*
$33,235.30	$11,269.42	$150,727.04	$ 3,759.96	$ 4,809.12	$ 1,271.16	$205,072.00	$237,581.82			
31.81	37.68	47.81	75.90	49.31	21.83	43.62	39.93			

equipment, supplies the principal apparatus for the maintenance crew. The tower on the car is operated by compressed air, and the platform is suitably insulated from the frame and cab to allow work to be handled without removing power from the line. The car is mounted on two four-wheel trucks and is capable of a safe speed of about 40 miles per hour in either direction.

The maintenance figures given below cover the year 1925 and are somewhat higher than the average for the several years past. The reason for this figure is that there is included the cost of stubbing 200 poles as protection against pole failures.

COST OF OVERHEAD MAINTENANCE

	1925	1926	1927
Cost per mile per year....	$179.32	$141.40	$179.85
Number of miles operated.	123.00	123.00	123.00

Average cost per mile, past 5 years	$144.85
Average cost per mile, 1915–1927.	154.56
Poles and fixtures.	39.50 }
Feeders.	5.10 } Per cent
Trolley.	32.20 } of total
Bonding.	23.20 }

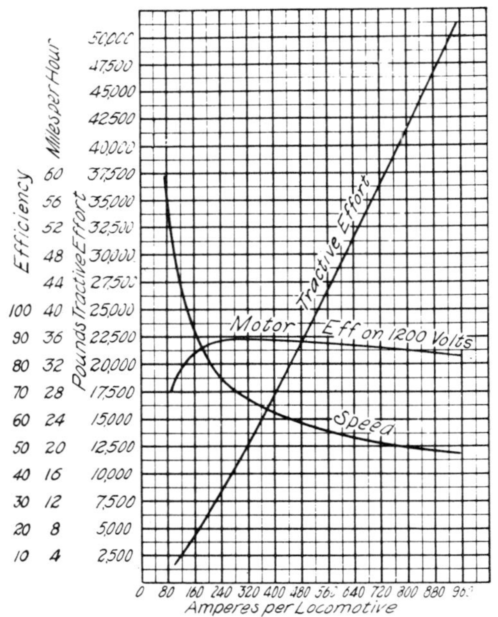

Fig. 18. Characteristic Curves of Passenger Locomotive

The Electrification of the Butte, Anaconda & Pacific Railway

TABLE 6

BUTTE, ANACONDA & PACIFIC RAILWAY

Operating Expenses—Comparison of Six Months' Steam Operation—December, 1912, to May, 1913, inclusive, with Six Months' Electrical Operation, December, 1913, to May, 1914

		Total 6 Months	AVERAGE FOR 6-MONTHS' PERIODS		
			1913	1912	1911
Maintenance of way and structure,	1913 1914	$ 63,316.64 75,857.03	$ 66,945.57	$ 81,284.00	$ 62,028.28
	Decrease	$ 12,540.39*			
Maintenance of equipment,	1913 1914	$133,475.43 133,952.88	$132,596.33	$109,495.65	$103,796.27
	Decrease	$ 477.45*			
Traffic expenses,	1913 1914	$ 4,164.53 3,604.22	$ 4,224.42	$ 4,371.95	$ 3,727.60
	Decrease	$ 560.31			
Transportation expenses,	1913 1914	$333,516.33 250,527.46	$315,555.24	$259,948.95	$241,571.49
	Decrease	$ 82,988.87			
General expenses,	1913 1914	$ 17,062.31 25,107.60	$ 18,625.85	$ 17,646.52	$ 13,874.55
	Decrease	$ 8,045.29*			
TOTAL OPERATING EXPENSES,	1913 1914	$551,535.24 489,049.19	$537,587.41	$472,747.07	$424,998.19
	Decrease	$ 62,486.05			
Net operating revenue,	1913 1914	$121,578.28 265,653.68	$127,882.70	$103,692.27	$111,106.97
	Increase	$144,075.40			
Taxes,	1913 1914	$ 12,638.58 15,705.50	$ 12,319.29	$ 12,881.99	$ 12,306.88
	Increase	$ 3,066.92			
Operating income,	1913 1914	$108,939.70 249,948.18	$115,563.42	$ 90,810.28	$ 98,210.09
	Increase	$141,008.48			

†Decrease.   *Increase.

The NEW YORK CENTRAL ELECTRIFICATION

GENERAL ELECTRIC COMPANY
SCHENECTADY, NEW YORK

January, 1929

GEA-902

NEW YORK CENTRAL ELECTRIFICATION
Grand Central Terminal from 50th Street
In 1906 and in 1927

THE NEW YORK CENTRAL ELECTRIFICATION

THE New York Central system has very appropriately been called "The Greatest Highway in the World." Its immense terminals at New York and Boston handle a huge passenger and freight business to and from all parts of the globe. Leaving the eastern seaboard, the lines of this system reach into twelve states and two Canadian provinces. In these twelve states, is located approximately one-half the population of the whole United States. Sixty-four per cent of the manufactured products of the country is produced in these states, and a large part of all the bituminous coal. Some of the principal northern and midwestern cities reached are Montreal and Ottawa, Buffalo, Detroit, Cleveland, Toledo, Chicago, St. Louis, and Cincinnati.

The main line of the New York Central Railroad has an almost complete freedom from difficult grades. It is practically a water-level route, the only helper section being the short grade just west of Albany. Including leased and allied lines such as Boston & Albany, Michigan Central, Big Four, Pittsburgh and Lake Erie, and other roads, the New York Central system comprises a total of more than 16,400 miles of main tracks.

The earlier section of what is now the New York Central system was the Mohawk & Hudson Railroad, operating between Albany and Schenectady. This company was incorporated in 1826 and began operation in 1831. Shortly afterwards, a line was built from Schenectady to Utica, and later to Rochester and Niagara Falls. It was not until 1853, however, that the ten railroad corporations operating in this district were incorporated in what is now known as the New York Central Railroad Company.

The New York Central Railroad includes over 700 miles of four-track road, about 800 miles of three-track, and about 2200 miles of double-track line. Over the remarkable piece of roadway between New York and Chicago, the Twentieth Century Limited is operated in each direction daily, frequently running in three to six sections. The trip between these cities is made in twenty hours, and the trains are practically always on time. Numerous other finely equipped, high-speed trains are operated between Chicago and New York, handling an immense through traffic between these two cities.

ELECTRIFICATION

The electrification of the suburban zone of the New York Central Railroad around New York City was, when initiated, the most extensive electrification project ever attempted. Extensions of the electrified lines and additions to equipment from time to time still allow this Company to retain its position as one of the foremost exponents of heavy electric railroading.

The normal week-day passenger traffic movement in and out of the Grand Central Terminal, including both New York Central and New Haven trains, averages each day about 475 trains aggregating some 4000 cars. The maximum total movement reported for a single day is 800 trains aggregating 6200 cars. The number of passengers handled in both directions by all trains totals about 134,000 per day normal and as high as 166,075 maximum.

In addition to the extensive electrical operation around New York City, notable electrification work has been done on other parts of the system. The Michigan Central

The Main Concourse of the Grand Central Terminal

Railroad operates about 26 miles of track in the Detroit River tunnel and terminal, using twelve electric locomotives handling traffic between Detroit and Windsor, Ontario. The West Shore Railroad between Utica and Syracuse, a distance of 48 miles, was electrified in 1907, using multiple-unit cars for handling interurban passenger traffic. Practically all of this line is double-tracked. The most recent electrification is that of the new Cleveland Terminal by the Cleveland Union Terminals Company. It is expected that this project, which includes about 17 miles of line, will be completed in 1929.

ELECTRIC DIVISION

A study of the possibilities of electrification on the New York Terminal was begun by New York Central officials in 1899. In the meantime, legislation at Albany was enacted directing the abandonment of steam locomotives in the Park Avenue tunnel south of the Harlem River not later than July 1, 1908. Plans for electrification of this terminal, however, were so well advanced that contracts were placed for locomotives, substations, and other equipment in the fall of 1903, and the first electric locomotive was formally tested on the experimental tracks at Schenectady in November, 1904. The first scheduled multiple-unit trains began service in December, 1906, and electric-locomotive trains in February, 1907. The complete change of passenger-train motive power, extending as far as High Bridge on the Hudson Division and Wakefield on the Harlem Division, was completed in July, 1907, a full year in advance of the date specified by legislative enactment.

The initial studies by the company officials were made with a view to eliminating the undesirable conditions in the Park Avenue tunnel and, from the start, the program was built up around the movement of trains by electric power, accompanied by an almost complete application of electric power to other purposes around the terminal.

Briefly, the program included the complete reconstruction of the Grand Central Terminal district with a new station arranged for two-level operation; the construction of new streets over the depressed electrified tracks; the installation of two complete power plants with necessary substations; transmission and distribution; and the substitution of electric for steam locomotives on the main-line trains and of electric motor cars for the steam-drawn suburban trains. The problem was further complicated by the fact that the New York, New Haven & Hartford Railroad is a joint user of the tracks from Woodlawn for the handling of its trains to and from the Grand Central Terminal.

The initial electric zone included about 15 miles of route and 77 miles of single track. As now operated, the electric zone includes 63.73 miles of route and 360.23 miles of single track. The first electric locomotives, known as the class "S" locomotives, were delivered during the years 1906 to 1909 and included a total of 47 units. Each is equipped with four gearless motors, and at each end a four-wheel guiding truck. Some of these locomotives have been in operation for over 20 years and have run more than 600,000 miles each. These earlier locomotives are now being given their first general overhauling in connection with modernization of equipment and adaptation to switching service.

In the selection of the proper system for electrifying the Grand Central Terminal, the officials of the Railroad Company proceeded with great caution, bearing in mind the imperative necessity of uninterrupted operation. The following commission of experts was appointed to study the situation and make recommendations: W. J. Wilgus, Bion J. Arnold, Frank J. Sprague, George Gibbs, Arthur M. Waitt (later succeeded by John F. Deems). E. B. Katte, later Chief Engineer of Electric Traction, sat with the Commission as Secretary.

It was finally recommended that 660 volts, direct current, be used with a protected third rail. In this decision, the question of reliability had considerable weight, and the fact that this method of power distribution had been thoroughly tried out was regarded as of great importance. Furthermore, restricted clearances forbade the use of overhead wires, and legal obstacles prohibited the use of overhead trolley wires carrying high voltages within the limits of the City of New York.

The Twentieth Century Limited in the Grand Central Terminal

The Port Morris Power Plant

The Glenwood Power Station and Substation

POWER STATIONS

As a precaution against possibility of failure of power at the generating source, duplicate stations were located at Glenwood, near Yonkers, and at Port Morris. The initial equipment of each station included sixteen 625-horsepower boilers with superheaters and mechanical stokers, and four 5000-kilowatt steam turbine-generators. Provision was made for an ultimate increase in total capacity to 30,000 kilowatts. It is an interesting commentary on the progress of the art to note that, after nearly twenty years of service, these 5000-kilowatt units are being replaced by 20,000-kilowatt units which require no more space than was originally provided for units of one-fourth the capacity. Not only is the new equipment a great improvement as regards space occupied, but it is much more efficient and enables the company to produce electric power at a much lower cost. At the present time, the modern units handle all of the load, the older turbines being held in reserve. The equipment of both the power stations at the present time is given in the accompanying tables. The power-station units are designed for generating

Interior of the Port Morris Power Plant

110th Street Automatic Substation, Controlled from
Mott Haven Substation

three-phase, 11,000-volt, 25-cycle current, which is transmitted without change to the several substations.

At the Port Morris station, which is now considered the main generating plant, bituminous coal is used entirely. Provision is made for transferring the coal directly from the cars to overhead bins, a storage capacity of 3500 tons being available. At the Glenwood Station, which is located nearer to the residential section, the off-peak load is carried on coal-burning boilers, and the peak load on boilers burning fuel oil.

PRESENT BOILER EQUIPMENT

The present boiler equipment of the Port Morris plant consists of sixteen 625-horsepower and four 673-horsepower boilers, all equipped with underfeed stokers for burning bituminous coal. The Glenwood plant also has sixteen 625-horsepower and four 673-horsepower boilers, of which four are equipped with underfeed stokers for burning bituminous coal, six with chain grates for burning anthracite, and ten for burning fuel oil.

TRANSMISSION AND DISTRIBUTION SYSTEM

Under the present conditions of operation, power is transmitted at 11,000 volts to the nine original substations, all of which are equipped with synchronous converters and are manually operated. Additions have been made to the equipment from time to time so that these original stations now contain a total of 66,500 kilowatts.

During the last three or four years, it has been found necessary to increase the substation capacity because of additional traffic. This has been done by the addition of new substations of the automatic type, located approximately midway between the older stations.

Interior of 110th Street Substation

TRANSMISSION LINES

The 11,000-volt, high-tension lines are carried in ducts throughout the congested districts, and on steel poles located on the right-of-way, in the outside sections. Low-tension power is fed from the substations to the third rails by underground feeders. The third rails act as the main d-c. feeders and are connected together at intervals through circuit breakers located in circuit-breaker houses. The Yonkers Branch, recently placed

Automatic Substation at Wakefield

in service, is fed from Kingsbridge and Glenwood substations. Three new substations are planned for supplying power to the West Side tracks when the electrification of tracks in this district is completed.

THIRD RAIL

The contact conductor is known as the Wilgus-Sprague under-running third rail and was first used by the New York Central. It is particularly designed to safeguard employees and others from accidental contact. It is also arranged so that the contact surface is not exposed to sleet or snow. This insures freedom from tie-ups in bad weather. The rail itself is of the bullhead type weighing 70 pounds per yard. The contact surface is located 2¾ inches above the top of the running rail and the center line 2 feet 4¼ inches from the gauge line of the nearest running rail. This rail is used at all points except where intricate switch layouts prohibit

Interior of Scarsdale Substation, Controlled from Tuckahoe Substation

the use of a continuous conductor near the level of the track. At such points, a rigid overhead conductor is used. Gaps are left in the third rail opposite substations to facilitate sectionalization and the isolation of any defective portion of the contact line. Flexible ribbon bonds are soldered to the side of the third rail. The track bonds are 16.8 inches long, pin-expanded into 1-inch holes drilled in the track rail. On the main line, both rails are double-bonded; but in the yards, only one of each pair of rails is bonded.

Substation No. 1B at 43rd Street. 2000-kw. Synchronous Converters

Synchronous Converters at Substation No. 5, Irvington

POWER STATION EQUIPMENT

	No. Units	Kw.	
Port Morris	2	5,000	11,000 volt, 25 cycle, 3 phase
	3	20,000	11,000 volt, 25 cycle, 3 phase
Glenwood	4	5,000	11,000 volt, 25 cycle, 3 phase
	1	20,000	11,000 volt, 25 cycle, 3 phase

SUBSTATION EQUIPMENT

Substation		No. Units	Capacity	Total Kw.	
No. 1.	50th Street	4	1,500		
		1	2,000	14,500	
		1	2,500		
		1	4,000		
No. 2.	Mott Haven	3	1,500		
		1	2,000	10,500	
		1	4,000		
No. 2a.	110th Stret	2	2,000	4,000	automatic
No. 3.	Kingsbridge	3	1,000	5,500	
		1	2,500		
No. 4.	Glenwood	3	1,000	5,500	
		1	2,500		
No. 4a.	Hastings	1	2,500	2,500	automatic
No. 5.	Irvington	2	2,000	6,500	
		1	2,500		
No. 5a.	Phillipse Manor	1	2,500	2,500	automatic
No. 6.	Ossining	3	1,000	8,000	
		2	2,500		
No. 6a.	Harmon	2	2,500	5,000	automatic
No. 7.	Bronx Park	3	1,000	5,000	
		1	2,000		
No. 7a.	Wakefield	1	2,000	2,000	automatic
No. 8.	Tuckahoe	3	1,000	5,500	
		1	2,500		
No. 8a.	Scarsdale	1	2,500	2,500	automatic
No. 9.	White Plains	3	1,000	5,500	
			2,500		

Total	85,000 Kw.

Manually controlled	66,500 Kw.
Automatically controlled	18,500 Kw.
Traction Substations Total	85,000 Kw.

SUBSTATIONS FOR LIGHTING AND POWER

Substation		No. Units	Capacity	Total Kw.
No. 1a.	50th Street	4	1,500	6,000
No. 1b.	43rd Street	4	2,000	8,000
				14,000

600 VOLT DIRECT CURRENT
100 TON ELECTRIC LOCOMOTIVE
B-B 200/200 4GE286A 600V.
NEW YORK CENTRAL RAILROAD
SWITCHING SERVICE

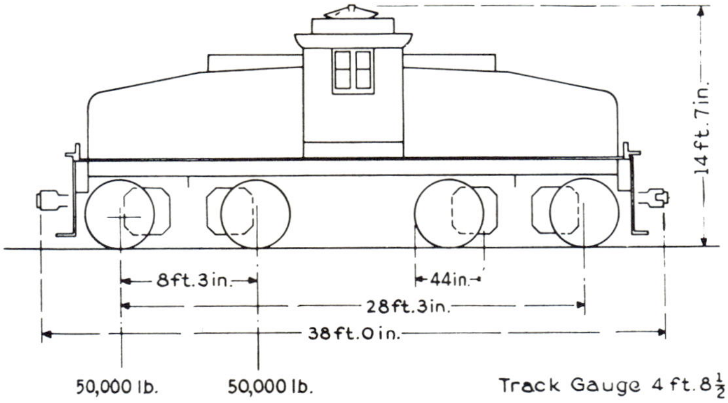

LOCOMOTIVE CHARACTERISTICS
600 VOLTS

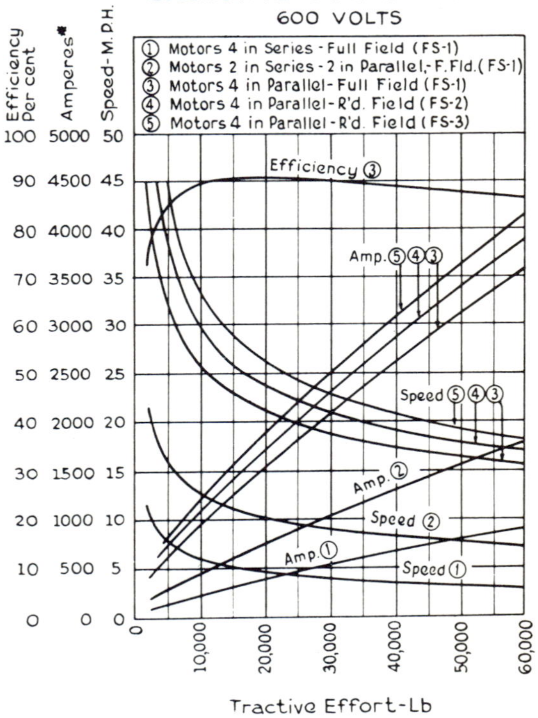

LOCOMOTIVE DATA

Weights-Lb.

Total (Excluding Sand)	200,000
On Drivers	200,000
Per Driving Axle	50,000
Cab, Platform and Trucks	126,045
Traction Motors (Including gearing)	36,100
Other Equipment	37,855

Traction Motors

Number	4
Type	GE-286-A
Rated Voltage	600/1200
Method of Drive	Single Cushion Gear
Gear Ratio	72/17 = 4.235
Ventilation	Forced

Locomotive Ratings

	One Hour Blown 120°C. Rise by Res. Full Field (FS-1)	Continuous Blown 120°C. Rise by Res. Full Field (FS-1)	Rd. Field (FS-3)
Tractive Effort-Lb.	34,100	25,260	18,820
Coef. Adhesion	17.05%	12.63%	9.41%
Speed M.P.H.	18.3	19.75	26.85
Horse Power	1665	1330	1350
Amperes*	2300	1840	1840
Tractive Effort at 25% Coef. Adhesion	50,000 lb.		
Maximum Safe Speed	40 M.P.H.		

Control   Type PCL (S.U.) 3 Speeds F.F. 6 Speeds R.F.
Current Collector, Third Rail Shoe and Overhead 3rd Rail Collector
Braking   Air
Train Heating Equipment,   None

First Locomotive Built	1926
Total Number in Service	7
Years Placed in Service	1926
Road Engine Numbers (Class Q)	1250-1256 Incl.

*Note:- Current values shown do not include auxiliaries.

Locomotive Data, Class Q, 100 Ton

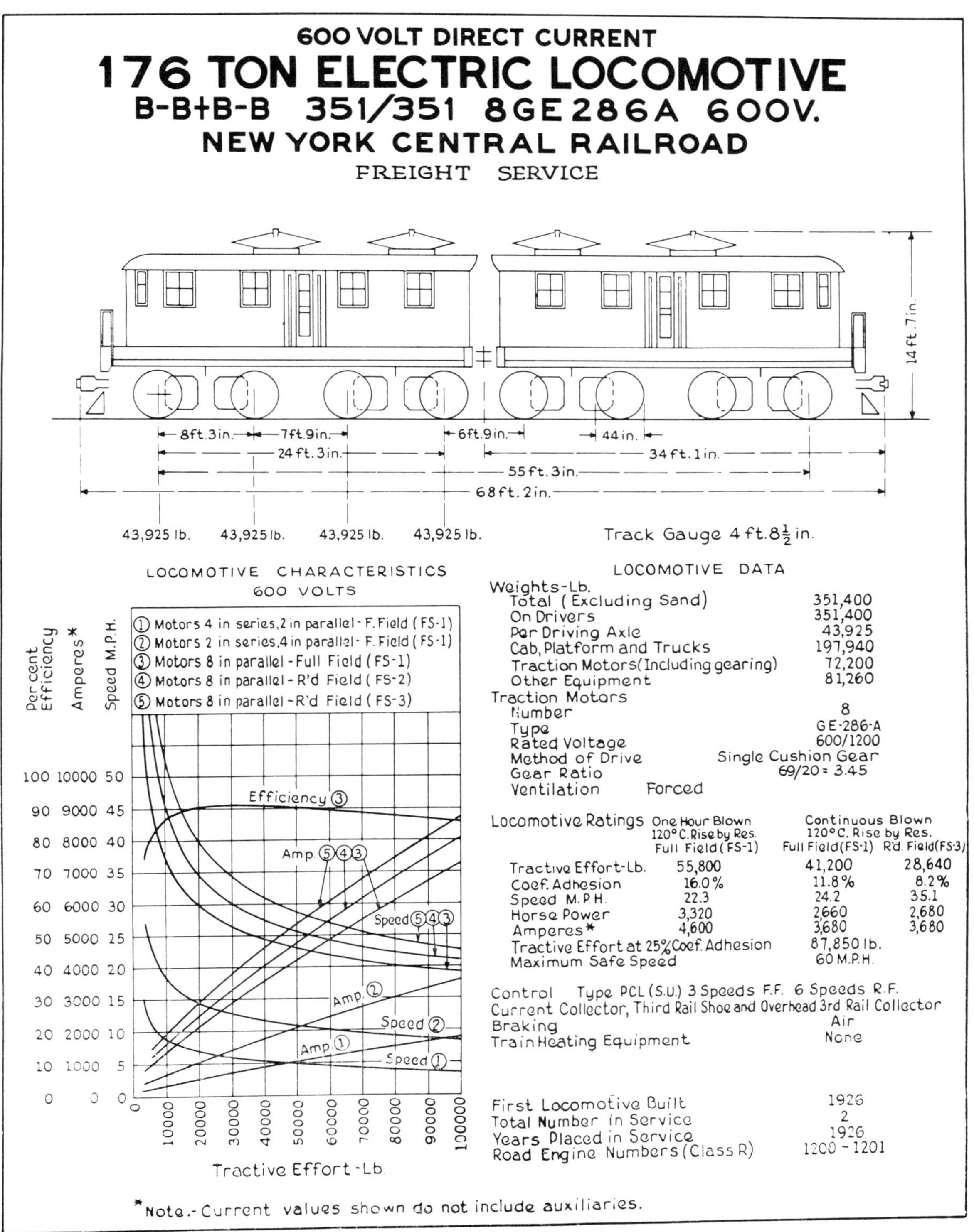

Locomotive Data, Class R, 176 Ton

600 VOLT DIRECT CURRENT
113 TON ELECTRIC LOCOMOTIVE
2-D-2 225/139 4GE84A 600V.
NEW YORK CENTRAL RAILROAD
PASSENGER SERVICE

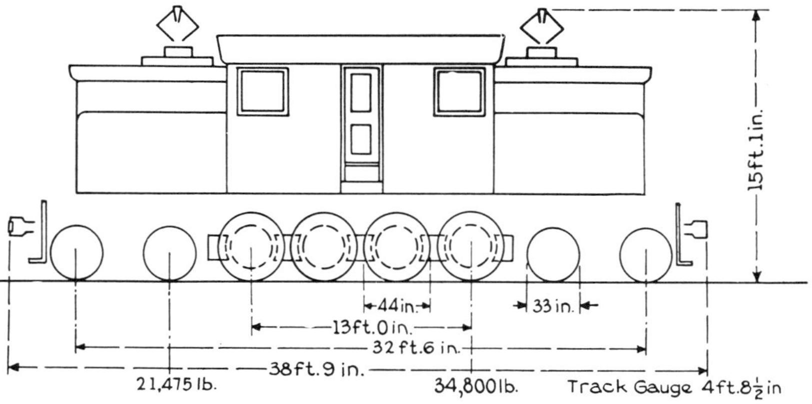

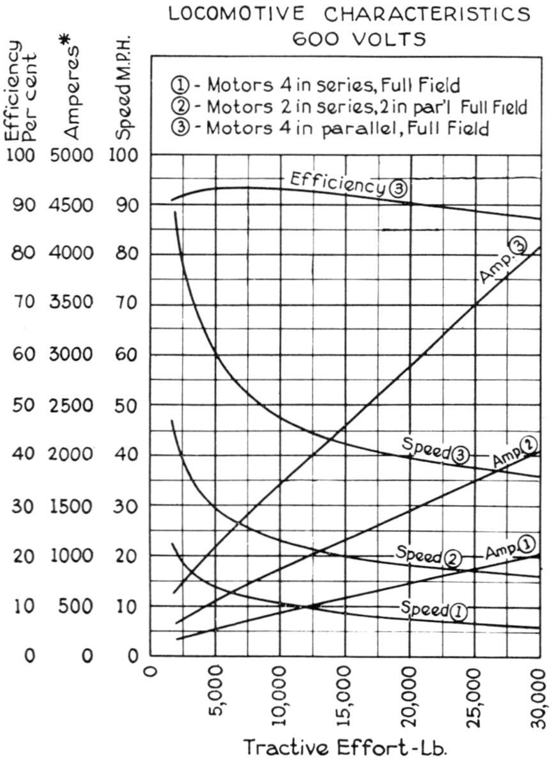

LOCOMOTIVE CHARACTERISTICS
600 VOLTS

LOCOMOTIVE DATA

Weights-Lb.	
Total	225,100
On Drivers	139,200
Per Driving Axle	34,800
Cab, Platform and Trucks	168,800
Traction Motors	40,760
Other Equipment	15,540

Traction Motors	
Number	4
Type	GE 84 A
Rated Voltage	600
Method of Drive	Direct
Gear Ratio	Gearless
Ventilation	Natural

Locomotive Ratings	One Hour-Unblown 75° C. Rise by Therm. Full Fld (FS-1)	Continuous-Unblown 120°C. Rise by Res. Full Fld (FS-1)
Tractive Effort	15,200 lb.	4,870 lb.
Coef. Adhesion	10.92%	3.5%
Speed	41.8 M.P.H.	61.0 M.P.H.
Horse Power	1695	792
Amperes*	2300	1060
Tractive Effort at 25% Coef. Adhesion		34,800 lb.
Maximum Safe Speed		60 M.P.H.

Control	Type M-(M.U.)-3 Speeds F.F.
Current Collector, Third Rail Shoe and Slider	Pantograph
Braking	Air
Train Heating Equipment	None

First Locomotive Built	1904
Total Number In Service	35-N.Y.C.R.R.
Years Placed in Service	35-1906
Road Engine Numbers (Classes S-1 & S-2)	1100 to 1134 incl.

*Note:- Current values shown do not include auxiliaries.

Locomotive Data, Classes S-1 and S-2, 113 Ton

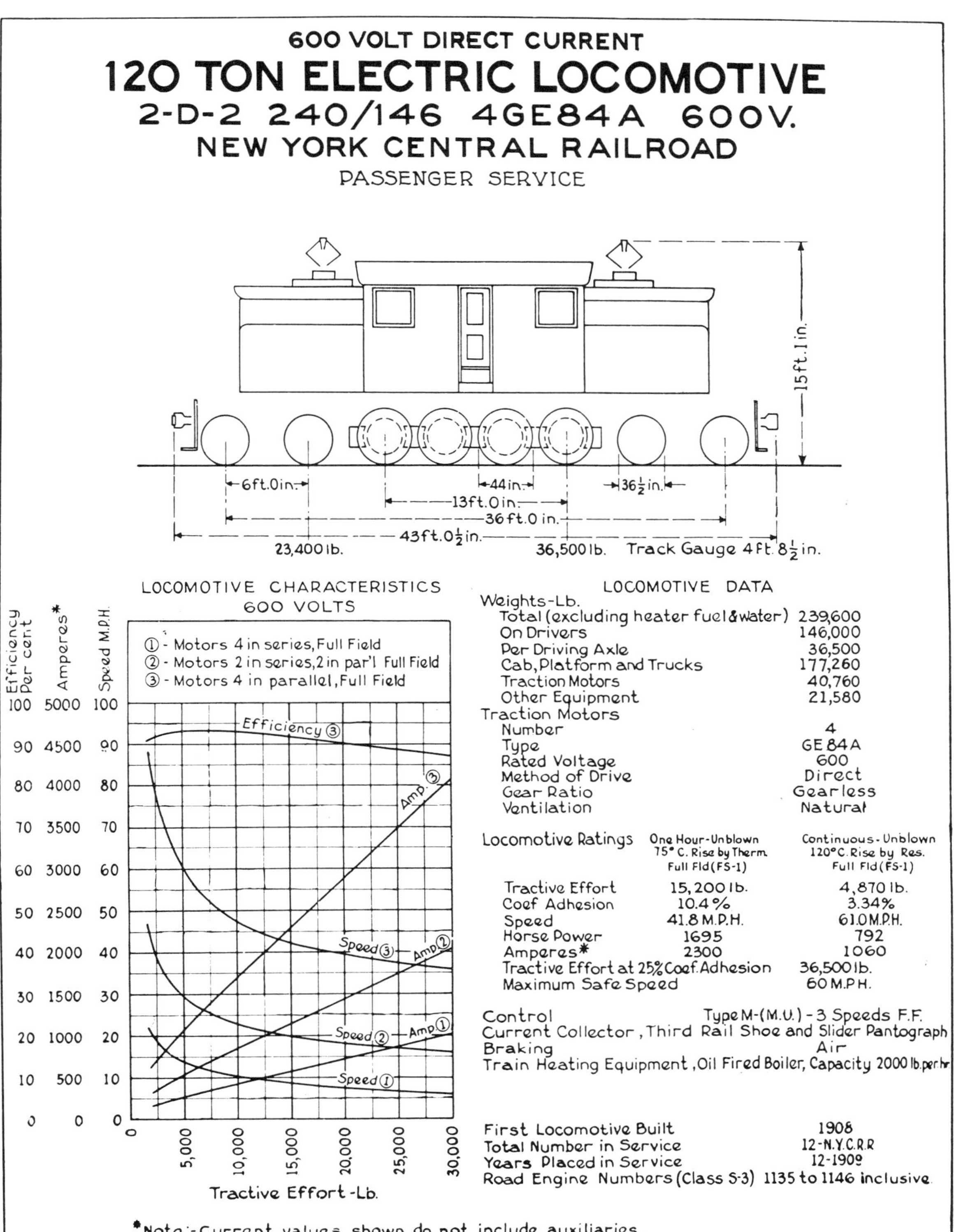

Locomotive Data, Class S-3, 120 Ton

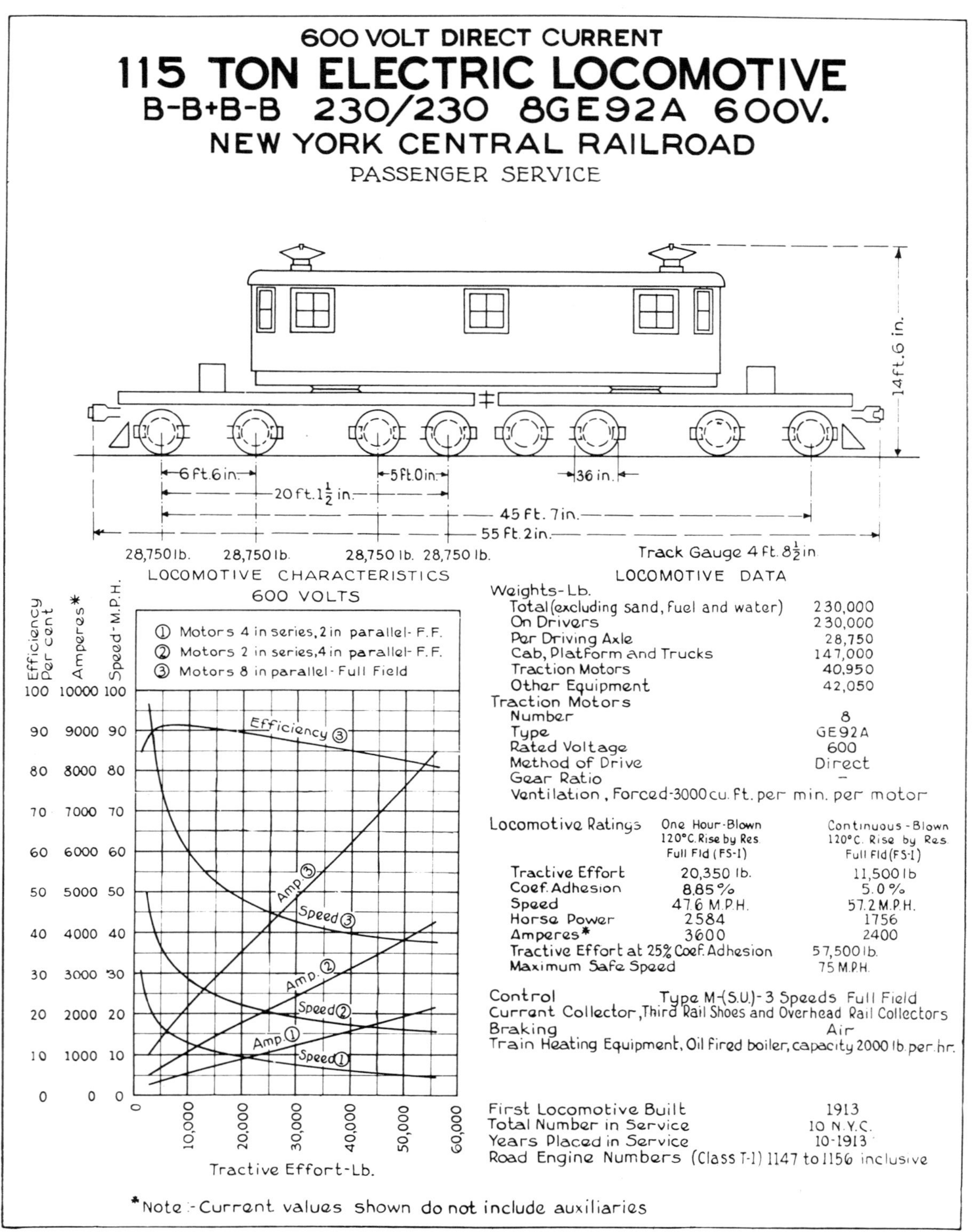

Locomotive Data, Class T-1, 115 Ton

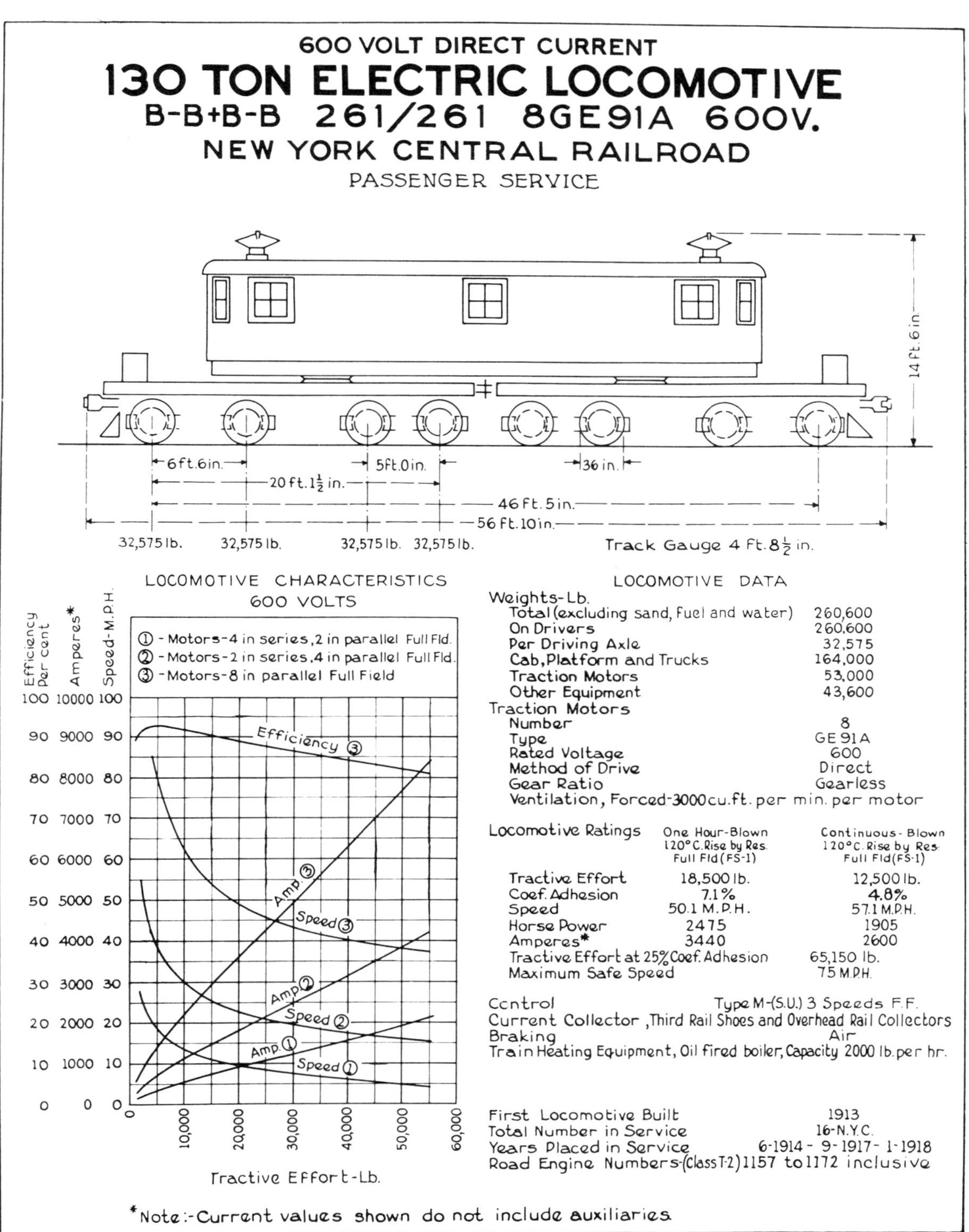

Locomotive Data, Class T-2, 130 Ton

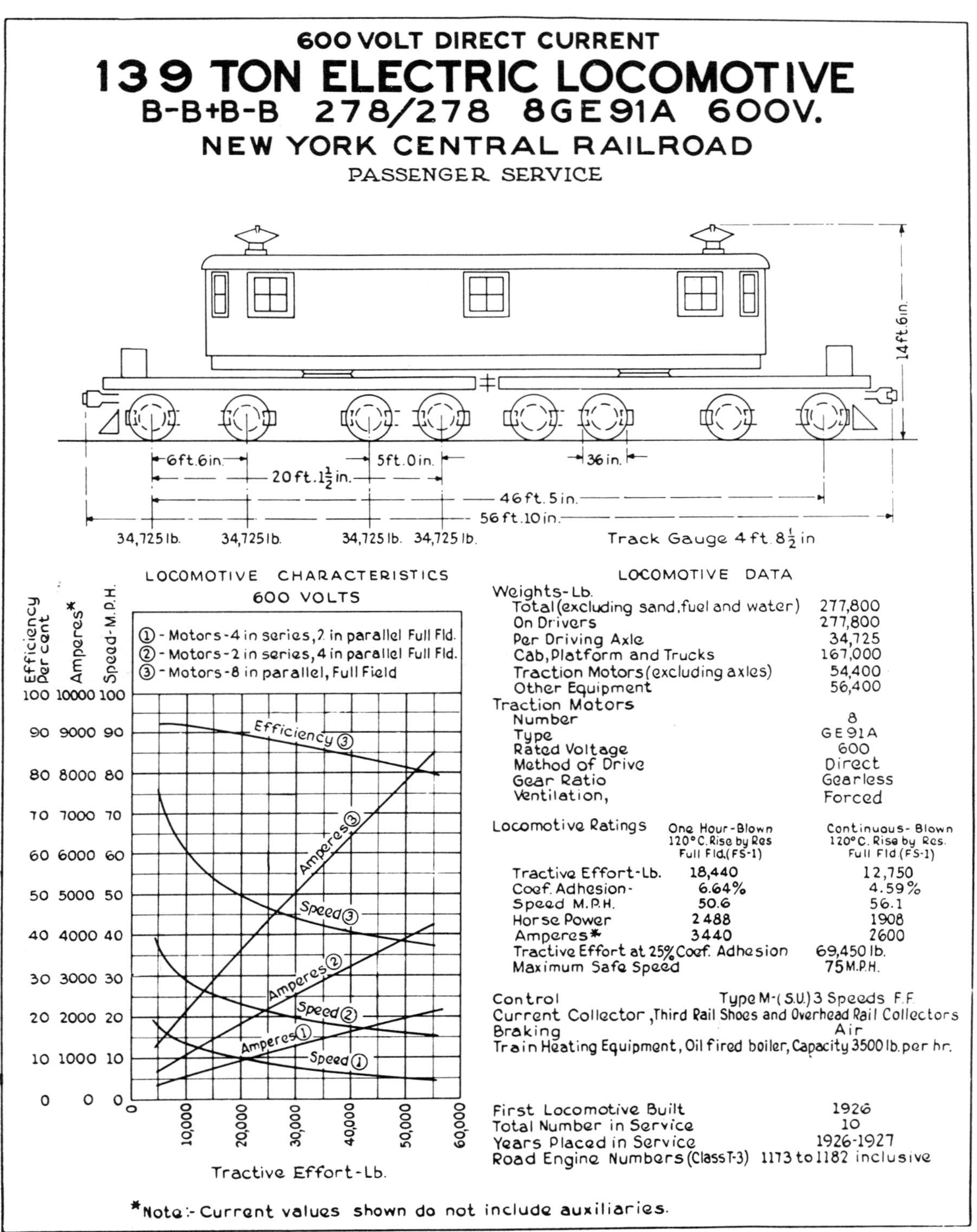

Locomotive Data, Class T-3, 139 Ton

The First New York Central Locomotive on Test

LOCOMOTIVES

The first locomotives used on the New York Central terminal were known as Class "S." The first of these units was given initial tests in October, 1904. This locomotive was known as No. 6000 and was tested for several months under various conditions of loads, speeds, and weather. The Class "S" engine is of the gearless type built with four driving axles, each equipped with a gearless motor with the armature keyed to the axle, and with guiding wheels at each end. The 6000 type, upon which the initial tests were made, was built with a single guiding axle, front and rear. Later it was decided to change this to a two-axle truck, and all units of this type of locomotive now have a two-axle guiding truck at each end. The original design weighed 94½ tons complete, while the present locomotives weigh 112½ tons with about 70 tons on the driving axles. The normal one-hour rating is 1700 horsepower, giving a tractive effort of 15,200 pounds at 41.8 miles per hour. In comparison with the 171-ton steam locomotive which was then displaced on heavy passenger trains, this locomotive had the advantage of much higher horsepower rating, a reduction in weight, and a lower weight per driving axle. It was built to operate equally well in either direction.

The first order of these locomotives, delivery of which began in 1905, was for 35 units. Before delivery was completed, however, the number was increased to 47 units, and the last locomotive was delivered in 1909.

With the extension of electrification from the temporary terminals at High Bridge and Wakefield to present locations at Croton and White Plains, North Station, additional equipment consisting of ten 115-ton passenger locomotives, was ordered, and was delivered in 1913. These are also of the gearless type but designed to carry all the weight on driving wheels. Each of the eight axles is driven by a gearless motor. The increased capacity gave the necessary power for handling the gradually increasing train weights. These locomotives

Class T-1 115-ton
Locomotive

Class Q 100-ton
Switcher

Class S-2 113-ton
Locomotive

Class T-3 139-ton Locomotive

Class T-2 130-ton Locomotive

Twentieth Century Limited with Class T-2 Locomotive.   View Shows Main-line Signals

were tested for a maximum safe speed of 75 miles per hour and are rated for continuous operation up to about 57 miles per hour with a tractive effort of 11,500 pounds.

The following year, the first of 16 additional units was placed in service. These are of similar design, but have a total of 130 tons, all on the driving wheels, to handle heavier trains. The most recent of the gearless passenger locomotives, consisting of 10 units placed in service in 1926 and 1927, are of the same design with slightly greater total weight.

The eight-motor locomotives, known as the Class "T", now handle most of the through passenger trains in and out of the terminal. The Class "S" locomotives are used for passenger-train switching around the terminal and between Grand Central Terminal and Mott Haven Yards, and for some of the through trains on the Harlem Division.

Many features of the eight-motor locomotive follow closely those of the Class "S", but the arrangement of the running gear and cab is radically different. The frame of the locomotive is made up of two platforms which carry the draft gear at their outer ends and are articulated at the center of the locomotive. The axles are assembled in four-wheel trucks of which one is secured rigidly to each of the platforms near its inner end and one is placed near the outer end of each platform and supports it through a center bearing. This permits rotary motion but not lateral motion of the truck. The cab is mounted on center plates, one on each of the two platforms.

The control is of the three-speed type. The two motors on each truck are permanently connected in parallel, and the four pairs are successively connected in three ways just as the four motors of the earlier-type locomotive are, the resulting combination being: four pairs in series, the motors of each pair in parallel; two groups in series, the four motors

Class R Freight Locomotive

of each group in parallel; and eight motors in parallel. The addition of reversing contactors for four additional motors increased the number of contactors in the main cab. The cab is divided into three compartments. The end compartments contain accommodation for the crew, and space for the controller, brake valves, etc., and the train steam-heating apparatus, which is divided, the boiler being in one end of the locomotive and the oil and water tanks in the other. The middle compartment has a passageway at each side, and the apparatus space is between these passages. The center part of the floor space is occupied by the blower and air compressor with their respective motors. On the partitions at the end of the compartment (center), are placed the motor cutout switches, switch and fuse for auxiliary circuits, compressor-governor fuse and switch, ammeter shunt, connection boxes, tube resistances for the control circuits, and the main switch.

The contactors are suspended at a height of about 6 feet 6 inches from the floor in two rows extending the length of the compartment, placed back to back facing outward, with room between for inspection of the connections at the back. The passageways are protected from arcing of the contactors

Armature of Gearless Motor, Class T Locomotive

by shields, hanging in front of the contactors, which can be opened upward when the contactors are inspected. The rheostats are placed directly above the contactors.

The trains are heated by an oil-fuel boiler of the vertical, fire-tube type. Water is fed by air pressure from a tank having a capacity of 5600 pounds of water. Fuel is supplied by gravity from a tank containing 102 gallons of fuel oil, which is located in the top of the water tank. The supply of fuel, and of air or steam, to the burner is regulated by hand.

Freight Locomotive with Train

FREIGHT AND SWITCHING LOCOMOTIVES

In anticipation of the electrical operation of the West Side tracks, two road-freight and seven freight-switching locomotives of the geared type were ordered in 1925 and delivered in 1926.

The running gear of the road locomotives consists of two swivel-truck units coupled by an articulated joint. The equipment consists of eight motors with a gear ratio to permit a maximum emergency speed of 60 miles per hour. The two cabs are of the box type, and the total weight of the locomotive is approximately 175 tons, all on the driving wheels.

The switching locomotive is of steeple-cab construction mounted on two-swivel equalized trucks, each equipped with four motors and geared for a maximum speed of 40 miles per hour. The running gear is similar to a half-unit of the freight locomotive. The total weight of the locomotive is 200,000 pounds.

Switcher with Train

Suburban Train with Motor Cars

MOTOR CAR OPERATION

The greater part of the local suburban passenger business is handled in multiple-unit motor cars. The initial equipment of the electric zone included 125 passenger motor cars, and 55 similar cars which were used as trailers. As the electrical service was extended, these trailer cars were all equipped with motors and control, and all subsequent cars for the electric zone were equipped for electrical operation. The earlier cars were 62 feet in length, and each was equipped with two 200-horsepower motors and type "M" multiple-unit control. These cars weighed about 51 tons each. Later cars are somewhat heavier and, during 1924 and 1925, a rebuilding program was instituted which provided for the lengthening of all the original motor cars and converted trailers then in service to approximately 69 feet over all. The weight was increased to about 65 tons, and the seating capacity from 70 to 82 or 100 passengers. It had been found that the margin in capacity of the electric equipment would permit this increase in weight without change in motor equipment. During the reconstruction, an intermediate relay was added, permitting the operation of 15 cars per train.

The more recent electric equipments include Type "PC" pneumatically operated control in place of the Type "M" which was originally furnished. Cars are normally operated in trains of from two to twelve units depending upon the volume of traffic, which

Suburban Level, Grand Central Terminal

varies throughout the day. All cars are motor cars, rather than a combination of motor cars and trailers as used on some roads. There is now in service, or on order, a total of 346 motor cars, and some of the original equipments have been run nearly 600,000 miles each.

SPECIAL EQUIPMENT

When steam operation was abandoned in the electric zone, an electric wrecking crane was designed to be used in the Grand Central Terminal and on the electric zone. The crane weighs 370,000 pounds, and was designed to meet the special conditions existing in the terminal, such as restricted clearances, 135-foot radius loops, and the avoidance of excessive concentrated loads on the upper-level tracks carried on steel work. It is propelled and operated electrically.

There is a 100-ton crane at each end, both of which may be operated at the same time if necessary. The maximum reach of the boom is 24 feet 2 inches and at this radius, with outriggers set, the 100 tons can be lifted and swung laterally 6 feet 6 inches either side of the track center; at the radius of 13 feet 8 inches, the same load can be moved to any point within a 180-degree swing of the boom.

Four GE-69-C 200-hp. motors are used for propulsion, one mounted on each of the four trucks. The motors are identical with those on the earlier multiple-unit cars except that a different gear ratio is used. A Sprague General Electric master controller is provided at each end to operate the 40 contactors, which are arranged to connect the motors in series, series-parallel, and parallel on third-rail current.

The crane is equipped with air brake sets for each pair of trucks, hand brakes, etc., and conforms with the U. S. safety appliance standards. Portable searchlights, which can be plugged into receptacles at the corners of the body, are provided.

185-ton Electric Wrecking Crane

New York Central Building

Airplane View of Upper New York City Showing Hudson and Harlem Rivers, New York
Central Tracks, and Mott Haven Yards

View of Harmon Shops from the South

SHOP FACILITIES AND INSPECTION
HARMON

The principal repair shops for the Electric Division are located at Harmon, where the change is made from steam to electric locomotives and vice versa. All heavy repairs, both to locomotives and motor cars, are made in this shop. This plant not only includes the large electrical repair shop, but also a roundhouse and complete terminal facilities for the steam locomotives. The organization for the care of the steam locomotives, however, is entirely separate and is a part of the steam-operated Hudson Division north of Harmon. In addition to the main electrical repair shop, there is also a local power house which supplies the roundhouse and shops with power, heat, and light. There is, furthermore, a running-inspection shed, through which all locomotives pass upon their arrival at the terminal.

This inspection shed is 209 feet long by 24 feet wide and houses a single track with a pit. In addition to the running inspection which each locomotive receives at this point, provision is made for supplying the heater boilers with oil and water and for refilling the sand boxes on the locomotives. No third rail is installed in this shed, but a contact device is provided for supplying 600-volt current to move the locomotive.

The main shop building is of the transverse type, through which 17 tracks pass. Access is thus provided to both ends of the shop. West of the car shop proper, is a machine shop 182 feet by 66 feet, and directly south of this shop is another building, 140 feet by 66 feet, which houses the storeroom, oil room, and blacksmith shop.

Harmon Shops, Interior of Locomotive Shop

Harmon Shops, Inspection Shed

Harmon Shops, Jack for Armature Removal

The locomotive shop proper is located to the east of the car repair shop, in which are two tracks provided with hydraulic jacks and connected with the car shop by means of transverse pits. There are two jacks, one of 40-ton capacity and the other 75-ton, both of the one-cylinder, telescopic type. The capacity of both of these jacks can be raised considerably by increasing the base pressure in the hydraulic line. No overhead cranes are located in the locomotive repair shop, as the armature and wheels are handled by jacks through the transfer pits to the car shop, where a crane is available for transferring the equipment to the transverse track across the north end of the car and machine shop.

East of the locomotive shop are located the paint shop, sheet-metal shop, and paint-storage room. Here the cars are washed and painted. A carpenter shop and storage room also adjoin this shop. North of the paint shop are the sandblast house and paint-spray house where equipment is prepared and painted.

Harmon Paint Shop

White Plains Shops, Battery Room

White Plains Shops, Exterior View

North of the car shop, but detached from it, is a wheel-press building with crane for handling wheels and axles.   Small rooms on convenient locations are devoted to armature repairs, air-compressor repairs, air-brake equipment repairs, welding, pipe work, train-heating boiler repairs, and contactor and control overhauling, together with office space. Acetylene gas and inflammable material are stored at points removed from the shop in order to reduce fire hazard.

WHITE PLAINS SHOPS

Well-equipped shops are also provided at White Plains North Station, where the transfer is made from steam to electric locomotives on the Harlem Division. This shop is more particularly intended for handling light repairs and inspection on multiple-unit cars.

White Plains Shops, Interior View

Inspection and light repairs, however, are also given to the electric locomotives reaching this point. The inspection shed covers three tracks, all provided with pits for practically the entire length. In the rear, on one side, is a room for handling repairs and inspection to storage batteries and for calibrating thermostats; while on the other side is a room devoted to light repairs, calibration, and inspection of air valves, contactors, etc., in connection with Type PC control. This room contains complete provisions for testing both locomotive and motor-car jumper cables.

A number of special machines are used to care for the operations in this shop. Among these are a small refrigerating unit for the calibration of the car thermostats, an automatic device for testing locomotive jumper cables, two motor-operated,

White Plains Shops, Car Jack

25-ton jacks for lifting car bodies from the trucks, and a greasing machine which includes electric heating elements to facilitate handling heavy compounds.

It is the practice of the inspection staff to anticipate possible interruptions to service; and any defect which is discovered on one car is usually a signal for the checking up of this piece of equipment on all cars. A careful record is kept of delays in the electric zone, and this shows an unusual freedom from delays due to electric equipment. In addition to the inspections given at Harmon and White Plains, some attention is also given to motive power and rolling stock in the Grand Central Terminal. For inspection and light repairs on the motor cars handling the service on the Yonkers branch, a small shop is maintained at High Bridge near the Sedgwick Avenue Terminal.

SIGNALS

With the rebuilding of the Grand Central Terminal, accompanied by the change from steam to electric operation, it was decided that for traffic reasons radical changes in the signal equipment then in use were necessary. The operation of the old signals would also be deranged by the use of the track rails for the return of the

White Plains Shops, Equipment for Testing Motor-car Jumper Cables

**White Plains Shops, Equipment for Testing
Locomotive Jumper Cables**

propulsion current. A new automatic signal and electric interlocking equipment was therefore adopted for the entire suburban zone. The signal circuits are operated by alternating current, and the influence of propulsion currents is prevented by the use of reactance bonds which permit the passage of direct current as desired, but, where necessary, interrupt the passage of the signal current.

MAINTENANCE OF EQUIPMENT

From the beginning of electrical operation, an efficient organization has been maintained by the New York Central Railroad Company for the repair and inspection of all electric rolling stock. From 1908 to the end of 1927, the electric locomotives used in the electric zone had operated a grand total of 38,404,000 miles. Records show that the cost of maintaining these locomotives during this entire period has averaged approximately 9 cents per locomotive mile.

Included in this figure are many items which might be termed extraordinary maintenance in connection with heavy repairs to the original class "S" locomotives which, after more than 20 years of service, are now undergoing the first back shop repairs. About half of these locomotives have already been overhauled.

Since starting electrical operation, the multiple-unit car equipment, consisting of 125 motor cars and 55 trailers at the beginning of operation and now totaling 336 motor cars, has made a total of 125,600,000 miles up to the end of 1927. The cost of maintaining these cars over this entire period has averaged approximately 5 cents per car-mile. There is now under way a program for rebuilding the first 180 cars. A portion of this expense is charged to maintenance and, therefore, in a way constitutes an extraordinary expenditure.

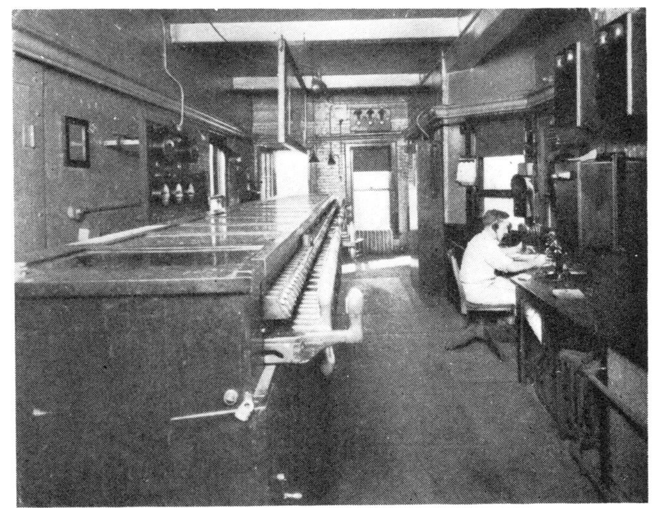

Interior of Signal Tower

View of Right-of-way Showing Third Rail

DATA ON ELECTRIC LOCOMOTIVES

Type	Classification	No.	Road No.	WEIGHT LB.		ONE HOUR RATING			CONTINUOUS RATING			First Built
				Total	Drivers	T.E.	M.P.H.	Hp.	T.E.	M.P.H.	Hp.	
S1–S2	2–D–2–225/139–4GE84A	35	1100–1134	225100	139200	15200	41.8	1695	4870	61.0	792	1904–6
S-3	2–D–2–240/146–4GE84A	12	1135–1146	239600	146000	15200	41.8	1695	4870	61.0	792	1908–9
T-1	B–B + B–B–230/230–8GE92A	10	1147–1156	230000	230000	20350	47.6	2584	11500	57.2	1756	1913
T-2	B–B + B–B–261/261–8GE91A	16	1157–1172	260600	260600	18500	50.1	2475	12500	57.1	1905	1914–18
T-3	B–B + B–B–278/278–8GE91A	10	1173–1182	277800	277800	18440	50.6	2488	12750	56.1	1908	1926
Q	B–B–200/200–4GE286A	7	1250–1256	200000	200000	34100	18.3	1665	25260	19.75	1330	1926
R	B–B + B–B–351/351–8GE286A	2	1200–1201	351400	351400	55800	22.3	3320	41200	24.2	2660	1926

ELECTRIC OPERATION

Grand Central Terminal	to Highbridge	December 12, 1906
Grand Central Terminal	to Wakefield	January 29, 1907
Wakefield	to Mt. Vernon	February, 1907
High Bridge	to Yonkers	April 6, 1908
Wakefield	to N. White Plains	March 16, 1910
Yonkers	to Glenwood	December, 1910
Glenwood	to Hastings	February 1, 1911
Hastings	to Tarrytown	November 19, 1911
Tarrytown	to Croton	February 22, 1913
Through trains	to Harmon	June 20, 1913
Sedgwick Avenue	to Getty Square, Yonkers	February 1, 1926

Combination Oil-electric Storage-battery Locomotive Used in Switching Service

OIL-ELECTRIC LOCOMOTIVES IN SERVICE ON THE NEW YORK CENTRAL R. R.

In anticipation of needs for self-propelled locomotives on parts of its lines not provided with an electric distribution system, the New York Central has contributed largely to the development of the oil-electric type of locomotive.

Three designs are now in operation in and about New York City to determine their adaptability to three types of service; namely, yard switching, freight haulage, and passenger service.

SWITCHING LOCOMOTIVE

The first type is a 128-ton combination oil-electric storage-battery locomotive with provision for operating from the third rail or overhead trolley. In normal service, the 218-cell battery is used to assist in acceleration and for operation when the engine is shut down. A 300-hp. Ingersoll-Rand engine is sufficient to keep the battery properly charged. Motor and control equipment identical with that used on the Class "Q" locomotive permits operation from the 660-volt supply when in the electric zone. This unit has given most satisfactory service in the various duties required in the switching yards.

FREIGHT LOCOMOTIVE

The 145-ton, 750-hp. oil-electric locomotive now operating on the Putnam Division of the New York Central is the first of this type to be used in road-freight service.

The running gear is a 2-D-2 design, each of the four driving axles being equipped with a GE-286 motor identical with that used on the electric freight and switching locomotives. Sufficient capacity is provided for handling freight trains of the weights common on this division; that is, from 500 to 550 tons. The schedule maintained is approximately the same as with steam locomotives.

The oil engine is a four-cycle, six-cylinder Ingersoll-Rand design, developing 750 hp. at 500 r.p.m. It is of the solid-injection type, the fuel being delivered to the cylinders through a distributor which is timed to register with the power stroke of each cylinder.

750-horsepower Oil-electric Freight Locomotive Used on Putnam Division

The control provides for operating the locomotive alone, or in multiple with another of the same type. Provision is made for operating in several motor combinations.

Compressed air for the brakes is furnished by a motor-driven compressor, and lighting and control circuits are supplied by a motor-generator set together with a 32-volt, 135-ampere-hour storage battery.

PASSENGER LOCOMOTIVE

The first oil-electric locomotive to be designed for road-passenger service has also a 2-D-2-type running gear similar to the freight locomotive, but with a somewhat heavier equipment, and a 900-hp. McIntosh & Seymour oil engine.

Sufficient capacity is provided for handling the regular passenger trains over the grades of the Putnam Division. It will make the same running time as is now made by steam locomotives, and in general it is intended to duplicate their performance.

The oil engine, designed and built by the McIntosh & Seymour Corporation, is a four-cycle, air-injection Diesel of the 12-cylinder "V" type. The engine is direct-connected to the generator through special flexible couplings. Its full-load rating is 900 brake horsepower at 300 r.p.m. with a 10 per cent overload capacity.

The electric equipment includes a main generator and an auxiliary generator direct-connected to the engine, four GE-286 traction motors, control equipment, electric auxiliaries, lights, and instruments. The auxiliary generator supplies separate excitation at 250 volts for the main generator, as well as power for the auxiliaries. A regulator maintains practically constant voltage on this auxiliary generator throughout the range of engine speeds.

Three running combinations of the traction motors are used—series-parallel, parallel, and parallel with reduced fields. Provision is made for train-line couplers at each end of the locomotive, permitting the operation of two locomotives in multiple with the control of both from operator's position. The speed of the locomotive is regulated by the operation of the throttle, which automatically establishes the field strength of the generator which is most suited for the existing load.

For heating the train, an oil-fired steam boiler is provided similar to that now used on the electric locomotives. The 32-volt supply for lighting and control circuits is obtained from a motor-generator set driven from the 250-volt auxiliary circuit. A 150-ampere-hour storage battery, floating on the line, supplies lighting and control circuits when the engine is not in operation.

900-horsepower Oil-electric Passenger Locomotive in Service on the Putnam Division

WEIGHTS AND DIMENSIONS OF OIL-ELECTRIC LOCOMOTIVES

OIL-ELECTRIC-STORAGE-BATTERY SWITCHER

Weight locomotive complete	257,000 lb.
Weight on drivers	257,000 lb.
Traction effort 1-hour rating	34,000 lb.
Maximum tractive effort (25% coef.)	64,250 lb.
Maximum speed	40 m.p.h.
Length inside knuckles	46 ft. 8 in.
Height over cab	14 ft. 8 in.
Width over all	10 ft. 2 in.
Total wheelbase	34 ft. 1 in.
Rigid wheelbase	8 ft. 3 in.
Diameter driving wheels	44 in.
Engine	Ingersoll-Rand 300 hp.
Battery	Electric Storage Battery 680 amp. hr. (6 hr. rating)
Mechanical parts	American Locomotive Co.
Electric equipment	General Electric Co.

OIL-ELECTRIC FREIGHT LOCOMOTIVE

Weight locomotive complete	295,000 lb.
Weight on drivers	175,000 lb.
Tractive effort 1-hour rating	30,600 lb.
Tractive effort continuous	20,800 lb.
Maximum tractive effort (25% coef.)	43,750 lb.
Maximum speed	40 m.p.h.
Length inside knuckles	52 ft. 1 in.
Height over cab	14 ft. 9½ in.
Width over all	10 ft. 4 in.
Total wheelbase	42 ft. 10 in.
Rigid wheelbase	17 ft. 6 in.
Diameter driving wheels	44 in.
Diameter truck wheels	30 in.
Engine	Ingersoll-Rand 750 hp.
Mechanical parts	American Locomotive Co.
Electric equipment	General Electric Co.

OIL-ELECTRIC PASSENGER LOCOMOTIVE

Weight locomotive complete	350,000 lb.
Weight on drivers	180,000 lb.
Tractive effort 1-hour rating	28,000 lb.
Tractive effort continuous	16,000 lb.
Maximum tractive effort (25% coef.)	45,000 lb.
Maximum speed	60 m.p.h.
Length inside knuckles	59 ft. 4 in.
Height over cab	14 ft. 8½ in.
Width over all	10 ft. 0 in.
Total wheelbase	49 ft. 4 in.
Rigid wheelbase	18 ft. 6 in.
Diameter driving wheels	44 in.
Diameter truck wheels	30 in.
Engine	McIntosh & Seymour 900 hp.
Mechanical parts	American Locomotive Co.
Electric equipment	General Electric Co.

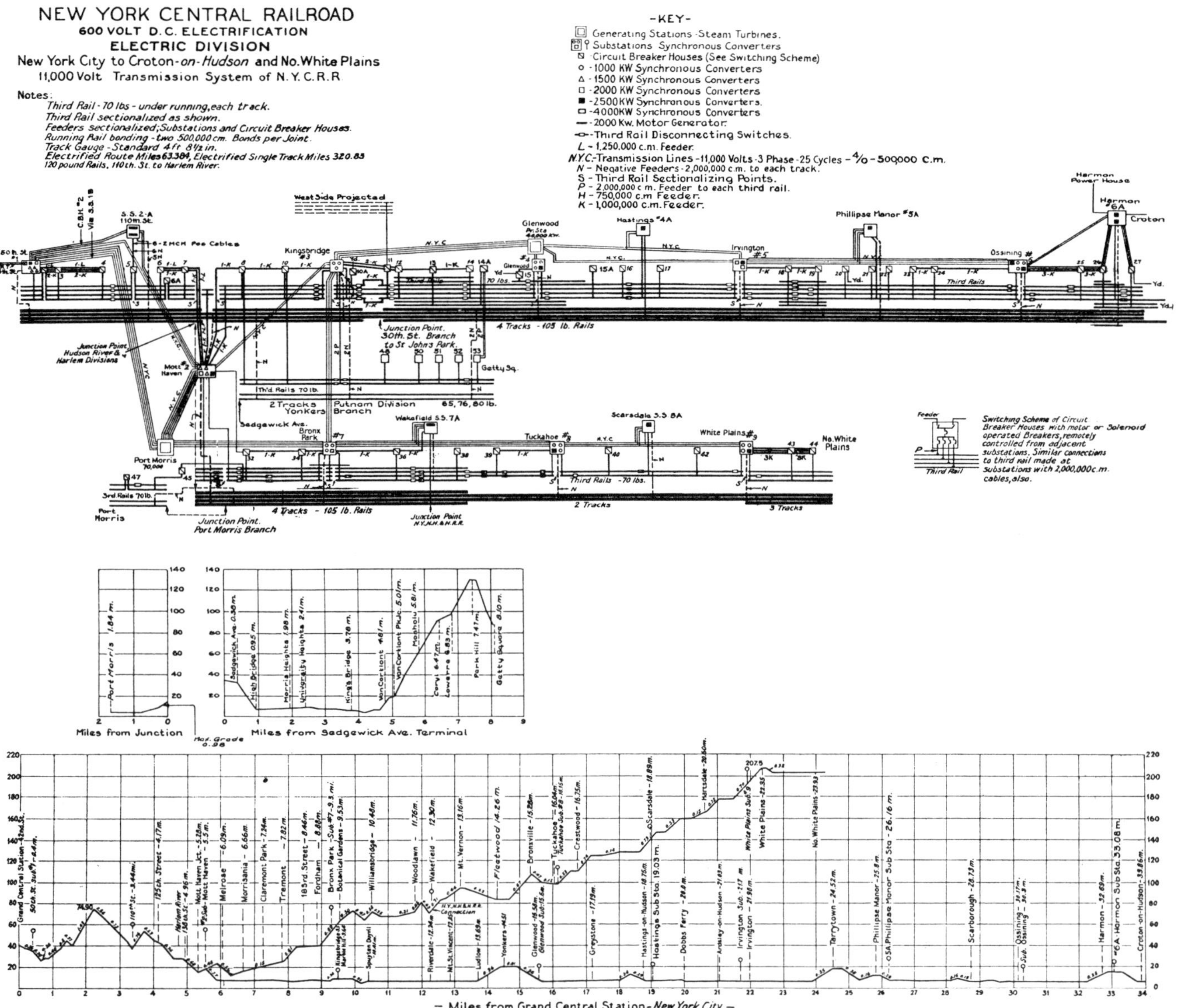

Schematic Diagram and Profile, New York City to Croton and North White Plains

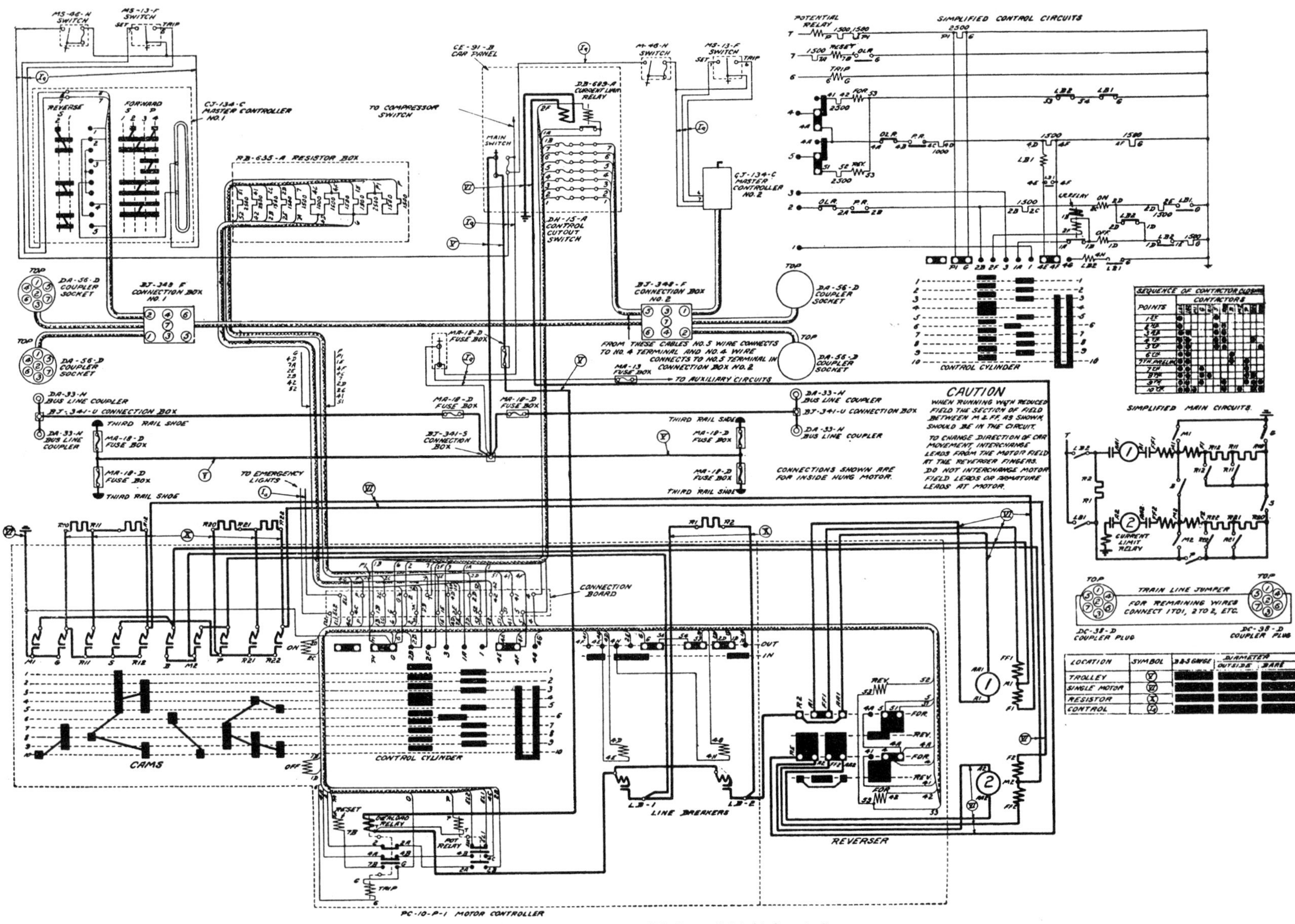

Simplified Wiring Diagram, PC Control, Multiple-unit Cars

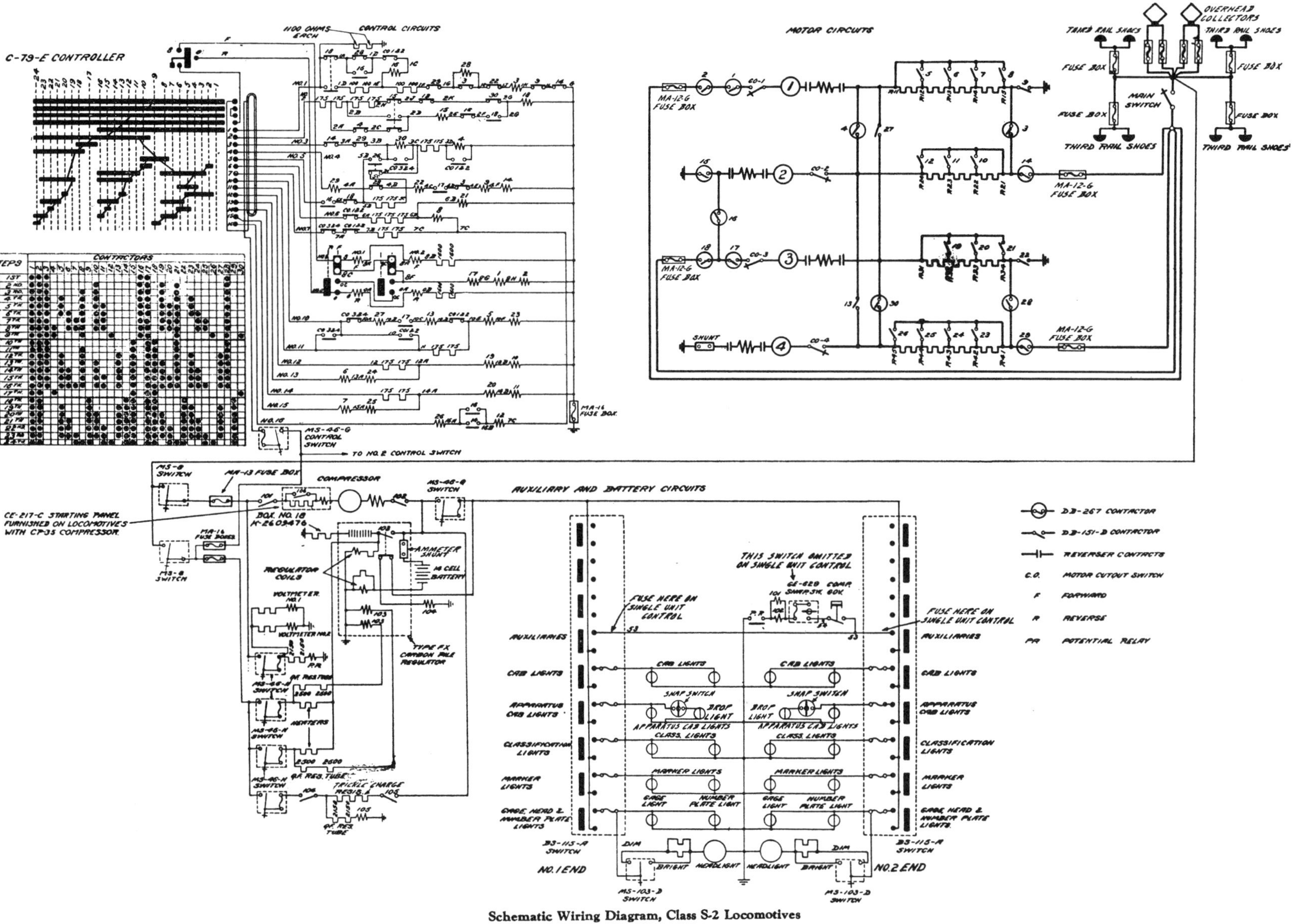

Schematic Wiring Diagram, Class S-2 Locomotives

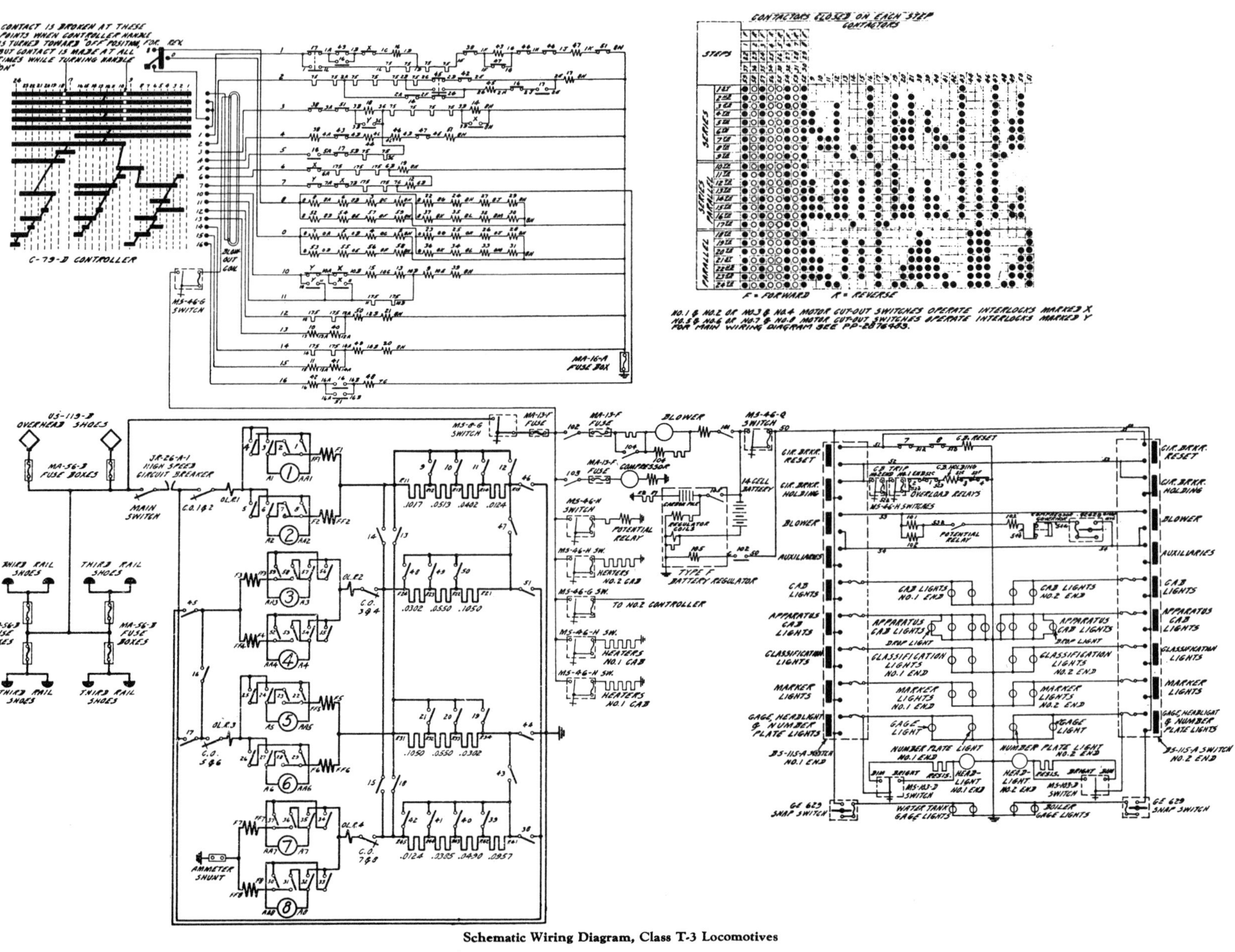

Schematic Wiring Diagram, Class T-3 Locomotives

GENERAL ELECTRIC
REVIEW

"Where lofty mountains once held sway
Electric power now makes its way."
—*Anonymous*

A View Along the Great Northern Railway, with Mount Index in the Background.   An extensive Electrification
and tunneling program is now being carried out on the Cascade Division of the Railway

LARGEST SINGLE-UNIT FREIGHT LOCOMOTIVE IN SERVICE
(See pp. 472, 474, 477, and 483)

GENERAL ELECTRIC
REVIEW

Vol. 30   October, 1927   No. 10

THE GREAT NORTHERN RAILWAY EXTENDS ELECTRIFICATION

The vast railroad systems of the United States constitute one of the greatest industries in the world today. Probably no other business has been favored with such an array of highly competent officers and men as the transportation systems of this country. Upon them rests the work of moving the ever-increasing freight and passenger traffic that has contributed so vitally to the growth of industry and to the widening of social life in America.

During the past fifteen years the transaction of railroad business has been handicapped however by constantly increasing cost for labor and materials, but in spite of these discouraging conditions the personnel of the railroads has attacked the problem with a will and has made remarkable progress in reducing the costs of operation and at the same time improving service.

The efficient handling of freight outside of the terminals is largely dependent upon the speed of movement attained. This speed in turn is affected by the character of the road and its profile, and the character and condition of the motive power and rolling stock. If a volume of business exceeding the capacity of the tracks is to be handled, delays are unavoidable.

The passenger business depends upon the frequency and speed of the train schedules, the attractiveness of the equipment, and in some cases upon the scenic attractions along the right-of-way.

Millions of dollars have been spent and more are being expended annually to improve the track and road bed, to lay heavier rails, reduce grades and curvatures, and to purchase new motive power and rolling stock, and on a number of roads to carry out extensive electrification programs.

Electric locomotives are now operating in every department of the transportation system: main-line freight and passenger business, switching yards, suburban and terminal electric zones, and more recently with the oil-electric locomotive and the gas-electric car, the handling of light-traffic branch-line business. Electricity has demonstrated its ability in every field to handle heavier trains at higher speeds, thus in one stroke increasing the capacity of a given set of tracks, expediting the handling of business,

reducing the cost of labor and material, and thereby improving the net revenue.

Advantages are also found in the lower cost of electric power as compared to locomotive fuel, the elimination of smoke, cinders and dirt, and a great reduction in the cost of maintaining electric as compared with steam locomotives, the advantages accruing from the use of regenerative electric braking on grades, and a general improvement in business resulting from the more attractive equipment.

In localities where there is an abundant supply of hydro-electric energy, cheap power is available even in competition with the low rates of coal which are in effect at this time. In other localities, great networks of power lines are now tied together and an abundant supply of power is available from central-station companies largely equipped with steam-generating stations. The reliability of this power supply and the extensive reserve behind it make it preferable to isolated-plant supply. Furthermore, the railroad company in electrifying its lines is relieved of the heavy expenditures for building a power station of its own and in some cases is able to purchase power delivered to the trolley line at the voltage required for locomotive operation.

The improvements being made by the Great Northern Railway on its Cascade section include, with the electrification, the building of a ten million dollar tunnel for the purpose of grade and curve reduction and the building of a new cut-off 16 miles in length. These will have a very decided effect in reducing the cost of operation, and it is expected that the electrification alone will produce sufficient increase in the operating revenue to more than justify the investment in the electrical equipment. The entire character of the Cascade crossing is being changed from a heavy-grade high-curvature district where severe winter conditions are encountered, to a comparatively high-speed high-capacity line.

The officers and engineering staff of the Railway are to be congratulated on the far-sighted policy which will enable them in a single progressive move to effectively reduce grades, curves, and at the same time take advantage of the many economies incident to electric operation.   W. D. B.

Great Northern Improvement Program

Scope of Project—New Electrified Zone—Reduces Grades and Curves—America's Longest Tunnel

By Col. FREDERICK MEARS

Assistant Chief Engineer, Great Northern Railway

COINCIDENT with the electrification of the Great Northern tracks over the Cascades, a most important program of grade and curve reduction and the elimination of snowsheds is being carried out between Wenatchee on the east slope and Skykomish on the west. These projects call for the expenditure of many millions of dollars.

The most important feature of this work is the long tunnel, now about half completed, between Berne and Scenic. This tunnel is 7.79 mi. long, and is by far the longest railroad tunnel on the American continent.

The electrification which is a part of the tunnel project will extend over all of the mountain grades in the Cascade Division, and will make possible a material reduction in running time of both passenger and freight trains.

The contract for building the tunnel was placed with A. Guthrie & Co., Inc., and the work was started in December, 1925. It was estimated at that time that the bore might be "holed through" by November, 1928, or about three years from the time of letting the contract. To date, the work is about up to schedule in spite of the necessity for timbering soft

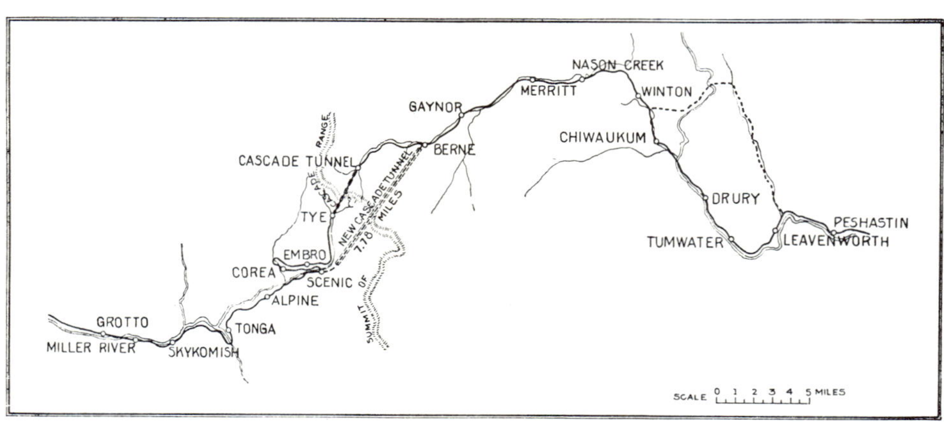

Fig. 1.   Map of the Great Northern Railway Through the Cascade Range, Showing the Location of the Construction Work on the New Cascade Tunnel and a New Line Between Peshastin and Winton

When completed, the new tunnel will afford the following advantages:

(1) Permanent protection from snowslides.

(2) Elimination of heavy expenditures for maintaining snowsheds.

(3) Reduction in operating costs through heavy snow belt during winter months.

(4) Shortening the distance by several miles.

(5) Elimination of much heavy curvature.

(6) Lower summit elevation and lessening total of rise and fall.

Although this improvement will involve an outlay in excess of $10,000,000, the expenditure can be fully justified by the elimination of the snowsheds, with their high maintenance cost and constant fire risk. The improvement in grade and track alignment, reduction in rise and fall, and the benefits from electrification are also sufficient in themselves to justify this capital expenditure.

ground at the start and encountering water in the Pioneer tunnel in quantities as high as 9000 gallons per minute. On this portion of the work, however, the drifting is up grade and the water drains naturally on a 1.56 per cent grade. Fortunately, very little water has been found in the East Portal workings and the Mill Creek shaft, where a provision for gravity flow is not possible.

All of the work is being carried on by electric power or by compressed air supplied from electrically-driven compressors. For handling the excavated material, more than ten miles of narrow gauge railroad has already been constructed. In the main tunnel the tracks are 36-in. gauge and 20-ton General Electric mine type locomotives are used equipped with gathering reels and flexible cable for extending the working range beyond the end of the trolley supply. In the Pioneer tunnel, 6-ton locomotives of the same type are used on a 2-ft. gauge track. These tracks run from both portals to the dumps and the locomotives are also used for discharging material from the Mill Creek shaft. In all, there are 39 locomotives, taking power from a 250-volt trolley system. The trolley is supplied from eight synchronous motor-generator sets suitably located and having a total capacity of 1500 kw.

Energy is supplied to all three camps at 2300 volts, 3-phase, 60 cycles, being transmitted to Scenic over a 13,200-volt line from the Great Northern substation at Skykomish. The Berne and Mill Creek workings receive power over an extension of this line from Scenic.

COMPARISON OF OLD AND NEW LINES
BERNE TO SCENIC

	O'd Line	New Line	Favorable to New Line
Length	17.67 mi.	9.99 mi.	7.68 mi.
Maximum curve	10 deg.	6 deg.	...
Total curvature	2128 deg.	187 deg.	1941 deg.
Maximum grade	2.2%	2.2%	...
Summit elevation	3382 ft.	2881 ft.	501 ft.
Total rise westward	546 ft.	45 ft.	501 ft.
Total fall westward	1325 ft.	824 ft.	501 ft.
Snowsheds, total length	6.04 mi.	0.0 mi.	6.04 mi.
Bridges, total length	0.23 mi.	0.04 mi.	0.19 mi.
Tunnels, total length	3.66 mi.	7.79 mi.	...

The extension of the electrification east to Wenatchee will be pushed rapidly in order that it may be ready for operation by the time the long tunnel is completed.

Chumstick Cutoff

Another improvement which is going forward on the Great Northern within the proposed electric zone is the construction of a new line between Peshastin

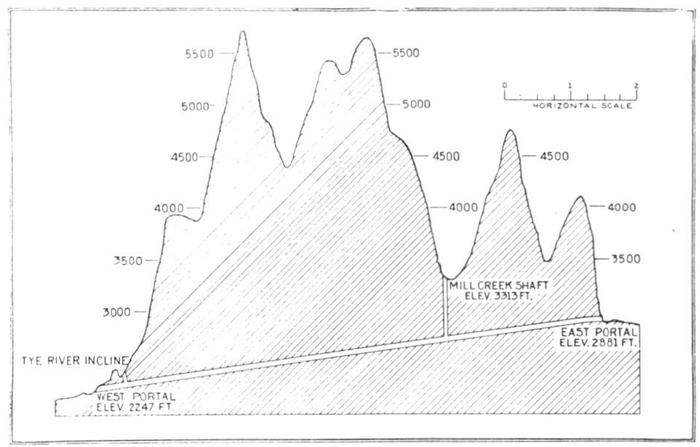

Fig. 2. Longitudinal Section of New Cascade Tunnel

and Winton, Washington. The present line between these points, 17 mi. in length, for the larger part of the distance runs through a narrow canyon and has 76 curves with a total of 2060 deg. curvature. The new line has a total of only 24 curves totaling 636 deg. The old line has maximum curves of more than 9 deg., while the new cut-off will not have any curve in excess of 3 deg.

The grades on the present line include six miles of 2.2 per cent compensated. On the other hand, the new line, besides being 1.02 mi. shorter, has no grade in excess of 1.6 per cent compensated. All of these factors assist in giving a line of fairly high-speed operating characteristics.

Fig. 3. A View in the Pioneer Tunnel Near the West Portal, Showing a 6-ton Mine-type Locomotive Flowing Through Water Which at Times Was Encountered in Very Large Quantities

The new line runs through an open country, thus eliminating the necessity for snowsheds, and reduces winter operating costs.

Fortunately, the old line passes through an unpopulated region and no difficulties due to abandonment of line will be encountered. The estimated cost of the new line is $3,600,000.

A. Guthrie & Co., of St. Paul, have undertaken the contract for this new line and completion will be in time for electric operation with the opening of the new tunnel.

The advantages of the new line are summarized in the following table:

DATA ON CHUMSTICK LINE
PESHASTIN TO WINTON

	Present Line	New Line
Length of line	17.22 mi.	16.20 mi.
Maximum curve	9 deg. 30 min.	3 deg.
Total curvature	2060 deg.	636 deg.
Number of curves	76	24
Maximum grade	2.20%	1.60%

Power for Great Northern Electrification Supplied by Puget Sound Power & Light Company

Power Resources of Territory—Reasons for Railroad Purchasing Rather Than Generating Power—Electric Operation Estimated to Require 25,000 Horse Power

By G. E. QUINAN

Chief Engineer, Puget Sound Power & Light Company

WITH approximately one-sixth of all the potential undeveloped water power of the United States within its borders, the State of Washington not only leads all other states in the Union in hydro-electric possibilities but in the application of electricity to commercial, rural, and domestic purposes as well. In estimating the water power resources of the country, the United States Geological Survey finds that the State of Washington has a minimum of 4,932,000 horse power and a maximum of 8,670,000 horse power available in the rivers and streams of the state.

It is estimated that somewhat less than 700,-000 horse power of water power has been developed to date and that this represents a per capita production of almost 0.4 horse power for every man, woman, and child in the state. It is interesting to note that estimates of per capita development in California are almost the same and that these two states lead all other states in this respect.

The figures just quoted do not of course take into consideration the steam plant capacity, more than 100,000 horse power of which is developed within the state and used largely as a substitute for water power when the streams are low in the fall and winter months, and also as a standby in case of accident to the water-power generating machinery or transmission lines.

Some idea of the extent to which electricity is utilized in Washington may be obtained from the fact that a survey conducted by the National Electric Light Association disclosed that but three per cent of the farms of the United States are electrified, whereas a similar survey conducted in the State of Washington showed that more than 50 per cent of the farms of that state make use of electric light

and power service, while more than 70 per cent of the farms situated west of the Cascade Mountains are electrified. More than 35,000 farms are served by the Puget Sound Power & Light Company alone, while at the close of 1926 nearly 17,000 electric ranges—almost one for every five resident customers—were connected to its lines. These figures are unequalled in any other territory in the world.

It may be a matter for thought why, in a state so wealthy in hydro-electric resources and wherein electric power is of such universal application, the Great Northern Railway did not prefer to construct its own power plant rather than purchase electricity from a power company.

As a matter of fact, the railroad company has found it doubly advantageous to buy power from a company having large power resources. By so doing, it is assured of a greater continuity of energy supply, for the power company's plants are not only interconnected among themselves but, in addition, are inter-connected with the power plants of other systems so that all possibility of interruption resulting from accident to any single generating station is virtually eliminated.

Furthermore, it has been found that the railroad company can purchase power much more cheaply than it can produce it for the reason that any power station that could be constructed of capacity large enough to serve the demand of the railroad would, of necessity, be idle a great part of the time, while the interest, operating expense, and depreciation charges would go on just the same. On the other hand, by purchasing power, the Great Northern Railway has to pay only its own proportion of such overhead costs while the balance is distributed among thousands of other customers of the power company.

Still another advantage which the railroad secures by purchasing power from a large central station company lies in the fact that regenerative braking can be adopted. Under this plan of operation, the motors which drive the locomotives up grades and along level stretches, become generators when the train is going downgrade and then produce electricity instead of consuming it. The current so generated is fed back into the power system and, naturally, must be absorbed at some point or other. In actual practice, part of this current might be absorbed by other trains but the amount would be so small that regenerative braking would prove uneconomical on a railroad served by a single power plant operated for railroad purposes only. Under the present arrangement, the power produced by regenerative braking is fed back into the power company's general system and is absorbed by other customers.

This method of braking represents a further substantial economy in operating costs since retarding the speed by operating the traction motors as generators greatly reduces the wear and tear on the wheels, brake-rigging, and brake shoes.

The Puget Sound Power & Light Company, which furnishes the Great Northern Railway with power for its electric operation, comprises a system of thirteen hydro-electric generating plants which, with subsidiary steam plants, has a total capacity of approximately 250,000 horse power, and the territory served extends from the British Columbia boundary line on the north to the Columbia River on the south and as far east as Wenatchee.

It is estimated that when the electrification of the Great Northern Railway has been completed from Skykomish to Wenatchee (Wash.), a distance of 82 miles, and is in full operation, the railroad requirements will be about 25,000 horse power.

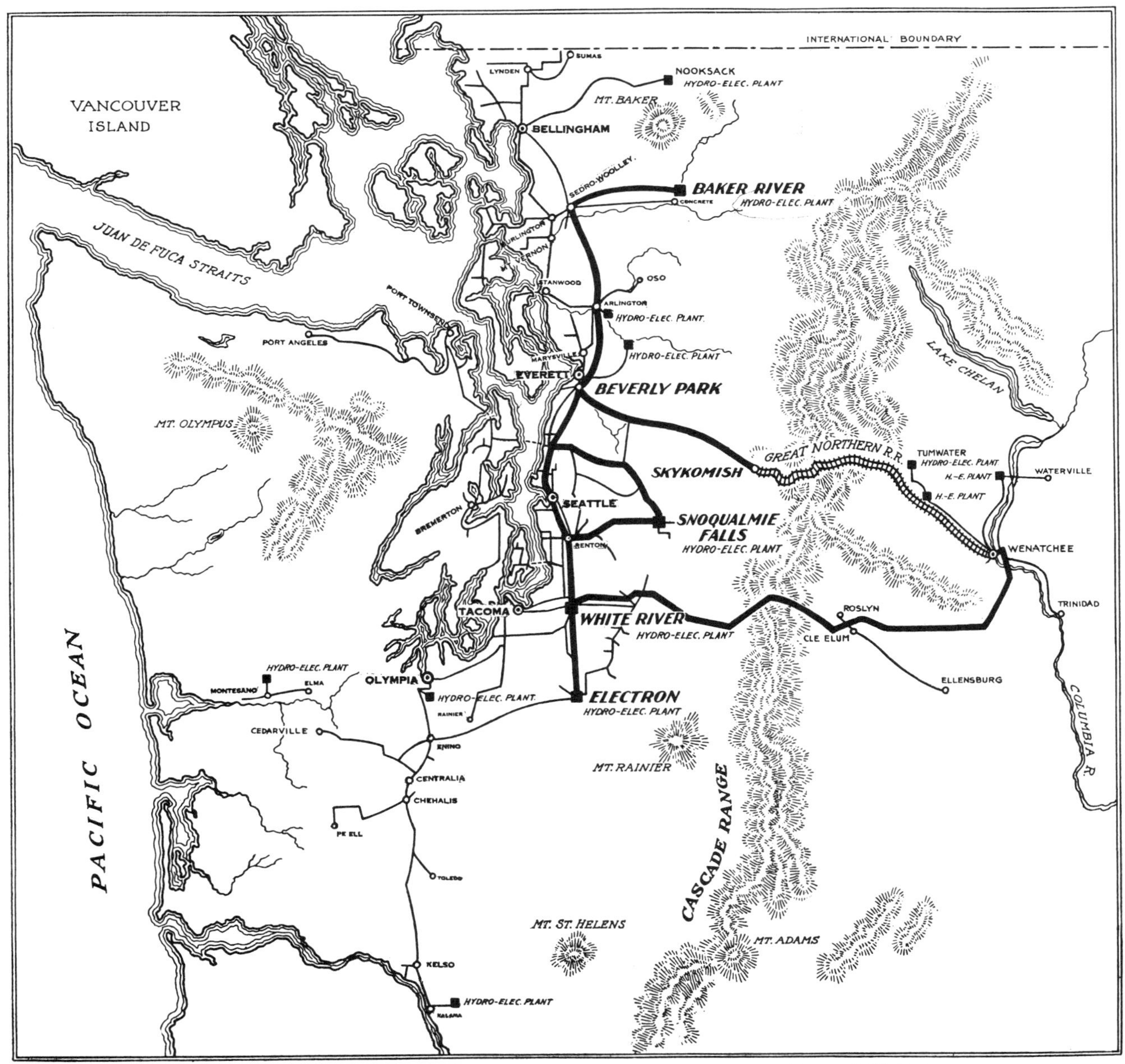

Fig. 1.   Map Showing the Relation of the Inter-connected System of the Puget Sound Power & Light Company to the Great Northern Railway Electrification

Fig. 2.   White River Hydro-electric Plant of the Puget Sound Power & Light Company, Which is One of the Plants in This System That Furnishes Energy for the Electric Operation of the Great Northern Railway

Fig. 3.   Generating Room of the White River Hydro-electric Plant

Motor-Generator Type Locomotives for Great Northern Railway

Single-phase A-c.-D-c. Locomotives to Handle Present Freight and Passenger Traffic—Mechanical Features of Construction—Electrical Converting and Driving Equipment—Control System and Auxiliaries

By ROBERT WALSH

Locomotive Division, Railway Equipment Engineering Dept., General Electric Company

MUCH interest has been manifested by both engineers and laymen in the new tunnel through the Cascade Mountains and the extended electrification which is being made by the Great Northern Railway in that region. A number of new and interesting developments have occurred during the progress of this work; and amongst these new developments the two motor-generator type locomotives, which have recently been built, supply their quota of interest. It is the purpose of this article to describe, briefly, the points relating to

Fig. 1. End View of One of the New Single-phase Locomotives. (A side view is shown in the frontispiece of this issue)

these locomotives which might be of interest, without going at all deeply into the fundamental design of the locomotives.

Motor-generator type locomotives, possessing as they do an extreme flexibility of control, lend themselves particularly well to certain types of railroad operation. Until the present developments are completed, the Great Northern locomotives will be used in both freight and passenger service between Skykomish (Wash.) and the present Cascade tunnel, which is a distance of 24.6 miles. They will then be operated

between Skykomish and Wenatchee. When electrified, this route will be about 72 miles in length and will include the new 7¾-mile tunnel and a new cut-off which will reduce a larger part of the present maximum grade of 2.2 per cent to 1.6 per cent. Incidentally, these are the largest single-unit motor-generator type locomotives that have yet been built.

General

The locomotive is of the geared motor type and has the converting apparatus and cab mounted on a cab-underframe, which in turn is supported through two center plates on two trucks. The trucks are articulated and each truck has three driving axles with an extension of the truck resting on a single-axle radius-bar guiding truck.

Single-phase power is obtained from the trolley at 11,000 volts, 25 cycles, and is transformed to 2300 volts. A synchronous motor operated at 2300 volts drives, through a flexible coupling, two direct-current generators which are connected in series and supply current at 1500 volts potential to the traction motors. The speed of the locomotive is chiefly controlled by varying the voltage of the generators, additional speed being obtained by two field-shunting positions.

The data in Table I indicate the general features of the mechanical design of the locomotive.

TABLE I

LOCOMOTIVE DIMENSIONS

Classification	$1-C+C-1$
Gauge	4 ft. 8½ in.
Total weight	518,000 lb.
Total weight on drivers	409,800 lb.
Weight per driving axle	68,300 lb.
Dead weight per driving axle	16,100 lb.
Weight per guiding axle	54,100 lb.
Total wheel base	58 ft. 8 in.
Maximum rigid wheel base	15 ft. 4 in.
Diameter of driving wheels	55 in.
Diameter of guiding wheels	36 in.
Length overall (inside knuckles)	73 ft. 9 in.
Width overall	11 ft. ¾ in.
Height over pantograph (locked down)	15 ft. 3 in.
Number of motors	6
Type of motors	GE-290-A
Minimum radius of curvature	250 ft.

Mechanical Construction

The box-type cab is 63 ft. in length and has sides and ends of ³⁄₃₂-in. steel plate riveted to a structural framework stiffened by bolster bars and a ¼-in. steel plate floor. The bolster bars are bolted and riveted to the cab-underframe at two places 31 ft. 1 in. apart.

The cab-underframe is made up of four 18-in., 45.8-lb., shipbuilding channels riveted together with bars so as to form two I-beams which extend the entire length of the cab. In addition to the bolster bars and cross-plates which stiffen and join the two I-beams, steel plate is riveted along the top and bottom, making an air duct through which air is supplied to all the motors.

An interesting piece of shop practice was accomplished during the building of the cab-underframe. Clearance conditions did not permit the use of 18-in., 45.8-lb., shipbuilding channels above the trucks where the center plates are situated. It was therefore decided to cut a piece of metal, approximately 17 ft. long by 9 in. wide and tapered at the inner end, out

Also, because of the heavy snowstorms that are experienced in the Cascade Mountains, the louvers are so made that they can be closed during the storms. Movable vanes in the roof of the cab are provided which allow the air discharged from the converting machinery to be disseminated inside the cab, when the louvers are closed, instead of being emitted through the roof hatches as is done normally. The interior of the engineman's compartment is insulated with cork in order to make him comfortable during extremely cold weather.

The roof is made of No. 8 tank steel and has three separate hatches so as to facilitate the removal of the converting apparatus and compressors from the cab.

Fig. 2.   The Trucks of a Great Northern Locomotive

Fig. 3.   Articulated Joint Between the Trucks Shown in Fig. 2

of the end of each channel near the neutral axis and then bring the divided surfaces together in a welded joint. This was done very successfully at the Schenectady plant of the American Locomotive Company.

There is an engineman's compartment at each end of the cab; and between each are located the direct-current control apparatus compartment, starting motor and regenerative braking exciter, main direct-current generators, traction-motor blowers and motor, synchronous motor, transformer blowers and motors, main transformer, compressors and alternating-current control apparatus compartment in the order named. The two control apparatus compartments are completely enclosed and apparatus can be reached only by opening doors or taking off covers. The louvers are placed in the cab sides opposite the control apparatus compartments. This is done so that any rain that may be forced through the louvers will hit only the sheet steel covering the compartments and then run down to the floor of the cab.

Although the speed of the locomotive at the continuous rating is only 18.6 miles per hour, the trucks have been so designed that the locomotive may be run at a much higher speed and still retain good riding qualities. A speed of 45 miles per hour was attained on the test track and at this speed the riding qualities of the locomotive were exceptionally good.

The side frames, end frames, air ducts, and transoms of each driving truck are combined in a single steel casting which, together with the articulated joint, take all buffing and hauling stresses. The complete trucks are mounted on semi-elliptic springs equalized in four groups arranged so as to give three-point suspension to each truck. The two axles on both sides of the articulated joint are side-equalized only, thus forming suspension at two points, while the driving axle on each truck is equalized to the center plate of its adjoining guiding truck which gives the equivalent of the single-point suspension. This makes certain that the weight carried by the guiding trucks (which is necessary for good guiding) be of a constant value irrespective of external conditions. The traction motors are so mounted that the "weight shifting" will be practically negligible regardless of the tractive effort exerted by the locomotive.

Provision is made for lubricating most of the wearing parts on the trucks by means of the Dot system of lubrication.

These mechanical features of construction furnish in part the background for the locomotive's electrical characteristics, listed in Table II. The various electrical units are described in the remainder of this article.

TABLE II
ELECTRICAL CHARACTERISTICS

Voltage at trolley (25 cycle)................... 11,000
Tractive effort, one-hour rating............... 67,200 lb.
Horse power, one-hour rating................ 3,300
Speed at one-hour rating, full field............ 18.2 m.p.h.
Tractive effort, continuous rating............. 60,500 lb.
Horse power, continuous rating.............. 3,000
Speed at continuous rating, full field.......... 18.6 m.p.h.
Tractive effort at 30 per cent coefficient of adhesion................................... 120,600 lb.
Gear ratio.................................. 21/82
Voltage at synchronous motor (single-phase)... 2300
Voltage of each of main generators (d-c.)...... 750
Voltage of starting motor (d-c.).............. 120
Voltage of main exciter (d-c.)................. 65
Type of control (non-automatic)....... { Electro-pneumatic Multiple-unit

Converting Apparatus

An air-blast transformer* is used to transform the current collected at the trolley from 11,000 volts to 2300 volts. Two blowers, each driven by a single-phase repulsion motor, supply air to the transformer. In case of the failure of one blower, the other will deliver sufficient air to the transformer under ordinary conditions, though indicating lights are installed in the engineman's compartments to inform him of such failure.

The motor-generator set is comprised of five units mounted on two shafts, three units being mounted on one shaft and two on the other. The two shafts are coupled together by means of a Fast flexible coupling which allows for angular and offset misalignment. The units comprising the motor-generator set are listed according to the functions that they perform in the following order:

(1) A synchronous motor operating on 2300 volts and having three-phase stator windings, though designed for single-phase operation. The shaft of this motor has $\frac{1}{32}$-in. end-play and is mounted on two bearings, an extension of the shaft carrying the main exciter.

(2) A 65-volt direct-current exciter that supplies the control current, the excitation for the main generators and regenerative braking exciter, and battery charging current. This exciter is overhung on the shaft of the synchronous motor.

(3) Two 750-volt generators connected in series and supplying current to three groups of traction motors, each group of which consists of two motors connected in series. The magnet frames of these two

*Described by G. L. Mower on p. 483 of this issue.—EDITOR.

generators are bolted together; and both armatures are mounted on a single shaft carried by two bearings. An extension of this shaft carries the combined starting-motor and regenerative exciter. The shaft has an end play of $\frac{1}{32}$ in.

(4) A combined starting-motor and regenerative exciter that is used as a single-phase series motor in order to start the motor-generator set, or as a direct-current generator to excite the fields of the traction motors during regeneration.

In order to start the motor-generator set it is only necessary for the engineman to press a button

Fig. 4. Parts of the Flexible Driving Gear Used on the Great Northern Locomotives

situated within easy reach. The synchronous motor then synchronizes automatically in one minute, with normal voltage on the trolley.

Traction Motors

Six GE-290-A-750/1500-volt forced ventilated, railway-type motors are geared to the six driving axles. These motors have box frames, twin gears and commutating poles, and are supported on the axles by axle brackets and bearings and on the transoms by spring nose supports. The trucks of the locomotive are so constructed that each motor can be dropped into a pit after the removal of the journal boxes, shoes, pedestal tie bars, axle brackets, motor nose suspension springs and motor ventilator flanges. Each motor receives 3500 cu. ft. of air per min. from the main air duct which is inside the cab-underframe and runs from No. 1 motor to No. 6 motor.

Cushion-type gears are used in order to equalize the stresses in the gears and pinions as much as possible and to absorb the shocks which, with a solid gear and pinion, are delivered on the teeth. The gear is made up chiefly of two parts, a cast-steel center and a forged steel rim. The gear center is prevented from turning inside the rim by numerous leaf springs

Fig. 5. Current-collecting and Auxiliary Equipment Mounted on the Roof of the Cab

placed in slots in the rim and center, allowing a small movement between the two. The pinions are made of forged steel. One pinion is mounted on each end of the armature shaft.

Control

The control used is of the well-known electro-pneumatic type arranged for non-automatic, multiple-unit operation.

Current is collected by means of two spring-raised, air-lowered, slider pantograph trolleys. One trolley has sufficient current-carrying capacity, two being provided so that under abnormal conditions both may be used or, in the event of one failing, the other will be available. It is possible for the engineman to unlock or pull down either or both trolleys from each engineman's compartment.

A master controller is placed in each engineman's compartment. This controller has a main cylinder with 26 notches and a braking cylinder with 16 notches. The first 24 notches of the main cylinder control the shunt fields of the two main generators, and the last two notches control the current in the traction motor field circuits. The 16 notches on the braking cylinder control the shunt field of the regenerative braking exciter. When the locomotive is motoring, the main cylinder only is used; when the locomotive is regenerating, all of the notches on both cylinders, with the exception of the two field-shunting notches, can be used. This gives an extremely flexible control during braking; and, as each of the 26 notches of the main cylinder are running notches, the flexibility of control during motoring is also remarkably good. Regeneration is established automatically when the voltage across the main generators is equal to the voltage across the traction motors. This balanced-voltage condition is obtained by manipulation of the controller handles. In order that the locomotive may on occasion pull a heavier train at lower speed, a small switch mounted on the master controller changes the motor grouping from the three groups of two in series to two groups of three in series. It is not possible to use this connection to regenerate, or shunt the current in the traction motor fields. One side of each main generator is grounded in order to give a maximum potential above ground of 750 volts on the traction motor circuits.

During the testing of the locomotive, regenerative braking operation was carried out with the help of a New York Central Class H-10 steam locomotive. Various tests were made with the steam locomotive pushing the Great Northern locomotive; and it was found that regeneration could be established at any speed up to 40 miles per hour. The steam locomotive, with the throttle wide open, was brought down to a speed of three miles per hour by means of the regenerative braking.

There is a high-speed circuit breaker in each of the main generator circuits. These breakers not only protect the main generators but give overload and short-circuit protection to the traction motors. They serve also as line breakers and can be opened and closed by means of a push-button within reach of the engineman.

Electro-magnetic contactors control the compressor motors and traction-motor blower motor. The contactors for the blower motor are actuated by push-button switches within reach of the engineman when in either operating compartment. There are no contactors in the transformer-blower motor circuits; these motors start up immediately the trolley touches the overhead wire.

The heaters in each engineman's compartment are in two separate circuits, each controlled by a separate switch, so that a certain amount of heat regulation is possible.

A voltage regulator, connected in the circuit of the shunt field of the main exciter, keeps the voltage at the brushes of this exciter at 65 volts. A battery is provided of sufficient capacity to keep the lights burning in the locomotive for a reasonable length of time and to energize the necessary contactors used in starting up the motor-generator set.

In addition to the usual air gauges there are various meters situated in full view of the engineman. These are the following: two direct-current ammeters, one in the traction motor armature circuit and the other in the traction motor field circuit; an alternating-current voltmeter and alternating-current ammeter, indicating the voltage and current of the synchronous motor; an equalizing voltmeter, and a speedometer.

thus overheating in the event of one fuse blowing, a temperature relay in the circuit opens the contactors when the windings of the motor reach a predetermined temperature.

Air Brakes

The locomotive is equipped with Westinghouse double-end, straight and automatic air-brake equipment together with air signalling equipment. Because of the regenerative feature of the locomotive, the brake equipment includes an automatic control switch and regenerative interlock. The automatic control switch insures that an emergency application of the brakes can be made at all times. The regenerative interlock prevents a service application of

Fig. 6. Regenerative Braking Test in Which a Steam Locomotive Served as a Substitute for a Loaded Train on a Down Grade

Overload relays and fuses in the main and auxiliary alternating-current circuits give protection against overloads and short circuits. Air-operated sanders, bell ringers and whistles are controlled by valves at the engineman's position.

Auxiliary Apparatus

The locomotive equipment includes two 540-volt, single-phase, two-stage compressors. Each compressor has a capacity of 100 cubic feet of free air per minute. The power supplied to the motors is taken from a tap off the main transformer and both motors are cooled by air taken from the transformer blowers. Connected to the same tap off the transformer are the heaters and transformer blower motors.

Two blowers supply the air for the six traction motors. One 720-volt, three-phase, squirrel-cage induction motor drives both blowers. Power is obtained for this motor from the three-phase windings of the synchronous motor. In order to prevent the operation of the motor as a single-phase induction motor, and

the brakes on the locomotive during regenerative braking but does not prevent an application of the brakes on the train.

Location of Apparatus

On the Great Northern locomotive an attempt has been made to give free access to all the apparatus that requires inspection and attention. In addition to this, as much as possible of the direct-current control apparatus is housed in one enclosed compartment; and the same plan is carried out with regard to the alternating-current control apparatus, leaving the center of the cab free for the motor-generator set, transformer, compressors, etc.

The direct-current control apparatus compartment is at the No. 1 end of the locomotive and is entered through a door opening into the No. 1 end engineman's compartment. In this compartment are the field-shunting and regenerative-balancing resistors enclosed in a heat-insulated compartment. Ventilation is provided through two flues which reach to the roof of the locomotive. The reversers, series-parallel switch, overload relays and all the contactors in the main traction-motor circuits are placed above and alongside this resistor compartment.

The traction motor blowers and blower motor are placed underneath the Fast coupling. Both blowers are set in the main air duct and discharge in opposite directions.

At the No. 2 end of the locomotive is the alternating-current control apparatus compartment which is entered through a door opening into the No. 2 end engineman's compartment. This compartment contains the contactors in the synchronous-motor circuits and the starting-motor circuit, the tap-changing resistor, various relays, and main generator and regenerative exciter-field resistors. In a small compartment inside this main compartment are the electro-magnetic contactors used for the control of the main generator- and regenerative-exciter voltages.

The engineman's compartments are connected by two aisles which run the entire length of the locomotive cab. The apparatus not in either of the control compartments can be easily reached from one or the other of these two aisles. Doors are placed at the ends of each aisle to keep the noise of the rotating machinery out of the engineman's compartments.

The mechanical portions of these locomotives were built at the Schenectady Works of the American Locomotive Company. The steel castings forming the truck beds were made by the Commonwealth Steel Company. The General Electric Company designed the locomotives and manufactured the equipment at various plants, the installation of equipment and test being made at the plant in Erie (Pa.). At the time of writing—August 13, 1927—one locomotive has been shipped to Skykomish (Wash.); another is being tested, and work is proceeding on two more locomotives very similar to the two described in this article, which have recently been ordered by the Great Northern Railway Company.

Prof. Elihu Thomson Awarded the Faraday Medal

The Institution of Electrical Engineers, of Great Britain, has recently awarded the Faraday Medal to Prof. Elihu Thomson, one of the founders of the General Electric Company and Director of its Thomson Research Laboratory at Lynn, Mass. This is the third of England's highest scientific and engineering honors to be bestowed upon Prof. Thomson, and he is the only scientist in the world who has received all three of these awards: the Hughes Medal (in 1916), the Kelvin Gold Medal (in 1924), and the Faraday Medal (in 1927).

Hughes Medal   Kelvin Medal   Faraday Medal

Air-blast Transformers for Great Northern Locomotives

Mechanical and Electrical Service Requirements—Unusual Features of Construction Incorporated—
Compactness, Strength, and Capacity Combined—Provision for Varied Operating Conditions

By G. L. MOWER

General Transformer Engineering Dept., Pittsfield Works, General Electric Company

THE motor-generator type locomotives for the Cascade Electrification of the Great Northern Railway, described elsewhere in this issue by Mr. Walsh, each includes as an essential part of its equipment an air-blast transformer of unusual design. This unit furnishes the electrical tie between the 25-cycle, 11,000-volt, single-phase overhead catenary system and the locomotive's 25-cycle synchronous motor-generator set which in turn converts the output of the transformer from 2300 volts alternating current to 1500 volts direct current for application to the traction motors. Each of these air-blast transformers is rated: 25 cycles, 3285 kv-a., 11,000 volts 2420/568 volts//150 volts.

Fig. 1. Exterior View of the Air-blast Transformer Mounted on Its Side as in the Locomotive. The portions of the coils projecting beyond the core are rigidly braced by the many adjusting screws

The electrical design was complicated by the varied operating requirements that had to be met, which will be briefly outlined later. The mechanical construction also was by no means simple because the space in the locomotive available for the transformer placed sharp restrictions upon its allowable dimensions. In order to meet this installation requirement, the transformer was not set upright in the usual manner, but was laid on its side with the long dimension perpendicular to the length of the cab. This arrangement permitted of a passageway between the transformer and the side wall of the locomotive. The height of the transformer was limited by the roof of the cab. These space restrictions required a very compact design. A very low core build and an abnormally high coil build were therefore used, resulting in the coils being approximately square instead of the conventional rectangle.

The standard steel-housed type of air-blast transformer construction was employed but the design was modified to permit the unit to be installed on its side, as shown in Figs. 1, 2, and 3. The necessary mechanical strength was obtained by riveted angle-iron braces, arranged on each side of the core. The four angle irons adjacent to the core were notched at the upper end to serve as lifting lugs. The complete unit rests on substantial angle irons which also provide means for attaching it to the car frame.

The portion of the coils enclosed by the core is supported against mechanical strains by the core structure itself. The part of the coils not enclosed by the core is braced against mechanical forces by means of an adjustable steel structure, which in turn is rigidly secured by the core clamps and steel housing. Special care was taken in the design of these units to make all parts absolutely tight, in order to withstand the continual vibration encountered in railway service. For example, special locking devices were used on all core bolts. The individual strands of conductor, in both the high- and low-voltage windings, are adequately braced every few inches by use of the so-called "wavy" spacing strips and channels. All these coil braces, as well as the coil leads, are secured against vibration. To protect the windings from the absorption of moisture which might enter with the cooling air, and also to increase their rigidity, the coils received a special varnish treatment and the assembled coil stacks were given vacuum varnish treatment followed by a varnish dip while hot.

The transformers were as carefully designed thermally as mechanically, *i.e.*, they were so designed that the cooling air effectively and efficiently dissipates the heat generated by the coils and core.

The coils, when assembled in the insulating barriers and supporting channels, have every strand of each conductor exposed on one or the other side to the cooling air blast. In other words, no conductor is blanketed on both sides by insulating material, except for very short distances. Then too, as the complete windings are entirely inclosed in insulating material and separated from the core by ample air ducts, the temperatures of the core and windings are practically independent of each other.

The core is cooled by the air blast passing across

the inside edges of the laminations and by natural radiation from the outside edge.

When an air-blast transformer is mounted upright in the standard manner, the air enters at the bottom and comes out at the top. In these locomotive transformers the air circulates through the interior in the same manner, except that instead of entering at one end and coming out the other it is blown in at the bottom, deflected at an angle of 90 deg., and after passing through the coils, is again deflected to come out the bottom at the other side.

Earlier in this article mention was made of the fact that the varied operating requirements to be met

(6) It must supply from a special 150-volt tertiary winding the current drawn by the starting motor of the locomotive's motor-generator set. This current amounts to 4000 amp. at the start and tapers to 1500 amp. in two minutes, after which the load is cut off. The winding has a capacity for five successive starting operations in a 30-min. period, then it must be cooled before being operated again. There is practically no other load on the transformer when this tertiary winding is in use. Its open-circuit voltage is 150 with 11,000 volts impressed on the primary. Two taps are provided to give 120 and 90 volts under the same conditions.

Fig. 2.   High-voltage End of the Transformer

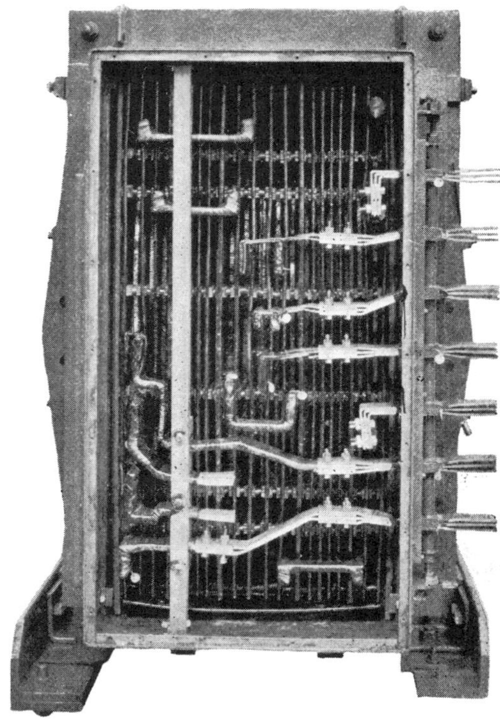

Fig. 3.   Low-voltage End of the Transformer

necessarily complicated the electrical design. An outline of these requirements follows:

(1) With 11,000 volts on the primary, the transformer must deliver 3160 kv-a. continuously.

(2) With 10,500 volts on the primary, it must deliver the same load (3160 kv-a.) continuously.

(3) With 9350 volts on the primary, it must deliver 3160 kv-a. for ten minutes and 3950 kv-a. for one minute, in either case with the windings at their normal temperature when the specified load is applied.

(4) Also, with voltages below 9350, it must operate continuously at reduced capacities using the full secondary winding.

(5) With 10,000 volts on the primary, a tap connection on the secondary must supply 125 kv-a. at approximately 568 volts (turn ratio) for operating auxiliaries, such as blower motors, heater circuits, etc. This load is continuous, but is reduced in proportion to the voltage when it is less than 10,500.

These locomotive air-blast transformers were designed and tested in accordance with A.I.E.E. Standards. The following operating characteristics are of interest:

(1) Volume of air 7,000 cu. ft. per min. at 40 deg. C.

(2) Air pressure 2 oz. per sq. in.

(3) Operating Conditions (approximate):

Kv-a.	High Voltage	Low Voltage	Power-factor (Leading)
3160	11,000	2415	95
3160	10,500	2305	95
2820	9,350	2310	95
3160*	9,350	2100	80

*Ten minutes load.

The actual net weight of each transformer is 26,850 lb.

The dimensions are 88 in. by 53½ in. floor space and 78 in. high.

It can be said in conclusion that since they occupy less space and weigh less than oil-immersed transformers, air-blast transformers are especially adapted for service on electric locomotives.

THE
ELECTRIFICATION
OF THE
MEXICAN RAILWAY

The Electrification of the Mexican Railway

PART I

By J. B. COX

Transportation Engineering Department, General Electric Company

THE electrification of the Mexican Railway (Ferrocarril Mexicano) is of special interest as being the first undertaking of this nature carried out in old Mexico. The author of the present article made the initial study of the problems involved in 1921 and a contract was signed for the construction work and for the electrical equipment in 1922. The work was completed and electrical operation started in 1925.

The operation has been so conspicuously successful that it would now seem to be of general interest to describe many of the details of construction and to give such operating data as are available.

The main line of the Mexican Railway extends from Mexico City to the Gulf Coast at Vera Cruz; it is 264 miles in length, and there are six branch lines. Details are given in Table I:

TABLE I

STANDARD GAUGE (4 ft. 8½ in.)

	Miles
Vera Cruz to Mexico	264
Apizaco to Puebla	29
Ometusco to Pachuca	29
Pachuca to Ixmiquilpan	51
	373
Sidings and Second Track	74
	447

NARROW GAUGE

Huajuapam Branch (3 ft.)	56
Zacatlan Branch (2 ft. 6 in.)	30
Huatusco Branch (2 ft.)	20
	109
Total Mileage	556

From Mexico to Esperanza the line follows the general contour of the plateau, resulting in frequent reversal of gradients, but none exceeding 1.5 per cent. The elevation at the terminus in Mexico City is 7346 ft. The highest point on the line is near Acocotla, 95 miles from Mexico, with an elevation of 8320 ft., making a rise of about 1000 ft. From this point to Esperanza, a distance of 58 miles, the drop is 240 ft. with the surface undulating as before.

At Boca del Monte (the Mouth of the Mountain), 3.8 miles east of Esperanza, the plateau ends suddenly and the descent for the following 19.0 miles to Encinar is very rapid. At Santa Rosa the line enters the Valley of the Rio Blanca and the grade becomes normal on to Orizaba.

From Orizaba to Paso del Macho the drop is considerable, though much less rapid than that just described. In the 35 miles there is a descent of 2466 ft. There are some comparatively long sections of tangent track, and the curves, except in the Baranca, are not unusually numerous or seriously sharp. Fig. 1 shows the general contour of the main line, Fig. 2 the original profile with uncompensated grades, and Fig. 3 the curvature on the 16.5 miles of heaviest grade.

In Fig. 4 is shown a map of the system including the electrified section. Fig. 5 is a general view of the power plant and Fig. 6 shows the general character of the country.

The productiveness of the country is quite varied in character: Coffee, corn, wheat, sugar cane, bananas, oranges and other semitropical grains and fruits grow in abundance. The soil and the climate seem well suited for a most successful agricultural development, and the possibilities for water-power development along the line of the railroad, combined with the many other attractive advantages, should leave little doubt as to the eventual prosperity of this section.

The section from Paso del Macho to Vera Cruz, 48 miles in length, is a gradual descent from an elevation of 1560 ft. to sea level, the ruling gradient being approximately 1.7 per cent and the alignment normal.

History

The promotion, construction and operation of this road, the first to be built in Mexico, has all been in close synchronism with the interesting, if tumultuous, history of the country. The original charter was obtained in August, 1855, under which a road was to be constructed from Vera Cruz, on the Gulf of Mexico, and across country via Mexico City to Acapulco, on the Pacific Coast. About 3½ miles of line extending from Mexico City to Guadalupe, a suburb, was built and opened to traffic on January 1, 1857. In August of the same year the original concession was taken over by Don Antonio Escondon, whose elder brother, Don Manuel Escondon, was the really dominant factor in the enterprise; but who, realizing that his advanced age would be likely to prevent his seeing the project completed, as was actually the case, placed his younger brother in direct charge of the undertaking.

In December, 1857, the services of Capt. Andrew Talcott, a graduate of West Point, of the class of 1818, with an extensive experience in government service and in the building of early American railroads, was engaged as chief engineer to take charge of the location and construction of the line.

Within 30 days Capt. Talcott was on the ground with three assistants and two brigades of engineers, consisting of 12 men each, and an exploring party of

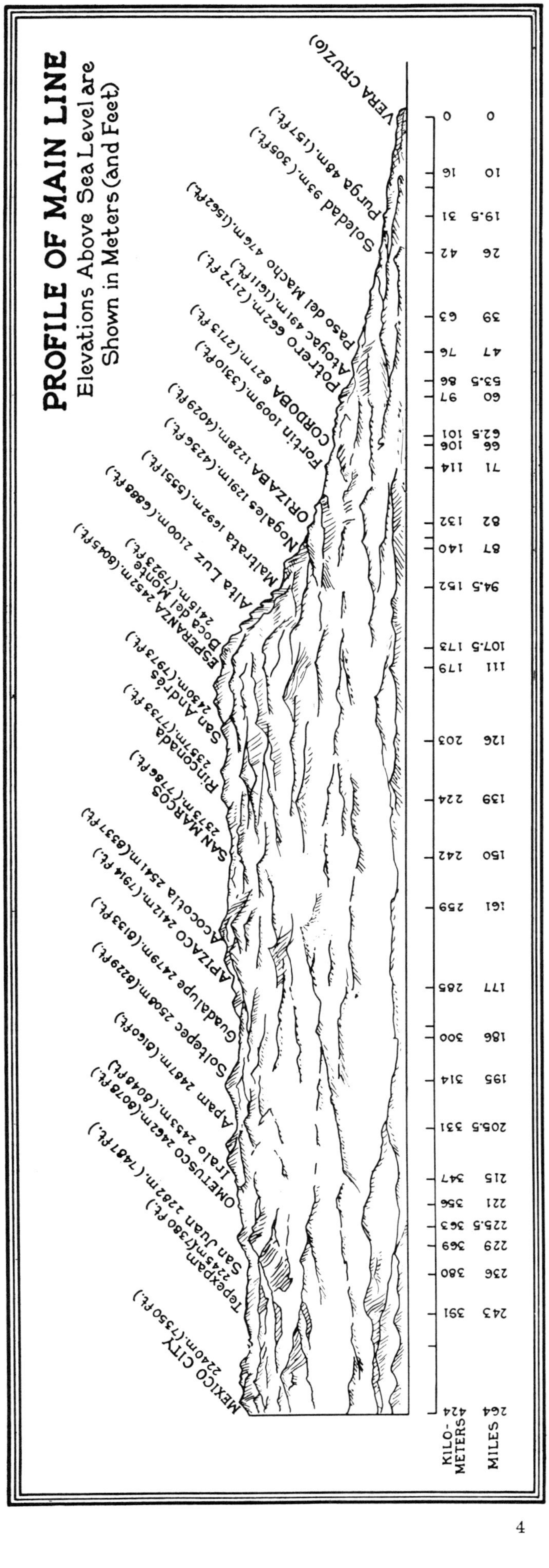

PROFILE OF MAIN LINE
Elevations Above Sea Level are Shown in Meters (and Feet)

Fig. 1. Graphic Profile of Line Between Mexico City and Vera Cruz

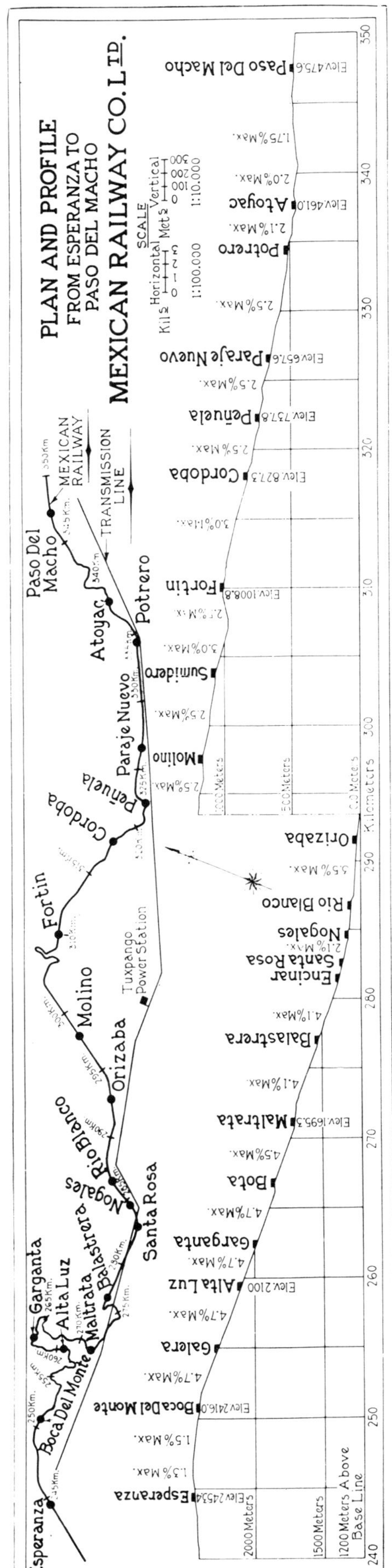

Fig. 2. Profile of Electrified Section

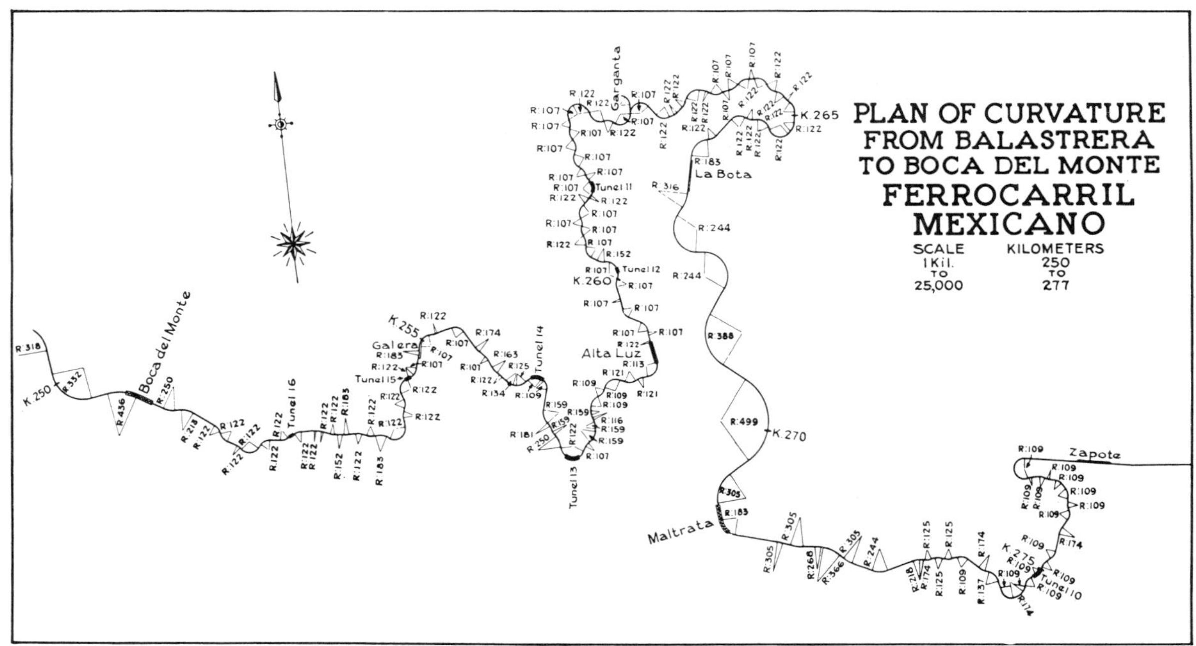

Fig. 3. Plan of Curvature from Balastrera to Boca Del Monte on the Ferrocarril Mexicano

Fig. 4. Map of System, Showing Location of Electrified Zone

Fig. 5.   Tuxpango Power Plant, which Supplies Power to the Mexican Railway

Fig. 6.   General Panoramic View of Electrified Section

five men ready for work. However, before the survey had been well started an internal revolution overthrew the constitutional government resulting in a struggle between the contending parties which seriously retarded the work. So it was not before March, 1859, that Capt. Talcott forwarded his report covering the survey of the route and the estimated cost of construction, maintenance, and operation of a railway from Vera Cruz to Mexico City.

Much careful work was done in determining the location of the line between Encinar and Boca del Monte. The route surveyed was approximately 19 miles in length, though the surface of the country was favorable for a considerably longer route, which would have reduced the ruling grade, but at an increased cost of construction. The question was analyzed from a purely economical standpoint. More tons could be handled with the same motive power if the grade was reduced and the cost of fuel per ton-mile would be less; but the longer line would cost more to construct and the maintenance of the line would be greater. It was desired to find the point which would secure the minimum cost of operation. It is interesting to note that a locomotive weighing 25 tons, with a tender weighing 20 tons, loaded, was considered in these calculations; one such locomotive being thought capable of hauling a 130-ton train from Vera Cruz to Orizaba. With a second engine of equal weight, but specially constructed for helper service, a train of the same weight could be taken from Orizaba to Boca del Monte.

It was considered that the most economical grade, so far as working power was concerned, changed as the adhesion of the locomotive changed, and that the adhesion varied from 14 per cent to 30 per cent, also that with an adhesion of 30 per cent a grade of 2.9 per cent would be most economical; or that with an adhesion of 20 per cent a grade of 2.3 per cent would be most economical; or that with adhesion of 14 per cent a grade of 1.9 per cent would be preferable. Increasing the grade to 4.6 per cent was estimated to increase the cost of power only 7.2 per cent with an adhesion of 20 per cent; that is to say, as the adhesion diminishes the cost of working increases.

The maintenance of way was considered at that time usually to be as large an item of operating expense as that of power, and therefore the most economical operation would be obtained by a grade exceeding that which would cost least for power, even if the cost of construction were not less. It was estimated that in a mountain road of this kind, a grade of 4.6 per cent would be 10 per cent shorter, and the cost of construction less; and that the saving in cost, together with the saving in maintenance, would fully compensate for the additional power required for operation. The extent of the saving would depend on the amount of tonnage which would be taken over the line. The line was, therefore, surveyed to have a ruling grade of approximately 4.6 per cent.

For many months after Capt. Talcott's report had been made no definite action was taken because of the internal conditions of the country. No construction work was done under the grant of August 31, 1857. A new grant was obtained from the existing government on April 5, 1861, and Capt. Talcott was called on to return to Mexico, which he did in March, 1862.

In the meantime, owing to the unsettled conditions of the Mexican Government, there had been a joint intervention in Mexican affairs by European powers, and Spanish soldiers had been put in charge at Vera Cruz in December, 1861; and these were soon followed by French troops. By this time about 9 miles of track had been constructed between Vera Cruz and Tejeria, from which point transportation to Mexico City and intervening settlements was conducted on the old Spanish highways, which had been allowed to deteriorate until almost impassable during the rainy season. The French army, requiring improved transportation, seems to have been responsible for the further extension of the tracks from Tejeria to Soledad. This definitely determined the route via Orizaba. The arrival of Maximilian in Mexico City in June, 1864, gave impetus to negotiations that Antonio Escondon had under way with English capitalists, which finally resulted in a contract, dated August 19, 1864, between the Imperial Railway Co., Ltd. and Smith Knight & Co., for the construction of a railway from Vera Cruz to Mexico City and a branch railway to Puebla, according to the plans and specifications of Capt. Talcott. Immediately afterward, definite plans for energetic construction of the remainder of the road were begun; the terms of the transfer of the road calling for its completion by April, 1869.

The present Mexican Railway was incorporated August 20, 1864 as the Imperial Mexican Railway Company, Ltd., under the government of Emperor Maximilian I.

After the downfall of Maximilian in 1867, and the reëstablishment of the republic, it was necessary to revindicate the former concessions. Accordingly on November 27, 1867, a new contract was made with Senor Escandon on terms more favorable than were contained in the former contract.

The railroad was finally completed on December 31, 1872, under the Escandon grant, 9 years after his first contract was made and 18 years from the date of the original concession. The road was formally inaugurated and opened for through traffic on January 1, 1873, by President Sebastian Lerdo de Tejada. The cost of construction was unusual and extremely high. The road had thus been in operation for about 51 years previous to the electrification of the Mountain Division which is the subject of this article.

With the comparatively settled conditions which gradually came about with the ascending of Porfirio Diaz as president, the property became more prosperous. Before the beginning of the disturbance leading to his abdication the property had been brought into splendid condition. However, the revolution of 1910 suddenly brought an end to this prosperity and resulted in the road being taken from its owners for operation by the new government in November, 1914, under which control it remained for about five years; first until August, 1916, when it was returned, but was again seized in April, 1917, and not returned until June, 1920.

When the property was returned to the owners the line and the equipment were found to be in very poor condition, as practically no new apparatus or supplies had been purchased and the stores had been depleted. Seventeen stations along the line had been burned or seriously damaged and the old personnel of the organization had been dispersed and the discipline of the working forces had become much demoralized. On again taking charge of the road in 1920 the owners found many of the locomotives and cars to be in an inoperative condition and there was little material or supplies on hand with which to make repairs. New difficulties were also encountered in the nature of strikes, which added greatly to the already difficult task of handling the increasing traffic.

In the fall of 1921 the business on the railway reached a point where it became very difficult to get the traffic over the mountain division from Orizaba to Esperanza which had always been the proverbial bottle neck. On October 25, a total of 14 trains, two of which were passenger, an aggregate of 4648 tons, was taken up the mountain, establishing a record for the division and indicating that the economic capacity of the single-track line with existing type of motive power had been reached.

The Electrification of the Mexican Railway

PART II

By J. B. COX

Transportation Engineering Department, General Electric Company

Electrification

IN November, 1921, a study of the mountain division was begun for the purpose of determining the results that might be expected from the electrification of this congested district. About two months were spent in looking over the line and equipment, studying the conditions and securing operating data and costs. An equal time was required to analyze these data, estimate the cost of electrification, the savings in operating expenses that would result, and to prepare a report which was submitted in April, 1922.

The unsettled conditions that had existed in the country for the preceding ten years, and the taking over of the railroad by the government from 1915 to 1920, rendered the records for any of this entire period unsuitable for forming a basis for the usual method of estimating the traffic that might reasonably be expected over the line for the following years.

Operating expenses had also been vitally affected during the interval by substantial increases in wages as well as by unusually expensive working agreements insisted on by newly formed labor organizations.

The semiannual reports of the Mexican Railway for the six months ending December 31, 1920, (the first period of operation after the return of the property by the government) compared with a similar period of 1913 (the last six months of operation by the owners prior to government operation for which the records were available) indicates increased costs as shown in Table II.

The comparative costs of the items that would be most directly affected by electrification for the same period are given in Table III.

An analysis of the comparative costs indicated that the motive power in use on the system should receive careful consideration.

The management of the railway suggested that the months of September and October, 1921, should be taken as a basis for the study, since the traffic conditions and operating costs during that period were more representative of anticipated future conditions than any other period for which records were available.

The mountain district constituting the line between Orizaba and Esperanza, a distance of 29.5 miles, was then operated as a separate district, and accurate operating expenses and statistics for steam operation were readily available for comparison with corresponding estimated costs of electrical operation.

The line between Orizaba and Paso del Macho was also included in the original study, but since this was operated with the remainder of the line on into Vera Cruz, and the result of electrification could not be so definitely determined until an exact schedule of operation had been decided on, only an approximate estimate was made for this section.

Of the 29.5 miles between Orizaba and Esperanza, the 19 miles between Encinar and Boca del Monte, which had been given such careful consideration in the original survey, again became the determining factor relative to motive power.

TABLE II

	1913	1920	INCREASE	
			Amount	Ratio
Maintenance of way and structures	$195,755	$379,652	$183,897	1.94
Maintenance of equipment	235,607	625,256	389,650	2.65
Conducting transportation	720,148	1,563,682	843,485	2.17
General expense	105,120	119,760	94,640	1.90
Total operating expenses	$1,256,630	$2,768,350	$1,511,672	2.20
Gross receipts	2,484,018	3,504,847	1,020,829	1.41
Net receipts	1,227,388	736,497	490,891	0.61
Operating ratio	0.51	0.79	....	..

TABLE III

	1913	1920	INCREASE	
			Amount	Ratio
Repairs to locomotives	$88,875	$280,463	$191,588	3.15
Enginemen and roundhouse	72,931	236,673	163,742	3.24
Fuel for locomotives	244,202	359,071	114,869	1.45
Train service	80,295	200,008	119,713	2.49
Total	$486,303	$1,076,215	$589,912	2.21

The actual rise in the 19 miles is approximately 3500 ft., equal to an uncompensated grade of 3.5 per cent. With the exception of the first 2.5 miles of this heavy grade just out of Encinar there is practically no tangent track, but continuously reversing curves, many of which are on a radius of 251 ft. equivalent to 16.5 deg.

In locating the line it was apparently intended not to let the uncompensated grade exceed 4 per cent as a maximum and to keep the maximum curve at 16.5 deg. During the study it was learned that some new consolidation-type locomotives, that had been recently purchased and were temporarily being used on this division, had failed to handle satisfactorily the weight of train they had been calculated to handle on the heavy grade.

These engines were expected to be capable of taking a trailing load of 250 tons up the mountain grade. It was found, however, that it was not practicable for them to take more than 175 tons, which represents a coëfficient of adhesion of approximately 20 per cent on a grade of 4.7 per cent. Since the profile did not indicate a grade in excess of 4 per cent or curvature greater than 16.5 deg. at any point, an investigation was made which indicated that there were certain points on the line where the engines stalled owing to the slipping of drivers, and as there was no indication that the condition of the rails at this point was responsible an engineer was sent to check the grade.

It was found that short sections of track from 300 to 500 ft. in length showed actual uncompensated grades as high as 4.4 per cent which, when properly compensated for curvature at the rate of 0.045 per deg., would make the maximum grade 5.24 per cent. The average uncompensated grade for the 1.24 miles, which represented the section of greatest difficulty was found to be 3.95 per cent; which when compensated for 16.5 deg. curvature, at the rate of 0.90 lb. per degree, is equivalent to a grade of 4.7 per cent. Accordingly this was taken to be the ruling grade for the division in the specifications for electric motive power.

The average weight of the passenger trains over the road was 215 tons but these trains varied from 165 to 350 tons.

The 32 steam locomotives that had usually been used for handling both freight and passenger trains on this division were four-cylinder Fairlie engines of English build. These engines were designed especially for mountain service, having pack-saddle type tanks for fuel oil and water over a double ended boiler, which was mounted on two 3-axle swivel trucks, all the weight being on the drivers.

The engines gave the impression of two 3-axle switching locomotives coupled with cab ends together.

The fire box was in the middle of the engines and contained two oil burners, the cab being over the central portion and the engineer located on one side of the boiler with the fireman on the opposite side. The engines ran equally well in either direction, and having a comparatively short rigid wheel base, with all weight on the drivers, at once deprived the electric locomotive of three of its usually boasted advantages.

The 32 engines were all of the same general type but of variable ages and weights as shown in Table IV.

TABLE IV

5	Weighing with full tanks					167,428 lb.
12	"	"	"	"		216,540 lb.
10	"	"	"	"		221,000 lb.
2	"	"	"	"		267,885 lb.
3	"	"	"	"		305,835 lb.

The first five of the above engines were not being used at the time, as ten new locomotives of the consolidation type had just been received and some of these were being substituted temporarily.

The weight of these new locomotives is given in Table V.

TABLE V

Weight on drivers	170,540 lb.
Weight on guiding axles	21,952 lb.
Weight of tender, loaded	119,775 lb.
Total	312,267 lb.

During the months of September and October, 1921, there had been taken over the division a total of 474 trains southbound with an aggregate tonnage of 108,749 gross metric tons, and 622 trains with aggregate gross metric tonnage of 197,220 northbound. The total hours of elapsed time, or the hours for which the engine and train crews were paid, between Orizaba and Boca del Monte, where the helper locomotives on the freight trains were usually left off, were 1574 for the southbound and 2756 for the northbound traffic; making the average times for each train over the 25.4 miles as given in Table VI.

TABLE VI

	South	North
Running	2 hr. 30 min.	3 hr. 39 min.
Delayed	49 min.	45 min.
Elapsed	3 hr. 19 min.	4 hr. 25 min.

This represented an average schedule speed of 7.66 m.p.h. and 5.7 m.p.h. respectively for the southbound and northbound trains, and an average delay of 47.4 minutes per train or 25 per cent of the running time per train.

Practically all trains, both freight and passenger, required two engines. In the case of the passenger trains both Fairlie engines were placed at the head of the train with a box car between, and with the freight trains an engine was placed at each end.

The average weight of the trains up grade was 317 metric tons, or 350 U. S. tons. The down grade tons were considerably less as almost two-thirds of the traffic was north bound.

The average wage of the enginemen and trainmen on the Mexican Railway at the time, based on an 8-hour day, or 100 miles, was approximately as set forth in Table VII.

TABLE VII

	Pesos Per Day	Dollars Per Day
Engineers	12.00	$6.00
Firemen	6.00	3.00
Conductors	11.00	5.50
Brakemen	5.28	2.69

The total cost of wages on the Orizaba-Esperanza division for the two months—September and October, 1921—was, in U. S. currency, as shown in Table VIII.

The cost of locomotive service, less wages of enginemen, for the two months is given in Table IX.

The locomotive performance combined for the two months is shown in Table X.

The corresponding estimated costs for the same passenger service and an equal freight tonnage with the electric locomotives proposed for the replacement of the steam engines is given in Table XI.

The operating data and actual costs of the steam operation for the months of September and October, 1921, as given in the accompanying tables, were taken as a basis for estimating the saving that might be expected to result from the electrification of the Orizaba-Esperanza district.

Only the items of operating costs which would be most vitally affected were considered. The estimate as submitted in the report is shown in Table XII.

The estimated cost of the electrification of the 29.5 miles, Orizaba to Esperanza, is shown in Table XIII.

TABLE X

LOCOMOTIVE PERFORMANCE

Average for September and October, 1921

ORIZABA-ESPERANZA DISTRICT

	Total or Average in Km. or Mexican Pesos	Equivalent in Miles or U. S. Dollars
Distance operated	47.4	29.5
Locomotives assigned	37	37
Locomotives in service	26.5	26.5
Kilometers run:		
Passenger	27,961	17,386
Freight	53,252	33,112
Work	3,176	1,975
Light with caboose	57,043	35,470
Light	50,563	31,440
Miscellaneous	94	58
Total	192,089	119,441
Barrels fuel oil consumed	33,518	33,518
Cost:		
Fuel oil per barrel-Mex	2.18	$1.09
Valve oil per liter	0.49	0.28
Car oil per liter	0.25	0.14
Illuminating oil per liter	0.45	0.26
Waste per kg	0.34	0.15
Grease per kg	0.66	0.30
Kilometers run per:		
Barrel of fuel oil	5.730	3.561
Liter valve oil	38.010	13.421
Liter car oil	28.230	9.968
Kg. waste	173.400	48.881
Kg. grease	209.000	58.917
Cost per km. run:		
Fuel oil	$0.38480	$0.30942
Lubricants	0.02889	0.02323
Labor repairs	0.47795	0.38433
Materials repairs	0.13847	0.11134
Enginemen	0.18720	0.15053
Hostlers and wipers	0.03631	0.02920
Total	$1.25362	$1.00805
Total cost of:		
Fuel oil	$73,929.09	$36,964.50
Lubricants	5,551.14	2,775.57
Repairs labor	91,814.67	45,907.33
Repairs material	26,601.19	13,300.55
Enginemen	35,966.00	17,983.00
Hostlers and wipers	6,981.62	3,490.81
Total	$240,843.71	$120,421.76

TABLE VIII

	September	October	Total	Rate Per Year
Engineers	$5,788	$6,490	$12,278	$73,668
Firemen	2,687	3,017	5,704	34,224
Conductors	2,140	2,395	4,535	27,210
Flagmen	721	768	1,498	8,934
Brakemen	3,847	4,344	8,197	49,146
Total	$16,183	$17,014	$32,197	$193,182

TABLE IX

	September	October	Total	Rate Per Year
Fuel oil	$19,413	$17,552	$36,965	$221,790
Repairs	30,426	28,782	59,208	355,248
Enginehouse	1,206	2,185	3,391	20,346
Lubricants	1,364	1,412	2,776	16,656
Total	$52,409	$49,931	$102,340	$614,040

TABLE XI

ESTIMATED OPERATING COSTS OF ITEMS DIRECTLY AFFECTED BY ELECTRIFICATION

Based on Tonnage Carried During Months of September and October, 1921

ORIZABA-ESPERANZA DISTRICT

	FREIGHT				PASSENGER
PROPOSED TRAIN RATING, TRAILING	600 TONS	600 TONS	900 TONS	1200 TONS	300 TONS
NUMBER OF ENGINE CREWS PER TRAIN	1	2	2	2	1
Gross tons trailing per year, northbound	1,053,756	1,053,756	1,053,756	1,053,756	......
Average tons per train, northbound	540	540	810	1,080	300
Total number of trains, northbound	1,951	1,951	1,301	977	521
Locomotive units per train	2	2	3	4	1
Locomotive unit miles per trip	120	120	180	240	60
Locomotive unit miles per year	234,120	234,120	234,180	234,480	31,260
Locomotive unit miles, work and miscellaneous	23,480	23,480	23,480	23,480	3,140
Total	257,600	257,600	257,660	257,960	34,400
Cost per trip, enginemen (U. S. dollars)	$9.68	$17.60	$18.48	$19.36	$8.56
Total cost per year	18,886.00	34,338.00	24,043.00	18,915.00	4,460.00
Cost per trip—trainmen	11.88	10.80	11.88	11.88	10.80
Total cost per year for trainmen	23,178.00	21,071.00	15,454.00	11,607.00	5,627.00
Total cost per trip—wages	21.56	28.40	30.36	31.24	19.36
Wages per year	42,064.00	55,409.00	39,499.00	30,522.00	10,087.00
Add 10 per cent for overtime and miscellaneous	4,197.00	5,541.00	3,950.00	3,053.00	1,009.00
Grand total, wages per year	46,267.00	60,950.00	43,449.00	33,575.00	11,096.00
Kilowatt demand	4,000	4,000	6,000	8,000	*
Approximate cost per kilowatt per year	$33.34	$33.34	$25.00	$25.00	......
Approximate cost per year	134,000.00	134,000.00	150,000.00	200,000.00	......
Cost of locomotive repairs per year	45,080.00	45,080.00	45,090.50	45,143.00	$6,020.00
Cost of locomotive repairs, enginehouse, per year	5,152.00	5,152.00	5,153.20	5,159.20	688.00
Cost of lubricants per year	2,576.00	2,576.00	2,576.60	2,579.60	344.00
Total cost per year	233,078.00	247,758.00	246,269.30	286,456.80	18,148.00
Grand total, including passenger	251,226.00	265,906.00	264,417.30	304,604.80	......
Maximum number of trips per day	10	10	7	7	2
Maximum gross tonnage per day	6,000	6,000	6,300	8,400	600
Normal number of trips per day	6	6	4	3	2
Normal tonnage per day	3,240	3,240	3,240	3,240	600

*No charge is made for power for passenger train since the purpose of the tabulated comparison is primarily to determine the desirable train weight to adopt.

It is assumed that the northbound tonnage will determine the number of train trips and that each train northbound will incur the expense of an entire round trip.

TABLE XII

	Steam	Electric	Saving	Ratio Steam to Electric
Wages of enginemen	$108,892	$31,354	$76,638	3.44
Wages of trainmen	85,290	23,191	62,099	3.68
Fuel and power	221,790	150,000	71,790	1.48
Repairs to locomotives	255,248	51,111	304,157	6.95
Enginehouse expense	20,946	5,841	15,105	3.57
Lubricants	16,656	2,921	13,735	5.70
Substation operation and maintenance	....	11,750	....	....
Maintenance distributing system	....	9,625	....	....
Total	$808,822	$285,793	$523,029	2.82

TABLE XIII

Ten 150-ton electric locomotive units	$1,420,000
One 6000-kw. substation	350,000
Thirty route-miles distributing system	430,000
Engineering and contingencies	220,000
Total gross capital investment	$2,420,000

The report accordingly indicated a probable saving of $523,029 per year by the expenditure of approximately $2,420,000, or a return of slightly more than 21 per cent on the gross investment, which included electric locomotives.

A similar study of the line between Orizaba and Paso del Macho was made at the same time, but as the probable savings indicated a return on the required investment only about half that estimated for the Orizaba-Esperanza district, the report recommended that only the latter be undertaken in the beginning.

After a very careful examination of the report by the operating department of the railway it was approved and recommended to the board of directors.

In October, 1922, a contract was made for the required equipment and materials, including the general supervision of the installation.

Actual work on the ground was begun in January, 1923, and the work was completed and all trains were being hauled electrically by January, 1925.

The work was almost entirely stopped from the middle of December, 1923, to May, 1924, by the rebellion that occurred at that time; just when the construction work had been fully organized and gotten well under way. This interruption caused several months' delay and considerably increased the cost of the work.

The work was done almost entirely with native labor which had to be trained. Three supervising engineers were placed in direct charge of the distribution, the substation, and the locomotives, respectively, reporting to the resident engineer of the railway Company, in coöperation with the general engineer of the contractor.

The Distribution System

The simple catenary system, with double 4/0 trolley on the main line and single 4/0 trolley in yards and passing tracks, similar to that used on the Chicago, Milwaukee and St. Paul, was adopted. Concrete poles were first selected for the supporting structure; but it was found that several hundred old 30-ft., 82-lb. rails, which had been replaced, were on hand and that there was no market for these where the price offered would justify handling and transportation charges.

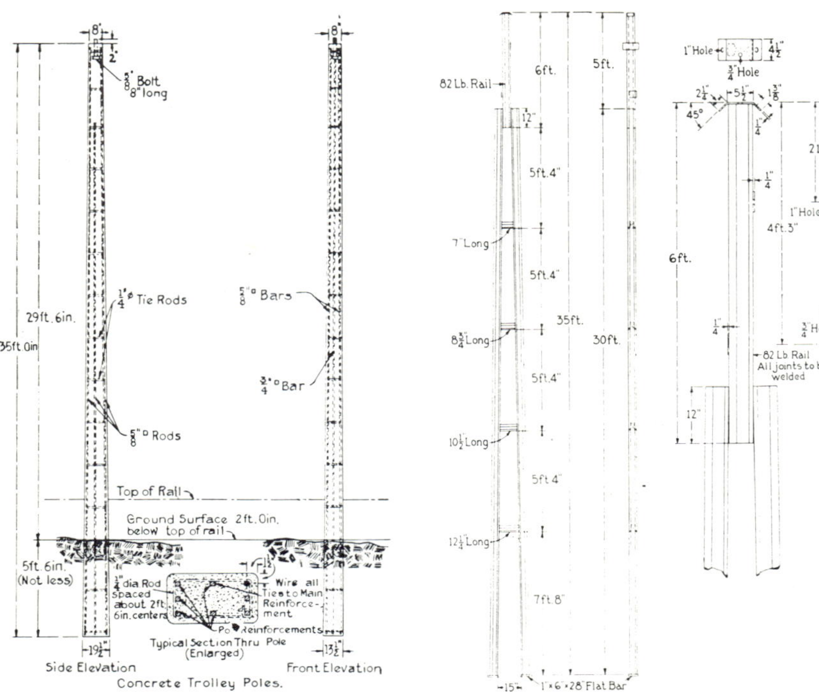

Fig. 7. Details of Concrete Trolley Poles

Fig. 8. Details of Welded Steel Pole Made from 62-lb. and 82-lb. Rails

TABLE XIV
DETAILED COST OF MAKING 405 CONCRETE POLES

Items	Quantities	Total Cost	Cost Per Pole
Cement at $1.05 per sack (including freight)	7 sacks per pole	$2,976.75	$7.35
Gravel at $3.60 per meter (including freight)		1,113.75	2.75
Sand at $1.00 per meter (including freight)		202.50	0.50
Reinforcement bars ¾-inch and ⅝-inch	69.3 tons	6,299.10	15.55
Reinforcement wire ¼-inch	2.1 tons	197.78	0.49
No. 6 welding wire	330 lb.	85.50	0.21
No. 9 welding wire	225 lb.	61.36	0.15
Old telegraph wire	1423 lb.	48.52	0.12
Electric current	Approx.	299.00	0.74
Oxygen	9 bottles	75.00	0.18
Carbide	154 lb.	8.70	0.02
Hut for storing cement, material		440.00	1.10
Forms and bottoms, material	9 forms	490.25	1.21
Other material for plant		322.13	0.80
Wages, Locomotive Dept.		569.50	1.41
Wages, Engineering Dept.		295.75	0.73
Wages, Eng. Dept.—bridges and buildings		153.00	0.38
Amount paid to contractor—cement work		1,612.00	4.00
Amount paid to contractor—reinforcement		776.05	1.92
Total		$16,026.64	$39.60
Overhead charges, superintendency, etc. 15 per cent		2,403.98	5.92
Grand Total		$18,430.43	$45.52

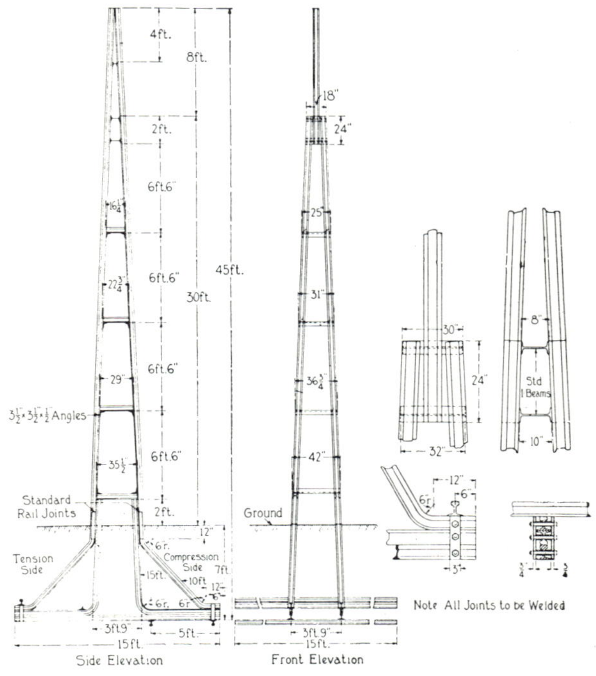

Fig. 9. Details of 45-ft. Welded Rail Tower for Orizaba Yard

Some sample poles were made up from these rails by electric welding and were tested for deflection and breaking strains, which resulted in a decision to use these as far as the rails would supply the demand. Of a total of 1920 poles made, 405 were of concrete as shown in Fig. 7. and 1515 were made up of old rails (see Fig. 8).

Detailed costs of each type of pole are given in Tables XIV, XV, and XX.

Unit costs of various items relative to the work in connection with the setting of poles are given in Table XVI.

All this work was done by contract, the unit price being fixed after sufficient experience had demonstrated a fair basis.

Details of the concrete poles are shown in Fig. 7. Figs. 8 and 9 show respectively the dimensions of the welded steel poles and towers which were made in the railway shops from old rails which had seen many years of service. Fig. 10 shows some interesting special construction work typical of that used on

TABLE XV
DETAILED COST OF MAKING 1419 RAIL POLES

Items	Quantities	Total Cost	Cost Per Pole
82 and 62-lb. rail at 1 ct. per lb..		$20,575.50	$14.50
$\frac{3}{16}$-plates	5,500 lb.	50.00	0.03
No. 6 welding wire	871 lb.	226.86	0.16
No. 9 welding wire	4,114 lb.	1,103.48	0.78
Old telegraph wire	12,770 lb.	469.35	0.33
Electric current, approximate..		1,443.00	0.02
Oxygen	9 bottles	75.00	0.05
Gasoline	100 gal.	28.12	0.02
Carbide	154 lb.	8.52	0.01
Installation of plant—materials		*5,582.13	3.93
Upkeep of plant—materials....		650.90	0.41
Wages, Locomotive Dept.		1,873.50	1.32
Wages, Engineering Dept.		2,750.00	1.98
Amounts paid to contractor....		6,901.50	4.86
Amounts paid for cutting		176.19	0.12
Amounts paid in compensation.		73.02	0.05
Total		$41,987.57	$29.57
Overhead charges, superintendence, etc., 15 per cent		6,298.13	4.43
GRAND TOTAL		$48,285.70	$34.00

*Including cost of two arc welding machines, $3,562.50.

TABLE XVI
DETAILED COSTS OF LABOR ITEMS OF CONSTRUCTION WORK

Number	Items	Unit Cost
405	Making concrete pole	$4.03
	Making concrete anchor	0.20
1120	Digging pole hole, earth	0.75
78	Digging pole hole, tepetate	0.95
521	Digging pole hole, loose rock	1.75
191	Digging pole hole, solid rock	8.00
	Average for 1910 holes	2.00
392	Setting concrete pole	1.70
1400	Setting rail pole	1.78
105	Distributing rail poles cutoffs	7.77
4	Towers Wimmer Bridge	43.75
42	Towers Orizaba yard	59.36
1483	Anchor holes	1.21

TABLE XVII
LABOR COST OF PUTTING UP TROLLEY, FEEDERS AND FITTINGS
ORIZABA-ESPERANZA 29.5 MILES

	Hours	Dollars	Cents Per Hour
Foremen	12,800	$7,953	62.1
Assistant Foreman	11,215	4,564	40.6
Linemen	34,612	9,563	27.6
Helpers	40,516	6,078	15.0
Laborers	43,769	4,658	10.6
Office Emp.	4,376	572	13.0
Total	147,288	$33,388	22.7

TABLE XVIII
LABOR COSTS OF MALTRATA SUBSTATION INSTALLATION—6,000 KW.

	Hours	Dollars	Cents Per Hour
Foremen	1,408	$1,308	92.9
Electrician 1st	4,868	2,237	45.7
Electrician 2d	5,214	1,490	28.6
Helpers	2,959	444	15.0
Mechanics	1,000	401	25.0
Pipe fitters	385	120	31.2
Storekeeper	524	57	10.9
Laborers	9,825	1,134	11.5
Operators	960	325	33.9
Total	27,143	$7,516	27.6

TABLE XIX
COST OF INSTALLING 11,551–250,000 CIR. MIL 14-INCH ELECTRICALLY-WELDED BONDS

2292 gallons gasoline	$736.56
78 gallons valve oil	93.60
34 gallons machine oil	57.12
1776 hours labor	6,177.49
Total cost	$7,064.77
Average cost per bond—cents	61.16

TABLE XX
DETAILED ESTIMATE OF COST OF MAKING 812 RAIL POLES
ORIZABA-CORDOBA

Items	Quantities	Total Cost	Cost Per Pole
82 and 62-lb. rail	1,363,023 lb.	$13,466.78	$16.585
Welding wire	11,340	678.40	0.835
Electric current, approx..	29,232 kw.	584.64	0.720
Oxygen	18 bottles	182.28	0.224
Gasoline	5 gal.	1.99	0.003
Carbide	640 lb.	34.80	0.042
Wages Locomotive Dept.		33.58	0.041
Amounts paid to contractor, labor		4,359.25	5.368
Amounts paid for cutting rail	3735 pieces	205.42	0.252
Amounts paid in compensation		9.65	0.011
Total		$19,556.80	$24.08
Overhead charges, superintendence, etc., 15 per cent		2,933.52	3.61
GRAND TOTAL		$22,490.32	$27.69

bridges; and Figs. 11, 12, 13, and 14 can be taken as general examples of the types of overhead construction.

Bracket construction was used where possible except where the poles supported feeder wires and it was desirable to avoid crossing over the tracks too often. In such cases, as between Boca del Monte and Alta Luz, the feeder cables were kept on the upper side of the track by having the poles continuous on that side irrespective of the curves, thus using cross-span supports where the curves were outward from the upper side of the slope. This also prevented interference with the magnificent view from the car windows overlooking the valley.

TABLE XXI
DETAILED ESTIMATE OF COST OF MAKING
33 RAIL TOWERS (Fig. 9)
ORIZABA–CORDOBA

Items	Quantities	Total Cost	Cost Per Pole
62-lb. rail	65,560 lb.	$892.38	$27.042
Iron beam	1114 lb.	60.63	1.837
Welding wire	1500 lb.	90.23	2.734
Electric current, approx.		71.28	2.160
Oxygen	2 bottles	24.40	0.739
Gasoline	0.66 gal.	0.28	0.008
Carbide	86 lb.	4.66	0.141
Wages, Locomotive Dept.		4.49	0.136
Amounts paid to contractor		1,320.00	40.000
Amounts paid for cutting	544 pieces	29.92	0.907
Amounts paid for	340 bends	425.00	12.878
Amounts paid in compensation		1.30	0.039
Total		$2,924.57	$88.62
Overhead charges, superintendence, etc. 15 per cent		438.68	13.30
GRAND TOTAL		$3,363.25	$101.92

TABLE XXII
DETAILED ESTIMATE OF COST OF MAKING
18 RAIL TOWERS
ORIZABA–CORDOBA

Items	Quantities	Total Cost	Cost Per Pole
40-lb. rail	4200 lb.	$57.65	$3.185
62-lb. rail	13390 lb.	182.22	10.123
82-lb. rail	22625 lb.	205.30	11.405
Iron beam	7130 lb.	388.01	21.555
Welding wire	830 lb.	49.60	2.755
Electric current, approx.		38.08	2.143
Oxygen	1 bottle	13.31	0.739
Gasoline	0.4 gal.	0.15	0.008
Carbide	46 lb.	2.54	0.141
Wages, Locomotive Dept.		2.45	0.136
Amounts paid to contractor		225.00	12.50
Amounts paid for cutting	297 pieces	16.34	0.908
Amounts paid in compensation		0.71	0.039
Total		$1,181.36	$65.64
Overhead charges, superintendence, etc., 15 per cent		177.20	9.84
GRAND TOTAL		$1,358.56	$75.48

In addition to the two 4/0 trolley wires, two 500,000 cir. mil positive feeders and one 4/0 negative feeder cable were installed from Orizaba to Boca del Monte. The feeders were carried on separate poles at four points where the rail line made long loops. The advantage thus gained was the reduction of feeder length from 29.5 miles to 20.4 miles. The single substation for the

Fig. 10. Special Overhead Construction on Bridge at Rio Seco

29.5 miles was located near Maltrata, which is almost midway in the feeder circuit. Only a single 500,000-cir. mil feeder was used between Boca del Monte and Esperanza as the grade here was comparatively light.

Fig. 11. Overhead Construction at Entrance to Paraje Nuevo Yard

A similar feeder was used from the substation to the middle of the Bota loop, making it unnecessary to install any feeders along the rail line between Bota and Alta Luz, where the curvature was greatest, since this loop was fed from both ends making the equivalent of a double-track circuit.

The voltage drop over the entire line, with a 665-ton freight train on the upgrade, indicates a maximum drop of 400 volts, or 13 per cent, the average drop being 235 volts or 7.6 per cent.

A single 250,000-cir. mil electrically welded bond was used throughout. Pressed steel track ties were in use over most of the line and were being used to replace wooden ties as required.

The trolley and feeder lines were sectionalized at Nogales, Maltrata, Alta Luz, and Boca del Monte.

At Orizaba the yards consisted of eight tracks, located between the shops on one side, and the station, storehouses, and roundhouse on the other side.

At many points the ground was soft and the use of guy wires objectionable. So towers were made up from 62-lb. discarded rails which were capable of supporting the wiring necessary for the 8 tracks. Special extensions were made which provided foundations at a reasonable cost and which rendered guying at any point unnecessary.

Fig. 12. View of Overhead Line South of Boca Del Monte

Drawings showing the dimensions of the 44 towers used in the Orizaba yard are shown in Fig. 9. Thirty-three similar towers were used in the Cordoba yard, detailed costs of which are shown in Table XXI. Other lighter towers also made from old rails, costs of

which are given in Table XXII, were used at bridges. The Metlac bridge on a 16-deg. curve, where 18 towers were required, is the longest.

There were seven tunnels on the first electrification, six on the Cordoba and two on the Paso del Macho extensions, a total of 15, all but two of which were on curves.

Fig. 13. Overhead Line in Nogales Station, Showing Span Construction Concrete Poles

The total cost of the 29.5 miles of distribution system, including poles and fixtures, was $462,011 or $15,661 per route-mile.

Fig. 14. 42,000-volt Transmission Line Crossing the Railroad Company's Tracks

In 1926 the trolley line was extended from Orizaba to Cordoba, 16 miles south, making a stub-end feed from the Maltrata substation approximately 29 route-miles in length; but feeder cut-offs at loops reduced the feeder to about 25 miles. This construction was similar to the original except that rail poles were used exclusively. Two 500,000-cir. mil copper feeders were used almost the entire distance. Detailed costs of this construction are given in Table XXIII. The total was $233,556 or $14,597 per route-mile. The estimated cost was $231,500, but did not include the complete wiring of the Cordoba yard as was done.

TABLE XXIII
DETAILED COST OF 25.9 KM. (16 MILES) DISTRIBUTION SYSTEM
ORIZABA TO CORONA

No.	Items	Amount	Per Route Mile
818	Rail poles, line	$22,656.46	$1,416.03
34	Rail towers, yard	3,456.17	216.57
22	Rail towers, bridge.	1,660.47	103.78
	Wire and fixtures	148,123.27	9,257.70
	Stone and cement.	1,855.37	115.96
	Work cars and equipment.	2,742.68	171.42
	Miscellaneous	9,085.27	567.83
	Total material	$189,588.69	$11,849.29
229	Work trains.	$14,011.82	$876.17
	Erection of poles and towers . . .	10,869.62	679.35
	Erection of wires, etc.	9,879.60	617.48
6008	Bonds installed.	2,513.36	157.09
	Engineering and supervision . . .	6,686.72	417.92
	Total installation	$43,967.12	$2,727.95
	GRAND TOTAL	$233,555.81	$14,597.24

The Electrification of the Mexican Railway

PART III

By J. B. COX

Transportation Engineering Department, General Electric Company

IN May, 1928, the electrification was extended from Cordoba to Paso del Macho, 18 miles farther south, making the total electrification 64 route-miles. The trolley construction on this last extension was the same as on the Cordoba extension, except that only a single 500,000-cir. mil copper feeder was used between Cordoba and Potrero and no positive feeder at all from the substation to Paso del Macho.

With the extension of the electric zone to Paso del Macho, a second substation was installed at Potrero, approximately 39 miles from Maltrata and 8.5 miles from Paso del Macho. The power demands for this portion of the line, however, are much lighter on account of the easier grades, so this station contains two 1500-kw. units which are similar in other respects to the original equipment. This station is

Fig. 15. Exterior of Maltrata Substation Equipped with Two 3000-kw.
3000-volt Motor-generator Sets

Non-ferrous materials were used for hangers and span wires and a copper-clad copper messenger on the last extension, as this section is nearing the seacoast, and it seemed advisable to use such material where steam locomotives are expected to operate at all frequently under the wires.

Substation Equipment

The original substation, located at Maltrata, contains two 3000-kw. 3000-volt d-c. three-unit synchronous motor-generator sets for supplying power to the original 29.5 miles electrified.

Power is purchased from the Puebla Tramway Light & Power Company at 42,000 volts, 60 cycles. Ample provision is made for housing all of the substation equipment, the transformers and high-tension switching occupying about one-half the building. The other half of the station is occupied by the motor-generator sets and switching equipment; each motor-generator set is protected by a high-speed circuit breaker and each of the outgoing feeders has the same protection.

also supplied from the 42,000-volt three-phase 60-cycle circuit which forms a part of the power company's network.

Each substation building provides the necessary space and foundations for a third unit when required. The equipment used is standard, being similar to that supplied the Chicago, Milwaukee & St. Paul, the Spanish Northern, and the Paulista Railways.

Fig. 15 shows the exterior of Maltrata substation and Fig. 20 an interior view of the same, showing the motor-generator sets and high-speed circuit breakers, while Figs. 16 and 17 are other interior views of the Potrero and the Maltrata substations.

Electric Locomotives

The initial motive power equipment for the Orizaba-Esperanza section included ten locomotive units suitable for handling both passenger and freight service. These are of the twin-geared 6-motor articulated truck type capable of operating at a maximum speed of 40 m.p.h. and provided with equipment for regenerative electric braking.

Fig. 16. Interior of Potrero Substation, Showing High-tension Switching Equipment

Fig. 17. View in Transformer Room, Showing Oil-circuit Breakers and Buses

Fig. 18. A 3000-volt 150-ton Six-motor Locomotive for Either Freight or Passenger Service

Fig. 19. Passenger Train with 150-ton 3000-volt Locomotive at Maltrata Station

The cab is of the box type mounted on two equalizer frames which in turn are carried upon three two-axle trucks. The motors are twin geared to each axle through cushion-type gears.

The motors are designed for 1500 volts per commutator; two being connected permanently in series. An unusual feature of this locomotive is the provision for removing the motor wheels and axle from any of the trucks without lifting the cab. These units are so constructed that the wheels, axle and motor can be dropped into the pit after first disconnecting the motor leads, or the wheels and axle may be taken out alone by propping up the motor and side frames.

of 50,000 lb. and 2700 line volts, corresponds to a speed range of from approximately 5½ to 26½ m.p.h., and correspondingly higher speeds at lighter loads.

The main motor circuits are protected by a high-speed circuit breaker which also serves as a line breaker as well as to give overload and short-circuit protection.

Current is collected from overhead slider pantographs, one of which is located at each end of the cab roof. These collectors have a range of from 15 ft. 5 in. to 24 ft. above the top of the rail. Fig. 18 shows a view of one of the locomotives and Fig. 19 one of the electric locomotives hauling a passenger train.

Fig. 20. Interior of Maltrata Substation, Showing Two 3000-kw. 3000-volt
Motor-generator and High-speed Circuit Breakers

The auxiliary machinery consists of a 3000/1500-volt dynamotor with a 65-volt control generator mounted on the shaft extension; a 1500-volt regenerative exciter set; two 1500/3000-volt motor-driven blowers and two 1500/3000-volt air compressors. The two blowers and the two compressors normally operate in series across the 3000-volt circuit with their mid points connected to the mid point of the dynamotor for equalization. The regenerative exciter set operates from the 1500-volt circuit of the dynamotor. The scheme of operation provides a means for operating one compressor or one blower from the 1500-volt dynamotor bus in case of failure of the other unit. This arrangement also permits operating the compressors and blowers in case the dynamotor fails.

The locomotives are equipped with electro-pneumatic control for non-automatic multiple unit operation. A master controller in the engineman's cab at each end is arranged to give a total of 31 accelerating steps, distributed through the three groupings of the motors, a full-field and two reduced-field running steps with each of the three combinations. This gives a total of nine running points which, for a given tractive effort

With the extension of the electrification from Orizaba to Paso del Macho, additional motive power was required and for this purpose two locomotives, duplicates of the original design, were used.

Table XXIV gives the electrical and mechanical data on these locomotives and Fig. 21 gives a dimensioned outline drawing.

Figs. 22 and 23 are included because of the general interest in showing the type of steam locomotive formerly in use.

Transmission Line

A 42,000-volt transmission line 17 miles in length was constructed from the Tuxpango hydroelectric generating station of the Puebla Tramway Light & Power Co. to the Maltrata substation. Twin lines of No. 1/0 aluminum cable are supported on steel A frames with anchor towers at proper intervals.

A similar line of approximately the same length, but with only a single set of conductors, is now under construction from the same generating station to the new substation at Potrero. In the meantime the power company's line to Vera Cruz, which the new line parallels, is being used and switching arrangements are provided in the substation for reciprocal use of the lines when desirable.

Electrical Operation

The Orizaba-Esperanza section has now been in complete operation electrically since January, 1925, thus making available the records for four full years of operating data and costs.

The great reduction in business resulting from the unsettled conditions caused by the disturbances of 1924, as well as new labor agreements and increased wages, had tended to make direct comparisons of operating costs look less favorable than they really were. A decrease in the tonnage to be hauled reduces operating costs to an extent, but unfortunately not nearly in the same proportion, and the capital charges remain practically the same. On the other hand, increased wages and higher costs of fuel and materials usually tend to make electrification comparatively more profitable.

The operation has been very satisfactory and successful throughout. No serious difficulties have been encountered with any portion of the equipment. This may fairly be measured by reference to the complaint bill for the usual guarantee period, which was less than three thousand dollars ($3,000.00).

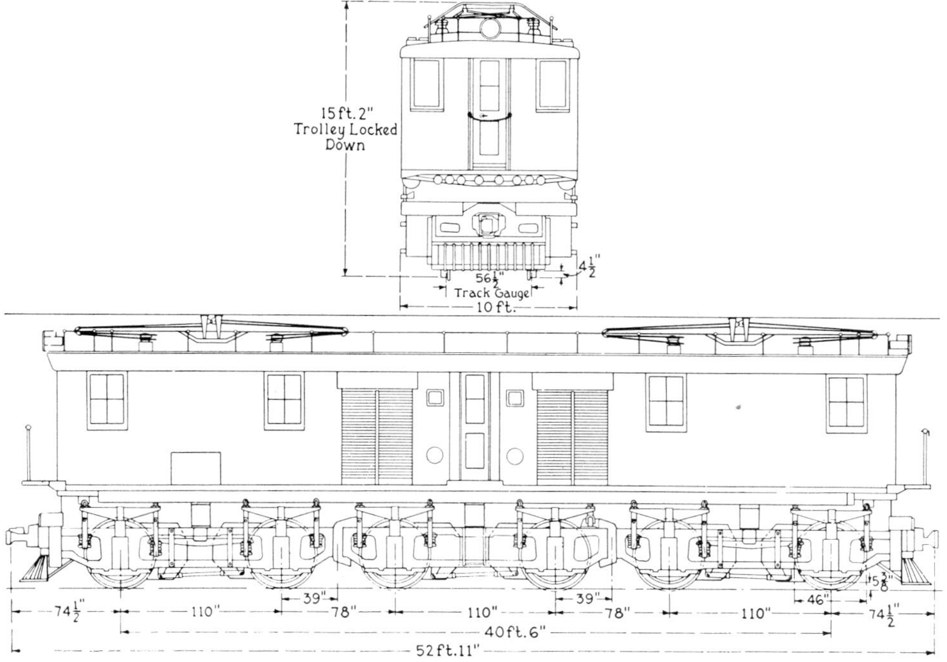

Fig. 21. 150-ton 3000-volt D-c. Locomotive for Mexican Railway.
Outline and Dimensions

TABLE XXIV

ELECTRICAL DATA

Nominal voltage of system	3000 v. d-c.
Tractive eff., 1 hr. blown (3000 v.)	54,000 lb.
Speed at 1-hr. rating, full field	19 m.p.h.
Total horsepower, 1 hr	2736
Tractive eff., continuous 3000 v. full field	48,500
Speed at continuous rating, 3000 v.	19.5 m.p.h.
Total horsepower, continuous	2520
Number of motors	6
Type of motors	GE-278-A-1500/3000 v.
Gear ratio	90/18
Tractive eff. at 30 per cent tract. coef.	92,700 lb.

MECHANICAL DATA

Track gauge	4 ft. 8½ in.
Wheel arrangement	0 4 4 4 0
Diameter of drivers	46 in.
Number of driving axles	6
Total wheel base	40 ft. 6 in.
Max. rigid wheel base	9 ft. 2 in.
Width overall	10 ft. 1½ in.
Height over trolley locked down	15 ft. 2 in.
Length inside knuckles	52 ft. 11 in.

WEIGHTS

Total weight on drivers	309,000 lb.
Dead weight per axle	12,150 lb.
Elec. and air brake equipment	135,000 lb.
Mechanical equipment	174,000 lb.

The general performance of the equipment may best be judged by the costs of maintenance, a fair average of which is given herein.

During the months of March and April, 1928, the traffic over the Orizaba-Esperanza section reached a new maximum, which was somewhat in excess of that for steam operation which had been attained during the months of September and October, 1921, and which was used as a basis in the original study. This offered a favorable opportunity for comparing actual results of electrical operation with that for steam operation, as well as to check the estimates in the report leading to the electrification.

Detailed tabulations of the operating records for March and April, 1923, with electrical operation were prepared for comparison with similar records as used in the report for September and October, 1921, with steam operation, as shown in Table XXV.

A summary of this comparison will be found in Table XXVI.

THE ELECTRIFICATION OF THE MEXICAN RAILWAY

Briefly stated, the 10 electric locomotives during March and April handled 36 per cent more ton-miles than were handled by more than double the number of steam locomotives during September and October, with 8 per cent less trains and in 40 per cent less train-hours on the road, and at 50 per cent of the corresponding total cost of steam operation for 26 per cent less tonnage handled. A saving of $67,102 was thus accomplished for the two months, or at the rate of $402,612 per year; this alone represents a return of more than 15 per cent on the gross cost of the electrification, including electric locomotives. However,

TABLE XXV

COMPARISON OF TRAFFIC DURING THE MONTHS OF MARCH AND APRIL, 1928, MAXIMUM MONTHS ELECTRICAL OPERATION, WITH SEPTEMBER AND OCTOBER, 1921, MAXIMUM MONTHS STEAM OPERATION

MEXICAN RAILWAY COMPANY—ORIZABA-ESPERANZA DISTRICT

	NORTHBOUND		SOUTHBOUND		TOTAL OR AVERAGE		PER CENT	
	Steam	Electric	Steam	Electric	Steam	Electric	Increase	Decrease
Passenger Service								
Number of trains	89	122	87	122	176	244	38	..
Number of cars	640	949	609	959	1,249	1,908	52	..
Number of tons	21,595	41,642	20,048	41,943	41,643	83,585	100	..
Number of train-hours	255	244	174	223	429	467	9	..
Average No. trains per day	1.46	2.00	1.43	2.00	2.89	4.00	38	..
Average No. cars per train	7.19	7.78	7.00	7.86	7.10	7.82	10	..
Average tons per train	243	341	230	344	237	343	..	..
Average hours per train	2.87	2.00	2.00	1.83	2.44	1.91	..	..
Per cent increase tons per train	...	40.32	...	49.56	...	44.72	..	..
Per cent decrease time per train	...	30.31	...	8.50	...	21.72	..	..
Freight Service								
Number of trains	533	404	387	363	920	767	..	16
Number of cars	4,086	5,448	3,903	5,484	7,989	10,902	37	..
Number of tons	175,625	195,357	88,701	137,095	264,326	332,452	25	..
Number of train-hours	2,656	1,167	1,492	1,084	4,148	2,251	..	46
Average No. trains per day	8.74	6.62	6.34	5.95	15.08	12.57	..	16
Average No. cars per train	7.67	13.48	10.09	15.11	8.68	14.25	64	..
Average tons per train	330	484	229	378	287	433	..	..
Average hours per train	4.98	2.89	3.85	2.99	4.51	2.93	..	..
Per cent increase tons per train	...	46.66	...	65.06	...	50.87	..	..
Per cent decrease time per train	...	41.96	...	22.33	...	35.03	..	..
Freight and Passenger Service								
Number of trains	622	526	474	485	1,096	1,011	..	8
Number of cars	4,726	6,397	4,512	6,443	9,238	12,840	39	..
Number of tons	197,220	236,999	108,749	179,038	305,969	416,037	36	..
Number of hours	2,911	1,411	1,666	1,307	4,577	2,718	..	40
Average No. trains per day	10.20	8.62	7.77	7.95	17.97	16.57	..	8
Average No. cars per train	7.60	12.16	9.52	13.28	8.43	12.70	50	..
Average tons per train	317	451	229	369	279	412	..	..
Average hours per train	4.68	2.68	3.51	2.69	4.18	2.69	..	..
Per cent increase tons per train	...	42.27	...	61.13	...	47.67	..	..
Per cent decrease time per train	...	42.73	...	23.36	...	35.64	..	..

TABLE XXVI

	STEAM OPERATION 1921 Sept. and Oct.	ELECTRIC OPERATION 1928 Mar. and Apr.	Difference in Amount	Advantage of Electric Operation Over Steam Operation in Per Cent
Number of trains run	1,096	1,011	85	8% less trains
Number of cars handled	9,238	12,840	3,602	39% more cars
Number of tons handled	305,969	416,037	110,068	36% more tons
Number of train-hours	4,577	2,718	1,859	40% less train-hours
Number of tons per train	279	412	133	48% more tons per train
Number of cars per train	8.43	12.70	4.27	50% more cars per train
Number of hours per train	4.18	2.69	1.49	36% less hours per train
Cost enginemen's wages	$17,982	$14,565	$3,417	19% less cost for enginemen
Cost trainmen's wages	14,222	10,721	3,501	24% less cost for trainmen
Cost fuel oil or power	36,965	31,140	5,825	16% less cost for fuel
Cost locomotive repairs	59,208	5,969	53,239	90% less cost for repairs
Enginehouse expense	3,391	1,945	1,446	42% less cost for enginehouse
Lubricants	2,776	92	2,684	97% less cost for lubricants
Substation operation	....	2,154	2,154	
Trolley maintenance	....	856	856	
Total cost items affected	$134,544	$67,442	$67,442	50% less cost for total

21

this amount does not represent the actual saving, since the cost of all classes of labor had considerably increased during 1922 and 1923, so that it is necessary to adjust the costs of the steam operation to have them indicate what they would have been if the increased traffic of March and April had been handled by steam and at the higher rate of wages, as was done by the electric locomotives.

The wages of mechanics and others employed in the repair and care of locomotives were also proportionally increased; but last year, and during the previous year, considerable reductions were made in this class of labor, in fact, to such an extent that no adjustment for wages in cost of repairs was considered necessary.

The average price paid for fuel oil during the months of September and October, 1921, was $1.09 per barrel,

Fig. 22. One of the 150-ton Fairlie-type Double-ended Oil-burning Steam Locomotives Formerly Used in the Electric Zone

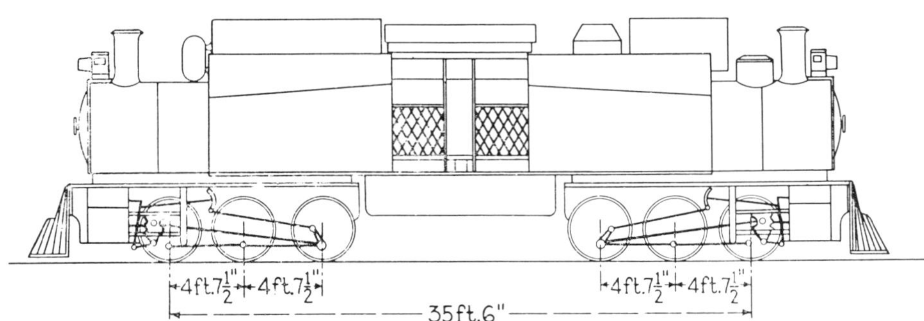

Fig. 23. Dimensions of Locomotive Shown in Fig. 22

Between October, 1921, and the end of 1923, and before the electrification had been completed, new contracts were made with practically all labor involved in these operating costs, under the terms of which the rates of pay were materially increased. Enginemen's and trainmen's wages were increased on an average of about 42 per cent, which higher rates were in effect in March and April, 1928. These increases are given in Table XXVII.

TABLE XXVII

	1921	1928	Per Cent Increase
Enginemen per round trip	$6.00	$8.88	48.0
Firemen per round trip	2.88	4.44	54.1
Conductors per round trip	5.50	7.20	30.9
Brakemen per round trip	5.50	7.20	30.9

but the price paid for it in March and April is given as $1.29, an increase of 18 per cent.

In adjusting the cost of steam operation for September and October, 1921, for the 36 per cent increase in traffic, it was considered inaccurate to assume that the cost would increase in the same proportion, since the number of trains required to handle the traffic are almost entirely determined by the northbound, or uphill traffic, which exceeded the southbound by 32 per cent during March and April. It is also possible to take considerably heavier trains down than up the mountain grade.

The adjustment for increased traffic was consequently made on the basis of the increased number of steam trains that would have been required to handle the northbound business.

The passenger trains running north in March and April numbered 122 as against 89 in September and October, an increase of 33 trains.

The freight tonnage hauled north for the same period was 195,357 and 175,625 tons respectively, an increase of 19,732 tons. At an average of 330 tons per train, which is the exact record for the steam locomotives, 60 additional freight trains would have been required to handle this excess freight tonnage, making a total increase of 93 trains, or 14.95 per cent. On an already congested single-track line with infrequent passing tracks, a 14.95 per cent increase in the number of trains would ordinarily considerably lengthen the

the 36 per cent greater tonnage handled; since any material increase in traffic should increase the savings also, and in a greater proportion. The increase in wages would also increase the savings, because of the increased tons per train and decreased hours per train with electrical operation.

This annual saving represents approximately 26 per cent on the gross cost of the electrification of the Orizaba-Esperanza district; this alone is a very satisfactory result. There are however other more indirect savings which cannot be so accurately segregated, such as wear on wheels and brake shoes, reduction of accidents from broken wheels due to over-heating

TABLE XXVIII

	STEAM	ELECTRIC	REDUCTION	
	Sept. and Oct.	Mar. and April	Amount	Per cent
Enginemen	$30,991	$14,565	$16,426	53
Trainmen	21,722	10,721	11,001	50
Fuel or power	50,139	31,140	18,999	38
Repair to locomotives	68,059	5,969	62,090	91
Enginehouse expense	3,898	1,945	1,963	50
Lubricants	3,191	92	3,099	97
Substation operation maintenance	....	2,154	....	..
Trolley operation maintenance	....	856	....	..
Total	$178,000	$67,442	$110,558	62

TABLE XXIX

	Steam	Electric	SAVING	
			Indicated	Estimated
Enginemen	$185,946	$87,390	$98,556	$76,538
Trainmen	130,332	64,326	66,006	62,099
Fuel or power	300,834	186,840	113,994	71,790
Repairs to locomotives	408,354	35,814	372,540	304,137
Enginehouse expense	23,388	11,670	11,718	15,105
Lubricants	19,146	552	18,594	13,735
Substation operation maintenance	....	12,924	....	....
Trolley operation maintenance	....	5,136	....	....
Total	$1,068,000	$404,652	$663,348	$522,029

time per train, and consequently increase the cost of wages and fuel; but since the enginemen and trainmen are paid by the trip, if made in ordinary time, and the run being unusually short, no allowance was made for this item. It was considered conservative to assume that all other costs of the items listed would be increased in approximately the same proportion as the number of trains operated, *i.e.*, 14.95 per cent.

When the costs of steam operation are adjusted on the basis outlined, the direct comparison between steam and electric operation for traffic handled in March and April, 1928, is as shown in Table XXVIII.

In order to compare directly these figures with the estimate in the original study on this subject the costs were placed on a yearly basis, as set forth in Table XXIX.

The above indicated yearly saving of $663,348 in favor of electrical operation is 27 per cent greater than the estimate, but this was readily accounted for by

while braking, which if fully valued would add many hundreds of dollars to the credit of electrical operation.

Perhaps the most valuable unlisted asset in the electrification is the increased capacity of the lines electrified. On March 18th, 5381 tons of freight and two passenger trains weighing 741 tons, making a total of 6122 tons, were hauled from Orizaba to Esperanza, which was a record for the district. The record day with steam operation was October 25, 1921, when 4008 tons of freight and two passenger trains weighing 640 tons, making a total of 4648 tons, were handled; giving 1474 tons or 31 per cent in favor of the electric operation; 14 trains were used in each case.

The total tonnage handled electrically on March 18th, north and south, was 9659 tons and that for October 25, 1921, by steam was 6532 tons. The excess for electric operation was 50 per cent. The electric train-hours were 64.6; and the steam train-hours were

83.4, a reduction of 18.8 train-hours, or 22 per cent with an increased tonnage handled of 50 per cent.

By increasing the train weight to 900 tons (metric), for which the line and equipment are capable, it would be practicable to handle over the present line double the tonnage handled on March 18th with no additional facilities except for locomotives, cars, and power.

The ten locomotives now in service were expected to be sufficient to handle a maximum of 4200 tons or, regularly 3600 tons in addition to two passenger trains per day in each direction between Orizaba and Esperanza.

heavy grade work this item will average between 40 and 50 per cent.

If the cost of the electric locomotives be deducted from the total cost of electrification the savings from electric operation, as shown, would be equivalent to an earning of 47 per cent on the net cost.

The entire 64 miles has been in full operation for about a year, but the records are not yet available for a comparison such as is given for the original electrification; and it will not be possible to have them so accurate as long as the 48 miles on the Vera Cruz end is operated by steam.

TABLE XXX

CLASSIFIED COST OF THE ELECTRIFICATION

District	Orizaba Esperanza	Orizaba Cordoba	Cordoba Paso del Macho	Total	Per Route Mile	Per Cent of Total
Route miles	29.5	16.0	18.5	64		
Substations	$452,725	.....	$234,194	$686,919	$10,733	19.0
Transmission	187,242	.....	75,888	263,130	4,111	7.3
Power distribution	318,233	148,072	167,022	633,327	9,896	17.6
Poles and fixtures	143,778	76,488	65,868	286,134	4,471	7.9
Houses	23,740	1,382	8,486	33,608	525	0.9
Engineering	61,260	6,687	26,578	94,525	1,477	2.6
Other expenses	25,937	927	2,430	29,294	458	0.8
Total	$1,212,915	$233,556	$580,466	$2,026,937	$31,671	56.1
Per route mile	$41,116	$14,597	$31,376	$31,670		
Locomotives including exchange				$1,580,000	$24,687	43.9
GRAND TOTAL				$3,606,937	$56,358	100.0

This maximum was exceeded by 1181 tons, or 28 per cent, on March 18th, and the average tons per day northbound for the month was 3350 tons, but all ten locomotives were used.

The earnings on investment as shown are for the gross investment including the cost of electric locomotives. Had new steam locomotives been purchased these would have been charged as renewals or betterments, and since sufficient new steam locomotives to handle an equal tonnage on a mountain district would cost approximately as much as the electric locomotives, it should be quite proper to deduct the cost of the locomotives from the cost of the electrification.

In the case of the Mexican Railway the cost of the electric locomotives was approximately 46 per cent of the gross cost of electrification, and usually for

Table XXX gives the segregated cost as prescribed by the Interstate Commerce Commission for each of the three sections, and the total costs for the whole electrification. These costs are taken from the official records of the railway company, with the exception of the item for the new transmission line now under construction, and the two additional electric locomotives recently delivered; these are estimated.

The original estimate contained in the report submitted in April, 1921, for the electrification of the entire 64 miles was $4,032,500.00. The original report did not contemplate the building of any transmission line by the railway company, and proposed that the transformers and a-c. switching be of the outdoor type, but included six more locomotive units than have been found actually required at the present time.

The Electrification of the Mexican Railway

PART IV

By J. B. COX

Transportation Engineering Department, General Electric Company

IN the concluding section of this article it should be explained that while the detailed operating costs, taken from the comparison between steam and electric performance, cover in each instance a period of only two months, the records for a considerably longer period of steam operation were carefully examined. The months of September and October, 1921, were selected by the management of the Railway Company as being most representative of the traffic conditions and operating expenses which it was expected would be likely to continue in the future if the steam locomotives were retained.

The country was just recovering from the depression caused by the revolutions that had existed for several years, and the road had been back in the hands of the owners only a little more than a year, so that there were really only four months' records that could be considered fairly representative of expected conditions. These months were July, August, September, and October, 1921. The operating costs that would be appreciably affected by electrification for these four months were recorded in the report in Table XXXI.

It was after a general study of these four months that September and October were selected for more detailed analysis for the purpose of preparing an estimate of results to be expected from electrification. The dispatcher's daily train sheets for the two months were gone over carefully and a complete record of each train movement prepared; from these data averages of running time, delayed time, elapsed time, and train weights were determined. A diagram was made up for checking comparative theoretical curves showing the probable elapsed time for steam and electric locomotives over the same profile.

TABLE XXXI

OPERATING COSTS OF STEAM OPERATION FOR FOUR MONTHS, 1921

MEXICAN RAILWAY COMPANY

	July	August	September	October	Total	Yearly Rate
Enginemen	$7,548	$9,625	$8,476	$9,507	$35,156	$105,468
Trainmen	5,745	6,720	6,707	7,508	26,680	80,040
Fuel	19,369	21,570	17,551	19,413	77,903	233,709
Repairs	24,887	27,523	28,832	30,426	111,668	335,004
Enginehouse	2,028	1,427	2,185	1,305	6,945	20,835
Lubricants	1,095	1,287	1,412	1,364	5,158	15,474
Total	$60,672	$68,152	$65,163	$69,523	$263,510	$790,530

Cost Per 1000 Ton-miles

	July	August	September	October	Total	Yearly Rate
Enginemen	....	....	$1.7301	$1.8818	....	....
Trainmen	....	....	1.3690	1.4861	....	....
Fuel	....	....	3.5826	3.8426	....	....
Repairs	....	....	5.8851	6.0226	....	....
Enginehouse	....	....	0.4460	0.2583	....	....
Lubricants	....	....	0.2882	0.2698	....	....
Total	....	....	$13.3012	$13.7614	....	....
1000 Ton-miles	....	....	4,899	5,052	....	....
Locomotive-miles	58,844	61,513	57,541	61,822	239,721	719,163

Cost Per Loco.-miles (Cents)

	July	August	September	October	Average
Enginemen	12.828	15.648	14.731	15.379	14.665
Trainmen	9.764	10.925	11.656	12.145	11.130
Power	32.918	35.069	30.502	31.403	32.498
Repairs	42.296	44.746	50.108	49.217	46.583
Enginehouse	3.447	22.320	3.797	2.111	2.897
Lubricants	1.861	2.092	2.454	2.206	2.152
Total	103.114	110.800	113.248	112.461	109.925

An examination of the four months' operating records indicated that the two months suggested by the management would be fairly representative.

In the case of electrical operation the months of March and April, 1928, were also selected for the comparison by the management of the railway because the traffic during those months was the heaviest in the history of the road, and it was considered that these two months were most desirable for comparing with the two months of steam operation that had been used in the report.

In this instance also the records for January, February, March, and April were gone over carefully to ascertain if there were any variations requiring consideration. Various other monthly records of electrical operation were also compared; but only the months of March and April were analyzed in detail, exactly as had been done in the report for September and October steam operation.

Table XXXII shows the operating costs of electrical service for the four months, and Table XXXIII the electrical operating cost for 39 months from October 1, 1925, to April 30, 1928, inclusive, covering practically the entire period during which the electrification has been in complete operation. Eight months of the year 1928 include the operation of the entire electrification from Esperanza to Paso del Macho.

A careful analysis of these figures will indicate that the total cost per ton-mile decreases as the total ton-miles increase, as would be expected. The power contract calls for a minimum charge which usually covers the demand (or ready-to-serve item of the power bill), so that in case of extremely light traffic for any month, the cost of this item remains fixed, making the cost of power on a ton-mile basis much higher. On the other hand, a considerable increase in traffic can usually be handled within the specified peak limit by the careful dispatching of trains, which increases the

TABLE XXXII

**OPERATING COSTS ORIZABA–ESPERANZA DISTRICT FOR FOUR MONTHS'
ELECTRICAL OPERATION, 1928**

MEXICAN RAILWAY COMPANY

	January	February	March	April	Total	Yearly Rate
Enginemen	$4,776	$5,517	$7,839	$6,726	$24,858	$74,574
Trainmen	2,850	3,619	6,010	4,711	17,190	51,570
Power	13,740	14,054	14,560	16,580	58,934	176,802
Repairs	2,888	2,534	2,251	3,717	11,390	34,170
Enginehouse	777	756	965	980	3,478	10,434
Lubricants	22	51	47	45	165	495
Substation	869	944	1,052	1,102	3,967	11,901
Distribution	439	269	444	412	1,564	4,686
Total	$26,361	$27,744	$33,168	$34,273	$121,546	$364,632

Cᴏsᴛ Pᴇʀ 1000 Tᴏɴ-ᴍɪʟᴇs

	January	February	March	April	Average	Yearly Rate
Enginemen	$0.9435	$0.9268	$0.9282	$0.9065	$0.9248	......
Trainmen	0.5631	0.6079	0.7116	0.6349	0.6395	......
Power	2.7143	2.3608	1.7241	2.2345	2.1925	......
Repairs	0.5705	0.4256	0.2665	0.5009	0.4237	......
Enginehouse	0.1535	0.1270	0.1143	0.1321	0.1294	......
Lubricants	0.0043	0.0086	0.0056	0.0061	0.0061	......
Substations	0.1717	0.1586	0.1246	0.1485	0.1476	......
Distribution	0.0867	0.0452	0.0526	0.0555	0.0582	......
Total	$5.2076	$4.6605	$3.9275	$4.6190	$4.5218	......
1000 Ton-miles	5,062	5,953	8,445	7,420	26,880	80,640
Engine miles	20,780	23,490	32,119	29,256	105,645	316,935

Cᴏsᴛ Pᴇʀ Lᴏᴄᴏᴍᴏᴛɪᴠᴇ-ᴍɪʟᴇ (Cᴇɴᴛs)

	January	February	March	April	Average
Enginemen	22.984	23.487	24.406	22.990	23.529
Trainmen	13.715	15.407	18.712	16.103	16.270
Power	66.121	59.828	45.331	56.668	55.782
Repairs	13.899	10.789	7.008	12.706	10.780
Enginehouse	3.739	3.219	3.004	3.349	3.293
Lubricants	0.106	0.217	0.146	0.154	0.156
Substation	4.182	4.018	3.275	3.767	3.755
Distribution	2.113	1.145	1.382	1.408	1.480
Total	126.857	118.120	103.265	117.145	115.045

load-factor, thus limiting the cost for extra power to one-tenth of a cent per kw-hr., a rate additional to the charge per peak demand.

The full four months of steam operation, as given in Table XXXI, compared with the four months of electrical operation, as in Table XXXII, gives a total saving of $141,964 for the four months in favor of electrical operation, or 54 per cent. This is at the rate of $425,892 per year, whereas the two-month comparison shows a saving of 50 per cent, or at the rate of $402,612, no adjustments being made in either case for increased tonnage or wages.

Unfortunately the record of the ton-miles for July and August, 1927, were not recorded in the report, rendering a proper adjustment for this term impracticable.

For the purpose of checking the savings shown herein, similar comparisons of the results shown on other electrified roads were prepared. Table XXXIV gives the yearly rate of operating costs for the Butte, Anaconda & Pacific Railway; two divisions of the Chicago, Milwaukee, St. Paul & Pacific Railroad; and the Paulista Railway of Brazil, together with that of the Mexican Railway, and a combined result showing the average result of all the five electrifications.

It will be noted that in every instance a substantial saving is shown in each item listed; the average saving varying per item from 41 to 70 per cent, with a total average saving of 52.7 per cent in favor of electrical operation.

These records of operating expenses, which in each case have been supplied and approved by the operators, should be an incentive alike to the electrical industry and the railroad operating fraternity for a mutual interest in the subject of railway electrification. A few hours' study of the operating costs, and a general inspection of the line and equipment will usually indicate whether or not a detailed study and estimate are worth while.

The figures for comparative costs of operation as well as for the cost of construction were taken from the official records of the Mexican Railway Co., Ltd., and were approved by them. The figures relating to the original estimate were taken from the original report. The comparison of operating costs are from a report asked for by the chairman of the board of the Mexican Railway Co., Ltd., who after inspecting the completed electrification in April, 1928, called the author of the report (a copy of which he held in his hand) and, pointing to the paragraph which predicted the savings that might be expected from electrification, said: "You have apparently done reasonably well in meeting the promises in the report thus far, and we have no doubt that the electrification does even more than promised so far as handling the traffic is concerned, but my directors wish to know if the savings accomplished are sufficient to justify the ex-

TABLE XXXIII

OPERATING COSTS OF ELECTRIFIED DISTRICT

MEXICAN RAILWAY COMPANY

	1925 Oct., Nov., Dec.	1926 Year	1927 Year	1928 Year	Total 39 Months	Average Yearly Rate
Enginemen	$9,221	$43,012	$54,992	$80,835	$188,060	$57,865
Trainmen	4,789	25,970	34,193	53,033	117,985	36,303
Power	40,531	163,668	164,840	195,680	564,719	173,760
Repairs	4,493	21,768	36,868	42,514	105,643	32,505
Enginehouse	5,644	11,562	9,998	16,810	44,014	13,543
Lubricants	747	2,173	668	733	4,321	1,329
Substations	4,966	15,130	12,831	18,309	51,236	15,765
Distribution	2,587	9,308	4,510	5,775	22,180	6,825
Total	$72,978	$292,591	$318,900	$413,689	$1,098,158	$337,895

PER 1000 TON-MILES

	1925 Oct., Nov., Dec.	1926 Year	1927 Year	1928 Year	Total 39 Months	Average Yearly Rate
Enginemen	$0.94925	$0.98075	$0.95431	$0.81630	....	$0.89458
Trainmen	0.49300	0.59217	0.59337	0.53555	....	0.56124
Power	4.17243	3.73194	2.86056	1.97605	....	2.68132
Repairs	0.46253	0.49637	0.63979	0.42932	....	0.50254
Enginehouse	0.58102	0.26363	0.17350	0.16975	....	0.20932
Lubricants	0.07690	0.04955	0.01159	0.00780	....	0.02055
Substations	0.51122	0.34500	0.22266	0.18489	....	0.24373
Distribution	0.26632	0.21224	0.07826	0.05832	....	0.10551
Total	$7.51267	$6.67165	$5.53405	$4.17758	....	$5.22380

	1925 Oct., Nov., Dec.	1926 Year	1927 Year	1928 Year	Total 39 Months	Average Yearly Rate
1000 Ton-miles	9,714	43,856	57,625	99,026	210,221	64,683
Engine-miles	37,898	199,424	231,895	355,093	824,310	253,633
Cost Repairs per Engine-mile (Cents)	11.855	10.915	15.898	11.972	....	12.816
Per 100 Tons on Drivers	7.903	7.277	10.599	7.982	....	8.544

penditure made. Will you obtain all the operating data necessary for March and April this year for a comparison with September and October, 1921, and make us a statement showing whether or not the savings are as favorable as predicted?"

The operating costs for the Orizaba-Esperanza district have been kept during electrical operation precisely as they were during steam operation, so that the comparison between steam and electric operation herein is perhaps more direct and more free of adjustments than any other such comparison on record. The railways of Mexico are generally operated with standard American equipment and by almost identical methods, so that the operating costs are for all practical purposes as comparable as they would be on any American road. The cost of supplies are slightly higher and wages are about proportional for the amount and character of the work done.

The steam locomotives formerly used were well adapted to the service at the time they were purchased, and the later ones which had almost exactly the same weight on drivers as their electric successors were about as efficient for this mountain service as any modern locomotive not equipped with superheat and water-heating equipment. It should be mentioned here that about 30 per cent of the locomotive-miles made on the Orizaba-Esperanza district during September and October, 1921, were made by the ten new Consoli-

TABLE XXXIV

COMPARATIVE OPERATING COSTS AND SAVINGS OF STEAM ROAD ELECTRIFICATIONS

BUTTE, ANACONDA & PACIFIC RAILWAY

	Steam	Electric	REDUCTION	
			Amount	Per Cent of Steam
Enginemen....	$112,817	$71,225	$41,592	37
Trainmen.....	159,442	116,486	42,956	27
Fuel or power.	340,455	164,509	175,946	52
Repairs.......	134,771	92,278	42,493	31
Enginehouse..	32,301	18,639	13,662	42
Lubricants....	10,531	4,942	5,589	53
Other supplies	6,289	4,552	1,737	28
Water........	5,350	1,194	4,156	..
Substations...	......	16,400	......	..
Trolley & trans.	......	17,816	......	..
Total.....	$801,956	$508,041	$293,915	36

MEXICAN RAILWAY

	Steam	Electric	REDUCTION	
			Amount	Per Cent of Steam
Enginemen....	$185,946	$87,390	$98,556	53
Trainmen.....	130,332	64,326	66,006	50
Fuel or power.	300,834	186,840	113,994	38
Repairs.......	408,354	35,814	372,540	91
Enginehouse...	23,388	11,670	11,718	50
Lubricants....	19,146	552	18,594	97
Other supplies	......	......	......	..
Water........	......	......	......	..
Substations...	......	12,924	......	..
Trolley & trans.	......	5,136	......	..
Total.....	$1,068,000	$404,652	$663,348	62

CHICAGO, MILWAUKEE, ST. PAUL & PACIFIC RAILROAD

HARLOWTON-AVERY DIVISION

	Steam	Electric	REDUCTION	
			Amount	Per Cent of Steam
Enginemen....	$561,406	$327,230	$234,176	42
Trainmen.....	473,223	319,056	154,167	33
Fuel or power.	1,200,017	763,720	436,297	36
Repairs.......	943,654	338,326	605,328	64
Enginehouse..	221,044	87,028	134,016	60
Lubricants....	18,671	15,185	3,486	19
Other supplies	25,207	7,604	17,603	69
Water........	26,196	......	26,196	..
Substations...	......	108,881	......	..
Trolley & trans.	......	64,812	......	..
Total.....	$3,469,418	$2,031,842	$1,437,576	41

OTHELLO-TACOMA DIVISION

	Steam	Electric	REDUCTION	
			Amount	Per Cent of Steam
Enginemen....	$328,626	$136,715	$191,911	58
Trainmen.....	365,542	164,919	200,623	55
Fuel or power.	705,016	322,348	382,668	54
Repairs.......	479,782	141,910	337,872	70
Enginehouse...	82,056	31,867	50,189	61
Lubricants....	7,870	7,080	790	10
Other supplies	10,515	5,528	4,987	47
Water........	16,860	......	16,860	..
Substations....	......	63,686	......	..
Trolley & trans.	......	37,047	......	..
Total.....	$1,996,267	$911,100	$1,085,167	54

PAULISTA RAILWAY

	Steam	Electric	REDUCTION	
			Amount	Per Cent of Steam
Enginemen....	$226,488	$63,232	$163,256	72
Trainmen.....	......	......	......	..
Fuel or power.	920,063	132,950	787,113	85
Repairs.......	141,876	24,032	117,844	83
Enginehouse...	174,518	34,867	139,651	80
Lubricants....	26,714	5,425	21,289	79
Other supplies.	75,188	26,669	48,519	65
Water........	......	......	......	..
Substations...	......	29,993	......	..
Trolley & trans.	......	29,261	......	..
Total.....	$1,564,847	$346,429	$1,218,418	78

COMBINED RESULT

	Steam	Electric	REDUCTION	
			Amount	Per Cent of Steam
Enginemen....	$1,415,283	$685,792	$729,491	51.5
Trainmen.....	1,128,539	664,787	463,752	41
Fuel or power.	3,466,385	1,570,367	1,896,018	55
Repairs.......	2,108,437	632,360	1,476,077	70
Enginehouse...	533,307	184,071	349,236	65.5
Lubricants....	82,932	33,184	49,748	60
Other supplies	117,199	44,353	72,846	62
Water........	48,406	1,194	47,212	97.5
Substations...	......	231,884	......	..
Trolley & trans.	......	154,072	......	..
Total.....	$8,900,488	$4,202,064	$4,698,424	52.7

dation engines herein listed. This fact, however, would not materially affect the cost of locomotive repairs for those months, since the shop was behind with such work at the time and proceeded at the regular rate throughout the period.

The original report did not enter into the subject of new steam locomotives as the introduction of the ten new Consolidated locomotives into the service had made it evident that these would not sufficiently increase the capacity of the line or accomplish the desired saving. A report was then requested, showing what might be expected from electrification. At the time (October, 1921) the improvements which have recently been made in the economy of steam locomotives had not been brought to their present state of perfection. Modern locomotives had been considered by the management at the time the ten new Consolidated locomotives were purchased, but the electrification looked so favorable and offered so many additional advantages that no detailed comparison was required.

In general, where electrification has been compared with most modern steam operation, the cost of locomotives very nearly balance, thus reducing the gross cost of electrification from 40 to 50 per cent.

However, modern steam equipment would show a considerable saving over the old steam locomotives, which amount would of course be deductable from the saving that electrification would accomplish over the old steam locomotives. For instance, in the case of the Mexican Railway the savings expected from electrification over the old steam locomotives per year was estimated at $520,000. Had the mountain district been equipped with the largest steam locomotives with all the most modern improvements, it would have been possible to have handled the existing traffic at a considerable reduction in operating expenses, ordinarily about half the saving estimated for the electrification, which would have given about the same rate of return on the required investment for the new steam locomotives as had been predicted for the electrification. But the management realized that even with the adoption of the most modern and best adapted steam locomotives, the capacity of the single-track line between Orizaba and Esperanza might soon be reached and that double-tracking would have to be considered. The cost of a second track on a steep mountain side with seven tunnels would be a very expensive undertaking, estimated for the thirty miles involved at approximately $5,000,000, or about double the cost of electrification. Double-tracking would have increased the capacity of the line beyond the expected requirements of the near future, but would not have accomplished a saving in operating expenses which, alone, would have been at all satisfactory for the expense involved; whereas the electrification, costing much less and meeting any anticipated requirements, promised sufficient saving in operating expenses to make the investment attrac-

tive, even had it promised no additional advantages, such as increased capacity and improved conditions generally. In many such instances it is questionable if an economic mistake has not been made in this very matter of double-tracking congested districts and purchasing more powerful steam locomotives, which though increasing the capacity of the line and showing marked savings in operating expenses, cost more than electrification would have cost, and accomplish much less saving. Such mistakes have been largely due to the failure of the electrical manufacturer and the power producer to familiarize themselves with practical steam railway operating problems sufficiently to be able to present the full advantages of electrification to the aggressive steam-operation official. The power producer has been inclined to stick too closely to the standard power contract when discussing rates for railway electrification, he being afraid of the effect of possible peak loads on his plant, has been inclined to insert protective clauses in the contract which have been equally alarming to the railway manager as to the effect on his pocketbook. Happily the general tendency for the consolidation of the many smaller power companies into larger companies and the interconnection of these larger corporations physically as well as financially, is rapidly leading to material economies and greater reliability which will enable the power producer to supply any necessary peak demand without greatly increasing his investment, and thus be able to offer a dependable service at an attractive rate.

The object of presenting the results of the electrification herein described is to give true information to all of those who are interested. There are many sections of railway line that might be electrified with equally satisfactory results, but a careful study of the actual conditions is necessary to definitely determine the extent of the advantages to be expected.

It will be of interest to note the following quotations from comments made in communications from Mr. W. T. Ingram, Resident Engineer and Assistant General Manager of the Mexican Railway, and Mr. C. I. Luque, Superintendent of Transportation of the line, to both of whom the author is greatly indebted for their whole-hearted coöperation, not alone in securing the data for this article, but for their able support throughout the original study, the carrying out of the construction, and the initial operating period.

From Mr. Ingram:

"Referring to yours of the 19th, please note that our chief accountant has orders to put on a man to make up the statements you require for the Orizaba-Cordoba and Cordoba-Paso del Macho electrifications, dividing the total costs into material, labor, freight and duties. We will also prepare the statement for you based on the information furnished by the locomotive superintendent. This report shows very steadily that the cost per ton-kilometer between Orizaba and Esperanza was about 1½ centavos for steam, and ¾ centavos for electric operation.

"As regards the effect electrification has had on track maintenance, it would be impossible to say what this is in dollars and cents, but there is no doubt that the life of the line has been increased and the same applies to labor. No reduction has been made in the track force, but we have very much better track and this has meant freedom from accidents, less wear and tear on equipment and an improvement of train schedule."

From Mr. Luque:

"The electrification of the Mountain Section has meant to the Transportation Department the reduction of the operating problems peculiar to heavy-grade railroading to those of level roads.

"During the four years that electricity has been used as motive power we have been able to reduce not only train and engine crews to nearly one-half of what we had during steam operation but also telegraphers and other employees.

"There is an absolute dependability on the running time of trains handled with electric locomotives, which makes the work of the train dispatcher a matter of certainty in figuring out meeting and passing points, which with steam operation was only a guess.

"From the moment the train is ordered to round house and yard forces, time is calculated exactly— no allowances for getting up steam, caulking flues, cleaning fires, watering, etc., to which a steam engine that has been on the road and must be 'returned to the road as soon as ready' is wasted.

"Meeting points are made with precision unknown before, and as to safety and simplicity of operation, it is unsurpassable.

"On a railroad like ours, where traffic conditions have not been the best, it is quite a serious matter to acquire modern cars and coaches at the rate it is done elsewhere per annum, yet, perforce, we have to put up with weak or rather light old equipment which is a drawback in the operation of long tonnage trains. In spite of this handicap and considering our very heavy 4½ per cent grades, we have operated with 50 per cent of such 'soft shell' equipment without yet having destroyed or burst a car; very few draw-heads pulled off, chargeable really to 'age' defects and not to rough handling, which is a hard matter to control with a 150-ton locomotive ahead of and another behind 15 to 20 cars on a train, were it not for the ease and flexibility of the multi-motored electric engine.

"The regenerative braking is another very important feature on our electric locomotives—to bring down our grades trains of 30 to 40 cars without using air or hand brakes is something which when first told to our men was not believed. Even today after so many years one often wonders, as these long trains marshal down the steep slopes of the mountain, at this marvelous performance at an even speed, without jerking, shoving, and pulling like they used to do when controlled by compressed-air brakes. The expense of changing brake shoes, cooling off wheels, flattening of same, etc., has disappeared in its entirety.

"Were it not for the electrification of the mountain, we would have to operate the second division as a division instead of as so many districts as we do now. Divisional officers and offices are now a thing of the past, and our line is operated for all practical purposes as one division instead of two. What used to be a matter of discomfort and even concern to our passengers going through tunnels on account of smoke has also disappeared."

Freight Train on the Mexican Railway, Ascending 4.7-per cent Grade between Bota and Alta Luz

Mexican Railway Company Freight Train Hauled by Two 150-ton Electric Locomotives

Electrification of the Mexican Railway

ONE of the most interesting electrifications ever undertaken is that of the Mexican Railway Company, Ltd., on the single-track line between Mexico City and Vera Cruz. This line, which is 264 miles in length, exclusive of branch lines, was, at the time of its construction, one of the most difficult engineering problems ever encountered. At its maximum elevation, the road reaches a height of 8323 feet above sea level. It is significant that the 30-mile section between Esperanza and Orizaba was chosen for the initial electrification. This is by far the most difficult section because of heavy curvatures and grades reaching 4.7 per cent ruling and 5.25 per cent maximum.

This section of the road, locally called the Maltrata Incline, traverses a remarkably scenic country under the shadow of Orizaba Peak, one of the several extinct volcanoes in the immediate

One of the 150-ton, 3000-volt Direct-current Locomotives

Running Gear of 150-ton Articulated Type Locomotive

Mexican Railway Company 3000-volt Electrification. View at Nogales Station, Showing
Concrete Poles and Cross-span Construction Over Two Tracks

vicinity which range in height from 17,000 to 18,000 feet.

After the success of the original installation had been demonstrated, the electrification was extended to Paso del Macho, making a total distance of 70 miles.

The most recent type of steam locomotive replaced by electric locomotives weighs 150 tons and was designed especially for this division. It is known as the Fairlie type, and is an oil-burner. These engines are double-ended and have a three-axle driving truck at each end. with all the weight on the drivers.

The original motive-power equipment for electrification includes ten 150-ton, 3000-volt, d-c. locomotives, used for both freight and passenger duty. Because of the severe grades and heavy curvatures, ranging from 12 to nearly 16 degrees, the speed of both passenger and freight trains is limited.

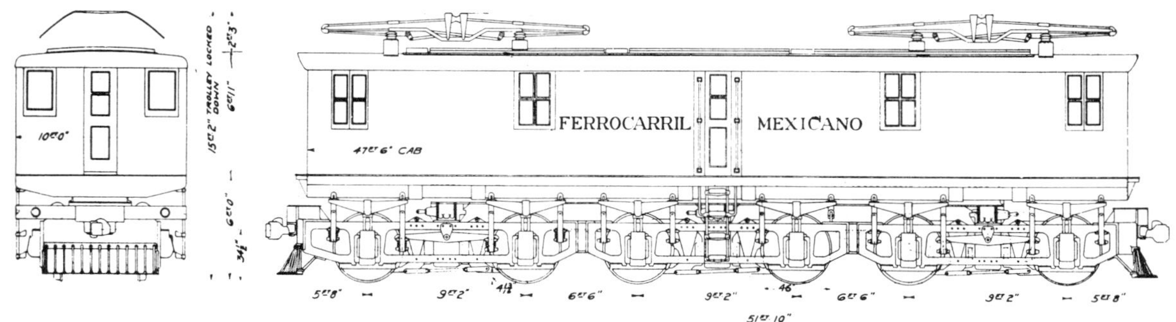

Outline and Dimensions of 150-ton, 3000-volt Type of Locomotive for the Mexican Railway Company, Ltd.

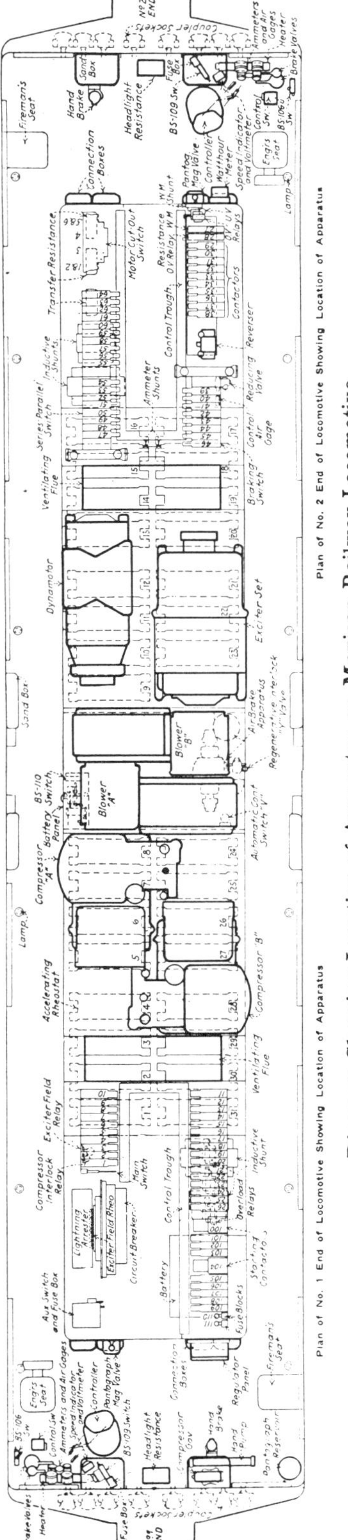

Diagram Showing Location of Apparatus on Mexican Railway Locomotive

In the substitution of electric locomotives for steam, there were several unusual conditions. First, the steam engines replaced have practically the same weight as the electric locomotives now in use; second, they have all the weight on the drivers; and third, they operate equally well in either direction. Nevertheless, in making the substitution, ten electric units have replaced 23 steam locomotives.

The two principal reasons for the greater capacity of the electric locomotives are the greatly increased speed in service on grades, and the higher percentage of availability. Whereas electric locomotives are available approximately 90 per cent of the time, the steam locomotives would ordinarily be available only about 30 per cent of the time. It has further been found that one electric locomotive can handle the normal passenger trains of eight cars on grades, whereas two steam locomotives were formerly used. This is due partly to the lack of steaming capacity on the long grades for the continuous pull, and partly to the faster schedule for passen-

View Looking Down into Auxiliary Machinery
Compartment

View Showing Overhead Construction and
Steel Poles

ger trains. The greater continuous capacity of
the electric locomotives has also made it possible
to handle heavier freight trains with two electrics than was possible with two steam engines.
Where two steam engines handled a 360-ton
train, two electrics are now handling a 660-ton
train at a higher speed.

An analysis of the operating speeds on the upgrade run shows that one of the passenger trains
which formerly required two hours and 50 minutes for the 30-mile run is now handled in one
hour and 50 minutes, an increase in schedule
speed of from 10.2 to 16 miles per hour. A typical freight run shows a decrease in running time

Passenger Train with 150-ton Electric
Locomotive at Maltrata

of from four hours to two hours and 25 minutes,
or an increase from 7.3 to 12.1 miles per hour.

While it was not expected that much improvement in speed would be shown on the down-hill
run, as a matter of fact, the running time of most
of the trains has been reduced. This is due to
the elimination of stops for fuel and water and
for cooling wheels and brake shoes. It will be
appreciated that the schedule speeds, mentioned heretofore, require actual running speeds,
not including stops, approximately double that
of steam.

Substations

Two substations, one at Maltrata and the
other at Portrero, furnish power to the lines.
The original 30 miles were fed from the substation at Maltrata. This substation contains

One of the 150-ton Fairlie-type, Double-end,
Oil-burning Steam Locomotives

two 3000-kilowatt synchronous motor-generator
sets with necessary transformers and switc ing
equipment. The second substation, at Portrero, is
a duplicate of the one at Maltrata except that it
contains two 1500-kilowatt synchronous motorgenerator sets. The total substation capacity
for the electric zone is thus 9000 kilowatts.

Locomotives

There are ten 150-ton, 3000-volt locomotives
on this road, which replaced 23 steam locomotives ranging in weight from 110 to 150
tons. The mechanical and electrical features
of these locomotives are as follows:

Nominal voltage of system . . . . 3000 v. d-c
Tractive eff., 1 hr. blown (3000 v.) . . . 54,000 lb.
Speed at 1 hr. rating, full field . . . . 19 m.p.h.
Total horsepower, 1 hr. 2736
Tractive eff., cont. 3000 v., full field . . 48,500
Speed at continuous rating, 3000 v. . . . 19.5 m.p.h.
Total horsepower, continuous 2520
Number of motors 6
Type of motors . . . . GE-278-A-1500/3000 v.
Gear ratio 90/18-5.00
Tractive eff. at 30% tract. coef . . . . . . 92,700 lb.

MECHANICAL DATA

Track gauge . . . . 4 ft. 8½ in.
Wheel arrangement 04440
Diameter of drivers . . . . 46 inches
Number of driving axles 6

**Passenger Train Hauled by Two Double-ended
Steam Locomotives up 4½-per cent
Grade North of LaBota**

Total wheel base . . . . 40 ft. 6 in.
Max. rigid wheel base . . . . 9 ft. 2 in.
Width overall . . . . 10 ft. 1½ in.
Height over trolley locked down . . . . . . 15 ft. 2 in.
Length inside knuckles . . . . 52 ft. 11 in.

WEIGHTS

Total weight on drivers . . . . 309,000 lb.
Dead weight per axle . . . . 12,150 lb.
Elec. and air brake equipment . . . . 135,000 lb.
Mechanical equipment . . . . 174,000 lb.

Each locomotive is of the twin-geared, articulated-truck type. A single cab is mounted on two equalizer frames which, in turn, are carried upon three two-axle articulated trucks. A motor is geared directly to each axle with twin, cushion-type gears.

Exterior of Maltrata Substation

The six motors, with which each locomotive is equipped, are of the box-frame, twin-geared, cummutating-pole, railway type with forced ventilation. They are designed to operate two in series on a 3000-volt circuit, or 1500 volts per commutator. The windings are therefore insulated for 3000 volts to ground. An 18-tooth steel pinion is mounted on each end of the armature shaft, and these mesh with 90-tooth cushion-type gears on the axle.

An unusual feature of the design of this locomotive is the provision for removing the motor, wheels, or axle from any of the trucks without removing the cab. By disconnecting the motor leads and jacking up the motor and the side frames, the wheels and axle and finally the motor can be lowered into a pit.

Interior of Maltrata Substation

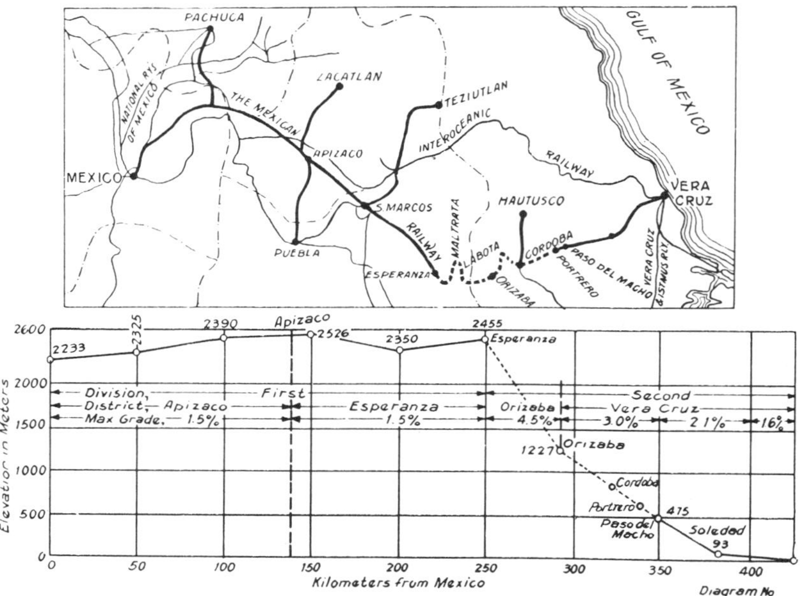

**Map and Profile of Mexican Railway between Mexico City and Vera Cruz.
Electrified Portion Indicated by Dotted Lines**

The power for the operation of the auxiliaries is provided by a 3000/1500-volt dynamotor which carries a 4-kilowatt, 65-volt control generator mounted on a shaft extension. The two blower motors and the two compressor motors are normally operated in series across the 3000-volt supply using the mid-point of the dynamotor for equalization. This scheme allows the operation of the compressors and blowers directly from the trolley in case of failure of the dynamotor, and of one compressor or blower in case of the failure of the other machine.

An exciter set, used for regeneration, is driven by a 1500-volt motor operated from the 1500-volt dynamotor bus. If it is not necessary to operate the blowers at maximum capacity, they can also be operated on the 1500-volt circuit by connecting them in series.

The control generator supplies current at 65 volts for lights, headlights, foot-warmers, and control circuits, and for charging the storage battery.

**View of Maltrata and Grade Section with
Orizaba Peak in Background**

ELECTRIFICATION
OF THE
SPANISH NORTHERN
RAILWAY

GENERAL ELECTRIC COMPANY

Fig. 1.   View of the Pajares Substation Which Furnishes Power to Southern End of the Line

ELECTRIFICATION OF THE SPANISH NORTHERN RAILWAY

IN order to overcome unusually severe traffic conditions, the Northern Railway of Spain electrified 38.5 miles of its tracks in the year 1924. This portion of its lines extends from Ujo, which is 816 ft. above sea level, to Busdongo, which is just across the ridge of the southern slope of the mountains and is 4050 ft. above sea level. This electrified section is part of the single-track line running from Gijon on the coast, south through Oviedo and Leon, and joining the main line from France to Madrid at Venta de Banos.

This remarkable stretch of railway was built about 40 years ago under the direction of a prominent Spanish engineer. In the electrified section the road goes through 71 tunnels, most of which are on curves and which have an aggregate length of 16.8 miles. The longest tunnel, La Perruca, a short distance north of Busdongo, is on tangent track and has a total length of 10,080 ft. The longest tunnel on the curved section is El Orria, which has a length of 3475 ft. and turns through three-quarters of a circle.

It is interesting to note that in Spain the track gauge differs from that of neighboring countries. There it is 5 ft. 6 in. while in France and the remainder of Europe the American standard of 4 ft. 8½ in. is almost universally used.

The initial contract for this electrification was awarded to the Sociedad Iberica de Construcciones Electricas, the Spanish representatives of the International General Electric Company, and provided for six 3000-volt loco-

Fig. 3.   Tangent Track Leaving the North End of the Cobertoria Classification Yards

motives, two 2-unit, 3000-kw. substations, and overhead line material for the complete project. In addition to the items listed, six additional locomotives have been ordered from other manufacturers. Power is purchased from the hydro-electric system of the Electra de Viesgo Company at 30,000 volts, three-phase, 50 cycles. This energy is transmitted over the lines of the railway company to substations located at Pajares and Cobertoria.

Fig. 2.   Relief Map of Terrain Between Busdongo and Campomanes

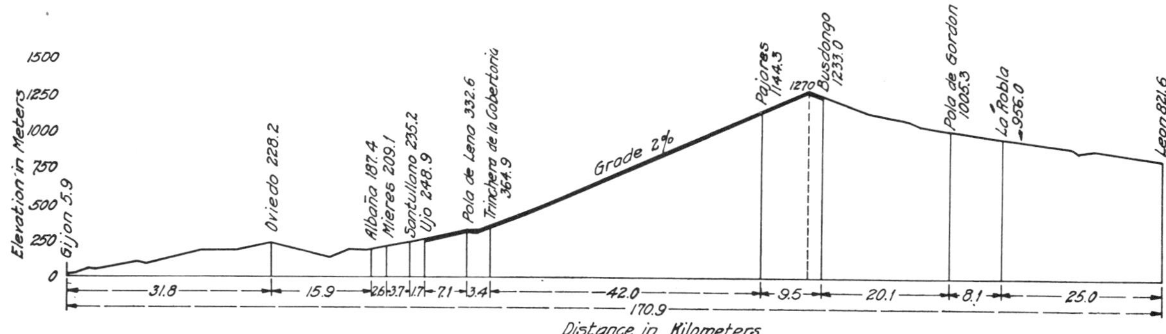

Fig. 4.   Profile of the Division of the Railway Including the Electrified Section
Indicated by the Heavy Line

Locomotives

The locomotives which the General Electric Company has constructed for this service are of the swivel-equalized-truck design and weigh 89.5 tons, all on the driving axles. With this type of locomotive the pulling stresses are transmitted through the platform of the locomotive instead of through the truck frames as is the case with the articulated type.

The cab is supported through center plates on two 3-axle trucks. Six motors geared one to each of the six driving axles give a total capacity of 1550 h.p. Hauling a 330 metric-ton train up the two per cent grade at a speed of 35 km. per hr. requires a tractive effort of 22,000 lb. The maximum speed on level tangent track is 40 km. (24.8 miles) per hr. with a train of 1655 tons, while the maximum emergency speed of the locomotive is 60 km. (37.2 miles) per hr.

The auxiliary apparatus and control mechanism are housed in a box-type cab which extends the full length of the locomotive. The platform, built up of structural steel members which are securely braced and riveted, is covered by a steel floor $\frac{3}{8}$ in. thick. At each end an operating compartment for the engineer is partitioned off from the apparatus room in the center. Current is collected by either of two slider-type, air-raised, gravity-lowered pantographs mounted on the roof.

When descending grades, the locomotive is held back by regeneration; five of the motors becoming generators while the sixth generates their exciting current. The locomotives are also equipped with vacuum brakes, but these are used only in emergencies and in bringing the train to a complete stop. On this railway, although practically all the passenger coaches are equipped with power brakes, the freight cars have only individual hand brakes which must be applied by the trainmen when a braking effort is required in excess of that which will slip the wheels of the locomotive. In actual freight service it is customary to have a man stationed on every fourth car to assist if necessary in braking the train. At present an average freight

Fig. 5.   Electric Locomotive and Train at Ujo, Showing Main-line and Yard Overhead

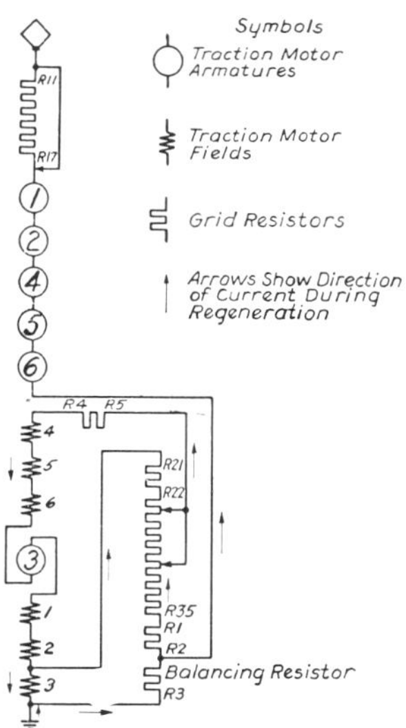

Fig. 6. Simplified Wiring Diagram, Showing Regenerative Braking Connections

train consists of 28 to 36 freight cars of 15-ton capacity, which requires a large crew.

The normal train movement is "loaded" up-grade (from Ujo to Busdongo) and "empty" down-grade, although trains loaded to the rated capacity of the locomotive are also handled on the down grade. Favorable comments have been made by Spanish engineers on the easy riding qualities of these locomotives.

Their ratings, dimensions, and weights are given in Table I.

TABLE I
ELECTRICAL DATA

Nominal voltage system 3000
Tractive effort, cont. . . . . .26,500 lb.
Tractive effort 1 hr., blown . . . . .27,100 lb.
  At 30% coefficient . . . . .53,700 lb.
Total h.p., continuous 1550
  One hour 1550
Speed, continuous . . . . .21.9 m.p.h.
  One hour . . . . .21.6 m.p.h.
Number of motors 6
Gear ratio . . . . .4:1 or 72:18

MECHANICAL DATA

Track gauge . . . . .5 ft. 6 in.
Width . . . . .9 ft. 8½ in.
Length . . . . .46 ft. 0 in.
Max. rigid wheel base . . . . .11 ft. 6 in.
Diameter of drivers . . . . .39⅜ in.
Total wheel base . . . . .35 ft.
Number of driving axles 6
Height over trolley down . . . . .13 ft. 5 in.

WEIGHTS

On drivers (total) . . . . .179,000 lb.
Per driving axle .29,830 lb.
Electrical equipment . . . . .85,000 lb.
Mechanical equipment . . . . .94,000 lb.

Motors

The motors are of the commutating-pole box type with the air inlet at the top. Ready access to the armature, pole pieces, and field coils is provided through the pinion end. Large hand-holes allow easy inspection of the commutator and brush-holders. The bearings are waste-lubricated and an ample supply of oil is insured by auxiliary oil wells.

Louvres in the sides of the cab permit the entrance of air to the whole interior of the apparatus compartment. The blower drives air into the horizontal duct between the center channels of the locomotive platform. These ducts open through hollow center plates and flexible duct connections into the truck transoms, which connect with ventilating openings in the motors. The series method of ventilation is used; that is, air enters the top of the motor frame at the pinion end, is forced over the armature and field coils, returning through the commutator and armature core to the pinion end, whence it is expelled through holes in the framehead. These motors are designed for operation at 1000 volts

Fig. 7. Curve on Main Line, Showing Poles on Inside of Curve Supporting Feeders and Overhead

Fig. 8. Freight Train Entering Station of Fierros from the North

per commutator and are insulated to operate three in series on 3000 volts.

The motor has a continuous rating of 258 h.p. at 1000 volts for a temperature rise of 120 deg. by resistance. The gears and pinions are of oil-tempered steel and have a reduction ratio of 72 to 18.

Control

The control is electro-pneumatically operated and is intended for non-automatic single-unit operation with the following connections: one group of six motors in series, or two groups of three motors in series.

Fourteen steps are provided for acceleration with six motors in series, ten steps with two parallel groups of three in series, and thirteen steps in regenerative braking. In starting, the six motors are connected in series with the line and an adjustable resistance. Sections of this resistance are short-circuited as the controller is moved from point to point over the series travel of the main handle until all the resistance is cut out and the six motors are in series directly across the line. Then, as the accelerating handle is moved to the first

series-parallel notch of the controller, a pneumatically operated transfer switch reconnects the motor circuits in the series-parallel arrangement with the resistances again in series. The short circuiting of the resistance is then repeated until the motors are in the full series-parallel position.

All the motor switching is performed by air-operated contactors. They are closed by compressed air and opened by a heavy spring. An arc chute and blow-out coil insure proper rupturing of the arc. An electro-pneumatically operated reverser is interlocked with the line contactors.

For speeds above the full-series and full-parallel connection, two reduced-field positions are provided. Both reduced-field positions can be obtained in either of the full-running positions. This is accomplished by moving a selective handle on the master controller. This controls contactors which connect an inductive shunt across the field. In emergencies three of the motors may be cut out and the locomotive operated with the remaining three.

Regeneration is accomplished by using one motor to excite the fields of the other

Fig. 9. Interior of the Cobertoria Substation, Showing Two 1500-kw., 3000-volt Motor-Generator Sets, and Switching Equipment

five. The remaining five motors are connected in series and regenerate to the line in proportion to the field excitation. Only one combination of motors is used for regeneration but, by means of the 13 steps which are provided, a speed range from 20 km. (12.4 miles) per hour to the maximum operating speed of the locomotive is obtained.

Regenerative braking is accomplished by the same controller, contactors, and resistors as are used during motoring. This simplifies the control and makes economical use of the apparatus. A balancing resistance is used to protect the motors, to stabilize the excitation, and to compensate for line-voltage changes. When starting to regenerate, the main handle of the master controller is moved to the *off* position, and the selective handle then thrown to the braking connection. This same handle is used to select the motoring, reduced-field, and regenerative-braking connections. Upon setting the selective handle for the braking connection, a transfer switch is thrown by compressed air. This rearranges the circuits to give the connections necessary for regenerative braking. The

Fig. 11. Cobertoria Substation

main handle may then be notched up until the desired braking value is obtained. The master controller is mechanically interlocked so that no false manipulation is possible.

Auxiliary Equipment

Power for the operation of the control circuits, lights, cab heaters, air compressors, exhausters, and for charging the storage battery is furnished by a 10-kw., 65-volt generator direct connected to a 25-h.p., 3000-volt motor. A blower mounted on the extended shaft of the motor-generator set furnishes air for the ventilation of the traction motors.

As a reserve there is provided a storage battery of sufficient capacity to operate the control, an exhauster, and the lighting system for one hour. A reverse-current relay is placed in the circuit between the battery and the generator to prevent the discharge of the battery.

The compressor, which furnishes air for the controls, pantographs, whistles, and sanders, is operated from the 65-volt circuit, and is controlled by a governor which starts and stops it automatically, thereby maintaining the pressure between certain predetermined values.

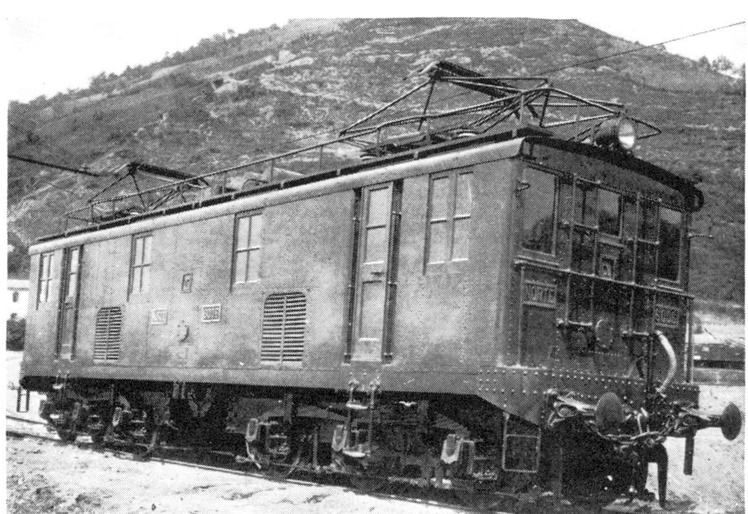

Fig. 10.   One of the Six Direct-current, 3000-volt, 1550-h.p., 90-ton Locomotives

Fig. 12. Electric Locomotive Hauling a Typical Freight Train
Over a Bridge Near Fierros

Two exhausters, both of which operate from the 65-volt circuit, maintain the vacuum-brake system on the locomotive and the passenger coaches. Normally one exhauster operates at low speed, while the other is shut down.

A high-speed circuit breaker is connected ahead of all other apparatus in the main motor circuits. In case of a short circuit on any part of the apparatus, or of a heavy overload, the circuit breaker trips and opens the circuit. The high speed with which the breaker opens greatly reduces the liability of damage from either short circuit or heavy overload. In addition to protecting the locomotive, it also protects the generating units in the substation by quickly reducing any heavy power demands. The breaker has no mechanical latches or triggers. It is tripped electro-magnetically. The blow-out consists of a powerful magnetic field which, combined with a narrow arc chute, quickly breaks the arc caused by opening the circuit.

An overvoltage relay is connected across the regenerating motors in series with the high resistance, and is so arranged that when the motors generate a predetermined voltage this relay opens, tripping out the high-speed circuit breaker and dropping out the resistance contactors during regeneration so as to open the field of the motors. This furnishes protection against overvoltage in case of interruption in the return circuit

Substation

Power from the 30,000-volt lines is converted to 3000 volts direct current in two substations, one of which is located at Cobertoria, 5.9 miles from Ujo; the other at Pajares which is the same distance from Busdongo, the southern end of the electric zone.

Each of these stations contains two 3-unit, 4-bearing, 1500-kw., 3000-volt, direct-current motor-generator sets with the necessary transformers and switch gear. Provision is made for the future installation of a third unit in each station. The outgoing positive feeders are amply protected by the addition of high-speed circuit breakers in each line.

Transformers

Two three-phase oil-cooled transformers rated 30,000/3500 volts, 1900 kv-a., 50 cycles are installed in each of the two substations. Four

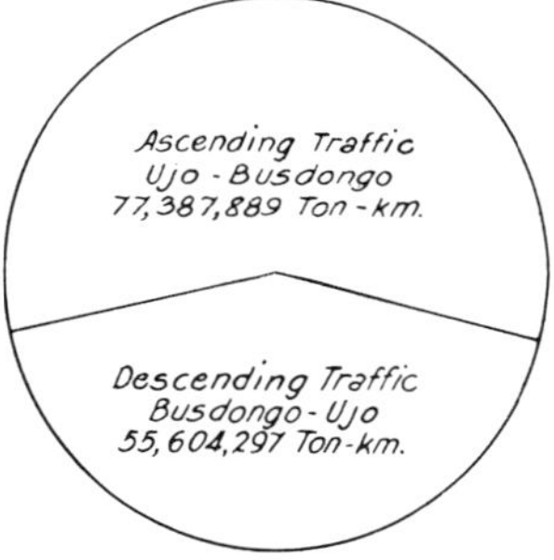

Fig. 13. Diagram Showing Proportions of Ascending
and Descending Traffic for the Year 1925

[8]

$2\frac{1}{2}$ per cent taps are provided in the high-voltage winding to compensate for variation in the transmission line voltage and 50 per cent starting taps in the low-voltage winding for starting the motor-generator sets.

Motor-Generator Sets

The direct-current generators are designed for 1500 volts per commutator and are permanently connected in series for 3000-volt operation. They are separately excited from a small 125-volt generator mounted on one end of the set. The series field of each main generator is designed to provide flat compounding from no load to 50 per cent overload. They are equipped with commutating poles and compensated windings to insure sparkless commutation under all load conditions.

Excitation for the synchronous motor is provided by a second 35- to 150-volt direct-current generator placed on the opposite end of the set. It has a series winding which carries the 3000-volt line current so that the motor-field excitation varies in proportion to the load on the set. This insures correct power-factor with varying loads, and also insures stable operation under heavy overloads. These sets handle 150 per cent load for two hours, or 300 per cent load for five minutes. They also operate inverted to take care of regeneration.

Overhead and Line Construction

The overhead construction is of the modified flexible catenary type designed by the General Electric Company and installed under the supervision of the Sociedad Iberica de Construcciones Electricas. This overhead is known as the twin-catenary type and comprises two 4/0 copper wires flexibly suspended side by side from the same $\frac{1}{2}$-in. diameter steel messenger by independent loop hangers. These supports are spaced 15 ft. apart and are alternately connected to each contact wire. Thus the distance between adjacent hangers is 7.5 ft. With this construction, because of the four contacts secured by the double-pan collector and the twin-trolley wire, current is collected under all conditions without visible sparking. Porcelain insulation is used throughout. Steel poles spaced at intervals of 150 ft. on tangent track, with reductions on curves, support the brackets carrying the messenger. Brackets on the poles carry the positive feeder and the negative return wire, while in tunnels these are carried on iron-bracket supports.

It is possible on account of the unusually circuitous route which the track follows to improve the distribution by running the feeder across the ends of several loops that are necessary to conform to the limiting grade. One of these cut-offs is 1.24 miles in length across about 4.35 miles, while two others about 0.30 miles long join the ends of another loop of about the same length.

As it was deemed advisable to put in concealed bonds, it was necessary to install special fish plates throughout the electrified section. Each rail joint is bonded by 12-in. 4/0 copper bonds, and at every 1000 ft. a 4/0 steel cross bond 76 in. long is put in.

To protect the system, sectionalized construction is used. Because of the character of the country—mountains, curves, and tunnels—and of the fact that there must not be any interference with normal operation, all construction work was done at night.

Fig. 14. Transformer Room at the Cobertoria Substation, Showing Transformers, Oxide-film Lightning Arresters, and High-tension Buses

Operating Data

All of the data on electric operation refer back to the year 1925, the first year in which the Pajares grade was operated wholly electrically. The data for steam operation are deduced from

tonnage. This performance record was due to the greater capacity of the electric locomotive which permitted the hauling of trains up the practically continuous 2 per cent grade with single locomotives.

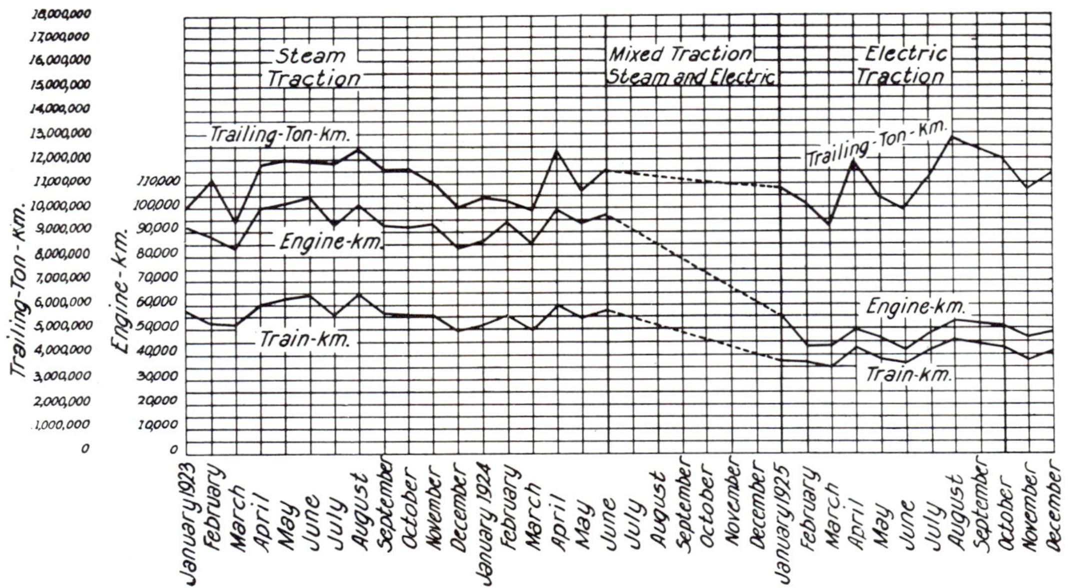

Fig. 15.   Curves Showing Variation of Traffic Statistics for Steam and Electric Operation

figures obtained during the year 1923. The change-over was made during the year 1924 so that during that year operations were partly steam and partly electric.

During the year 1925 the electric locomotives were operated 363,096 miles. Of this amount 302,886 miles represented the handling of trains and the remainder switching and light engine movements. The traffic handled totaled 90,700,660 ton-miles in both directions. The consumption of electric power for hauling this traffic totaled 9,173,847 kilowatt-hours delivered to the purchase point at Cobertoria by the power company (La Electra De Viesgo).

For the year 1923, the period selected for comparison with the electric operation, the steam engines then in service were operating a total of 704,000 locomotive-miles, while the traffic handled, 92,600,000 ton-miles, differed but slightly from that handled in 1925. The number of engine-miles with electric operation was therefore only 51.6 per cent of that with steam operation while hauling nearly the same

The comparative statistics are made the basis of several graphical comparisons, Fig. 15 plotting the values for ton-km., engine-km. and train-km. operated over the period from January, 1923, to December, 1925. The first portion of this curve applies to steam traction; a period of seven months in the central portion covers mixed steam and electric traction, and the balance of the chart the all-electric operation. It is interesting to note that the curve for ton-km., while somewhat fluctuating from month to month, remains fairly constant over the period. The number of engine-km. and the number of train-km., however, are greatly reduced. The chart, Fig. 13, shows graphically the portion of traffic handled with and against the grade. In Fig. 17 a graphic comparison is presented of the engine-km. made by electric locomotives handling the 1925 traffic with the engine-km. that would have been required by steam operation.

With regard to the consumption of electric power, the following figures are calculated, based on performances of the calendar year 1925:

Power consumption per engine-mile..   25.27 kw-hr.
Power consumption per ton-mile of trailing train....................101.17 watt-hr.
Power consumption per ton-mile of total train.....................   77.7 watt-hr.

The electric energy for the year 1925 was purchased at Cobertoria substation at a rate of 10 centimos per kw-hr., corresponding to a cost of $1.18 per 1000 ton-miles of total train.[1]

The energy purchased represents the requirements over and above the amount returned to the overhead line by regenerated power from the descending trains. It is not possible to determine the amount of regenerated power actually utilized, but a large percentage is taken up by ascending trains. From readings of the instruments on the locomotives, however, and taking into account the efficiency of the line and other factors, it is calculated that the regenerated power absorbed by ascending trains was 10 per cent of the total energy delivered at Cobertoria.

Since records of the actual coal consumption for the Pajares grade had been combined with those for the entire division, it was necessary to resort to calculations to determine what amount would have been consumed on this electrified grade during 1925 had it been steam operated. In order to determine this figure as accurately as possible, four separate calculations were made.

[1] Based upon rate of exchange of 15.2 cents per peseta.

The first calculation was based on coal consumption per virtual engine-km.[2] These figures were deduced from data covering a period of one month, giving the following monthly averages:

1921   0.421 kg. per ton-km. (1.36 lb. per ton-mile)
1922   0.360 kg. per ton-km. (1.16 lb. per ton-mile)
1923   0.344 kg. per ton-km. (1.03 lb. per ton-mile)
1924   0.324 kg. per ton-km. (1.045 lb. per ton-mile)

A consistent improvement is shown over this period. This is claimed to be due in part to more efficient handling of the locomotives, but principally to improvement in the grade of fuel used.

The second calculation was made on the basis of the coal consumed per actual engine-km. These data, which are compiled beginning in 1921, also show the tendency to decrease over the total period. These figures which are calculated to give total kilograms of coal per engine-km., are as follows:

1921 49.1 kg. per engine-km. (174 lb. per engine-mile)
1922 42.3 kg. per engine-km. (150 lb. per engine-mile)
1923 41.0 kg. per engine-km. (145 lb. per engine-mile)
1924 37.9 kg. per engine-km. (134 lb. per engine-mile)

The third calculation was based on practical tests performed with trains on the upgrade. In order to get these data, a series of tests was run

[2] Some European authorities have deduced a formula for taking into account the grades curvature in an attempt to reduce all energy consumption to a basis of tangent level track. The following formula is given by an Italian engineer:

$$L_v = L_r + \frac{h + \Sigma\, pl}{5}$$

where

L_v = Virtual length in kilometers
L_r = Real length in kilometers
h = Difference of level in meters between two points
l = Length of curves in kilometers
p = Coefficient of radius of the curve

The following values are given for p:

Radius of curve meters...	1000	800	600	400	300	200	180
Values of p............	0.5	0.8	1.2	2.0	2.8	4.2	4.5

Fig. 16.   Freight Train with 90-ton Locomotive at Cobertoria

[11]

in July, 1921, with various trains running from Ujo to Busdonogo. For each of these trains the coal consumption was calculated for starting and cleaning fire, getting up steam, and maintaining the fire during operation. The results of

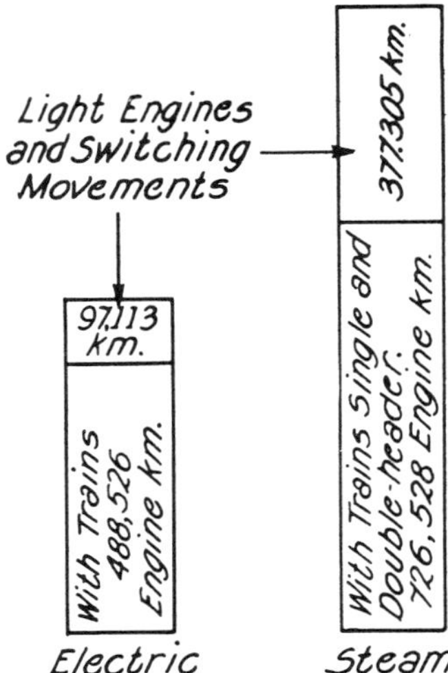

Fig. 17. Graphic Comparison of the Engine-km. Required to Handle the Same Traffic by Electric and by Steam Operation

this calculation give a mean consumption of 1.09 lb. per ton-mile of train. Three grades of fuel were used:

- 40 per cent Ujo briquettes
- 40 per cent Cobertoria briquettes
- 20 per cent small size bituminous coal from Asturias

Furthermore, the experiment showed that each train on the down grade consumes about 2200 pounds of coal and that the engine running light or performing switching service has an average consumption of 35.5 pounds per mile. The figures arrived at by this method are somewhat less than the two preceding calculations, but this is explained by the fact that stand-by losses were not considered, neither was the coal consumed through the cleaning of fires taken into account nor the starting of fires in engines after repairs. A further error is involved in the fact that trains do not always operate with the maximum load assumed in the calculations.

The fourth calculation was made by attempting to determine the decrease in the amount of coal delivered to the coaling stations at Leon, Oviedo and other points between the year 1923, the last year of operation exclusively by steam,

and the year 1925. As previously explained, the adjoining divisions at each end of the electrification were formerly supplied with coal from the same coaling stations as the Pajares grade. Figures obtained for this calculation show that there was a decrease of 37,600 tons of fuel due to the electrification. It is not believed, however, that these figures accurately reflect true coal consumption, since the traffic conditions of the other lines quite probably show considerable variation for the two periods, even though the traffic over the grade division was approximately the same.

To sum up, the most satisfactory figures obtained by the several methods indicate that an average consumption of 114 tons of coal per day would be required had steam locomotives been used on the electric division during the year 1925.

Assuming this daily average, the total consumption during the year 1925 would have been 41,800 tons. Since the actual electric energy was 9,173,847 kw-hr., it will be seen that this corresponds to 9.18 lb. of coal per kw-hr. Inasmuch as the purchased energy is supplemented by the regenerated power from the down trains, the comparison might in effect be represented by:

$$4.173\tfrac{5}{8}0.9 = 3.723 \text{ kg. (8.2 lb.) coal} = 1 \text{ kw-hr.}$$

STEAM OPERATING FIGURES

The steam locomotives displaced on the Pajares grade were as shown in Table II.

The capital represented by these locomotives is calculated from the 1924 prices, which were exceptionally low, as follows:

Price of 30 locos., 3,154,305 lb. $719,181
Price of 30 tenders, 1,079,100 lb. 126,745

Total. $845,926

From this figure the interest and depreciation charges are calculated using 7 per cent interest and depreciation (on a basis of 25 years' life.)

Coal Consumption

Estimates for cost of coal during 1925 are based on prices in Asturias increased by a charge for loading and unloading and a 5 per cent overhead for general expenses as follows:

		Per Ton
Briquettes. . . . . .80 per cent		$8.62
Grain (Granos). . . . . .10 per cent		7.57
Small size (Menudos). . . . . .10 per cent		5.25
General average.		$8.18

TABLE II

STEAM LOCOMOTIVES

Type	Service	No. of Engines	LB. WEIGHT EACH		LB. TOTAL WEIGHT	
			Engine	Tender	Engine	Tender
Series 1 651–89........	Express	1	76,285	26,400	76,285	26,400
Series 2 731–60........	Passenger	3	108,900	36,300	326,700	108,900
Series 2 663–82........	Freight	26	105,800	36,300	2,751,320	943,800
Total............		30			3,154,305	1,079,100

Engine Maintenance

The estimated maintenance expenditures for steam locomotives per locomotive-mile had this division been steam operated in 1925 are based on the general averages for the year 1922 as follows:

Routine up-keep in roundhouses and
    sheds......................... 8.14 cents
Major repairs.......................11.02 cents

      Total........................19.16 cents
                      per locomo-
                      tive-mile

The personnel necessary for operating the Pajares grade with steam locomotives numbered about 35 engine crews with 5 extra crews used for helper service. Table III gives the total annual expense which would have been required for steam operation of the Pajares grade during 1925.

COST OF ELECTRIC TRACTION

Table IV gives in some detail the total cost of the electric installation, including locomotives, substations, and distribution equipment.

In comparison with Table III, giving the costs of steam operation over this grade section, Table V gives the annual expenditures involved with electric operation. It should be noted that in this table several assumptions are made, for example: first, there has been practically no maintenance on the substation save for lubrication of the motor-generator sets. It is expected, however, that the renewal of oil in the transformers, replacement of brushes, etc., may cause an annual expenditure of $760 for each station. This accounts, therefore, for the $1520 charged against substation maintenance. Second, in the maintenance of overhead, the assumption is made that it would be necessary to renew two

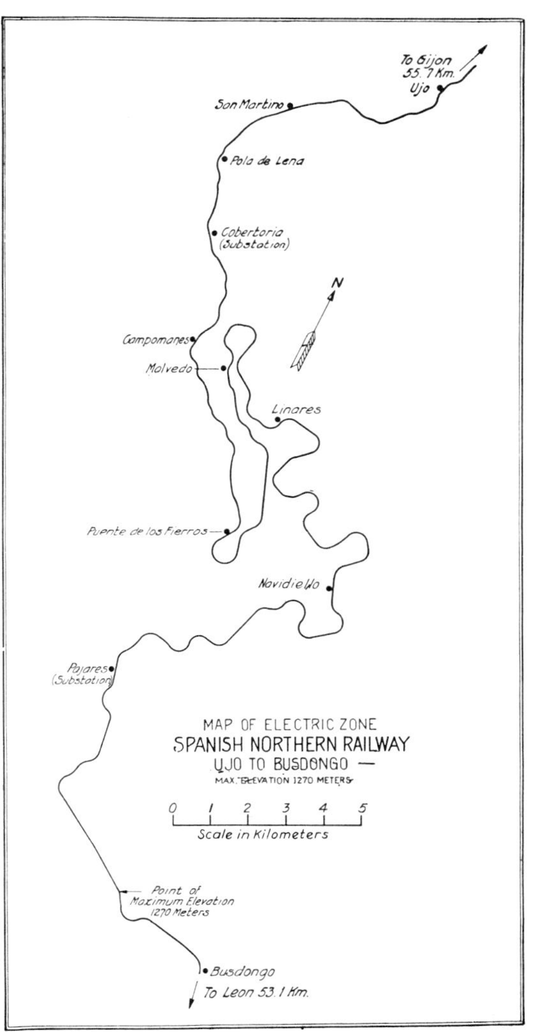

Fig. 18. Map of the 38.5-mile Electrified Section
of the Railway

kilometers of wire annually, at an estimated cost of $1125. In general, therefore, it is evident that the figures given are very conservative.

[13]

RESULTS OF ELECTRIC OPERATION

The report calls attention to a number of conditions which affect any comparison that may be attempted between steam and electric operation. In the first place, the cost of the installation was comparatively high, since the equipment was purchased in 1920 when material prices were at the high peak. In the second place, the price of electric energy during the year 1925 was not very advantageous since the traffic anticipated did not materialize and consequently the purchase of power was penalized to some extent by certain features of the power contract. Installation of the power limiting device, together with the gradual increase in traffic, is expected to reduce the cost of energy approximately 20 per cent.

It is also regarded as of great importance that the use of electric locomotives permits handling nearly double the traffic which could have been handled with steam. A summation of the report gives the following direct advantages secured by electrification, as follows:

(1) The substitution of 12 electric locomotives, having a weight of 1043 tons and a total continuous rating of 18,960 h.p., for 30 steam engines and tenders with a total operating weight of 2932 tons and with 29,590 h.p.

(2) A saving of 55 per cent in the cost of power required for operation.

(3) A reduction in the engine-miles by 47 per cent, which, taking into account the respective operating weights, represents a reduction of 83 per cent in the ton-mileage of the motive equipment.

(4) A saving of 73.5 per cent in the cost of repairs and upkeep for locomotives.

(5) A saving of 63 per cent in crew expense.

(6) A reduction of 31 per cent in the cost of moving a ton-mile. The actual figures are 0.646 cents per ton-mile for steam, and 0.436 cents per ton-mile for electric operation. This decrease amounts to an overall saving of approximately $182,000 in annual operation obtained by electrification.

The railway and electrical fraternities will find the report of the engineering staff of the Spanish Northern Railways highly instructive and a most valuable contribution on the subject of railroad electrification.

TABLE III

ANNUAL EXPENSES STEAM OPERATION

Interest and depreciation for the motive equipment (7 per cent)	$59,200
Coal consumption	310,400
Engine maintenance	131,600
Operating personnel	78,400
Total expenses for 1925	$579,600

TABLE IV

COST OF ELECTRIC INSTALLATION

Contact lines (62 km.)	Electric material (including rail bonds)	$288,100
	Poles, brackets, and supports	105,800
	Installing the line (including tools and the material)	133,600
		$527,500
Transmission line 30,000 volts (14 km.)	Electric material	$7,800
	Steel poles	17,400
	Erection	13,700
		$38,900
Substations	Electric equipment	$329,400
	Auxiliary equipment	37,800
	Buildings, etc.	77,400
	Erection	12,400
		$457,000
Locomotives	Twelve locomotives (including extra expenses)	$1,464,000
Power limiting device	Material and erection	14,200
Grand total		$2,501,600

TABLE V

COST OF ELECTRIC OPERATION

Interest and depreciation of the installation (7 per cent) $175,000

Energy Consumption 140,000

Trolley Lines . . . . { Personnel . . . . $ 9,580 . . . .
                                  Maintenance 2,420 12,000

Substations . . . . { Personnel . . . . 6,180 . . . .
                                  Maintenance 1,520 7,700

Locomotives . . . . { Engine Crew . . . . 39,200 . . . .
                                  Maintenance and repairs 34,800 64,000

       Total per year $398,700

Saving over Steam Operation $180,900

Fig. 19.   Steam Locomotive Formerly Used
in Freight Service

Direct-Current Locomotives for the Imperial Government Railways of Japan

By A. Bredenberg, Jr.

Railway Equipment Engineering Department, General Electric Company

The United States has been the great proving ground for railway electrification. There are here present a combination of the talent necessary, the manufacturing facilities required, and the reasons for electrification which are: the high cost of maintenance, labor, and fuel for steam operation; the limitations placed on greatly increased tonnage movement by inadequate parallel trackage, heavy grades, or severe climatic conditions; and the smoke nuisance in tunnels and at terminals. All the types of electric systems that showed promise have been tried out on a practical scale. As the result, the governments of England, France, and Holland have officially accepted the high-voltage direct-current system for their electrification programs; and installations are in operation, or contracted for, in Spain, South Africa, South America, Australasia, Mexico, and Japan. The following article details in particular the control equipments of the locomotives for the initial 1500-volt direct-current electrification in Japan.—Editor.

Two direct-current locomotives have recently been completed for the Imperial Government Railways of Japan. The track gauge of this railway system being 42 inches, considerably smaller than is standard in this country, necessitated a very compact design widthwise. This narrower gauge also lends added significance to the locomotive weight, 132,000 lb., which is carried entirely on the drivers. The tractive power is furnished by four motors each directly geared to a driving axle. Thus equipped, the locomotives are capable of hauling 670 tons up a one per cent grade at 15 miles per hour.

For the present, the locomotives will operate on the Tokaido line between Tokyo and Yokohama at 1200 volts. Eventually, they are to operate on the extension of this electrification at 1500 volts direct-current.

While the narrow gauge prevented the use of parts exactly like those in use in this country, where the gauge is 4 ft. 8½ in., the design is very similar to the design of locomotives used successfully on various American railroads.

The running gear consists of two-axle main trucks supporting the superstructure on centerplates. The truck has cast-steel transoms which carry a hollow centerplate and have openings provided with collars at the sides held against the motors in such a manner that

air delivered by a fan in the cab passes down through the centerplate into the hollow transom and thence to the motors.

Equalization of the load on the journals is provided for by semi-elliptic springs and by coil springs in series with the leaf spring which tends to produce an easier riding truck.

The width of the locomotive is determined by a strict clearance line, and by the necessity

TABLE I

PRINCIPAL DATA OF LOCOMOTIVE

Trolley voltage.........	1500, 1200, or 600 volts
Track gauge...........	42 in.
Length over bumpers....	37 ft. 2 in.
Length over cab........	29 ft. 0 in.
Total width...........	9 ft. 4¼ in.
Total height (Trolleys locked down)........	12 ft. 10 in.
Total wheel-base........	26 ft. 0 in.
Rigid wheel-base........	8 ft. 6 in.
Diameter wheels........	42 in.
Weight locomotive (all on drivers).............	132,000 lb.
Weight per axle........	33,000 lb.
Number of motors......	4
Tractive effort; one-hour rating (1500 volts)....	17,800 lb.
Tractive effort; continuous rating (1500 volts).	17,300 lb.
Starting tractive effort; 25 per cent coefficient of adhesion..........	33,000 lb.

for keeping within such clearance lines on certain specified curves.

The draft and buffing are taken care of by what is known in this country as European type draft gear and buffers; although the details are in accordance with the Imperial Government Railways' standards. Provision is made for substituting American type draft gear which eventually may be the Japanese standard.

The construction of the platform of structural channels and plates follows the method used in this country.

volts the motor and resistance connections are commutated so that the same speed is obtained on 600 volts as on 1200 volts.

Fig. 4 illustrates the master controller used. It has two speed combinations with ten steps in the first combination and eight steps in the second. This gives an ample number of operating steps for a locomotive of this size and allows the torque increments between steps to be so proportioned as to obtain smooth acceleration. The first nine steps in the first combination and the first seven steps in the second combination are resistance steps, i.e.,

Fig. 1.   1500/600-volt Freight Locomotive for Imperial Government Railways of Japan

The cab is of the box type which lends itself best to housing the type of equipment required by the necessity for operation at the same speed on 600 volts as on 1200 volts.

The control equipment for these locomotives is of particular interest as it embodies several new features of design. Outstanding among these features are a new form of high-speed circuit breaker for locomotive service and a new type of electro-pneumatic contactor unit for controlling the motor and resistance circuits.

Operation

These locomotives are designed to operate on 1500, 1200, or 600 volts. They may be operated either in single unit or with two locomotives in multiple. On 1500 and 1200 volts the same control and motor connections are used, the speeds obtained being approximately proportional to the voltage. On 600

with resistance in series with the motors. The 10th and 18th steps are running steps with all the accelerating resistance short circuited.

The control voltage for energizing the master control circuits is obtained from the midpoint of a dynamotor with a 2:1 voltage ratio. This dynamotor is operated by trolley voltage. Thus with 1500 volts on the trolley the nominal control voltage is 750 volts and with 1200 volts on the trolley it is 600 volts. For operation of the locomotive on 600 volts, the control circuits are disconnected from the dynamotor and connected directly to the trolley.

On 1500 or 1200 volts the motors are connected in two groups, each group having two motors connected in series. Thus the motors are operated all four in series in the first combination, and in two multiple groups of two motors in series in the second combination. On 600 volts the motors in each group are connected in parallel. The motors are then operated in two series groups of two motors in multiple in the first combination, and all four motors in multiple in the second combination.

As a result of these two operating connections, the same voltage is applied to the

Fig. 2.   Side View of Truck with Motors Assembled

individual motors when operating on the 600-volt section of the line as on the 1200-volt section. Thus the same running speeds are obtained on both voltages.

The change in connections described is accomplished by means of an air-operated commutating switch. For 600-volt operation this switch changes each two-motor group from the series connection to the multiple connection. It also divides up the accelerating resistance into several sections and reconnects these sections into a number of series groups, each group having two sections in multiple. By this means approximately the same resistance steps are obtained on 600 volts as on 1200 volts.

When transferring from the first motor combination to the second, the transition is accomplished by means of contactors. In transfer; first, part of the accelerating resistance is cut back in circuit; then, one pair of motors is short circuited while the other pair of motors is maintaining torque on the locomotive. Finally, all four motors are connected in two multiple groups with resistance in the circuit. By this method of transfer, torque is never lost in going from the first to the second combination or from the second to the first. It provides smooth operation of the train during transfer and prevents any jolts or damage to draft gear.

Current Collection

The locomotive will operate from an overhead trolley wire. Each is equipped with two pantographs similar to those used on the Chicago, Milwaukee and St. Paul Rwy., the Paulista Rwy., and others. Each trolley has two independent pans with sliding contacts. The contacts are of copper and are easily renewed. The ends of the pans are provided with long horns to prevent fouling the overhead if the pan should run off the trolley wire. The operating range is about 6½ ft., and throughout the range the pressure on the trolley wire is held approximately constant.

The trolleys are air raised and gravity lowered. A hand pump is provided for raising the trolleys when there is no air pressure on the locomotive. This pump may be used either to operate the trolleys directly or to pump air into a trolley reservoir from which air pressure may be obtained later for operating the trolleys. This reservoir may either be pumped up from the hand pump or from the air compressors if the latter are running. A globe valve is connected in the reservoir line which allows air pressure to be maintained in the reservoir for several hours. It will thus rarely be necessary to operate the hand pump.

Main Circuit Switches

The switches in the main motor circuits consist of:

 17 electro-pneumatic contactors
 1 reverser
 1 main switch
 1 motor cutout switch
 1 commutating switch.

Fig. 3.   End View of Truck with Motors Assembled

Contactors

Electro-pneumatic contactors are used to make and break the main motor circuits, to transfer the motor connections when passing from one motor combination to another, and to short circuit the starting resistors when accelerating. Figs. 5 and 6 illustrate this contactor.

It will be seen that the elements of the contactor are mounted on an upright insulated rod. This rod is fastened at the top and bottom to angle-irons in the locomotive by means of U-bolts. This method of support gives considerable flexibility in mounting the contactors in the locomotive. The operating mechanism of the contactor consists of a magnetically controlled air cylinder which operates a piston and rod that in turn operates the movable contact through an insulator. Both contact tips are alike and are cut from a rolled copper section. The contactor has a narrow arc chute with arc suppressor plates which together with the blowout coil give a very effective blowout.

The construction of the contactor with the electro-pneumatic operating mechanism, together with the narrow arc chute and method of mounting, results in a very compact unit which is comparatively light in weight and requires considerably less room for mounting than previous types of contactors of the same capacity.

this shaft being operated by the air cylinders. The contacts are made by fingers mounted on insulated rods on each side of the main shaft. This construction gives a line of reversers for different numbers of motors and of different capacities which have many parts in common.

Fig. 4.   Master Controller with Cover Removed

Fig. 5.   Electro-Pneumatic Contactor

Fig. 6.   Electro-Pneumatic Contactor with Interlock

Reverser

A four-motor electro-pneumatically operated reverser is provided for reversing the traction motors. This device is of a new design that is quite simple in construction. It consists of a series of cylindrical castings which are mounted along an insulated shaft,

Main Switch

A hand-operated knife-blade switch is placed in the circuit ahead of the main motor equipment. It carries the entire traction motor current and is used to isolate the main part of the equipment when it is desired to test out the control auxiliary circuits, etc.

This switch is mounted on an insulated rod similar to those used for the contactors, and can be mounted if desired on the same angle-iron supports as the contactors.

Motor Cutout Switch

A hand-operated motor-cutout switch is provided for cutting out one pair of motors in

Fig. 7.   Pneumatic Commutating Switch

case one of the motors is damaged. The locomotive can then be operated by the two remaining motors, either in single unit or in multiple with another locomotive. This switch is very simple in construction and consists of a single-pole double-throw knife-blade switch mounted on an insulated rod similar to those used for the contactors and main switch. The switch carries a number of finger type interlocks which commutate the control circuits for operation with motors

Fig. 8.   High-speed Circuit Breaker

cut out. It is mounted on the same angle-iron supports as the contactors.

Commutating Switch

A commutating switch is provided to change the motor, resistance, and auxiliary

circuit connections so that full-speed operation may be obtained on half the normal operating voltage. This switch is air-operated and controlled by hand-operated valves. It is quite similar in construction to the reverser, some of the parts being interchangeable.

The switch, Fig. 7, has contacts for changing the connections of each two-motor group and for dividing up and paralleling the accelerating resistance for operation on low voltage. There are also auxiliary contacts to commutate the compressor and blower connections to run at full speed on half voltage and to change the control voltage connection from the mid-point of the dynamotor to the trolley circuit.

Protective Apparatus

The protective apparatus for these locomotives consists of the following:

1 high-speed circuit breaker
1 overload relay
1 protective relay
1 lightning arrester
Fuses for auxiliary and control circuits.

High-speed Circuit Breaker

Short circuit and overload protection is obtained by a high-speed circuit breaker, Figs. 8 and 9, which is connected in the main

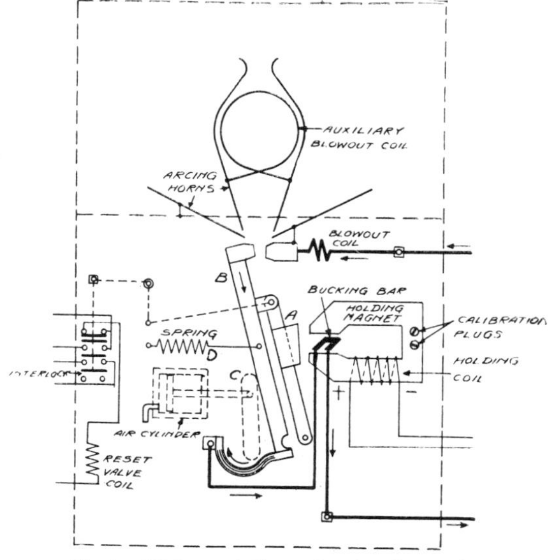

Fig. 9.   High-speed Circuit Breaker Connections

motor circuit directly after the main switch. This is a new form of high-speed circuit breaker for locomotive service. It has several features which make it a distinct improvement over those which have hitherto been applied to electric locomotive service.

In the first place the size and weight for a given capacity have been greatly reduced.   It operates on the same principle as those which have previously been described in this magazine;* viz., the armature, operating the movable contact, is held in the closed position magnetically against the tension of strong springs and is released under short circuit or overload by the shifting of the magnetic flux in the holding circuit, due to the action of a bucking bar which carries the entire traction motor current.

Former locomotive high-speed circuit breakers have been closed by a magnetically operated mechanism.   This circuit breaker is closed by an electro-pneumatically operated mechanism.   Furthermore, the closing mechanism has a trip-free feature.   This is obtained by making the movable contact arm separate from the armature and pivoting it from the armature arm.   Thus in closing, referring to Fig. 9, the air-operated closing lever C pushes the armature A against the holding magnet which then holds the armature in against the tension of two strong springs.   The closing lever, while closing the armature, at the same time holds the movable contact B open.   When the air closing mechanism is released, it in turn releases the contact arm, allowing the contact to close by means of the tension of the springs D.   With this trip-free feature, if the contacts should close on a short circuit, they would open immediately and would not be required to wait until the closing mechanism was released as the contacts cannot close until the

Fig. 10.   Overload Relay

closing mechanism starts to drop back.   This is a very important advance in high-speed circuit breaker design.

As in former circuit breakers this one has a strong magnetic blowout with a narrow arc

* "New Type of High-speed Circuit Breaker," by J. F. Tritle, GENERAL ELECTRIC REVIEW, April, 1920.

chute which will effectively open very heavy short-circuit currents.

The tripping point of the circuit breaker is set at the desired value by means of adjustable plugs in the magnetic circuit.

When the circuit breaker opens on short circuit or overload, interlocks open the line

Fig. 11.   Protective Relay

contactors.   These contactors cannot then be reclosed until the circuit breaker has been reset, which is done on the first point of the master controller.

Overload Relay

An overload relay is provided for overload protection of the individual motor circuits. This relay, Fig. 10, has two series coils either of which will operate the relay contacts.   One coil is connected in each two-motor circuit. When the motor current exceeds the setting of the relay, the relay contacts are opened against the compression of the resetting springs.   This opens the holding circuit of the high-speed circuit breaker, thus causing it to drop out.   Operation cannot then be resumed until the master controller has been turned back to the first notch.   The relay contacts automatically reset as soon as the overload current is removed.

Protective Relay

When operating from the 600-volt section of the line with the main and auxiliary circuits in the low-voltage connection, protection is afforded in case the locomotive runs onto the 1500 or 1200-volt section of the line and the operator fails to throw the commutating switch to the high-voltage connection.   In this event the high-speed circuit breaker protects the main part of the equipment while a protective relay protects the auxiliary circuits. This relay, Fig. 11, is placed in circuit ahead of all the auxiliaries.   It has two coils, an operating coil and a trip coil, and one set of contacts. The contact arm and the operating armature are independently pivoted but are connected together by a trip catch so that normally the relay operates simply as a shunt contactor, closing when voltage is applied and

Fig. 12.   Operator's Position Showing Master Controller, Air Valves, Gauges, etc.

opening when voltage is removed. In the high-voltage connection the trip coil is not connected in circuit. In the low-voltage connection the trip coil is connected in series with the operating coil and is calibrated to trip out the trip catch at about 700 volts.

The following sequence of operations results if the locomotive passes from the low-voltage to the high-voltage section of the line and the commutating switch is not thrown to the high-voltage position. First, the relay contacts open when the dead section of the line is reached. Then, when the high-voltage section is reached, the trip coil operates, tripping out the trip catch and preventing the contacts from closing when the operating coil picks up its armature. A small relay is used to short circuit the operating coil in the de-energized position. This slows up the operating coil and allows the trip coil to operate first.

This scheme gives a very effective protection for the auxiliary circuits as the high potential cannot be applied even momentarily to the auxiliary circuits until the commutating switch has been thrown to the high-potential connection.

Fuses

A cartridge fuse is placed in circuit ahead of all the auxiliaries including the protective relay. The individual auxiliary motors, the control circuits, lights, etc., are protected by cartridge fuses in the auxiliary switches.

Lightning Arrester

Protection from damage by lightning is secured by means of an aluminum-cell lightning arrester especially designed for railway service. This arrester is connected to the trolley circuit ahead of all the apparatus.

Auxiliaries

The control voltage on 1500 or 1200-volt operation is obtained from a dynamotor with a 2:1 voltage range.

Compressed air for the air brakes and pneumatic control apparatus is obtained from two 750-volt air compressors each having a capacity of 35 cu. ft. per min. On 1500 or 1200

Fig. 13.   Apparatus Compartment Showing Location of High-speed Circuit Breaker

volts the two compressors are connected in series, and the lead connecting the compressors is connected to the midpoint of the dynamotor. This balances the load between the two compressors and also provides a means of cutting out one compressor and operating with the remaining compressor in case of emergency.

On low-voltage operation the compressors are each connected directly across the line thus obtaining full-speed operation on half voltage.

Forced ventilation for the traction motors is provided by two blowers, one for each pair of motors. These blowers are driven by 750-volt motors which are connected in series for 1500 or 1200-volt operation and in parallel on 600 volts.

Each operating cab also contains enclosed hand-operated switches for the auxiliary, control, and light circuits.

There is an aisle connecting the two operating cabs on either side of the apparatus compartments. In the center of the apparatus cab is a compartment containing the accelerating resistors. This compartment extends from the floor to the roof. The air for ventilating the resistors enters through openings in the bottom of the compartment and is vented through a ventilator in the roof. On either side

Fig. 14. Apparatus Compartment Showing Location of Contactors, Cutout Switch, Commutating Switch, Reverser, and Resistance Tubes

Fig. 15. Apparatus Compartment Showing Location of Relays and Resistance Tubes

Location of Apparatus

An idea of the location of the apparatus in the locomotive cab may be obtained from Figs. 12 to 15. The cab is of the box type with the apparatus compartments in the center of the locomotive and an operating cab at either end.

A master controller is located on the left side of each operating cab and is constructed for operation by the right hand. Directly before the operator is a gauge panel containing an ammeter, voltmeter, and air gauges. In one cab is a mercury watthour-meter for measuring the power input to the locomotive.

of the resistor compartment is a compartment for the control and auxiliary equipment.

The dynamotor, compressors, and blowers are located on the cab floor. The high-speed circuit breaker, contactors, switches, relays, control resistance tubes, etc., are mounted above the motor-operated auxiliaries. This arrangement places the control equipment in a convenient position for inspection or repairs.

From the foregoing description, it may be seen that the principal features of the control equipment for these locomotives are: reduced space occupied, reduced weight, accessibility of parts, and general simplicity.

Fig. 1.   Electric Trains at Crescent Beach Station. Inbound train in the distance

Fig. 2.   General Arrangement of Revere Street Station, Showing Overhead Bridges

Fig. 3.   View of East Boston Terminal, Looking Toward Ferry Slip

Fig. 4.   Crystal Cove Near Winthrop Beach Station, Before Electrification

Electric Operation of the Boston, Revere Beach and Lynn Railroad

Statistics—Description of Railroad System—Cost of Electrification—Electric Train Equipment
Power Substations and Distribution System—Signal and Traffic Equipment

By W. D. BEARCE

Transportation Engineering Department, General Electric Company

INTERESTING figures have recently been made public by the Boston, Revere Beach and Lynn Railroad, which began electric operation during November, 1928. The passenger revenue for May, June, and July of this year shows an increase of 10.2 per cent over the same period of the previous year. The actual number of passengers carried increased 10.3

changes have taken place in the character of the population and the country through which the road operates. About two years ago the railroad properties came under a new management* known as the Eastern Railway Associates, controlled by Hemphill & Wells and the American Equities Co. Plans were immediately prepared for renovating the entire system.

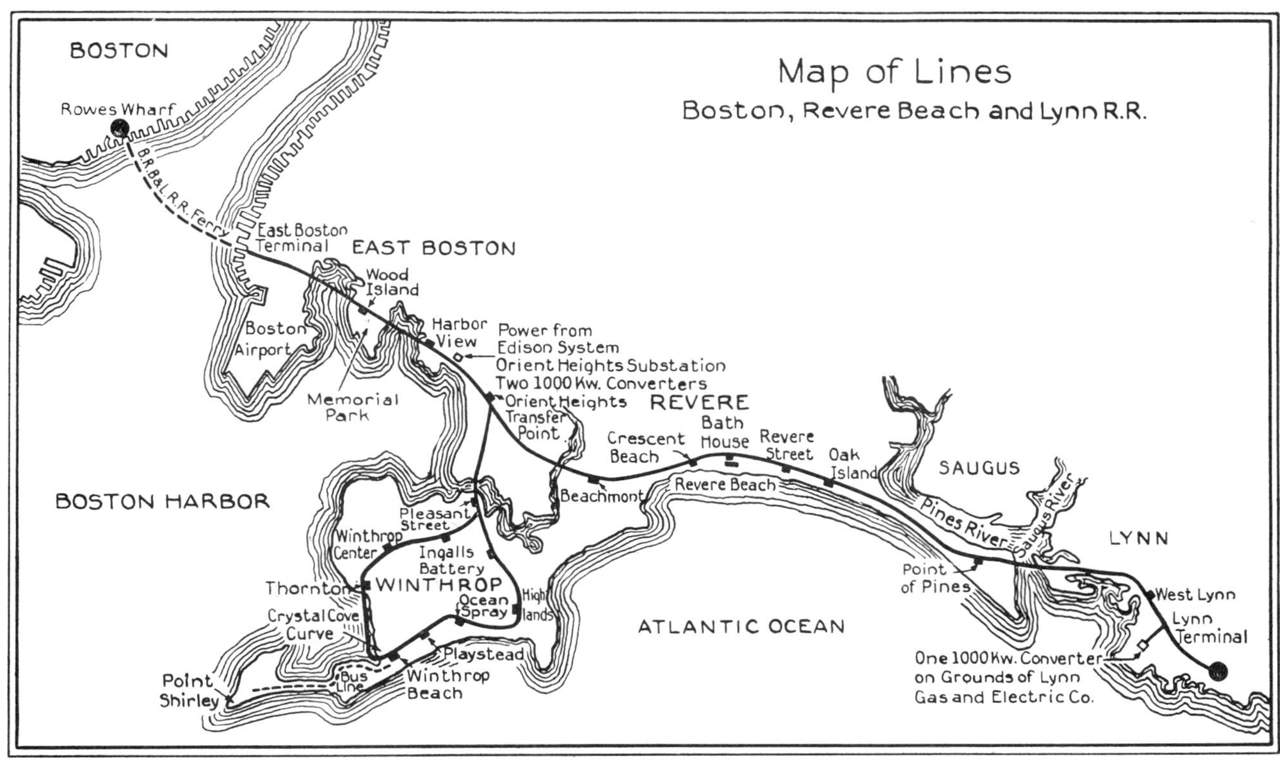

Fig. 5. Map of Boston, Revere Beach and Lynn Railroad System

per cent. This improvement is particularly gratifying since other New England electric railways report a decrease in revenues of about 3 per cent for the same period. There was an increase of 1.58 per cent in car-miles operated, so the increased riding must be for the most part attributed to the faster, more regular, and cleaner service provided by the electric trains.

The railway operating expenses, despite an increase in miles operated, decreased 18.8 per cent for the first 6 months of 1929. The combination of increased riding with reduced cost of operation has resulted in a decided improvement in net income.

The "Narrow Gauge," as this road is popularly known, has been one of the important rapid-transit passenger lines for the greater city of Boston for more than fifty years. During that period, great

The steam locomotive power at the time of the change-over consisted of 26 locomotives which had been in operation for many years. The other rolling stock included 96 passenger coaches which were in fairly good physical condition.

The Boston Terminal of this line is at Rowe's Wharf, which is connected with the East Boston Terminal by ferry. The ferry service is handled by four large ferryboats with schedules arranged to meet all trains. The total mileage of this system between the East Boston Terminal and Lynn, and around the branch line to Winthrop, is 13.12 mi. of route with 34.48 mi. of single track.

The communities served include several of the most frequented resorts, such as Revere Beach and

---

*The officers of the new company are: Gardner F. Wells, president; Geo. W. Wells, vice-president; and Albert W. Hemphill, treasurer.

Winthrop, and the traffic, therefore, in addition to a large percentage of commuters, comprises an appreciable holiday movement to these resorts. Since electrification, the management has been particularly pleased to note an increase in the number of commuters, as well as the holiday business.

The improved service provided by electric operation includes six and seven-car express-train units operating during rush hour and two or three-car trains operating throughout the day on a 15-minute schedule. During the year 1927, more than 13 million passengers were carried over this system.

In comparison with the former schedule operated by steam, a reduction of 15 min. has been made in the running time between Lynn and Boston. The regular running time between Lynn and Rowe's Wharf in Boston, including the ferry trip, is now 30

The expenditures for this conversion approximate $1,400,000 as shown in the following table:

Car equipment	$610,000
Substations	152,000
Overhead structures, lines, and feeders	277,000
Signal changes	90,000
Miscellaneous construction including engineering, interest charges, etc.	271,000
	$1,400,000

The direct economies resulting from these improvements, as shown by the operating costs for the first six months of 1929, are in the neighborhood of $160,000 or about 11.5 per cent on the investment.

Rolling Stock

It was decided, after a careful inspection of the existing cars, that they were in satisfactory condition to admit of their being remodeled and electrically

Fig. 6.   A Six-car Multiple-unit Train

min. as compared with previous schedule calling for 45 min. A proportionate reduction in running time has been effected for the citizens of the Winthrop section.

The new equipment was, of necessity, installed without interrupting the existing steam traffic. The erection of the overhead distribution system was largely done at night, when interruptions would occur only once an hour in each direction. It was found that approximately 60 multiple-unit motor cars would be sufficient to handle the service under electric operation. Provision was made for equipping and renovating these cars, a few at a time, making use of cars not required for the schedules. After some of the motor cars had been equipped and the distribution completed, partial service was provided with electric trains for a short time until the remainder of the cars were available for electric operation.

equipped. A total of 60 of these cars have been put through the shops and seven additional cars have been remodeled as trailers for use during peak-load periods. The interior of each car has been refinished and operating cabs placed at each end. Thirty 500-watt electric car heating units, consisting of two circuits with 15 units in series, are installed, controlled by a switch mounted at the motor end of the car. Twenty dome-type lighting fixtures are used in each car and these are provided with 32-volt lamps, all connected in series across the trolley circuit. Short-circuiting sockets insure continuous lighting in case of a burned out filament. The headlights used are street-car type portable units which can be attached to the hand rail at the front of each car by means of brackets. These headlights are equipped with 250-watt incandescent lamps with a three-way switch which permits dimming.

The motive power includes two GE-295A 600-volt railway motors which are mounted on a new Brill 177-E2 truck. The motors are of the commutating-pole type with provision for tapped-field operation. Each motor weighs, complete with gear, pinion, gear case, etc., 2770 lb. The normal one-hour rating is 60 hp. This motor is of modern design with longitudinal ventilating ducts in the armature, renewable carbonway brush holders and a multiple ventilating fan which is built integral with the pinion-end armature head.

Control

All cars are equipped with magnetic control, arranged for multiple-unit operation. The main controller is suspended underneath the car body and

60 passenger cars and the seven trailers, four service cars have now been equipped, each carrying two double-motor trucks and using platform-type control. The passenger cars, completely equipped, weigh 52,000 lb.

Substations

Power for the Lynn end of the electrification is furnished by a 1000-kw. 650-volt synchronous converter which is located in the power house of the Lynn Gas and Electric Company. The switching equipment for this unit is of the manual type and the station is operated and maintained by the power company's staff at a fixed charge. The Orient Heights station is located near the junction of the main line with the Winthrop loop. Power is supplied by the

Fig. 7. A Group of Turnstiles at a Prepayment Area

remotely controlled by a master controller, one of which is located in each operating cab. The electrical connections for multiple-unit control are made overhead by means of coupler sockets located at the ends of each car roof. A 2/0 bus line runs the entire length of each car and is connected to the trolley and the bus-line coupler sockets. All control circuits are supplied from the 600-volt trolley. Current is collected by a 11 ft. 4 in. trolley pole and carried down through the car near a corner post at the motor end.

Air Brakes

The air brakes are of the electro-pneumatic type, using a brake valve with an equalizing piston which provides for pneumatic service application, if for any reason the electric brake is inoperative. There are five positions of the brake valve as follows: release, holding, lap, service, and emergency. In addition to the

Edison Electric Illuminating Company to two 1000-kw. 650-volt synchronous converters equipped for complete automatic control. Two feeders furnish the two trolley wires leading to the East Boston Terminal; a second pair of feeders supply power to the main line going toward Lynn; and a third pair of feeders furnishes power to the Winthrop loop. Reclosing feeders of 2000-amp. capacity are used in the outgoing lines.

Power is supplied to this station by two 3-phase 60-cycle 13,800-volt incoming lines. These are equipped with manually-operated breakers which trip only on reverse current overload. The transformers and alternating-current switching equipment are located outside the station.

An unusual type of ventilation is used for these converters, which consists of a steel housing constructed over each machine in such a way that the converter itself causes a draft of air to flow through

Fig. 8.   Crystal Cove Curve, Showing Overhead Construction

Fig. 9.   Orient Heights Substation

Fig. 10.   Winthrop Center Station, and Two-car Electric Train

Fig. 11.   A 1000-kw. Portable Substation

this housing into a pit underneath the machine and thence through a stack leading through the roof of the station. The warm air from the machine is thus expelled through the roof and the temperature of the machine can be regulated by an adjustable damper located in the outgoing pipe. The housings for this scheme of ventilation are built in sections and can be easily removed without disturbing the converter.

The third substation is a portable unit which also contains a 1000-kw. converter of the same type as those used in the main substations. Provision is made for connecting this station either at the Orient Heights or the Lynn substation where 13,800 volts is available for the portable equipment. The converter is located in a closed section of a steel car, while the transformer and oil circuit breakers are mounted on the other end of the car on the open platform.

Distribution System

The overhead distribution is unusual in a number of respects, but in general represents the latest practice in 600-volt direct-current distribution. The catenary-supporting structures are steel bridges spaced at a maximum distance of 300 ft. apart. Signal and power wires are carried on steel cross-arms located at a height of 5 ft. above the top of the bridge. Unusually large foundations were necessary on account of the character of the soil. These are of concrete being 7 ft. 6 in. deep, 8 ft. long and 2 ft. wide and sunk 6 ft. below the surface. The foundations for the three track towers are 6 ft. by 9 ft. by 2 ft.

On curved sections, the trolley wire is held over the track by steel pull-off poles. These poles are also set in concrete and are braced laterally. Altogether there are 262 bridges and 161 pull-off poles. A feature of this installation is the use of corrosion-proof steel on account of the possibility of damage due to the salt air.

Ample conductivity is provided by a 500,000 circular-mil copper cable which serves both as a messenger and a feeder. This type of construction is used over the entire system. The contact wire supported from this feeder messenger is a 4/0 grooved trolley wire which is $99\frac{1}{2}$ per cent bronze and $\frac{1}{2}$ per cent cadmium. Messenger and trolley wire are bonded at intervals of about 600 ft. All hangers and castings are of non-ferrous material to eliminate possibility of corrosion.

Direct suspension is used in the yards and sidings and, to avoid corrosion in this type of construction, all span wires are of red brass. It was not found necessary to use a negative return as the tracks are all on private right of way and the bonded rails seemed to be ample for handling the return current.

The existing rails were $4\frac{1}{2}$ in. 60 lb. ASCE type and these are bonded with 4/0 $7\frac{1}{2}$-in. bonds, acetylene-welded. In some cases it was necessary to lower the grade under the bridges to provide additional clearance. Some changes were also made in the alignment to provide for speeds of from 35 to 45 miles per hour.

Signal Equipment

New signal equipment furnished by the Union Switch and Signal Company included a number of automatic block color light signals which are operated from the 2300-volt line through 60-cycle $\frac{3}{4}$-kv-a. distribution transformers.

Turnstiles

Some little time prior to the beginning of electric operation the prepayment system of fare collection was instituted at all of the principal stations. This system uses a total of 19 turnstiles with prepayment areas fenced off around the station. Provision is made for handling the maximum traffic with expedition at a minimum expense. At the Rowe's Wharf station, where only 250-volt direct current is available, two 5-hp. motor-generator sets are installed which deliver 600-volt current for operating the turnstiles at this point.

Two-Car Units for Lackawanna

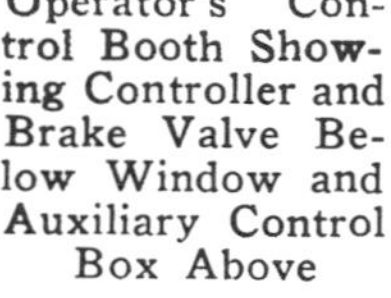
Operator's Control Booth Showing Controller and Brake Valve Below Window and Auxiliary Control Box Above

THE cars used in the Lackawanna suburban electrification incorporate a number of innovations, such as 1500/3000-volt motors for multiple-unit cars, motor ventilating air inlets in the roof of the car, 3000-volt heater circuits, and pantographs with self-aligning roller bearings. All but five of the motor cars have roller journal bearings and all cars are equipped with electro-pneumatic brakes.

There are 70 miles of line, including 160 miles of track, to be operated electrically and service will be provided by 141 motor cars and 141 trailers. Motor cars and trailers are semi-permanently coupled together in two-car units and standard M. C. B. couplers are used for coupling units together to make trains of from 2 to 12 cars.

Both motor cars and trailers are of all-steel construction except that the motor cars have aluminum doors, inside finish and roof sheets. All cars have vestibules with trapdoors but without diaphragms and the underframes are of the open channel center sill type.

The motor cars are 70 ft. 3½ in. long over the bumpers, seat 84 passengers and weigh 147,200 lb. The trucks are Commonwealth with wheel bases 8 ft. 6 in. long; the distance between center pins is 45 ft. The trailers are 70 ft. ¾ in., and 70 ft. 6 in. long, weigh 106,400 lb. and seat respectively 78 and 82 passengers. There are toilets in the trailers but none in the motor cars. Included in the 282 cars to be used in electric service are

six club cars, 15 combination baggage and passenger cars and two combination mail and passenger cars.

All but five of the motor cars are equipped with Hyatt roller bearings, the five having plain bearings. Five of the trailers have roller bearings and all of the remainder plain bearings. This arrangement permits making up one ten-car train completely roller bearing equipped and another ten-car train equipped entirely with plain bearings. The motor cars to be used in these two trains are provided with watt-hour meters so the power consumption of the two trains may be compared.

The interiors of the cars are finished in unusually light colors. The ceilings are cream and the upper side walls a light buff. The seats are light yellow rattan with dark green metal frames and mahogany side arms. The lower parts of the side walls are also dark green and the floors are battleship gray.

Motors and Motor Ventilation

The motors, and the method of ventilating them, are probably the most radical departure from the usual low voltage railway practice. Each motor develops 235 shaft horsepower (one hour rating) with 1500 volts impressed on the commutator and has a weight of approximately 6900 lb., including gears, gear case, axle linings and other motor accessories. At the same time, the motor is insulated for a working potential of 3000 volts to ground. There are

Electrification

Multiple-unit cars are the first in America to operate from a 3000-volt, direct-current, contact system

Interior of One of the Motor Cars

four motors on each motor car in pairs and connected permanently in series. The successful operation of a high voltage motor depends to a great extent on keeping the interior of the motor, particularly the commutator end, clean and free from road dirt, brake shoe dust, snow and other foreign material. To satisfy this requirement, the motor frame operates at all times either at or slightly above atmospheric pressure in order that loose commutator covers and similar conditions will not allow the entrance of foreign material. This condition could have been accomplished by the use of motor-driven blower sets, but it was desired to dispense with these blowers for the sake of simplicity because of the noise and vibration which it was expected they would produce in the motor car. It was also considered desirable to avoid air filters with attendant expense for cleaning.

Experiments made on the test track on a motor-trailer unit showed conclusively that snow and road dirt picked up by the moving train does not swirl around the cars at a height much above the center of the side windows. It was decided therefore to take air for ventilating the motors at each side of the roof at each end of the motor car, and pass it through a

An 8-Car or 4-Unit Train On the Electrified Section Between Hoboken and Newark, N. J.

1. Heater Connector Used Between Motor Car and Trailer. 2. One of the Roller Bearing Trucks. 3. The Seat Cushion Has Been Removed to Show the Heater Box. 4. The Only Electrical Apparatus Mounted Under the Trailers are the Heater Fuse and Switch Boxes. 5. Connections Between Motor Car and Trailer. 6. Outer End of a Motor Car—Note Dummy Receptacles at Right

settling chamber located above the vestibule. Louvres were located at the four corners of the motor car so that air drawn from the side of the car enters this compartment between the ceiling of the vestibule of the car and the car roof.

With this construction, the air is drawn into the louvres at a velocity of approximately 50 ft. per minute and on entering the comparatively large compartment fitted with baffles and located between the vestibule ceiling and the car roof, it decreases in velocity to a sufficient extent to deposit any dirt, snow or foreign material that may have been carried through the louvres.

From the settling chamber the air enters the ducts which carry it to the underside of the car flooring. In these ducts the air velocity is approximately 300 ft. per minute. Two ducts are carried from the compartment over the vestibule at each end of the car to the underside of the car, making a total of four such ducts. Each of these terminates in an opening which is suitably reinforced and is provided with bolts for the receiving of a ring to which the flexible air duct is strapped. This duct consists of two layers of canvas on either side of wire springs which prevent collapsing of the duct. The other end of the duct is clamped to the inlet casting on the motor which in turn is bolted to the commutator end framehead, use being made of a gasket to insure a tight joint.

The ventilating air is delivered to the center of the motor armature at the commutator end by suitable passages in the commutator end framehead. The ventilating fan is located at the pinion end of the armature. It draws the air through the center of the armature and forces it through the motor frame, past the exciting and commutating field coils to the commutator end of the frame, from which it is discharged to atmosphere through the outlet at top of the motor. Inasmuch as the discharge of this ventilating air always takes place at the commutator end, the entire frame is always somewhat above atmospheric pressure when the car is in motion. There is no tendency, therefore, for any foreign matter to be drawn into the motor.

The flexible air ducts are made of white canvas. painted on the outside with a weatherproofing com-

Under Side of Motor Car With One Truck Removed

pound having a relatively high ignition point and sufficient body to cool off any impinging sparks or brake shoe flakes that might set fire to canvas.

The four motor leads are brought out on the axle side of the motor. The leads do not cross the motor or touch any part which might cause abrasion. They are clamped to the motor at one end, to the car underframe at the other end, and the connectors between the motor leads and the car wiring are enclosed in insulating tubes clamped to the car.

The armature and axle bearings are of the constant-level, waste-packed type, insuring uniform lubrication at all times. Each motor is equipped with a 22-tooth pinion having a diametral pitch of 2¼ in., and drives a 59-tooth gear mounted on the axle. Four of these motors are mounted on each motor car and as each motor car handles one trailer in addition to itself, the total weight of the two-car unit handled by four motors is 253,600 lb. The 59-tooth gears are of the non-resonant type and effectively eliminate gear noise. Each motor complete, with pinion, gear, gear case, axle linings, and air ducts, weighs approximately 6900 lb. This is exclusive of the inductive shunts, which provide the reduced field or maximum speed running point on the controller.

Three two-car units (6 cars) carrying one-half passenger load when supplied with 3000 volts at the pantographs are designed to have a free running speed of not less than 67 m.p.h. on level tangent track. This is on the basis of 36-in. wheels, which is 2 in. less in diameter than the wheels are when new. New wheels are 38 in. in diameter and may be worn to 35 in. before the clearances under the motors become limiting.

Dynamotor, Air Compressor and Brakes

For control, operation of the air compressor, and auxiliary power, the 3000-volt current is stepped down by a 3000/1500-volt dynamotor which is hung on the underside of the car body on four rubber cushioned suspension bolts. The dynamotor has two 1500-volt commutators and armature windings connected in series and a separate 40-volt armature on the same shaft, all located between the two bearings for supplying power to the controls and for lighting. A ventilating fan which draws air through the entire set is mounted on the same shaft. The intake air passes through a centrifugal type air cleaner located outside the bearings.

The air compressor is driven by a 1500-volt motor which is connected across the low-voltage commutator of the dynamotor. It is of the center-gear type and has a displacement of 35 cu. ft. of free air per minute. It is hung under the car on a three-point cushion suspension similar to that used for the dynamotor.

Type UCE brakes are used on all cars. Electrically-operated magnet valves control the operation of the brakes and cause simultaneous application of brakes on all cars in the train.

Control

The master controllers located in opposite ends of each two-car unit are of the low-voltage drum type and the one which is in use actuates the 32-volt control circuits which govern the motor controllers throughout the entire train. The motor controllers are mounted under the cars. Each controller includes a reverser, cutout switches, accelerating relay, line potential relay and field shunting relay in addition to contactors for making the series and series-parallel motor combinations. The contactors are all cam-operated and the cam shaft is actuated by an air engine of the opposed air pressure type.

An automatic line breaker protects the high-voltage circuits from overload and short circuits. Additional protection is provided by an explosion chamber type main fuses mounted on the roof of the car. Three-thousand-volt fuse are also used to protect heaters and auxiliary apparatus.

The master controller is equipped with a deadman's release and emergency air brake application feature which functions if the operator's hand is removed from the controller. When the controller is moved to the full-speed position the acceleration of the train is controlled automatically and is limited by the current flowing in the motors. After the motor controller is advanced one position, it remains in that position until the current has dropped to 185 amperes before advancing to the next. The acceleration rate is adjusted to 1½ miles per hour per second with six-car trains and the maximum power at starting required by a 12-car train is 9,000 kw., or approximately 12,000 horsepower.

Above the window at the motorman's position is a push-button control box for operating the pantographs dynamotors, heaters, circuit breakers, control circuits, headlights, marker lights and vestibule lights. This is a low-voltage control which operates the low-voltage circuits directly and the high-voltage circuits through 3000-volt electrically-operated contactors.

Pantographs and Jumpers

The pantographs used have self-aligning roller bearings. This feature gives only three to four pounds difference in pressure against the contact wire between the up and down movement of the pantograph. The normal pressure against the wire is 28 lb. and the working range is from 15 ft. 6 in. to 25 ft. 3 in. above the rail. The locked down height of the pantograph is 15 ft. 3 in.

There is a grounding switch for each pantograph and the first duty of a man climbing to the top of a car is to close this switch, the operation of which grounds and hold the pantograph in the locked-down position. Fifty of the pantographs have single con-

tact shoes and the other 232 (there are two on each motor car) have double shoes. The pantograph pressure for the single-contact pantographs is 18 instead of 28 pounds.

Two train line jumpers for control circuits are mounted below the bumpers and used between units and two between motor car and trailer. There is also a third jumper between motor car and trailer for the 32-volt lighting and battery circuits. The jumpers used have plugs at each end and there are four sockets on each end of a two-car unit. This duplication of sockets avoids the necessity of crossing the jumpers over with the air hose connections.

There is a 3000-volt heater connection on the car roofs between the motor car and trailer. This is provided with a bronze tiller rope and unlatching device which automatically releases the plug on the motor car in case the cars are separated. The plug thus released does not have voltage on it since the trailers do not have pantographs.

Heaters

There is an electric resistance heater under every seat mounted in a steel box and the conduit carrying the feeder wires is extended along each side of the heater box to form a foot rest. The heating elements are mounted near the window end of the box, thus allowing ample creepage distance along the lead wires which enter at the aisle end of the box. Each heater box is connected to a ground wire in addition to being clamped to the car body.

The heat is controlled by thermostat and there are two heating circuits which can be turned on separately or together, depending upon the weather and at the discretion of the operator. The total heating load in each car is 28 kw. plus three heaters totaling 3½ kw. in the motorman's vestibule.

Lighting

The new motor cars are lighted by eleven, center-mounted, 50-watt lamps in corona bowl glassware and provide a lighting intensity on the reading plane of about nine foot-candles. The generator and lamp voltages are controlled by the same type of regulators that the railroad uses for its axle light equipment. The lights and heater circuits are controlled by Safety toggle switches in a metal cabinet in the regulator locker. There are two heater switches, two interior light switches, one switch for the vestibule lights and one for the marker lights. There is a Pyle-National headlight on each end of a two-car unit controlled from the motorman's position. The 300-ampere-hour lead batteries used are mounted under the motor car. This arrangement places this weight on driving instead of trailing wheels, makes the operation of the motor car independent of the trailer and avoids the voltage drop through connectors which makes proper battery charging difficult when the battery is on the trailer.

About half of the cars are now delivered and a number are in service on the Montclair branch and for the training of crews. The electrical equipment is being supplied by the General Electric Company and the motor cars were built by the Pullman Company. The equipment, with the exception of the motors, is shipped from Erie, Pa., to Chicago, where it is installed and the cars are shipped to the Kingsland, N. J., shops of the Lackawanna where the motors are installed. Heaters were supplied by the Consolidated Car Heating Company and the brake equipment by the Westinghouse Air Brake Company.

The trailers are made from steel equipment which

has been used in steam service. They are taken from service, a few at a time, and sent to the plant of the American Car & Foundry Company, Berwick, Pa., where they are fitted with vestibules similar to those on the motor cars. the steam heating apparatus is replaced with electric heaters and control equipment is installed.

All of the work of building and equipping the cars is being done under the direction of C. J. Scudder, superintendent of motive power and equipment, and E. M. Jenkins, master car builder. Specifications, inspection, and other engineering work in ·connection with the electrical equipment is being done by Jackson and Moreland, engineers, of Boston, Mass.

Automatic Control Equipment for 1500-volt Arc Rectifier Substations of the Chicago, South Shore and South Bend Railroad

First Installation of Rectifier Substations—Description of Mercury Arc Rectifier Equipment— Description of Control—Operation of Substation—Special Protective Features Necessitated by Use of Rectifiers

By E. L. HOUGH

Engineering Department, St. Louis Office, General Electric Company

THE rehabilitation of the Chicago, South Shore, and South Bend Railroad, formerly known as the Chicago, Lake Shore and South Bend Railway, which was undertaken in the summer of 1925, has progressed to the point where the power supply system has been rebuilt and most of the new equipment has been placed in service. As previously announced in the technical press, the electrical equipment has been changed from 6600 volts alternating current to 1500 volts direct current. One advantage of this change is that it permits the operation of South Shore trains with their own equip-

> *So far as we know, this is the first description of the automatic control of a mercury arc power rectifier. The instructive information given possesses more than the interest of novelty because the control functions strictly in accordance with the high standard previously set by the automatic control of rotary conversion apparatus.*—EDITOR

ment directly into the Chicago terminal area although the trains run over the tracks of the Illinois Central Railroad from Kensington, Ill., to the Loop District of Chicago. The Illinois Central railroad has placed its Chicago terminal electrification in service, the 1500-volt direct-current system being used.

Power supply for the South Shore lines is obtained from a 33,000-volt high-tension line which feeds eight substations located along the right-of-way. At these substations the voltage is stepped down and converted to 1500 volts direct current. In so far as economically feasible, automatic control equipments

have been employed in the substations. Where the presence of attendants was necessitated by other considerations, partial automatic control has been installed. A unique feature of the power supply system is the use of mercury arc rectifiers in four of the eight substations. This represents the first application of 1500-volt rectifiers and of 1500-volt automatic rectifier control in this country. A map of the route showing the location of both the converter and rectifier substations is given in Fig. 1.

Since the use of automatically controlled rectifiers is an innovation in this country, a brief description of the automatic control equipment for this installation will be of interest, particularly to those contemplating installation of this type of equipment. Many of the elements of the control parallel very closely those which have been used for some time in railway substation control equipments while others are peculiar to the rectifier station itself.

Each of the 750-kw. rectifier substations contains a single rectifier tank which is rated at 500 amp. 1500 volts. Fig. 2 shows the front, and Fig. 3 the back view of the control for such a substation. Power is supplied to the anodes of the rectifier by a step-down transformer which is connected double "Y" on the secondary and "Y" on the high-tension side. The transformer is also equipped with a tertiary winding. The transformer is connected to the high-tension line through an automatically operated oil circuit breaker and is protected by means of standard alternating-current overload relays. The 1500-kw. unit in Substation No. 4 at Furnessville is similar except that the rectifier consists of two tanks operated in parallel as a single unit. The connections are similar except for the use of anode transformers to provide for properly balancing the load between the anodes of the two tanks. For initial starting of the rectifier (bakeout) it is necessary to provide for the supply of low voltage

Fig. 1. Map of the Electrified Section of the Chicago, South Shore and South Bend Railroad, showing the location of both the rectifier and converter substations to the anodes. This is accomplished by connecting the anode leads to a terminal block provided with removable links which allow the insertion of a step-down or "bakeout" transformer between the main transformer secondary leads and the rectifier anodes.

The positive lead of the rectifier is taken directly from the cathode, the cathodes of the 1500-kw. unit being connected permanently in parallel. The positive lead runs through the instrument shunt, the relay shunt, two steps of load limiting equipment, a direct-current line contactor, and a "reversed" high-speed circuit breaker to the direct-current bus.

value thermostat control is employed. If the tank is not warm enough this thermostat energizes a contactor which applies current to the tank heaters. When the tank reaches a predetermined temperature the heaters are cut off. If, during operation, the temperature should exceed a certain higher value the thermostat functions to start the water pump and at the same time to open a solenoid valve which permits cooling water to flow through the tank jacket. Under normal conditions the tank temperature is thus maintained at the proper value. In the case of the two-tank unit thermostats are provided in each tank.

Fig. 2. Automatic Control Equipment for a 750-kw., 1500-volt Rectifier and One Reclosing Feeder (front view)

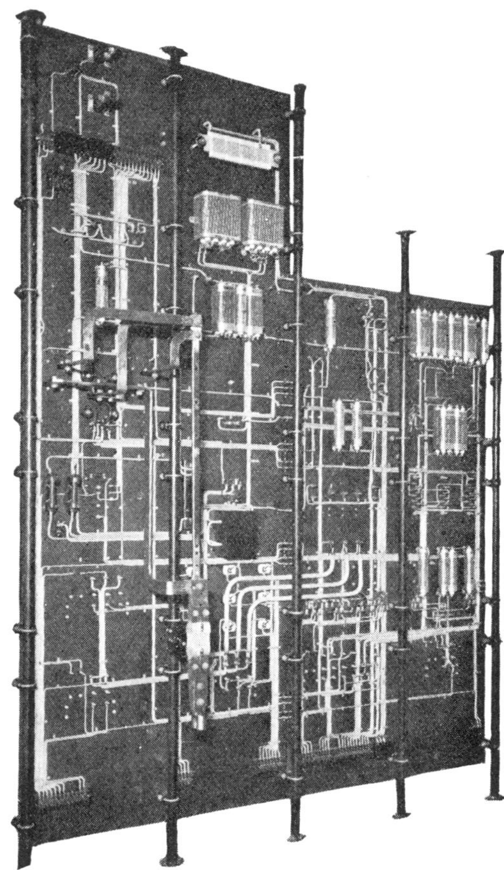

Fig. 3. Back View of the Equipment Shown in Fig. 2

The negative lead is taken from the "Y" points of the transformers, the two "Y's" being connected through an interphase transformer. The midpoint of the interphase transformer is connected to the negative bus through a saturation winding, which gives a compounding effect and then through a direct-current reactor, and a high-speed breaker.

A schematic diagram of the rectifier connections is shown in Fig. 4. Control power is obtained from a small three-phase transformer connected to the high-tension line just ahead of the oil circuit breaker.

The satisfactory operation of a rectifier depends upon maintenance of proper vacuum and temperature. Since the rectifier must be ready to go on the line at any time it is desirable to maintain the tank temperature and vacuum at an operating value at all times. In order to hold the tank temperature at the correct

Proper tank pressure, or rather vacuum, is maintained by a pumping unit consisting of a rotary pump and a Langmuir mercury condensation pump. When the rotary pump reaches its approximate running speed, a speed switch on its shaft makes contact to open the solenoid operated vacuum line valve. This valve serves to shut off the vacuum line when the pumps are not running and thereby prevent leakage through the pumps.

Devices are provided to start and stop the stations in accordance with load demand in a manner identical to the load responsive starting scheme employed in other automatic railway substations, and which consists of voltage and load indicating relays and time delay starting and stopping relays.

When the starting indication is given by the load responsive equipment the master contactor is energized and closed if the station is not being held off by the protective devices. The closing of the master contactor starts the small a-c. to d-c. exciting set which supplies power for the exciting arc of the rectifier. As soon as the exciter voltage builds up, an arc striking solenoid on the rectifier is energized and operates to strike the exciting arc. When the exciting arc circuit has been established as indicated by the exciting arc relay the solenoid is de-energized, thus allowing the exciting anode to rise and start the exciting arc. This arc is kept playing continuously as long as the rectifier is under load. It was originally intended to cut it off when the load was sufficient to maintain the arc, but it was found that the load fluctuated so rapidly and through such wide limits that this scheme could not be used in this particular installation.

Within a short time after the arc has been established the oil circuit breaker is closed by the operation of a reclosing relay similar to the one used for controlling oil circuit breakers in alternating-current reclosing service. As soon as the oil circuit breaker has closed, a circuit is made to close the negative high-speed breaker, the positive high-speed breaker, and the direct-current line contactor in order. This connects the rectifier to the direct-current bus through the load limiting equipment, and if the load is not excessive the load limiting resistor shunting contactors close to connect the rectifier directly to the bus.

Normally a station is shut down by the operation of the load responsive equipment. This causes the master contactor to drop out and in turn to open the oil circuit breaker and the direct-current circuit breakers and contactors. The stations are also provided with supervisory control of the carrier current selector type thus permitting the load dispatcher at Hammond to start and stop the stations.

Protection against alternating-current undervoltage, direct-current overload, severe alternating-current overload, load limiting resistor overheating, and delayed starting sequence is provided by an alternating-current undervoltage relay, direct-current overload relays, alternating-current overload relays, resistor thermostats, and a time delay starting protective relay, in a manner analogous to the protection provided for automatically controlled rotating

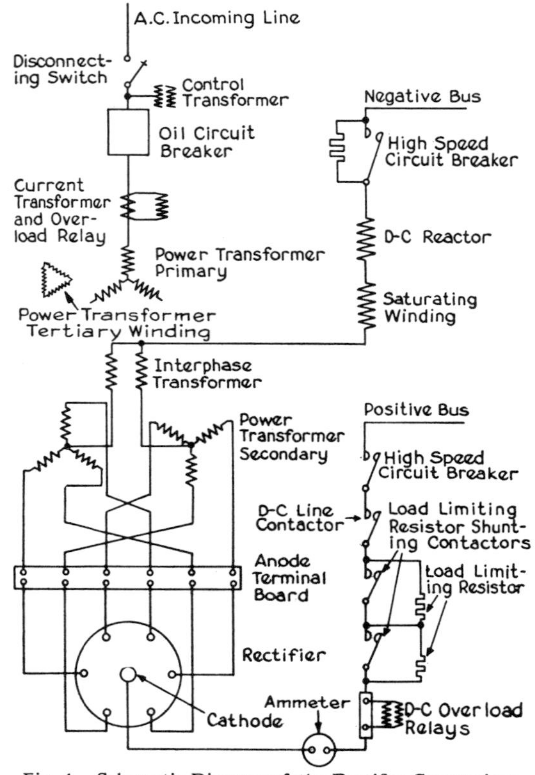

Fig. 4.   Schematic Diagram of the Rectifier Connections

apparatus. Single-phase starting and running protection is provided by means of a single- and reverse-phase relay of the potential type.

Failure of the exciting arc causes the arc striking equipment to endeavor to re-establish the arc and if this does not take place within a definite time the station is shut down and locked out. Extreme variations in tank temperature such as might be caused by failure of the cooling water or heaters shuts the station down and prevents restart.

SUBSTATION DATA

Station No.	Station Name	Location	Converting Units	Type of Control
1	Columbia Ave.	Hammond, Ind.	2—750-kw. Rotary Converters in Series	Partial Automatic
2	Gary	Gary, Ind.	2—750-kw. Rotary Converters in Series	Automatic
3	Wickliff	8.5 mi. east of Gary, Ind.	2—750-kw. Rotary Converters in Series	Automatic
4	Furnessville	9.5 mi. west of Michigan City, Ind.	1500-kw. Rectifier	Automatic
5	Eastport	Just east of Michigan City, Ind.	2—750-kw. Rotary Converters in Series	Partial Automatic
6	Tee Lake	9 mi. east of Michigan City, Ind.	750-kw. Rectifier	Automatic
7	New Carlisle	New Carlisle, Ind.	750-kw. Rectifier	Automatic
8	Grand View	1 mi. west of South Bend, Ind.	750-kw. Rectifier	Automatic

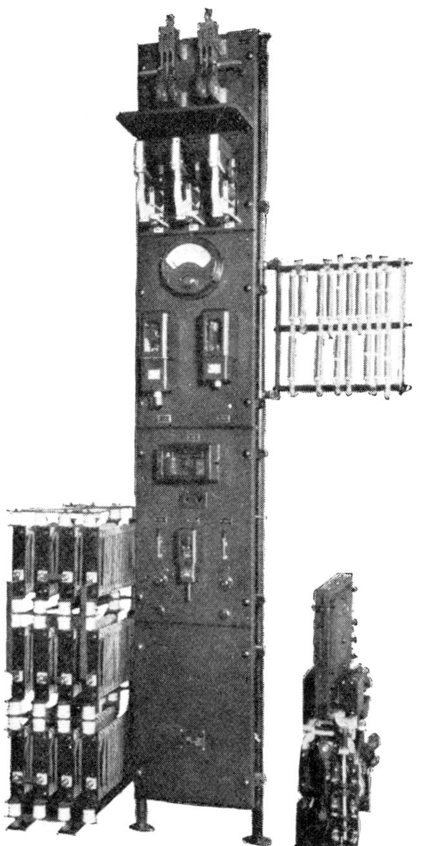

Fig. 5. Automatic Reclosing Feeder Equipment for
1500-volt, 2000-amp. Feeder

Although a rectifier is theoretically a valve which allows current to flow in one direction only, in practice there is the possibility of an occasional "arc-back." This phenomenon within the tank constitutes a short circuit on the direct-current side and on one or more phases on the alternating-current side. When an "arc-back" occurs it is desirable to isolate the rectifier from both the alternating- and direct-current systems. To accomplish this a high-speed circuit breaker arranged so as to trip on reverse current flow only is connected in the positive lead. With this arrangement an arc-back opens the d-c. side instantly and by means of an interlock on the high-speed breaker the oil circuit breaker is tripped at the same time. The tripping of the oil circuit breaker energizes the reclosing relay, which recloses the breaker after a time delay. If the rectifier does not arc-back normal operation is resumed. If a second arc-back occurs the process is repeated. After three arc-backs in succession within a definite time the station is shut down and prevented from restarting until an inspection has been made.

Automatic reclosing direct-current feeder equipments of the load indicating high-speed breaker type are provided for each station in order to isolate sections of the line in trouble. The complete equipment for a 2000-amp., 1500-volt automatic reclosing feeder is shown in Fig. 5.

Although the control of mercury arc rectifiers is materially different from the control of rotating apparatus, it is no more complicated and operates with the same reliability.

Electric train operation started on July 21, 1926, between Randolph Street and 67th Street. The first train, led by car 1127, is loading at what is now the upper level (South Shore Line) platforms of Randolph Street station.

GENERAL ELECTRIC
REVIEW

VOL. 30, No. 4 — APRIL, 1927

TO TRAVEL MORE RAPIDLY IN GREATER COMFORT AND SAFETY

A two-unit train consisting of two motor coaches each with a trailer on the Chicago Terminal Electrification of the Illinois Central Railroad. By multiple-unit trains up to ten cars in length, this railroad now furnishes to 25,000,000 passengers annually an electrified service that is 10 to 24 per cent faster than the former steam schedules

In This Issue: *A Series of Eleven Special Articles Describing the Chicago Terminal Electrification of the Illinois Central Railroad*

"I WILL"

says Chicago's motto

"WE DID"

said the Illinois Central

CHICAGO is jubilant over a lot of things this year. It is jubilant over the fact that the Illinois Central has electrified its tracks along the shore, between the towering skyline of Michigan Boulevard and the brilliant lake.

This is significant. For Chicago, the city made by the railroads, is now being made beautiful by the railroads. Last September the power was turned on, and the first electric trains sped over 37 miles of Illinois Central railroad. Now commuters ride more comfortably, and in 15 to 40 per cent less time.

General Electric supplied all of the control equipment and the air compressors as well as 260 of the powerful driving motors used in the new electric cars of the Illinois Central. Further evidence of Chicago's improvement is shown in the G-E lights on the famous State Street "White Way" and in the thousands of G-E street lights all over the city that are giving Chicago better illumination. Wherever G-E products go, their accomplishment arouses a just pride.

The electrification marks an epoch in the evolution of Chicago, for the city's improved area will be enlarged and property values increased all along the electrified line. It will have a far-reaching effect on residential and industrial developments, and on the ultimate beautification of the entire lake front.

Such stories of civic improvement are becoming more numerous. Public spirit and cooperation plus electricity can accomplish marvelous changes in any community.

GENERAL ELECTRIC

350-28B

General Electric Review

SCHENECTADY, NEW YORK

Member Audit Bureau of Circulations

Manager, M. P. RICE | Editor, J. R. HEWETT | Associate Editor, E. C. SANDERS

SUBSCRIPTION RATES:

United States and Possessions, $3.00 a year; Canada, $3.25 a year; Foreign Countries, $3.50 a year; payable in advance.
To Public Libraries and Students: Domestic, $2.00 a year; Canadian, $2.25 a year; Foreign, $2.50 a year; payable in advance.
Single copies 30 cents each.

FOREIGN REPRESENTATIVES:

Great Britain: General Electric Review,
5-6 Wenlock Rd., City Rd.,
London, N. 1., England

Japan: Maruzen Co., Ltd.,
Tokyo, Osaka, Kyoto, Yokohama, Fukuoka,
Nagoya, and Sondai

Entered as second-class matter, March 26, 1912, at the post office at Schenectady, N. Y., under Act of March, 1879.

Vol. 30, No. 4 | Published and Copyrighted 1927 by General Electric Company | April, 1927

CONTENTS

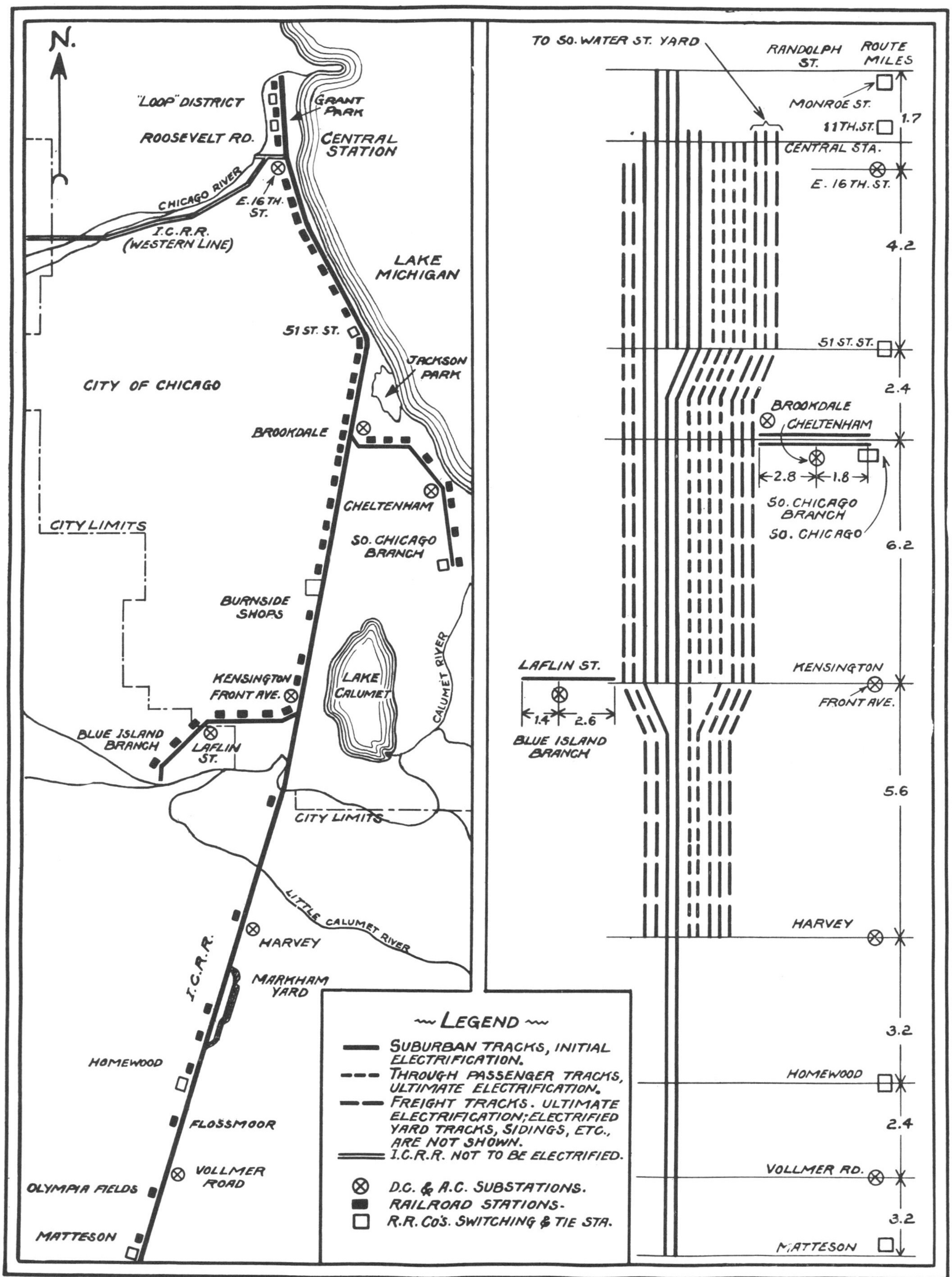

Map of the Chicago Terminal Electrification of the Illinois Central Railroad and Diagram of the Initial and Ultimate Electrified Tracks

General Electric Review

Vol. 30   April, 1927   No. 4

A NEW STANDARD OF SUBURBAN SERVICE

The fondest desires of many of Chicago's commuters have been brought more nearly to a reality by the suburban electrification of the Illinois Central Railroad, formally opened in August, 1926. By this far-sighted policy on the part of the management of the railroad, and the judgment and aggressiveness of its engineers, this progressive transportation company has made available to its millions of patrons a service which is not surpassed in this country or abroad.

An electrification of this magnitude and importance, involving the transportation of millions of passengers annually, requires an exactness of performance which can be obtained only by careful consideration of all phases of the problem, the combination of which provides a successful transportation system.

That all engineering features, as well as those equally important matters which relate to the traveling public, were fully considered and adopted only after the most careful study and investigation, is best shown by the information presented in this issue of the REVIEW by those engineers who successfully carried out the responsibilities for this important undertaking.

Recognizing that the contact of the traveling public with the railroad, and consequently its judgment of the service provided, would to a large extent be influenced by the type of car in which it travels and by the rapidity with which the journey is completed, careful thought and study was given to these two factors which so largely affect the success of a transportation system.

A notable feature of the car selected is the consideration given to the safety and comfort of passengers. The car body is of metal construction, using the highest grade of materials, and the spacious platforms are completely vestibuled and equipped with doors of a safety type.

That the comfort of the traveling public was given full attention is best shown by the provision of wide doors and aisles, comfortable seats with ample space between them, good ventilation, and excellent lighting facilities.

The reduction of 10 to 24 per cent in schedule running time made possible by electric drive is the best illustration of the desire on the part of the railroad company to provide the traveling public with modern rapid transportation.

Next to the rolling stock, the most important feature of an electrification of this magnitude is the power supply. The decision of the engineers responsible for the success of this exacting service to purchase power from existing power companies having several generating stations and transmission lines insures an uninterrupted supply of power and relieves the railroad company of the necessity of constructing and maintaining transmission lines on its own right-of-way. In addition, the railroad company obtains a more reliable power supply due to the larger number of generating stations and varied routing of transmission lines.

The same careful attention to detail with a view to insuring reliability of service was given to the conversion equipment in the substations. This installation is the first in which mercury-arc power rectifiers have been used for a steam-road electrification in this country. Synchronous converters in most cases are installed in the same station with the rectifiers. Special design features of these converters provide a close regulation of the voltage to comply with the railroad company's specifications.

The feeder distribution system is also an example of modern methods of power distribution to insure protection not only to the substation equipment but also to the motor equipment of the cars. The high-speed circuit breaker is the most important element in this protection.

The installing of overhead equipment on a railroad carrying such dense traffic as the Illinois Central was a notable achievement. One of the articles in this issue deals with this subject, describing the methods which were used to avoid all possible interruptions to the regular service.

The facilities for inspection and repairs are also discussed and here again the importance of uninterrupted service is emphasized.

Every detail of this installation was thoroughly studied and carefully worked out. The equipment involved was selected only after most careful investigations and tests, and its performance has fully justified the judgment and expectations of the engineers responsible for carrying out this undertaking.

Thus it has come about that the electrified suburban service on the Illinois Central Railroad is successfully providing a most exacting traveling public with a new era in transportation.   H. L. ANDREWS

Selection of System and General Features of Illinois Central Electrification

Origin of the Electrification—Extent of Program—Four Systems Considered—Suburban Trackage—
Institution of Electric Service—Traffic Totals

By W. M. VANDERSLUIS

Electrical Engineer, Chicago Terminal Improvement

ON July 21, 1919, the City Council of the city of Chicago passed what is commonly known as the "Lake Front Ordinance." This three-party contract between the city of Chicago, the South Park Commission, and the Illinois Central Railroad Company covered the release by the railroad company of its riparian rights along Lake Michigan, between East Roosevelt Road and 51st Street; extensive grade revisions by the railroad company in this territory, to permit of the construction of viaducts and subways to the lake; exchange of certain pieces of property; and the electrification of the railroad within the city limits. The approval of the War Department was required, as the filling of certain submerged lands was involved.

The ordinance which was finally approved by all concerned provided specifically for the electrification of the suburban service within the city limits by Feb. 21, 1927, the freight service north of East Roosevelt Road by 1930, the freight service south of East Roosevelt Road to the city limits on the main line by 1935, and the through passenger service of the Illinois Central and Michigan Central railroad companies by 1940, provided a certain proportion of the tenant roads then using the passenger station on East Roosevelt Road are electrically operated at that time.

After the passage of the ordinance and its acceptance by all parties, the immediate problem of the railroad company was to settle on the system of electrification to be used. In view of the apparent great differences in opinion among the engineers of the country as to the proper system, there was appointed by the president of the railroad, in 1920, a Commission to make recommendations covering the electrification as provided by the ordinance; *i.e.*, to include suburban, freight, and eventually through passenger electrification of the Chicago Terminal.

This Commission was composed of the late A. S. Baldwin, Vice-president, Chicago Terminal Improvement, Chairman; D. J. Brumley, Chief Engineer,

W. M. VANDERSLUIS

Chicago Terminal Improvement; Bion J. Arnold, Consulting Engineer; George Gibbs, Consulting Engineer; Dr. Cary T. Hutchinson, Consulting Engineer; and the writer, Engineer-Secretary. Hugh Pattison was retained as Electrical Engineer of the Commission in charge of the compilation of such data as required.

The Commission considered the following systems:

(1) 750-volt, direct current with third rail.
(2) 1500-volt direct current with overhead contact.
(3) 3000-volt, direct current with overhead contact.
(4) 11,000-volt, single-phase, alternating current with overhead contact.

Complete first cost, maintenance, and operation estimates were prepared to cover the four systems.

In September, 1922, the Commission recommended the 1500-volt, direct-current system with overhead contact, on the basis that it was a terminal electrification only, with no prospects for immediate extensions over adjacent main-line divisions. The recommendations were approved by the president.

The Commission was relieved of its duties and the work of electrifying the suburban service undertaken by the Chicago Terminal Improvement organization, with F. L. Thompson, Vice-president, and D. J. Brumley, Chief Engineer, in charge of the work. The firm of Gibbs & Hill was retained as Consulting Engineers, passing on all general electrical engineering matters and on important details.

The tracks electrified for suburban service cover the following on the main line south:

Randolph Street to 11th Street—1.3 miles, 2 main tracks and 1 equipment lead.
11th Street to 51st Street—4.9 miles, 6 main tracks.
51st Street to 115th Street (Kensington)—8.1 miles, 4 main tracks.
115th Street to Matteson—13.7 miles, 2 main tracks.

In addition to the station tracks for 46 cars at the northern terminus, Randolph Street, there is a storage yard for 56 cars just south of Van Buren

Street for day storage of trains that terminate there; day storage for 110 cars in the vicinity of 16th Street, where the light inspection shed is located; turnaround tracks for one train at 53rd and 69th Streets; night storage yard for 50 cars at Kensington; and night storage for 52 cars at Matteson.

There is a branch line to South Chicago leaving the main line at 67th Street with 4.5 miles of double track. Night storage for 72 cars is provided at 83rd Street and for 36 cars at South Chicago on this line.

A single-track branch line extends from the main line at Kensington to Blue Island, 4.4 miles, with night storage for 34 cars at that terminus.

gency movements at Homewood, near mile post 23 and at the south end of the storage yard at Matteson. When the permanent layout is put in north of 22nd Street, plants will be installed for the six-track four-track ending south of Van Buren Street and for the terminal layout at the new Randolph Street station now under construction.

Actual electric operation was started with four local trains each way between Randolph Street and Hyde Park on July 21, 1926, seven months before the time required by the ordinance. This service was gradually built up on the steam time-table basis, and on August 29, 1926, the first electric time-table was put into effect.

Reproduction of an Oil Painting Typifying Electrified Suburban Service at the
Chicago Terminal of the Illinois Central Railroad

Necessary track facilities are also provided at the electrical overhaul and heavy inspection shops, in Burnside Yard. These include a test track approximately a mile in length.

The final location of all suburban tracks on the main line will be on the west side of the right-of-way; but as the new through passenger terminal at East Roosevelt Road has not been started, all suburban tracks are located temporarily to the east of the present through-passenger layout between 8th Street and 22nd Street.

Interlocking plants are provided for the six-track four-track ending at 51st Street, the South Chicago Railroad connection at 67th Street, the four-track two-track ending and Blue Island Railroad Junction at Kensington, which also includes a double-track connection to the tracks of an electrified tenant line, the Chicago, South Shore and South Bend Railroad. Additional interlocking plants are installed for emer-

The electric schedules have decreased the old steam running time between terminals from 10 to 24 per cent, this decrease depending on the number and location of the intermediate stops. Additional trains have been added until there is at the present time a total of 475 scheduled trains on a normal week day, including trains of the C.S.S. & S.B. operating between Kensington and Randolph Street. The train-miles are about 215,000 a month and the car-miles are running about 870,000 a month. Approximately 25,000,000 revenue passengers are now carried yearly.

This service, with its heavy concentration of trains during the morning and evening rush hours, requires a most reliable power supply, a comparatively heavy distribution system with a flexible sectionalization scheme, and adequate equipment.

How this has been accomplished is described in the following articles.

Power Supply and Distribution System for Illinois Central Electrification

Principal Features—Power Purchased at Right-of-way—Distribution by Railroad—Sectionalization—Control—Supply for Miscellaneous Purposes

By G. I. WRIGHT

Assistant Electrical Engineer, Chicago Terminal Improvement

G. I. WRIGHT

THE most interesting features of the power supply for the Illinois Central electrification are:

(1) The power is delivered at the railroad's right-of-way by the power companies in the form in which it is used by the trains, *i.e.*, 1500 volts direct current; and these companies own and operate the conversion substations

(2) The magnitude and density of the train loads. Ten-car multiple-unit trains will be operated, each train having a motor capacity of 5000 h.p., drawing 3500 amp. or 5250 kw. during acceleration, and 760 amp. or 1140 kw. average. In addition, all freight switching and through passenger movements will be handled with electric locomotives in the electrified territory.

(3) The problem of conversion of alternating current from a very large capacity 60-cycle power supply system with short heavy a-c. supply lines into 1500-volt direct current to furnish a low-resistance direct-current distribution system with a service of exceptional reliability. This conversion is accomplished by the use of 3000-kw. synchronous converters and mercury-arc rectifier sets.

(4) The d-c. sectionalization system, which maintains high average voltage to the trains, automatically isolates short defective sections of the overhead, and gives the highest degree of protection to equipment and overhead yet obtained, by interrupting fault currents so quickly that these do not ordinarily attain a damaging value.

(5) The use of remote supervisory control for indication to, and control by, the railroad's power supervisor of all d-c. feeder circuit breakers in substations and at sectionalization points.

Power Generation and Transmission

One of the reasons for the Illinois Central's decision to purchase power from the Commonwealth Edison and subsidiary companies, rather than build its own generating plant, was the ability of the power companies to supply the railroad from several power plants, laying their lines over various routes and serving each substation from a sufficient number of lines to prevent an interruption on any one of them from interfering with the operation of the substation supplied.

The power for the electrification is generated at the Crawford Avenue, Calumet, Fiske, and Quarry Stations of the Commonwealth Edison Company, the first two being the latest and most efficient stations of this company. It is also generated at the Joliet and Blue Island Stations of the Public Service Company of Northern Illinois, while other stations of both companies are tied into the network and are available if needed. The railroad is thus relieved of the necessity for constructing and maintaining

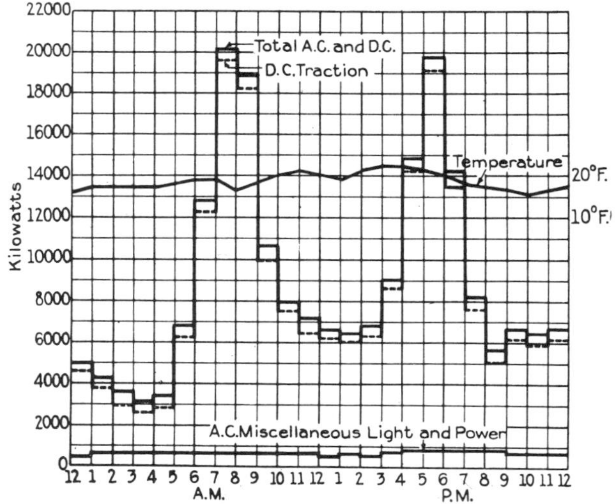

Fig. 1.   24-hour Load Curve of the Suburban Electrification System

transmission lines along its right-of-way, and obtains more reliable power supply due to the larger number of generating stations and varied routing of the lines.

The railroad's present load, as shown in Fig. 1, is about 20,000 kw. maximum hourly demand; and while this is large for a single consumer it is a comparatively small addition to the total load of the power companies. This naturally insures greater reliability and lower generating cost due to the use of larger units and better system load-factor.

The power supply to the substations is all 60-cycle, and in the Commonwealth Edison territory inside the city limits is by means of 12,000-volt, 3-phase underground feeders. Outside the city limits, in the Public Service territory, it is by means of 33,000-volt, 3-phase transmission lines.

Substations

The power is converted in substations owned and operated by the power companies and located either on their property or on property leased from the railroad. They were located (see frontispiece) particularly for the railroad's requirements, and in general

Vollmer Road..... One 3000-kw. synchronous converter set
    One 1500-kw. mercury arc rectifier set
Cheltenham....... Two 3000-kw. synchronous converter sets
Laflin........... One 1500-kw. mercury arc rectifier set
  Total installed capacity.... 42,000 kw.

Fig. 2. The Vollmer Road Substation of the Public Service Co. of Northern Illinois, Located in a High-class Suburban Residence District

Fig. 3. Interior View of Brookdale Substation Showing 3000-kw. 2-unit Synchronous-converter Sets

The operation of the substations by the power companies is the first case of this kind for a large steam road electrification. The power companies are here a "supply" company in the true sense of the word, supplying the energy to the consumer in the form and at the place where it is to be used. The railroad company is left to concentrate its activities on conducting transportation, which is primarily its business, and incidentally is relieved of a large investment in substation buildings and apparatus.

All the substations are arranged for manual operation and under the contract may be used to supply other customers, either railway or light and power. The buildings are attractive in appearance and roomy, and are laid out to permit of expansion to take care of future freight and through-passenger electrification of the railroad.

The incoming a-c. line and converter switchboards consist of truck-type equipments. The synchronous

are spaced six miles apart. The size and type of units are as follows:

16th Street...... Three 3000-kw. synchronous converter sets
Brookdale........ Two 3000-kw. synchronous converter sets
    One 3000-kw. mercury arc rectifier set
Front Avenue..... Two 3000-kw. synchronous converter sets
Harvey.......... One 3000-kw. synchronous converter set
    One 3000-kw. mercury arc rectifier set

converter sets consist of two shunt-wound 1500-kw., 750-volt, 60-cycle synchronous converters, permanently connected in series to make up 3000-kw. units. Each pair of converters and its air-cooled transformer are mounted on a common bedplate with the transformer between, thus making a most compact unit. As the a-c. switching is handled on the high-tension side of the transformer, the secondary leads between the transformer and the slip rings are reduced to the shortest possible length. The converters are equipped with flash barriers and high-speed circuit breaker protection, and have operated most satis-

Fig. 4.   Interior View of Harvey Substation Showing a 3000-kw. 2-unit Synchronous-converter Set and a 3000-kw. 2-unit Mercury-arc Rectifier Set

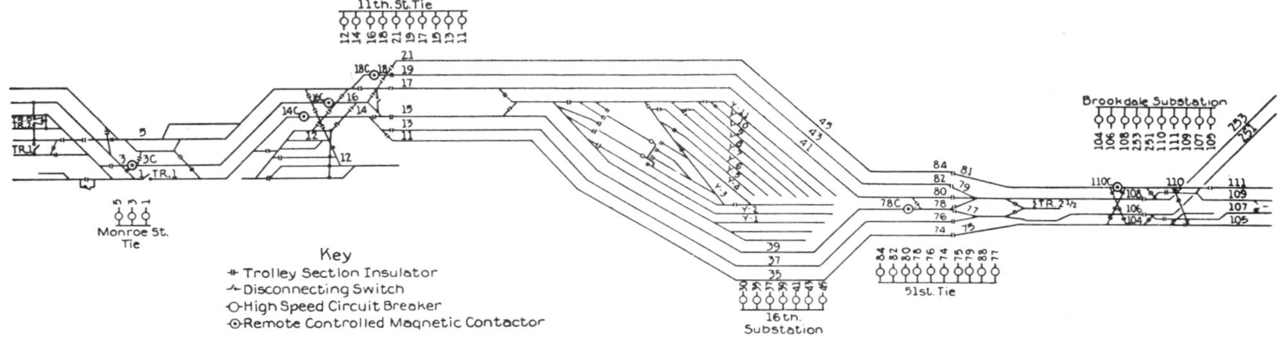

Fig. 5.   Diagram of 1500-volt Surburban Electrified Tracks,

factorily. Flashovers with their resulting damage have been practically eliminated. The overload ratings are 150 per cent rated load for two hours, 300 per cent for one minute.

The rectifier sets consist of two 750-kw. or two 1500-kw. 1500-volt bowls operating in parallel; and, in all cases but one, are installed in substations with synchronous converters and operate in parallel with the converters in the same substation. The rectifier overload ratings are 150 per cent rated load for 20 minutes, 300 per cent for one minute.

In order to meet the voltage-regulation requirements of the railroad, which are that the voltage at the substation bus must not fall below 1400 volts during all normal load conditions, it was decided to equip the converters with separate automatic excitation, using a specially developed scheme known as counter e.m.f. regulation. Each converter set is provided with its own exciter, the armature of which is connected permanently in series with the shunt-field coils of the converter. This combination is connected

across a c.e.m.f. motor bus for regulating the converter field current. This bus is common for all sets in a station. The voltage is regulated on all sets simultaneously by the c.e.m.f. set. The c.e.m.f. voltage is in turn controlled by an automatic voltage regulator connected to the 1500-volt d-c. bus, together with an automatic four-circuit motor-driven rheostat. The automatic voltage regulator works in the usual way, while the four-circuit rheostat compensates for varying a-c. supply voltage and also protects the machine against excessive reactive kv-a. at all loads.

The outgoing 1500-volt direct-current feeders are equipped with 2000-amp. high-speed circuit breakers, mounted in truck-type switching equipments. There is also a 3000-amp. high-speed circuit breaker in both positive and negative machine leads. The system is designed so that overloads and short circuits on the feeders will open the feeder circuit breakers involved and will ordinarily not affect the machine breakers. If, however, the total load distributed on several feeders is not sufficient to open the individual feeder breakers, but exceeds the capacity of the machine, the machine negative breaker opens and cuts in resistance which limits the current to 300 per cent of the normal rated capacity of the machine. If this load is maintained for more than four seconds, the positive breaker opens, disconnecting the converter from the bus. This selectivity between feeder and machine breakers is being obtained in all cases except where short circuits are very close to the substations.

Sectionalization of Distribution System

The distribution system of the railroad was laid out so that the wires over each track are separate electrically from those over adjacent tracks, and can be sectionalized at substations and at points half way between substations where there are crossovers in the tracks and interlocking plants to control train movements. This sectionalization is automatic in case of trouble on the distribution system, or can be obtained by opening the circuit breakers involved. At the sectionalization points between substations, the railroad has installed tie stations which consist of a bus connected to the trolley wire over each track through a high-speed truck-

and thus give better voltage at the trains than would otherwise be obtained. The tracks are usually operated in one direction only, and in the morning the north-bound tracks are the heavier loaded and in the evening the south-bound. The tie between all tracks thus serves to equalize the currents flowing and thus decrease the voltage drop.

Selectivity between short circuits and power loads is facilitated by the inherent characteristic of the high-speed circuit breaker which causes it to be more susceptible to short-circuit currents with a high rate of rise than to normal load currents. The circuit breakers open on most abnormal occurrences on the car equipment or overhead, such as motor flashovers, slight grounds of any kind, severe wheel slipping, etc. While these openings result in momentary power interruptions, they prevent any appreciable burning of the equipment or overhead and the trouble is thus much easier to repair than were the burning more extensive.

The automatic sectionalization of faulty sections is also assisted by the fact that the tie station breakers operate somewhat faster than those at the substations. This differential is obtained by energizing the

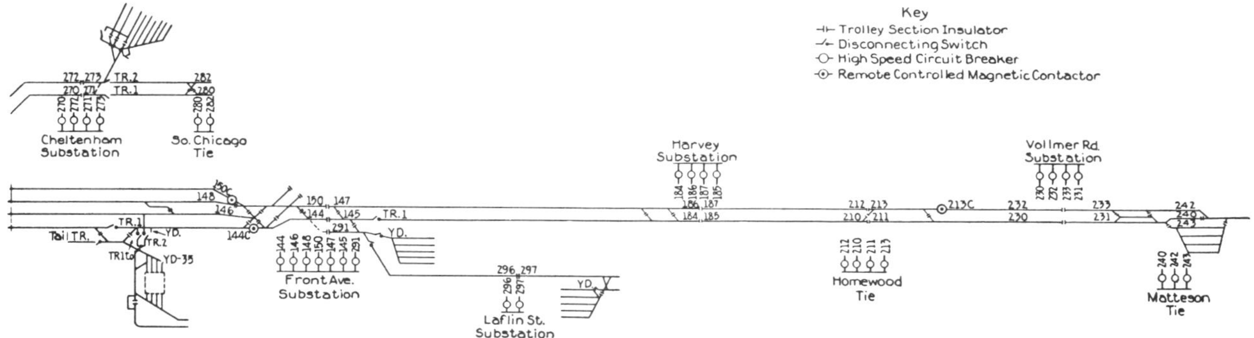

Showing Sectionalization at Substations and Tie Stations

type circuit breaker. In the event of trouble on any track, for example between 51st and Brookdale (Fig. 5), the circuit breakers at these two points feeding the trolley over this track would open automatically, thus killing this section; and if it were necessary to leave it dead for some time, the trains could be routed around this section by using crossovers at 51st and Brookdale, which are under the control of interlocking plant operators. In addition to sectionalizing the affected sections, the tie stations serve the purpose of tying the copper over all tracks together

Fig. 6. Control Desk of the Power Supervisor in the Power Supervisor's and Train Despatcher's Office

holding coils of the tie-station breakers from the 1500-volt trolley, whereas the holding coils of the substation breakers are energized from a constant-voltage battery source. With a short circuit or ground near the tie station, the voltage on the holding coils and the resulting flux is decreased, in effect lowering the tripping setting of the breakers which open before the substation breakers feeding the tie-station bus through other feeders. The high-speed breakers are uni-directional in tripping; *i.e.*, they trip due to load in the normal direction only. Reverse current tends to hold the breaker in and compensates for reduced voltage on those breakers on other sections feeding into the tie-station bus. There is therefore little difficulty in obtaining selectivity of breakers at the tie stations, the breaker feeding into the faulty section being the only one that opens. It should be noted that the selectivity which has been described is obtained in about 100th of a second. Selective operation that has been obtained in the past, that in alternating-current circuits, has always been by means of time-limit relays with consequent delayed operation.

To energize a section, the substation breaker is first closed and this impresses voltage on the associated tie-station breaker, causing it in turn to close automatically. This very simple system of automatic reclosing makes unnecessary the use of voltage-measuring or feeling-out apparatus.

The tie stations are unattended and therefore, although the circuit breakers are automatic reclosing, it was necessary to provide some system of remote indication and control.

Supervisory Remote Control

The railroad company has made a complete installation of supervisory control for all substation and tie-station circuit breakers serving the traction distribution system. The control and indication are centered in the railroad company's power supervisor's office, located in the Randolph Street building at the north end of the suburban lines, where knowledge of the entire power system is at once coördinated. The power supervisor and train dispatcher occupy a joint office and are in constant contact, which greatly facilitates the movement of trains in case of trouble and also expedites the reporting and correcting of troubles of all kinds. It is the power companys' responsibility to maintain sufficient power on the substation buses, and the railroad company directly controls all the feeders to its distribution system. In the event of failure of the supervisory control, or for any other reason, the substation operator can take over this control of his circuit breakers, operating them on orders from the power supervisor. Due to the number of circuit breakers in the ultimate installation, it was decided to install three groups of supervisory control with three line wires to each group. All these wires are in the regular railroad telephone cables.

Miscellaneous Light, Power, and Signal Power Supply

In addition to the direct-current supply, 2300/4000-volt, 4-wire, 60-cycle grounded-neutral distribution is also provided for miscellaneous station light and power and other uses. This is supplied from the traction substations, in which are 12,000/4000-volt transformers and oil switches for the railroad's feeders. Duplicate lines are provided on the most important portions of the system, lines being run overhead on the catenary structures. Where the loads are important, automatic throwover switches are provided, these operating on the failure of the preferred line. The 60-cycle a-c. signals are supplied with power by single-phase 2300-volt duplicate lines run on the catenary structures, fed from the traction substations through one-to-one ratio insulating transformers. The a-c. feeder switches are all operated manually by the substation operators on the orders of the railroad's power supervisor.

Induction feeder regulators are provided for the 4000-volt light and power substation buses, and the railroad can require regulators in individual feeders if found to be necessary.

In order to avoid paralleling the substations on the 4000-volt side, the light and power lines are sectionalized at points midway between substations and air-break pole-top switches are provided for emergency connections. The duplicate signal lines, however, are run through from substation to substation and are provided with feeder oil circuit breakers at each end. The breakers on opposite ends of the two feeders between substations are left open so that a failure of either line or either substation would not affect the other line. This has resulted in a very high degree of reliability of signal power supply.

Tie Stations and Supervisory Control for Illinois Central Electrification

Function of Tie Stations—Simplicity of the Equipment—Its Operation—Method of Centralizing
the Control—Interlocking Features of the Supervisory Control—Operation of the
Control—Its Results

By C. L. DOUB

Assistant Engineer, Chicago Terminal Improvement

AT certain locations between substations and at stub ends of the traction distribution system, the Railroad Company has provided switching and tie stations, which are commonly referred to as "tie stations." These stations have a three-fold purpose in that they provide for sectionalizing of tracks, they improve voltage regulation by the paralleling of feeders, and they also provide reduced distribution losses due to the more economical utilization of copper through paralleling.

Six tie stations are provided initially and additional stations will be provided at later times. Four of these tie stations, namely, Monroe Street, 11th Street, 51st Street, and Homewood, are at interlocking plants (or hand-operated plants). The other two, Matteson and South Chicago, are at stub ends of the distribution system, and serve primarily to parallel two-track sections, except that at Matteson a third feed is provided for a suburban coach yard. Monroe Street Station is at the stub end of the north terminus of the suburban electrification and provides for paralleling of feeds as well as for promoting flexibility of power supply. The 11th Street Tie Station is unusual in that it is located between a substation and stub end tie station. It is essential for the purpose of sectionalizing tracks, and, since it is less than one mile from East 16th Street substation, it is not of primary importance for voltage regulation or economy of energy. It is in a sense a point of power supply, since the entire feed north of this point is obtained through the tie station bus. This station is a temporary one and will be removed when suburban tracks through this territory are relocated and rearranged in connection with the building of a new through passenger station at Roosevelt Road (12th Street).

Tie Station Equipment

Feeders from the tie stations serve each track independently and each connects through a high-

C. L. DOUB

speed circuit breaker to the tie station bus. These breakers are rated at 2000 amperes continuously and have been demonstrated to have a rupturing capacity of over 50,000 amperes. Actual continuous loads are much below this capacity at the present time, and inasmuch as these loads, in general, consist only of interchange current between various feeders, they are naturally considerably lighter than corresponding substation feeder loads. The breakers, as are the substation feeder breakers, are truck mounted, together with the necessary control devices. This mounting promotes a simplicity of station design, with finished appearance. It assures a maximum of protection to maintenance men, as well as other employees at times requiring access to these unattended stations. Of special importance is the ease and safety of inspecting and maintaining the high-voltage equipment, since all parts are necessarily dead when such work is done. It is occasionally found desirable to take advantage of the ability to interchange equipment in a negligible time.

The high-speed breakers are of the type rather generally known at this time, in which the contacts are held closed by means of a holding coil constituting an electrical latch. Tripping of the breaker on overload or short circuit is effected by the series current creating a flux which "bucks" the holding-coil flux and allows powerful springs to open the contacts. Contacts are designed to have a minimum of inertia and therefore can be accelerated in the shortest possible time. In parallel with the "bucking bar" (the flux from which reduces the holding flux) is an "inductive shunt" consisting of a copper bar made inductive by being surrounded by iron laminations. Short circuit current is therefore choked back in the inductive shunt and caused to flow through the bucking bar, whereas current of normal loads distributes between the two paths in the ratio of their ohmic resistance. The current in the bucking bar only is effective in tripping the breaker, hence a higher value of total current is required for tripping on useful loads than on short circuits. That is, the breaker discriminates between short circuit and useful load. The various tie station breakers are set to trip on overloads of from 4000 to 6000 amperes, the settings depending on the conditions of the respective circuits, whereas they will trip on short circuits of about one-third or one-half of these values.

Fig. 1.   Exterior of Homewood Tie Station

All of the high-speed breakers have a trip-free closing mechanism. They are frequently called upon to close upon short circuits, and no difficulty has been experienced in such action. During initial testing and adjusting of the feeder system, dead short circuits were repeatedly put on lines at points immediately adjacent to breakers, and it has not been found necessary even to clean contacts after a large number of such interruptions.

Control of High-speed Breakers

Tie station breaker holding coils are energized normally from the feeder side of the respective breakers. Reset coil circuits are fed during the closing operation from the same 1500-volt control supply. The breaker thus provides automatic reclosing upon the principle of voltage restoration. That is, when a tie station and a substation breaker feeding a given section of track are opened by overload or short circuit, the tie station breaker remains open until voltage is restored on the section by the closing of the substation breaker. In the event of closing the substation breaker upon

an uncleared short circuit, the tie breaker will not even make a momentary attempt at reclosing because the short circuit will prevent voltage from building up at the tie breaker. This holding-coil circuit is under the control of the railroad power supervisor through the supervisory control system, by which he can open or close the 1500-volt control feed. The operation of his "trip" function opens the breaker or locks it out if already open, and the operation of his "close" function closes the 1500-volt control circuit to the point of supply, and allows the breaker to close when voltage is restored to the predetermined value. In ordinary cases of tripping, the power supervisor does not perform any operation of the tie breaker, simply allowing it to close automatically after the closing of the substation breaker.

In certain cases it is desired to close tie station breakers independently of other voltage supply on the section. This is essential north of 11th Street since there is no source of 1500-volt supply for these feeders other than the 11th Street Station. It is also required in connection with the remotely-operated contactors adjacent to tie stations, so that power may be restored to the short sections of feeders over interlocking tracks, when these sections are segregated from the substation supply by means of the contactors. To accomplish this, a scheme of control, commonly referred to as the "three control" equipment, is used. The supervisor has three control functions over these breakers; *viz.*, "trip," "close from feeder," and "close

Fig. 2.   Interior of 11th St. Tie Station Showing Ten Feeder Trucks.   Four of these are of the "three-control" and six of the "two-control" type

from bus." He may thus close these breakers by connecting the 1500-volt control circuit directly to the tie station bus. The feed may later be transferred to the feeder side of the breaker without opening the breaker. This control requires the use of "anti-pump" relays, so that in the event of closing of breakers upon short circuits they will not repeatedly reclose. These relays, however, do not lock out the breaker, but may immediately be reset for another closing by operation of the tripping function through the supervisory control.

The diagram, Fig. 3, shows the schematic circuits for the three-control trucks. The circuits for the ordinary "two control" truck are similar, except for the elimination of the anti-pump relays and the current for the breakers, by obtaining this supply from the 1500-volt lines.

Tie stations at 11th Street and 51st Street have ten circuit breakers and several contactors. Batteries are of 51-ampere-hour capacity, and are charged from a 1000-watt motor-generator set. Monroe Street Station, with three circuit breakers and one contactor, and Homewood Station, with four circuit breakers and one contactor, have each a 34-ampere-hour battery, charged from a 500-watt motor-generator set. Matteson and South Chicago tie stations have only three and two circuit breakers, respectively, and a 17-ampere hour battery each, charged by Tungar rectifiers.

The motor-generators are run from single-phase, 110-volt supply, and have automatic control panels. All charging equipment is operated continuously and actually carries the load of the tie station equipment, with batteries on floating charge. Batteries have sufficient capacity for carrying the station load for a reasonable time in case of failure of charging source. Batteries are relieved somewhat by having local indicating lamps fed from a separate lamp bus, which is cut off when no attendants are in the station. Relays are being installed in tie stations to give supervisory indication at Randolph Street in case of a battery being drained sufficiently to threaten complete discharge, so to assure the prompt dispatch of a maintenance man to the station.

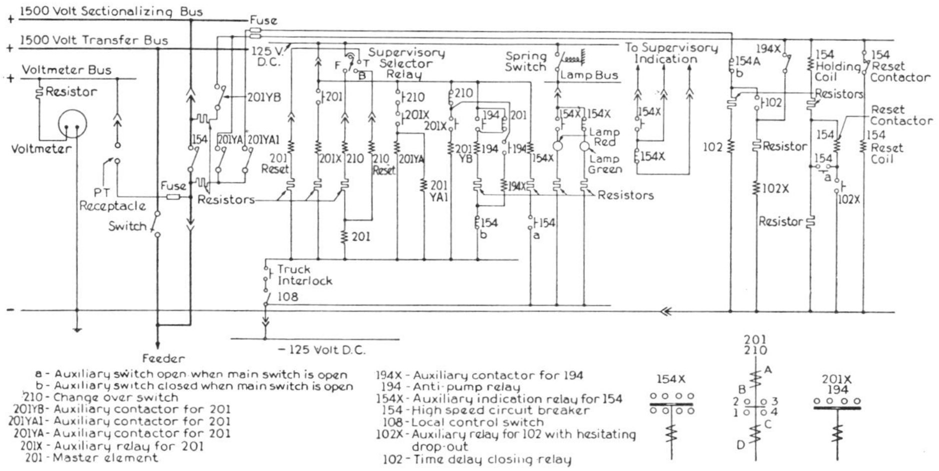

Fig. 3. Schematic Wiring Diagram Showing the Circuits Used on the "Three-control" Trucks

a - Auxiliary switch open when main switch is open
b - Auxiliary switch closed when main switch is open
210 - Change over switch
201YB - Auxiliary contactor for 201
201YA1 - Auxiliary contactor for 201
201YA - Auxiliary contactor for 201
201X - Auxiliary relay for 201
201 - Master element
194X - Auxiliary contactor for 194
194 - Anti-pump relay
154X - Auxiliary indication relay for 154
154 - High speed circuit breaker
108 - Local control switch
102X - Auxiliary relay for 102 with hesitating drop-out
102 - Time delay closing relay

relays for changeover from bus to feeder control. Since line voltage is variable, it is advisable to prevent application of low voltage to the reset coil, which might not be sufficient to close the breaker and would therefore allow the reset coil to be energized continuously and probably burned out. The time delay relay provides a voltage measuring feature, and will pick up only when voltage is high enough to complete the reclosing operation. The time delay of this relay is set at from five to ten seconds, so as to assure stable voltage conditions upon a section before the tie breaker attempts to reclose. The other 1500-volt devices are auxiliary to the reclosing operation and provide for momentarily increasing holding-coil current in order to assure sealing in of the breaker as well as providing for the proper de-energizing of the reset coil after the breaker has closed.

Tie Station Battery Supply

Tie stations contain 120-volt lead storage batteries of moderate capacity, primarily for operation of the auxiliary relays upon feeder trucks and the auxiliary contactor of the remotely-operated sectionalizing contactors. As previously explained, the station battery is relieved of holding-coil and closing-coil are being installed in tie stations to give supervisory indication at Randolph Street in case of a battery being drained sufficiently to threaten complete discharge, so to assure the prompt dispatch of a maintenance man to the station.

Transfer Bus

Each tie station is provided with an auxiliary or transfer bus and a 2000-ampere disconnecting switch to connect any feeder or feeders to this bus. In the event of removal of a circuit breaker truck for any considerable length of time, the corresponding feeder may be paralleled with any other feeder selected and the two fed through one breaker. This transfer bus also provides emergency closing of the ordinary two-control equipments without energizing feeders at the substation end; *i.e.*, voltage may be applied to the feeder side of such trucks momentarily through the transfer bus from some other feeder, thus providing control voltage for closing the circuit breaker. This circuit breaker will then remain closed by back feed from the tie station bus, after the transfer switch is opened. The transfer bus provides a simple but very effective emergency feed.

Remotely-operated Contactors

In conjunction with certain tie stations and sub-stations are installed remotely-operated contactors of 1500-ampere capacity, mounted upon catenary structures at special points of sectionalization of overhead wiring. These contactors are of the simple electromagnetically-operated type, and each is enclosed with an auxiliary contactor in a wooden housing. By their means sections of the 1500-volt feeders between substations or between substations and tie stations are normally tied but may be disconnected so that a comparatively long section serving regular track may be cut off if faulty, and power fed into the remaining section of the feeder serving short lengths of main and crossover tracks in interlocking plant limits. Since substations and tie stations are located at interlocking plants, each contactor is within a short distance of one of these stations and is controlled from a panel in the station. The contactor control panel is in turn connected with the supervisory control in the station so that the power supervisor has control and indication for all contactors. They aid greatly in prompt rerouting of traffic in cases of trouble.

Control and indication are provided between contactor and substation by three No. 14 wires from the station 120-volt battery circuits. The main contactor circuit operates on 1500 volts and is local within the contactor box, being closed by an auxiliary contactor with 1500-volt contacts and 120-volt operating coil, the latter being connected to the circuits from substations. Indication is obtained by one additional control wire only, connected through one interlock on the main contactor and serving both station and supervisory indications by means of an auxiliary relay on the control panel.

Contactors are provided with blowout coils and arc chutes, and would interrupt considerable load under emergency conditions. They are however, non-automatic in tripping, and overloads or short circuits are cleared by the high-speed breakers serving these sections. The contactor therefore serves merely as a remotely-operated disconnecting switch and generally is opened before power is restored to the section by means of the high-speed breakers.

SUPERVISORY CONTROL

The supervisory control is of the selector type. It was developed from the apparatus that has been used for a number of years by many railroads for selective ringing on train dispatchers' telephone lines.

Randolph Street Supervisor's Office

The supervisory control serves seven substations and six tie stations along the right-of-way. Six standard lamp and key cabinets designed for control and indication of twenty circuit breakers each are mounted directly upon a special desk in the supervisor's office

Fig. 4.   Supervisory Control Desk and Typical Apparatus Cabinets, Randolph Street Supervisor's Office

(Fig. 4). Present connections to these cabinets include 32 tie station circuit breakers, of which eight have three control functions each, 38 substation breakers, and nine sectionalizing contactors, a total of seventy-nine switches, in addition to checking keys for all of these devices. Provision is being made for addition of indication of other features in tie stations. These cabinets include a pair of red and green lamps for each device indicated, and an operating key for each control function; *i.e.*, one key for the "close" operation and one key for "open." Three keys are required for the "three-control" tie station feeder breakers. All operating keys are within easy reach of the supervisor when seated at the operating desk.

The operating apparatus, including selectors for receiving indications, lockout relays, control relays, etc., are mounted in ten small steel apparatus cabinets also located in the supervisor's office. The principal source of power for the supervisory control system is a 24-volt, 51-ampere-hour lead storage battery for lamps and local control relays, and a 192-volt,

6-ampere-hour lead storage battery for sending impulses over line wires to substations. Both batteries are kept on floating charge by Tungar rectifiers. The entire equipment, including lamp and key cabinets, apparatus cabinets, and storage batteries, occupies a space of about eight feet by fourteen feet.

The supervisory control equipment operates over three wires, two being required for the operating

Fig. 5. Interior of the 11th Street Tie Station Showing Two Supervisory Control Panels (at right , One Control Panel for Three Contactors (middle) and One Battery Charging Panel (left). 1000-watt motor-generator set for battery charging is shown above the board

and indicating impulses, and a third for a lock-out circuit to prevent two stations conflicting by sending codes at one time. The number of codes that can be used on one set of three wires is, however, exceeded by the amount of apparatus now and later to be controlled, and apparatus is arranged in three groups with separate control wires for each group. These groups operate independently, and control and indication may therefore be performed on them simultaneously. One supervisory group serves Monroe Street and 11th Street Tie Stations, and 16th Street Substation, lines being only about two miles long but serving a total of 24 switches, with 101 operating and indicating functions. The second group serves 51st Street Tie Station and Brookdale Substation on the Main Line, and then extends on the South Chicago Branch to serve Cheltenham Substation and South Chicago Tie Station. These line wires have a total length of about thirteen miles and serve 28 switches with 113 functions. The third group serves Front

Avenue, Harvey and Vollmer Road Substations, and Homewood and Matteson Tie Stations, all on the Main Line, and Laflin Street Substation on the Blue Island Branch. The length of route on the Main Line is about 29 miles and on the Blue Island Branch about three miles. The group serves 27 switches with 110 functions. In addition to the present 324 operating and indicating functions are 25 functions used for checking of indications at will.

All supervisory line wires are in telephone cables owned by the Railroad Company and installed along the right-of-way. Most of the wire is 16-gauge, but a small amount is 19-gauge. All wires, including laterals to stations, are in lead-covered cables, those on the north end of the terminal being in underground duct lines and the remainder being run overhead on catenary structures or on wood pole lines. Lines are thus free from inductive troubles, and have a maximum of protection from weather conditions and outside obstructions likely to cause grounds, short circuits, etc.

The groups and lines have been laid out to have sufficient capacity for the control of facilities for the freight and through passenger electrification contemplated, which will involve at least twice the amount of equipment described above.

Supervisory Control in Substations

Supervisory control apparatus installed in substations is owned by the Railroad Company and the supervisory devices proper are located upon panels separate from the 1500-volt feeder trucks. Certain auxiliary relays required in connection with the control of the truck are mounted directly upon the feeder truck panel, and the feeder trucks retain the ordinary hand control devices for the use of the substation operator. The control is so arranged that both the power supervisor and the substation operator must concur in closing by setting their respective devices in the closed position, but either party can open the breaker at will. Normally, complete control may be retained by the power supervisor, but the substation operator can trip the breaker in case an emergency should arise. He may also take over control of the breaker if requested to do so by the power supervisor. "Anti-pump" relays are required as auxiliary to the supervisory control feature to prevent the breaker closing and tripping repeatedly in case it should be closed upon a short circuit. These devices lock the breaker open when it trips automatically, and the power supervisor must perform a "trip" operation in order to reset the circuits for another attempt at closing. The closing operation may then be repeated at once.

Tie Station Supervisory Control

The supervisory equipment proper is identical to that used in substations and is mounted upon switchboard panels separate from feeder trucks (Fig. 5).

Auxiliary relays are also mounted upon feeder truck panels, and three-control breakers include anti-pump devices similar to those used for substation breakers.

Substation and tie station supervisory equipment are operated by means of a 24-volt tap from the station 120-volt lead storage battery. The power requirement for the supervisory control is very small, being required only for driving the one-twentieth horse-power motor of the motor sending key and for energizing the telephone type supervisory relays, all of which operate only when indications are being sent. The 24-volt tap is also drained slightly by the sending of the codes on the line wires, connections being arranged so that this battery serves during actual operation as a booster in series with the 192-volt storage battery at the supervisor's office.

Operation of Supervisory Devices

The selectors are operated by codes of impulses, each code consisting of three groups of impulses sent over two of the line wires. Each selector has four contact points corresponding to four different codes and thus controls four functions. Any selector will respond only to a specified basic code; for example, 8-3. This selector will then operate upon four codes based on these initial impulses; namely, 8-3-6, 8-3-8, 8-3-10, and 8-3-12. Operating keys in the power supervisor's cabinets govern the groups of impulses by closing contacts intermittently. They are set in each case for the established code and this code is sent simply upon turning the key and allowing it to return by spring action. About eight seconds is required for each code sent or received.

Indication from the substation to the supervisor's office is also performed by means of a code, but in this case the code must be sent by means of a fractional horse-power motor driving a code wheel similar to the hand-operated key. One driving motor serves four breakers (8 indications) by driving four separate code wheels through frictional clutches, which normally are held by latches while the clutches slip. Through suitable intermediate relays, interlocks upon circuit breakers start the driving motor and release the proper code wheel to send the code established for the indication required. Selectors at the supervisor's office which receive these impulses are identical with those in substations for operation of equipment, but by use of a scheme using polarized impulses, each selector governs eight indications instead of only four.

Lockout relays are arranged in the supervisor's office and substations so that it is impossible for two codes to be sent simultaneously on the line wires. These relays prevent a motor key starting while other codes are being sent, and cut off circuits from hand-operated keys. They also prevent two motors starting simultaneously. The relays, in effect, store up indications at substations and send them in successively when a number of operations occur at one time. Pilot lights upon the supervisor's key and lamp cabinets indicate when the group is locked out so that the supervisor will not perform operations at such times. An audible signal is also given while codes are coming in, to direct the supervisor's attention. Operation by the supervisor would, however, not cause any failures of codes coming in, since lockout devices are adequate to prevent any conflict.

Checking of Substation Equipment

In order that the supervisor may at any time check the conditions of any circuit breakers, thereby also checking the proper performance of the supervisory control, checking keys are included in the supervisor's lamp and key cabinets. Each key, through the operation of a selector in the substation, governs one motor key which in turn sends indications for four breakers. Checking consists of sending a reversed indication and then the correct indication for each device connected with the motor key governed, leaving the supervisor's lamps with the correct indication.

Group Operation

The supervisory control lends itself to certain group operation of circuit breakers and this has already been tried with success for the clearing or closing of a number of selected breakers by operation of one key only. This saves time in operation since about eight seconds is required for each code sent or received. The application is limited by the arrangement of codes and its use also tends to restrict the total number of codes that may be used upon one supervisory group.

Operating Results

Although this type of control has been used previously on a number of railway installations, this constitutes the largest application of the selector control yet made. In troubles involving a large number of circuit breakers, speed of operation would be somewhat greater by other more elaborate and more expensive systems of supervisory control available, and with a greater number of line wires. In general, however, this control has proved adequate for operating conditions on the Illinois Central system, and has given prompt and reliable service. Apparatus faults have not been excessive. There have been a few cases of troubles with line wires, although these have not been excessive in view of the fact that the rather extensive battery control wiring in substations and tie stations is tied together through the use of common batteries.

Rail Bonding of the Illinois Central Electrification

Preliminary Service Tests—Determination of Most Suitable Bond—Bonding Additional Tracks Not Electrified—Impedance Bonds—Special Bonding

By R. M. ALLEN
Power Supervisor, Chicago Terminal Improvement

R. M. ALLEN

AS there is considerable variation in the form of rail bonds and the method of applying them, the selection of the type best suited for a particular installation requires careful study of operating and maintenance conditions. The requirements are: the maintaining of a low-resistance contact between adjacent rail ends that will withstand the constant pounding of cars passing over the rail joints and permit of the expansion and contraction due to extreme changes in temperature, without appreciably interfering with the upkeep of the rail joints, such as the removal of splice bars, tightening of bolts, etc.

To facilitate the selection of the standard joint bond best suited for the Chicago Terminal, a test installation of 1600 bonds of seven different types was made on the terminal tracks in May, 1924. These bonds were closely observed, and in March, 1925, their resistance was measured. A careful study was made of the average resistance of each type of bond, the number of failures and their causes, obstruction to track repairs, etc., on the type of rail joint used by the Illinois Central. With this information and analyses of the economy and current capacity of the various types of bonds, a standard joint bond was selected.

The economic investigations consisted of determining the annual charges, including cost of energy loss in the return circuit, maintenance and depreciation, and interest on initial investment.

The resistance losses in the return circuit were estimated for various sizes and types of rail bonds. The cost of these energy losses were then calculated, assuming the cost per kilowatt-hour to be that derived from the total electrical energy used for traction purposes. The cost of these losses was added to the estimated maintenance and depreciation costs and interest on the investment. Fig. 1 is a set of curves showing the variation of these annual charges with varying bond size and with two different types of bonds, *viz.*, the short gas-weld type and the 30-in.

expanded pin-terminal type. It was concluded from a study of this curve that the energy losses in the return circuit would not be decreased materially by using bonds of larger copper cross-section than a No. 2/0 A.W.G. size. The interest and maintenance (including depreciation), however, increase rapidly with the size of bond. The total annual charges, therefore, will be a minimum for a certain size of bond, as seen in Fig. 1. The curves also show that the annual charge for the 30-in. pin-terminal type of bond is considerably greater than for the short bond.

The study of the current-carrying capacity of various sizes and types of bonds was thorough. Temperature limits were considered carefully, allowance being made for the fact that the bonds would be made of flexible annealed copper and could therefore be subjected to higher temperatures than are advisable for hard-drawn copper or insulated cables. Also, the effect of the close contact of the bond with the rail was considered; the conduction of heat from the bonds into the rails through the bond terminals and through the side contact being an important factor in cooling the bond. The magnitude of the rail currents was determined, as was also the minimum size of bond necessary to carry the maximum rail current that will exist in 1932, assuming two bonded rails per track in all cases. (Where single-rail bonding of a track is necessary, double-bonding per joint was assumed.)

The sizes of bonds decided upon as being of the smallest cross-section necessary to carry the current were No. 4/0 A.W.G. (212,000 cir. mils) for the short gas-weld type and 300,000 cir. mils for the 30-inch pin-terminal type.

Since the sizes of bonds selected for current-carrying capacity were larger than the sizes indicated to be most economical in annual charges, current-carrying capacity became the determining factor. The 30-in. pin-terminal bond was discarded in favor of the short gas-weld bond for economic reasons. Where long bonds are necessary, as in the bonding of special track work, 300,000 cir. mil flexible copper cable was decided upon as the conductor with the terminals welded on in the same way as for the short bonds.

Fig. 2 is a photograph of the standard joint bond first selected. The cable is No. 4/0, 127-strand copper, 7 in. between terminals when formed and 8½ in. between terminals unformed. The terminals are of copper tubing, 2½ in. long, bell-shaped where the cable enters. Both the terminals and the ends of the copper strands are welded to the rails with oxy-acetylene gas, a No. 10 gas tip being used. The bond is placed slightly to one side of the joint to clear the track wrench.

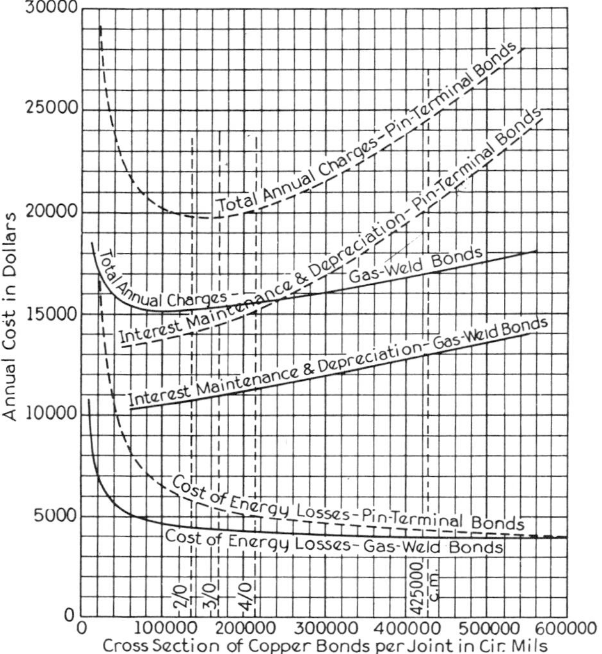

Fig. 1. Curves of Operational Costs of the 30-in. Pin-terminal and the 7-in. Gas-weld Types of Bond, Plotted to Aid in the Selection of the Bonds for the Suburban Tracks Only

These bonds however were found to be subject to damage due to boys turning the loop up over the rail so that trains ran over them. All replacements are therefore being made with standard U-type bonds, an example of which is shown in Fig. 3. The bond cable consists of two No. 1 A.W.G. flexible conductors, with an unformed length of 8 in. The terminals are of steel with copper sleeves.

Approximately 45,000 standard joint bonds were used, bonding 156 track miles.

One of the first considerations in the design of the negative return was the number of tracks to be bonded. The initial electrification, recently completed, included only the suburban tracks. Two freight tracks and two through-passenger tracks, extending the full length of the terminal, are to be electrified later. The bonding of these non-electrified tracks in order to utilize as many rails as possible in the return circuit was investigated and found advisable in

some sections due to voltage drop which was limited by electrolysis consideration. Increasing the size of rail bond does not materially affect the voltage drop because the resistance of the short bond is small compared to the resistance of the 33-ft. rails.

The bonding of additional tracks, not electrified, furnishes supplementary negative feeders connected to the rails of electrified tracks at cross bonds, thus

Fig. 2. Type of Standard Rail Joint Bond Later Superseded by the Type Shown in Fig. 3

utilizing the conductivity of the additional rails. No other supplementary feeders were used. The standard rails used by the Illinois Central weigh 90 lb. per yard and have an equivalent copper conductivity of approximately 936,000 cir. mils each, or 1,872,000 cir. mils per track.

Fig. 3. U-type Rail Joint Bond Eventually Selected as Standard

Another factor affecting the decision to bond additional tracks, not electrified, in certain sections, was the desire to use one standard size of bond throughout the terminal. In the sections where non-electrified tracks were bonded, the rail currents were greatest and a larger bond for standard rail joints would have been necessary than for other sections.

Fig. 4 is a diagram showing the bonded tracks.

Impedance Bonds

On all main-line tracks the rails are a part of the automatic signal circuits which are of 60-cycle alternating current. At intervals of approximately 2000 ft., the rail joints are insulated, separating adjacent signal blocks. The negative return must of course be continuous around these joints. This is accomplished by an impedance bond which consists of two coils of copper having low resistance and high reactance.

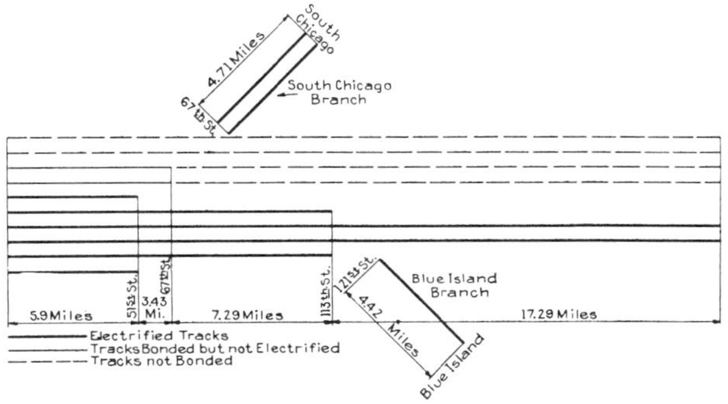

Fig. 4. Diagram of the Bonded and Not-bonded Tracks of the Chicago Terminal

Such a coil in a d-c. circuit would act as a choke coil. However, the traction current in each rail is equal and in the same direction, but in opposite directions through the two halves of the impedance bond. That is, the direct current flows from the neutral point of the impedance bond in both directions or from both directions to the neutral point of the impedance bond. The magnetizing effect of the direct current is therefore neutralized as long as the bonding is maintained in good condition and the current remains equal in the two rails.

Bonding of Special Track Work

At points where there is a large amount of special track work the switching of trains is controlled from interlocking towers. Within the limits of interlocking towers the signal blocks are short and insulated joints frequent, and the cost of impedance bonds at these points would be very large. Also the leakage of signal current through so many impedance bonds would be too great.

Single-rail track circuit was therefore resorted to within the limits of interlocking plants. One rail is used for traction energy without insulated joints and both rails used for signal circuits with insulated joints in only one rail. Each rail joint on the rail used for traction current is bonded with two standard bonds to obtain double current capacity. As previously stated, this does not decrease the voltage drop proportionally.

The bonding of frogs, switches, slip switches, and all special track work was done with 300,000-cir. mil bare cables in loom, taped at the terminal. In some cases where very long bonds were necessary, parkway cable was used and buried two feet under ground. To prevent excessive leakage of signal current and also to reduce electrolysis to a minimum, all special bonds were carefully insulated.

As far as was practical, every piece of special track work was carefully bonded for two reasons; to minimize the potential difference between rail and ground, thereby reducing electrolysis, and to maintain automatic signal protection against the breaking or removal of any special track work or part of it. Special terminals, and tools for applying them in the field, were designed. Most of the special bonds were cut and terminals applied in the storehouse, however.

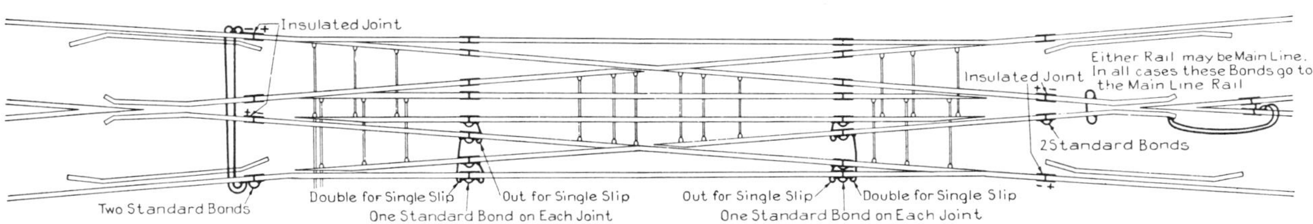

Fig. 5. Layout of Typical Slip-switch Bonding for Single-rail Track Circuit

Impedance bonds of 500- and 1000-amp. capacity were used in this installation, the capacity being expressed in amperes per rail.

The connections of the impedance bonds to the rails were made with 300,000-cir. mil bare cable covered with standard wood trunking when run along track, and in loom fastened to the side of a cross tie when run across track. The cable for these connections was cut and terminals applied in the storeroom, the same kind of terminal being used as for other special bonds. The rail end of the connection was welded to the rail and the other end bolted to the impedance bond, terminals being supplied on the impedance bond.

In most cases slip switches are operated from interlocking towers and are therefore bonded for single-rail track circuit. This increased the necessity of bonding every piece of track work. In double-rail track circuit, if a small piece of rail were not bonded, the other rail would supply a return circuit. In the bonding of slip switches the following conditions had to be obtained: All rails bonded must have a continuous circuit through the switch from all four tracks, and all main circuits double bonded. Fig. 5 shows the bonding of a double slip switch. It will be noticed in the illustration that some joints have only one bond. Where such is the case the single bond either feeds a short piece of rail and is not a part of the main circuit, or a parallel path is provided in the main circuit through another rail.

At the special track work where the Illinois Central crosses street railways, signal protection is impossible. Following the practice of the signal department, a bond was carried around street railway crossings. One 500,000-cir. mil parkway cable for each rail was used, terminating in a pothead at each end and attached to the rail with two 300,000-cir. mil, 127-strand bare cables. The pothead consists of a concrete pier for anchoring the parkway cable,

Structure Bonds

The overhead wires being supported by steel structures, it was necessary to connect every structure to the rail for protection. No. 1 parkway cable was used for this purpose, one end of which was welded to the rail and the other to the structure.

Each end of the structure bond was taped and coated with insulating paint to keep moisture from getting into the parkway cable. A one-foot loop was left in the cable at the rail end of the structure bonds to allow for movement of the rail.

Fig. 6. Concrete Potheads for Connection Between Parkway Cable and Rails

a terminal for the parkway and 300,000-cir. mil rail connections, and a space around the cable where the insulation is cut back and the space is filled with insulating compound, keeping moisture out of the insulation. The same type of terminal was used in all cases where 500,000- or 1,000,000-cir. mil parkway cable was connected to the rail except where such connections were made through an impedance bond. An installation of six of these potheads is shown in Fig. 6.

To reduce the potential between rails and ground at street railway crossings, a single impedance bond was installed on one track with the center point connected to the special track work. As far as possible, all parts of the crossing were then bonded together and a return circuit thereby established for a train anywhere on the crossing.

Cross Bonds and Negative Feeder Connections

Cross bonds, or bonds connecting the rails of all bonded tracks together, were installed at alternate signal bridges. The cross bonds are 500,000- and 1,000,000-cir. mil parkway cable connected to the neutral point of impedance bonds, Economically, cross bonds could have been placed much closer together but the effect on the signal circuit would not permit.

At points opposite the substation, connections for negative feeders were made to the neutral of impedance bonds, one to each track, and with 1,000,000-cir. mil parkway cables, buried two feet under ground. The other ends of these cables connected to a negative bus in a manhole on the right-of-way, this bus connecting to the substation negative bus by 2,000,000-cir. mil lead-covered cable run in duct lines.

Selecting the Traction Motors for the Illinois Central Electrification

Service Requirements—Ingenious Analysis of Motor Ratings *vs.* Train Weights for Most Severe Service
Prior to Availability of Car Weights—Determination of Final Motor Specifications—
Actual Schedules Exceed Calculated Schedules

By W. P. MONROE

Assistant Engineer, Chicago Terminal Improvement.

W. P. MONROE

THE suburban service of the Illinois Central in Chicago was considered extensive enough to warrant the purchasing of traction motors designed especially for its requirements. The motors would thus embody all the latest approved features, the development costs when spread over a large quantity of motors would not be excessive, and the obvious advantages of using a motor which exactly fits the requirements would be gained. Estimates indicated that motor equipments would be necessary for at least 260 cars in 1926, and for over 300 cars in 1932.

The classes of service to be electrified were known as local, express, and special. The local trains made station stops every 0.6 mile on the average. Express trains made high-speed non-stop runs up to 5.8 miles in length, followed by local runs, the entire trips averaging 1.0 mile between stops. The specials averaged 1.7 miles between station stops, but all trains made one or two fast non-stop runs of from 5.8 to 14 miles in length. On account of the advantage of flexibility in using interchangeable equipment, it was decided to use the same motors with the same gear ratios in all these classes of service, thus making all car equipment standard. The motors as applied must therefore be able both to acceler-ate the cars rapidly in order to provide a fast local schedule, and to propel the cars at a high balancing speed on long runs to satisfy the fast schedules of the express and special trains. In both cases, the requirements were set so as to shorten the then existing steam schedules very materially. Table I is a comparison of the steam schedules with the electric schedules as set up for a typical service and those actually obtained after electrification.

Rated Voltage

The 1500-volt direct-current system of electrification made possible the use of either 1500-volt or 750-volt motors, the latter connected in groups of two in series and insulated for 1500 volts. A careful study of different schemes of making up trains resulted in the decision to compose all trains of standard units, each unit consisting of a motor car and trailer car semi-permanently coupled, the car bodies to be identical in seating capacity and appearance, but the motor car to be equipped with four 750-volt motors (insulated for 1500 volts), one to each axle. This arrangement was adopted because the estimates showed it to be the most economical scheme. It was also concluded to be the most reliable scheme, although the manufacturers guaranteed the absolute reliability of the straight 1500-volt motor.

TABLE I
STEAM AND ELECTRIC SCHEDULES FOR MATTESON TRAINS

Distance from Randolph Street to Matteson 27.93 Miles

	STEAM SCHEDULES (1925)		ELECTRIC SCHEDULE REQUIREMENTS			ELECTRIC SCHEDULES ACTUALLY OBTAINED		
	No. of Intermediate Stops	Schedule Time in Minutes	No. of Intermediate Stops	Schedule Time in Minutes	Per Cent Decrease in Time Electricity vs. Steam	No. of Intermediate Stops	Schedule Time in Minutes	Per Cent Decrease in Time, Electricity vs. Steam
Local....................	34	80.0	33	72.5	9.4	*36	68.5	14.4
Express..................	25	79.0	25	63.5	19.6	*28	64.7	18.1
Special..................	14	64.5	13	53.0	17.8	*15	53.0	17.8
Golf Special.............	9	60.0	8	46.0	23.3	8	45.7	23.8

* A short time previous to starting electric operation, the station stops were increased to the numbers shown.

Operating Characteristics

As a result of an early but detailed study of the schedule requirements of electrified Illinois Central service, the decision to operate with an acceleration rate of 1.5 miles per hour per second, a balancing speed of 57 miles per hour, and a braking rate of 1.75 miles per hour per second was reached. These operating characteristics were found to be the most econom-

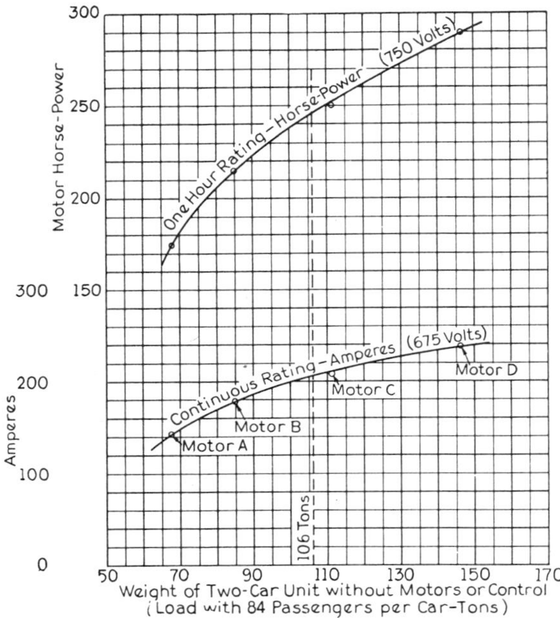

Fig. 1. Curves Plotted from Preliminary Calculations Made in Selecting Traction Motors for Suburban Service

Motor *A*—175 h.p. Motor *C*—250 h.p.
Motor *B*—215 h.p. Motor *D*—290 h.p.

Conditions: Motors to operate continuously in South Chicago local service, without coasting, and with two minutes' layover at terminals. R. m. s. current to equal continuous rating.

Average train—6 cars Wheel diameter—36 in.
Acceleration—1.5 m.p.h.p.s. Balancing speed—57 m.p.h.
Braking—1.75 m.p.h.p.s. Volts per motor—675

ical in meeting all the requirements of all the services while allowing a liberal margin for making up time and providing for coasting to save energy. They were adopted as fundamental requirements of the motor equipment.

Most Severe Service

The capacity of the motor to be specified was considered to depend upon the heating caused by the most severe service the motor had to furnish, commutation and other limits being temporarily neglected. All services were investigated carefully from this point of view. The manufacturers were asked for motor characteristic curves for a 750-volt d-c. railway motor (insulated for 1500 volts) of their latest recommended design for rapid-transit service, and of horse-power capacity which was judged to be approximately that which would ultimately be selected. This motor, which was of a field-control type, was applied on paper to each service, assuming the approximate weight of train and using an accelerating current and gear ratio to give the prescribed acceleration and balancing speed. A curve sheet

similar to Fig. 5 but including more information was drawn up from detailed speed-time calculations for a six-car train with full seated load. By reading from these curves the running time and (amperes) ^{2}— seconds for every run[1] in each service and summing them up, allowing for stopping times and layover, the r.m.s. current of each service was calculated. The trains were considered to be run without coasting because such operation will exist when trains are late and are making up time, this procedure being agreed upon when the requirements were set up. Also, a layover of two minutes was allowed at terminals, this time also being agreed upon as the minimum required. The class of service causing the highest motor r.m.s. current under these conditions was found to be the South Chicago local service. A motor performing satisfactorily in this service without overheating was desired.

Method Used for Determination of Ratings

The design of the cars, at this time, had not reached a stage where a close estimate of their weight, when built, was possible. Search was being made for lightweight materials, and other schemes for cutting down car weight were being discussed. The determination of motor ratings had to proceed without delay, however, in order that the motor specifications would be ready at the same time as the car specifications. A method was devised whereby the hourly and continuous ratings, as well as the weights and approximate costs, of the motors could be very quickly ascertained when an accurate estimate of car weight finally became available.

Fig. 2. General Electric GE-285A Traction Motor Selected for Suburban Service

Hourly rating—250 h.p. at 750 volts
Continuous rating—215 amp. at 675 volts
Weight with gears and gear case—7080 lb.
Weight of motor alone—6400 lb.
Type of ventilation—Self, multiple
Guaranteed safe peripheral speed of armature—8400 ft. per min.
Diameter of armature—18.5 in.
Gear ratio on I.C.R.R.—60/21

The method of motor determination which was used depends upon the apparent law of similitude which exists between the accelerating current of a motor and its root-mean-square current for a

[1] By "run" is meant a single train movement from start to stop.

particular length of no-coast run. The ratio of the accelerating current to the r.m.s. current was found to be practically a constant for direct-current field-control motors of similar design applied to various weights of car equipment, but with control and gear ratio adjusted for the same acceleration rate and balancing speed. This relation proved out by trial with a number of different-sized motors and assumed equipment weights covering a wide range. In the investigation which determined the most severe service, this ratio was found for the specified no-coast South Chicago local trip. It was assumed, then, that this ratio would also hold for all motors of the same general design when applied to this service. The accelerating current entering into the ratio was the short-field current giving the tractive effort necessary for 1.5 miles per hour per second acceleration. If a motor application is made to the most severe service in such a way that the accelerating current bears the same ratio to the continuous rating as the ratio determined as described, then the r.m.s. current in the service will equal the continuous rating of the motor, one of the conditions desired.

The manufacturers were asked for preliminary specifications and characteristic curves for several motors of their recommended design, but varying in horse power from 175 to 300. These motors were each applied to the most severe service in such a way that their continuous ratings were equal to their respective r.m.s. currents in this service. In order to make these motors fit the service, all with the same accelerating rate and balancing speed, the weights of the car equipments had to be varied, the smaller

Fig. 3. Westinghouse 587-D-5 Traction Motor Selected
for Suburban Service

Hourly rating—250 h.p. at 750 volts
Continuous rating—210 amp. at 675 volts
Weight with gears and gear case—6905 lb.
Weight of motor alone—6425 lb.
Type of ventilation—Self, multiple (dual type)
Guaranteed safe peripheral speed of armature—8400 ft. per min.
Diameter of armature—18.5 in.
Gear ratio on I.C.R.R.—60/21
Lubrication—Oil sealed

motors propelling the lighter cars. The proper weight of car for each motor was determined as follows:

Let R = ratio of short-field accelerating current to r.m.s. current for the service.

g' = Gear ratio as used by the manufacturer in plotting the motor characteristic curves.

g = New gear ratio which is to be found for correct application of motor in most severe service.

F_o = Starting tractive effort in lb. per motor.

F'_o = Starting tractive effort per motor as read from characteristic curve, with gear ratio g', and for starting current equal to $R \times$ continuous rating.

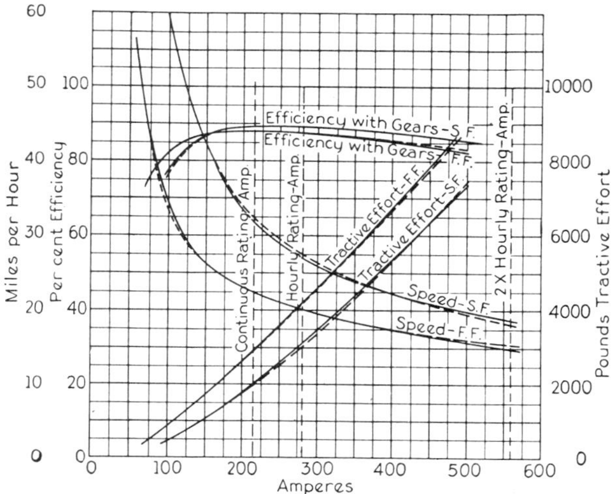

Fig. 4. Characteristic Curves of Manufactured Motor, GE-285A, in Full Lines and Design Motor, GEZ-1231, in Dotted. The motors are rated 750/1500 volts but the curves are plotted for 675 volts

Gear—60 teeth   Reduction—2.857
Pinion—21 teeth   Wheel dia.—36 in.
R.p.m. 26.7 × m.p.h.

a_o = Acceleration rate (in this case 1.5 m.p. h.p.s.)

W = Weight of car equipment per motor for correct application, in tons,—to be found.

Assuming 10 lb. per ton to be the train resistance during the acceleration period, [2]

$$a_o = \frac{F_o - 10\,W}{100\,W} = \frac{F'_o \dfrac{g}{g'} - 10\,W}{100\,W}$$

or

$$W = \frac{F'_o\,g}{(100a_o + 10)g'} \tag{1}$$

If F_f = tractive effort of motor for balancing speed (gear ratio, g).

V_f = balancing speed in m.p.h.

and n = number of motors in train,

then

$$F_f = 4W + \frac{W\,V_f}{6} + \frac{V_f^2}{3n} \tag{2}$$

for Sprague's train resistance formula.

Let F'_f and V'_f equal motor tractive effort and speed, respectively, for same current as F_f and V_f, but for gear ratio g'.

Then

$$\frac{F_f}{F'_f} = \frac{V'_f}{V_f} = \frac{g}{g'} \tag{3}$$

____

[2] During straight-line acceleration the train resistance was assumed constant at the value determined for the speed at the end of this period, thus allowing for high journal friction at the start.

Substituting in equation (2)

$$F'_f = W \frac{g'}{g}\left(4 + \frac{V_f}{6}\right) + \frac{V^3_f}{3nV'_f} \qquad (4)$$

Substituting (1) equation in equation (4)

$$F'_f = \frac{F'_o}{100a_o + 10}\left(4 + \frac{V_f}{6}\right) + \frac{V^3_f}{3nV'_f} \qquad (5)$$

All the terms in equation (5) are known except F'_f and V'_f. This equation, therefore, is a function of F'_f in terms of V'_f for the given conditions. The manufacturer's motor characteristic curve of tractive effort plotted against speed also furnishes a relation between F'_f and V'_f. If this curve and equation (5) are solved

If nW is found in this way for each of the motors submitted, a curve can be plotted of the horse-power ratings against the weights of train for application to the most severe service such that the r.m.s. current equals the continuous rating of each motor. This curve will be smooth if the motors are of the same design and if they are rated in the same way.

Application of Method

The foregoing procedure was carried through with motors of two manufacturers. Table II contains the calculations for four such motors. Item (7) in the table shows that the ratio of short-field accelerating

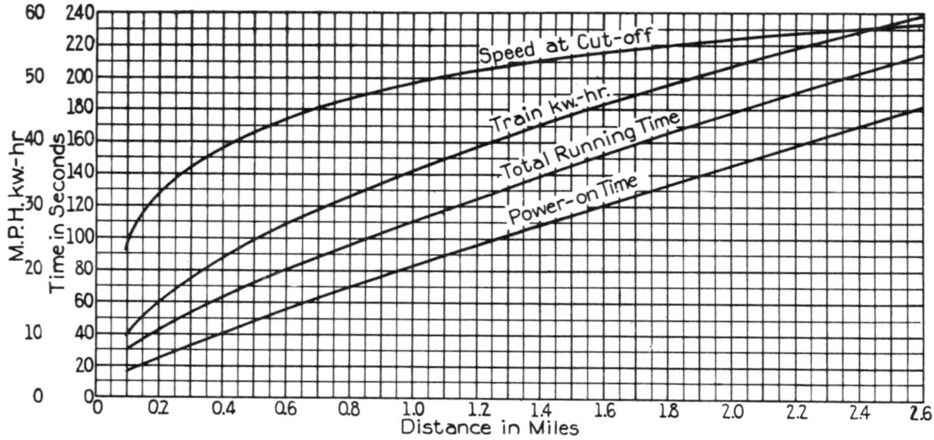

Fig. 5. No-coast Train Characteristic Curves

Six-car multiple-unit train (3 motor and 3 trailer cars)   Trailer weight—50.3 tons (with passengers)
Trolley voltage—1350 volts   Wheel diameter—36 in.   Acceleration—1.5 m.p.h.p.s. Braking—1.75 m.p.h.p.s.
Motor car weight—76.5 tons (with passengers)   Train resistance by Davis formula

as if they were simultaneous equations, the solution being easily obtained graphically, the values of F'_f and V'_f thus found can be substituted in equation (3) to get g. Substitutions can then be made in equation (1) and W obtained. This value of W multiplied by n gives the weight of train for the correct application of the motor from the heating standpoint.

current to the r.m.s. current of the most severe service, found previously to be 2.103, was used to obtain the accelerating currents from the known continuous ratings of the motors. Items (8) and (9) are a check to determine if the accelerating currents are within the safe commutating limits of the motors; if they were not within the limits, the motors would have

TABLE II

APPLICATION OF RAILWAY MOTORS TO SOUTH CHICAGO LOCAL SERVICE

Determination of Car Weights and Gear Ratios for Proper Application of Four Typical Motors

Item	(1)	Motor designation	Motor A	Motor B	Motor C	Motor D
"	(2)	Nominal rating, horsepower (750 volts)	175	215	250	290
"	(3)	Continuous rating, amp. (675 volts)	143	178	208	238
"	(4)	Hourly rating, amp. (750 volts)	192	240	280	320
"	(5)	Gear ratio for characteristic curves at hand, g'	3.26	2.86	2.37	2.625
"	(6)	Wheel diameter, inches	36	36	36	36
"	(7)	Short-field accelerating current = 2.103 × continuous rating	301	375	437	501
"	(8)	Corresponding full-field accelerating current, same tractive effort	252	309	360	423
"	(9)	Maximum full-field accelerating current for good commutation	265	330	360	440
		Comparison with Item (8)	O.K.	O.K.	O.K.	O.K.
"	(10)	Gross tractive effort for current of Item (7), read from curve = F'_o =	3630	4400	4900	6210
"	(11)	Solution of equation (5) with motor characteristics { V'_f =	51.9	52.4	60.0	60.9
		{ F'_f =	402	470	500	608
"	(12)	New gear ratio, from equation (3)	2.965	2.630	2.495	2.802
"	(13)	Train weight per motor, from equation (1), tons	20.62	25.28	32.30	41.45
"	(14)	Weight of loaded 2-car unit = $4W$ =	82.48	101.12	129.0	165.8
"	(15)	Weight of motors and control, tons	14.6	16.39	17.5	19.79
"	(16)	Weight of loaded 2-car unit without motors and control	67.88	84.73	111.5	146.01
		Check on Safe Speed				
"	(17)	Safe armature speed, r.p.m.	1880	1660	1500	1670
"	(18)	Safe corresponding train speed, m.p.h.	67.9	67.6	64.3	63.9
		Check on Calculations				
"	(19)	Tractive effort at 57 m.p.h. from $F'_f g/g' = F_f$ =	366	432	526	649
"	(20)	Train resistance from Sprague's formula (per motor)	372	435	528	650

had to be discarded or the acceleration rate lowered. In Item (16) is calculated the weight of a 2-car unit without motors and control, but with seated load, and these weights were used in plotting the horsepower and continuous rating curves in Fig. 1. The weight without motors and control is of greater convenience in computing than the total weight of the train. Items (17) and (18) are a check to determine if the motor, as applied, will operate within the safe armature speeds. Items (19) and (20) are a check on the accuracy of the calculations by comparing the balancing-speed train resistance, as read from a curve, with the calculated tractive effort, F_f.

Final Selection

When the final motor specifications were ready, they were given to the manufacturers who then submitted complete data on their proposed motors. They were investigated and found satisfactory. Contracts were then let for 263 General Electric motors and 262 Westinghouse motors.

When manufactured, the General Electric motor was designated GE 285-A, and the Westinghouse motor 587-D-5. The GE 285-A motor characteristic curves as obtained by test are shown in Fig. 4, compared with the guaranteed characteristics of the design motor GE Z-1231, as finally approved.

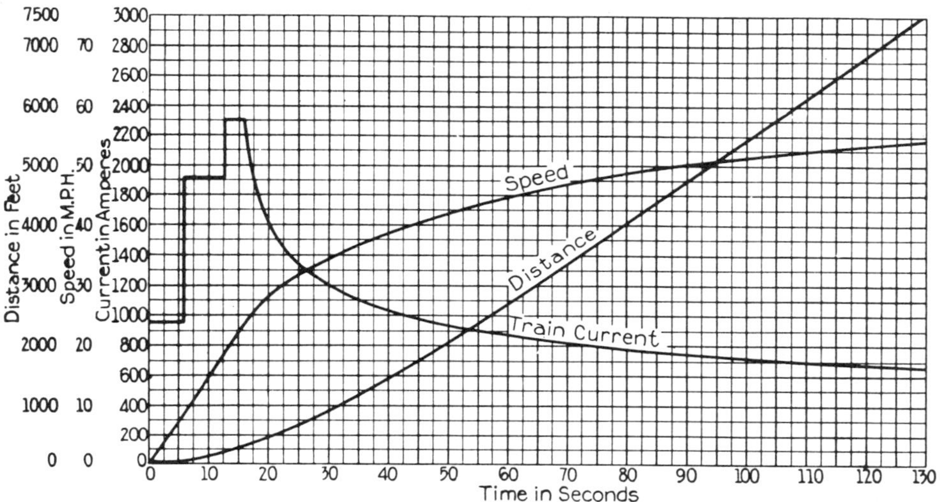

Fig. 6. Speed-time Train Characteristic Curves
Same conditions as named in Fig. 5.

Final Determination of Capacity

When the car design had reached the specification stage and an accurate estimate of car weight became available, the motor horse power and continuous rating were read from the curves in Fig. 1. This estimated weight was 106 tons for a loaded 2-car unit without motors and control. The horse power read from the curve for this weight is 246 at 750 volts. This figure was rounded to 250 h.p. for the specifications. (The actual weight of an Illinois Central electric 2-car unit when built was found to be 108.8 tons without motors and control, but including seated passenger load.)

Ventilation and Mechanical Details

Most of the mechanical details of the motors were decided upon independently of the calculations of motor capacity, the manufacturers' recommendations being followed in most cases. The type of ventilation, however, since it affects the ratings, was carefully considered before asking for the performance characteristics of the preliminary motors. The type approved was the kind of self ventilation known as "multiple ventilation."

Actual Operation

It is of interest that in actual operation the motors drive the trains at a balancing speed somewhat in excess of 57 miles per hour. Since the motor characteristics were carefully verified by complete factory tests, it is concluded that the train resistance used in the calculations is too large. The multiple-unit train resistance as given by W. J. Davis, Jr.,[3] seems to be nearly correct for Illinois Central trains. Table I shows to what extent the actual schedules are faster than the calculated schedules. The additional station stops, added since the required schedules were agreed upon, somewhat offset the effect of this higher balancing speed.

Figs. 5 and 6 are train characteristics calculated from the motor speed and tractive effort curves obtained from actual test data and using the Davis' train-resistance formulas. These calculated train characteristics are very close to those of actual operation as shown by observation.

(3) "The Tractive Resistance of Electric Locomotives and Cars", W. J. Davis, Jr., GENERAL ELECTRIC REVIEW, Oct. 1926, p. 685.

Underground Conduit System for Telephone, Telegraph and Signal Cables of the Illinois Central Electrification

Multiple-duct Conduits Used—411,410 Duct Feet Now Installed—Most Manholes Precast—Handholes and Other Accommodations for Laterals—Drainage Problem

By C. P. TRUEAX

Assistant Engineer, Chicago Terminal Improvement

C. P. TRUEAX

IN connection with the Illinois Central electrification, the railroad's plans contemplate the installation of an underground conduit system extending from South Water Street (the downtown terminal) to a point south of the Blue Island Railroad junction with the main line at 120th Place, a distance of 15.25 miles. This conduit will carry all low-voltage communication circuits; *i.e.*, telephone, telegraph, signal control, and other miscellaneous circuits such as supervisory control for substation and tie-station operation.

Up to the present time, work has been completed and cables have been pulled in and placed in service from 21st Street to 80th Street, from 93rd Street to 100th Street, and a short stretch under the Blue Island Railroad junction with the main line at 120th Place.

between opposite surfaces. Within the interlocking plant limits the number of ducts varies, depending upon the number of cables to be used. These sections range in duct numbers from 9 to 20, multiple-duct conduit being used in all cases to secure the advantages of first-cost economy, constructive simplicity, and ease in pulling cables. The linear and duct feet of the various sections of multiple-duct conduit installed are given in Table I.

With a track layout utilizing to a maximum the entire width of right-of-way, it was necessary to locate the conduit line between tracks having a spacing of thirteen feet. At several points along the right-of-way, offsets had to be made in the line to transfer it to another space between tracks in order to avoid obstructions such as suburban

Fig. 1. A Pile of Four-duct Multiple Vitrified-clay Conduit Delivered to the Site of the Work

With the exception of portions within the limits of interlocking plants, the conduit consists of 8 ducts, made up of two 4-duct multiple salt-glazed vitrified-clay conduit with square duct holes from $3\frac{1}{4}$ to $3\frac{1}{2}$ in.

station platforms and stairs and catenary structure foundations.

The vitrified-clay conduit is encased in a 1:3:5 mixture concrete protection having a thickness where parallel to tracks of four inches on the bottom, three inches on the sides, and three inches on the top. Where crossing under tracks the top protection is increased to six inches and reinforced with ½-in. reinforcement bars with longitudinal bars spaced one foot three inches and transverse bars spaced six inches.

At frequent intervals along the right-of-way there are subways having a concrete deck with track ballast laid directly on it. Where the conduit line crosses over these subways the concrete protection is laid on the subway deck and the top and side protection is increased and reinforced in the same manner as where crossing under tracks in order to protect the conduit in case of derailment. At locations where conduit with a large number of ducts crosses over subways, the sections are laid up in such a manner as to obtain an overall shape with upper corners bevelled in order to keep outside the clearance line.

Where the conduit is parallel to tracks, the depth varies from two feet to two feet eight inches from base of rail to top of concrete protection. On level roadbed the two-feet eight-inch depth is at manholes

Manholes are placed at an average spacing of 500 ft. for pulling and splicing chambers and for connecting and taking off laterals. Except for a few important locations where larger manholes, cast in place, are required, precast reinforced concrete manholes are used throughout. The use of precast manholes

Fig. 3. Manholes, Conduit, and Other Material Distributed Along the Right-of-way Prior to Installation

effected a decided saving over the cast-in-place type, not only in the cost of material but in the labor of installation.

In the close working quarters between tracks, excavations were made and the precast manholes lowered in place under heavy traffic conditions that would be very detrimental to the proper setting of the concrete of cast-in-place manholes due to the continual vibrations caused by passing trains.

Fig. 2. Precast Reinforced Concrete Manhole Showing Knockout for Laterals

with the conduit sloping both ways from a high point midway between adjacent manholes to provide duct drainage. Where the roadbed has a gradient, and also where the conduit crosses under tracks, the two-feet eight-inch depth is maintained with sufficient slope to drain the conduit.

TABLE I

Number of Ducts	Linear Feet	Duct Feet
8	34,200	273,600
9	2,130	19,170
10	1,700	17,000
12	3,475	41,700
16	1,360	21,760
18	410	7,380
20	1,540	30,800
Totals.......	44,815	411,410

The manholes were manufactured in accordance with the railroad's plans and specifications and appear elliptical in shape, the sidewalls being shaped to the arc of a 14-ft. diameter circle. The inside dimensions are six feet long, three feet six inches wide in the middle, and five feet high. The roof and side walls are four and one-half inches thick and the floor four inches thick. The entire manhole is reinforced with welded wire mesh reinforcement. Pulling-in irons are cast in the walls opposite and slightly below the duct entrances. A two-foot square opening is left in the ends for duct entrances. A certain number were manufactured with duct entrances in one end and one side to accommodate right-angle turns in the conduit line.

Because of not knowing beforehand all locations where laterals would be required, and also to simplify manufacture, a one-foot square section of reduced thickness (with reinforcing omitted) was provided in each side to form knockouts for laterals. For signal control laterals, parkway cable is used; and for telephone and telegraph laterals lead-covered cable is pulled through vitrified-clay, fiber, or creosoted-wood conduit, depending upon local conditions. In the manhole floor an opening thirteen inches square is left to be used for placing a floor drain or for building a sump hole as required. Either bolts or concrete inserts for bolts are cast in the manhole walls for attaching cable racks.

Excavations were made for manholes at the desired locations, then usually two flat cars carrying seven or eight manholes each were pulled out with a work train and the manholes lowered directly into their holes or deposited as near the site as could be reached with a derrick.

The telephone and telegraph cables are pulled in from manhole to manhole and laterals taken off only at these manholes. With the signal control cables, however, laterals are often required at frequent intervals between manholes. To provide outlets for these laterals, handholes are installed. These are octagonal in shape and the top is level with the base of rail. The bottom of the concrete protection forms the bottom of the handhole and the handhole, which is three feet five inches across inside flats, is cast of concrete as an integral part of the concrete protection. The ducts carrying telephone and telegraph cables are carried through the handhole without openings, but the ducts carrying signal control cables are ended flush with the inside walls of the handhole to make the cables accessible for lateral taps. The same cast-iron frames and covers are used on both manholes and handholes.

Drainage is an important factor in the successful operation of any underground conduit system, and is particularly so in the case of certain portions of this one.

Three general types of drainage are used, the elevation of the grade determining the type. In sections where the manhole floor is less than four feet above city datum, or lake level, a floor or side wall drain outlet is connected by a four-inch cast-iron drain pipe to an adjacent storm sewer. Where the manhole floor ranges in height from four to six feet above datum, a watertight sump is built under the opening left in the floor and all seepage water drains into this sump. When work is to be done in the manhole, a portable pump is used to pump it dry. Where the

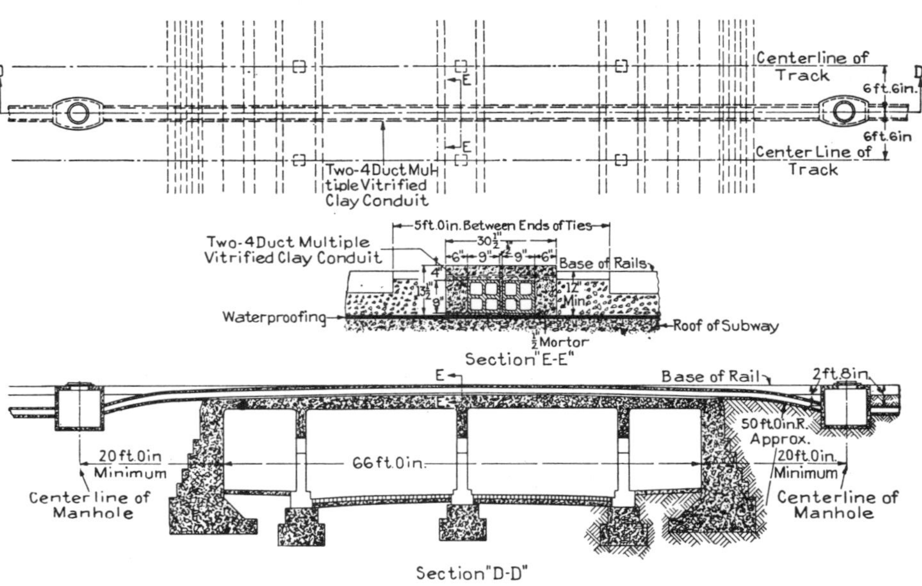

Fig. 4. Construction Diagram of Conduit Over Subway

manhole floor is over six feet above datum, a self-draining sump filled with crushed stone is located under the floor opening. Within the territory from 31st Street to 40th Street, where the surface of the roadbed is only a few feet above lake level, the drainage of manholes is accomplished by cast-iron drain pipe connected to a drain pipe running parallel to the tracks and forming part of a drainage system ·which handles the surface and subsurface water of the roadbed in this territory. North of 31st Street and from 40th Street to 43rd Street, though higher than the section just mentioned, the roadbed is too low to make the manholes self draining. There being no storm sewers accessible, the watertight sump type of drainage is used. The remainder of the territory through which the conduit line runs is on a fill sufficiently high that manholes will drain through the self-draining sump.

All precast manholes and all frames and covers were furnished and delivered to the site of the work by the railroad company. All other material and all labor was furnished by the contractor.

Design of Overhead Equipment for the Illinois Central Electrification

Catenary System Without Additional Feeders — Features of Suspension — Non-ferrous Alloys Used — A-c. Distribution — Determination of Stresses in Structures

By J. S. THORP

Distribution Engineer, Chicago Terminal Improvement

J. S. THORP

THE Illinois Central electrification includes, in its first stage, from two to six parallel tracks on the main line and one or two tracks on branches. There are about 110 track miles electrified along 38 miles of route. The electrification of the suburban service will be followed by electrification of the freight and through passenger service within the city limits. Present plans, therefore, anticipate as many as 15 main line tracks in parallel in some sections, and the ultimate electrification of about 415 track miles including yards and sidings.

Overhead catenary construction for 1500 volts direct current was chosen in 1922 by the electrification commission, appointed by the railroad in 1920 to make a report upon the choice of system. The design and layout of the distribution system were made by the permanent engineering staff.

Catenary System for Main-line Tracks

The catenary system over all tracks, in itself, provides the required current-carrying capacity without additional feeders. The distribution system allows for an average voltage drop of about twelve per cent in normal rush-hour service, with an all-day average drop estimated at three per cent. The average conductivity over every track, throughout the life of the contact wire, will be about 790,000 cir. mils copper equivalent. The system over all main tracks consists of a composite main messenger of high tensile strength, two bronze or copper grooved contact wires, and a hard-drawn copper auxiliary messenger. In the heavy traffic section north of 67th St., 3/0 bronze contact wires are used to obtain the best wearing qualities. On the remainder of the main line and on the South Chicago and Blue Island branches, 4/0 copper contact wires are used. The make-up of the catenary systems vary somewhat in other respects, as shown in Table I.

The normal height of the contact wire is 22 ft. above the top of the rail at structures, with a "hog" of three inches to insure against excessive sag under heavy current densities and high temperatures. This height is maintained south of 43rd St., except at a few points where passing under overhead structures. Because of the frequent present and proposed bridges over the railroad to give access to Grant Park and the new Lake Front Park, the contact wire north of 43rd St. (Fig. 1) has a normal height of 18 ft. 6 in. The minimum height of the contact wire is 16 ft. 6 in. and a gradient of one per cent or less with respect to the track is used where the height varies.

The auxiliary messenger is highly flexible, 19 strands in each case, which assures a contact line free from hard spots. It is hung from the main messenger by hangers spaced at 20- and 15-ft. intervals, for the respective catenary systems. Clips for the contact wires are spaced at half this interval and each contact wire supported from alternate clips. The bronze contact wire is therefore supported at 20-ft. intervals, and the copper contact at intervals of 15 ft. The two contact wires of a system hang side by side, with points of support staggered, but with no appreciable sag.

TABLE I

	North of 67th St.	South of 67th St.
Contact wires............	Two 3/0 bronze	Two 4/0 copper
Conductivity.............	80 per cent copper equiv.	
Composite main messenger	0.81 in. dia. 19 strands	0.81 in. dia. 19 strands
Hard-drawn copper auxiliary messenger........	200,000 cir. mil	1/0 A. W. G.
Hanger spacing..........	20 ft.	15 ft.
Ultimate strength of main messenger	31,500 lb.	31,500 lb.
Copper equivalent of system when new	838,900 cir. mil	898,700 cir. mil

The resulting contact system differs from those so far used by electric railroads in actual operation. The double-contact wire arrangement has been used previously, but suspended directly from the main messenger. The insertion of the stranded auxiliary messenger increases the flexibility of the system and practically eliminates "hardness" of contact. At the same time it gives positive connection between messenger and contact wires, and decreases wearing due to moving parts, as compared with the various forms of lifting hangers. The double-contact wire insures good contact with the pantograph at all times, and decreases materially the burning and pitting of the wire that results from minute, though invisible, arcing when a current-collecting device is used on a single wire.

No Auxiliary Feeders

The use of the relatively elaborate system comprised of four wires might be prohibitive for some installations, but in the present electrification the total copper would be required in any event for feeder capacity. It becomes advantageous, therefore,

Non-ferrous Alloys

The selection of a non-ferrous alloy for this particular installation was made after several years of tests throughout the eastern part of the United States. Various samples of alloys, both ferrous and non-ferrous, were placed in service on some of the eastern roads. After years of exposure to the atmosphere and smoke conditions existing in these localities, it was found only a few of these alloys were suitable for overhead work. The final selection was made from the few mentioned by an analysis of their electrical conductivity and strength, as fitted for this particular purpose.

Non-ferrous hangers and fittings are used exclusively, and all connections between the parts of the

Fig. 1.   View of Six-track Section at Junction of 18 Ft. 6 In. and 22 Ft. 0 In. Contact Wire Heights

to provide the electrical conductivity in such a way as to give the best mechanical arrangement.

The main messenger has a sag of 4 ft. 9 in. under normal conditions for the standard span of 300 ft. The resulting tension in the messenger is 7700 lb. for normal loading in still air at 60 deg. F. Under conditions of maximum loading (0 deg. F. with ice and wind) the tension will be 12,300 lb. The sags vary with span lengths in such a way as to maintain the same tension throughout a messenger. Pull-over construction is used for curves, of which there are relatively few.

The messenger is supported from the catenary structures by suspension insulators, two insulators being used at every support. The entire catenary system is below the supporting structure. This allows the use of suspension insulators instead of the pin insulators commonly used for heavy catenary systems. Furthermore, men may work on structures without danger of contact with live wires. This feature is of added importance in view of the use of the catenary structures for signals.

catenary system are fixed. For electrical purposes, the component parts are cross connected so thoroughly that they are, in effect, a single conductor. The minimizing of corrosion of fittings insures good electrical connections indefinitely as well as facilitating maintenance work.

The catenary construction over crossovers, sidings, and yard tracks is of simpler and less expensive construction than for the main tracks. A ⅜-in. seven-strand high-strength bronze messenger from which is suspended a single-contact wire is used. The messenger is independent mechanically of the main-line messenger, but the contact wires merge into the main-line contact wiring so as to avoid any crossing of contact wires and still allow the most advantageous method of wiring in each case. The contact wire used in the crossover system is either 3/0 bronze or 4/0 copper, depending upon the make-up of the adjacent main line. Crossover wiring is connected electrically to the adjacent main tracks, but sectionalized so as not to interfere with the complete sectionalization of the main tracks. In no instances have deflectors been used at the junction of the crossover and main tracks.

The yard construction is of the same design as the crossover wiring, but on account of the feeder capacity required, 4/0 contact wire was used irrespective of the contact wire over the adjacent tracks. In all except one yard, four, five, or six-track trusses are used as supports. The other, the 16th St. Storage Yard adjacent to the light inspection facilities, was built with some cross-span construction of six to nine tracks. The decision to use cross-span construction in this territory was one of economy based on the fact that the tracks are in a temporary position and are to be moved when the new through-passenger facilities are developed.

ends. As a part of the insulation, the contact wires are held apart by suitable spreaders at such points. Single-contact wires are used at crossovers and over sidings. Because of the fewer pantograph passes and lower speed of operation, they are insulated with wood-section insulators cut directly into the contact line.

A-c. Distribution System

The catenary structures carry three-phase four-wire 4000/2300-volt transmission lines for miscellaneous lighting and power loads, and single-phase 2300-volt transmission lines for supplying the signal system. All these are fed from substations of the Commonwealth Edison Company. There are duplicate

Fig. 2.   Details of Cross-span Construction in Weldon Yard

The cross spans as constructed have a maximum length of 104 ft. and have a sag of five feet at 60 deg. F. The supporting strand is of $\frac{3}{4}$-in. extra-high-strength galvanized steel. The strand serving as hanger to the insulator and the steady strand above the insulators are of $\frac{7}{16}$-in. Seimans-Martin. All connections to these wires are made with wire-rope clips as shown in Fig. 2. Non-ferrous material was not considered necessary for this construction due to the work being of a temporary nature.

Sectionalization

At important interlocking points, substations and tie stations are situated so as to come within the interlocking limits. The catenary systems are sectionalized at these points, and tied together through the substation or tie buses. The double-contact wire lends itself to air-gap ectionalization quite advantageously. At the desired point the contact wires are raised, alternately, high enough to insert a strain insulator in each without danger of the insulators fouling a pantograph. In this way the contact wires are continuous, and there are no additional dead

signal lines along the electrified part of the main line and a single circuit on the South Chicago Branch.

Duplicate three-phase lines are in operation from 12th St. to the 69th St. substation. A single three-phase line extends from 69th St. to the end of the electrified zone. Future provisions include an additional line between 69th St. and Harvey, the point of steam-electric changeover for future through passenger and freight electrification.

The transmission lines are fed from both ends in every case, and in general are sectionalized at midpoints between substations. At present there are from four to twelve No. 1 hard-drawn copper, triple-braid weatherproof wires along every section of the electrified route. These are carried on four-pin and six-pin angle-iron cross arms erected on the tops of the catenary structure columns. All designs are for the ultimate use of 2/0 wires. The wires are supported at normal heights of 33 and 36 ft., and have a normal sag of six feet in a 300-ft. span. The resulting maximum tensions in the wires are 1900 and 2500 lb. for each No. 1 and 2/0 wire, respectively.

Fig. 4.　Typical Four-track Section, 67th St. to Kensington

Fig. 6.　Tunnel Fittings at the South Chicago Undercrossing

Fig. 3.　34th Street Curve, Showing Long Trusses Made Necessary by Ultimate Track Arrangement

Fig. 5.　Curve Construction on Two-track Section

Control Cables and Messengers

In addition to the catenary and transmission wiring and signals, the catenary structures support multiple-conductor cables for signal-control circuits. There are as many as 32 No. 14 wires, in one or two cables, carried from an extra-high-strength steel messenger of one-half inch diameter. Along some sections of the line, two messenger and cable assemblies are used. These messengers have a normal sag of six feet for the 300-ft. span and the resulting tension under heavy loading is from 5100 to 7500 lb. for the several sizes. North of 80th St. these circuits are carried in a duct line instead of as an aerial cable.

Loading of Catenary System

The wire loading was based upon the assumed maximum condition of a coating of ice $\frac{1}{2}$ in. thick on all wires and hangers, with a wind pressure of eight pounds per square foot of projected area, including the ice. This pressure corresponds to an indicated wind velocity of about 72 miles an hour. As an alternative condition of maximum loading to cover extremely heavy winds, coincident with which there will not be a heavy coating of ice, a pressure of 20 pounds per square foot of projected area corresponding to an indicated velocity of about 119 miles an hour was assumed.

The loadings on flat surfaces of the structures were taken as 12 and 30 pounds per square foot for the two conditions, and ice on structures was not considered. The minimum temperature of still air was taken as 20 deg. below zero F. and a zero temperature coincident with maximum ice loading.

Catenary Structures

The layout and design of the catenary supporting structures allows for their extension over future electrified tracks, although at this time they are used over suburban tracks only. The effect is that structures were designed for the present with the future view of serving the entire right-of-way along a large part of the electrified route. This right-of-way has a minimum width of 200 ft. In places it is 250 and 300 ft. wide, exclusive of electrified yards. Bridges, having up to six columns, and up to 200 ft. long, without expansion joints, will be used. Individual bents span up to four or five tracks, ordinarily, with lengths of 60 to 70 ft. Longer bents are used frequently with a single span, in the ultimate, for the entire right-of-way width of 200 ft.

A complete rearrangement of tracks within the terminal district was made, preliminary to electrification, so as to make possible the ultimate maximum utilization of the right-of-way without extensive changes after electrification. Along a considerable part of the right-of-way this had the effect of practically reconstructing the railroad. Since the normal track spacing of 13 ft. does not allow room for columns

of catenary structures, a track spacing of 17 ft. was provided for columns at appropriate intervals where possible.

Types of Structures

North of Kensington, on the main line, built-up columns and trusses of latticed angle construction are used, which are shown in Fig. 4. The greatest number of electrified tracks are on this part of the line. Here, nearly all of the ultimate structures will have more than two columns, and the longest spans. In addition to the heavy catenary loading, certain of these structures carry signals for the several tracks.

South of Kensington, and on the Blue Island and South Chicago branches, the structures are made up of Bethlehem H-sections for columns and cross beams (Fig. 5). This section of the main line has only two electrified tracks at the start, and single columns with brackets are used. Between Kensington and Harvey, about six miles, additional columns will be erected, and cross beams will be joined to the columns as additional tracks are electrified. On the branch lines, where there are only one or two tracks, single columns and brackets or two-track portal structures are used.

Occasional three-column structures, required for combined signal and catenary use along the main line south of Kensington, are of the built-up type.

All steel used in the permanent structures (except the H-beams) is copper-bearing, having a copper content of from 0.15 to 0.25 of one per cent. Copper added in this amount has no effect on the physical properties of the steel while it is estimated the life will be increased from two to three times. The results obtained by the use of a similar copper-bearing steel in steel car and other construction indicated a rust-resisting quality which amply warranted the additional expense of $3.00 per ton.

Use of Models in Structure Design

In addition to the normal loads of wires and cables, and the ice and wind loads, structures were designed to carry an additional load of 1000 lb., parallel with the track due to a broken catenary messenger. This load will be limited by the slipping of the cable in the clamp. In view of the heavy values of the assumed loads and the infrequency of their probable occurrence, a maximum calculated stress of 20,000 lb. per square inch was allowed in the structural steel.

Certain standard sections for trusses and columns were adopted for all built-up bridges. In practically all cases the column sections consist of four 4-in. by 4-in. angles laced, with a depth across track of 15, 16, or 18 in. back to back, while the sections for the trusses are four $3\frac{1}{2}$-in. by $3\frac{1}{2}$-in. angles, legs out and laced inside, with depths of 3, 4, 5, and 6 ft. over all. Using these sections, a careful preliminary design was made for each type of bridge to be built.

Differences in loadings were met by the use of angles of different thickness.

The stresses in bents of the types used for these structures are indeterminate statically. The exact calculation of these stresses for structures of more than two columns was impractical on account of the time and labor involved. A mechanical solution of statically indeterminate structures, [1] developed by Prof. G. E. Beggs, of Princeton, seemed admirably suited to this problem. A set of Beggs' apparatus, consisting of six deformeter gauges and three microscopes, was purchased and used in designing these structures. In general, the mechanical determination of the stresses in a bent consists in obtaining the relation of the deflections, at various points on a cardboard model of the bent, to a known deflection made at the base of each column in turn.

its column by means of a clamp or a small pin, depending upon whether the column is to be considered as fixed or pin ended. These deformeter gauges are merely mechanical devices for making a given small horizontal or vertical movement or rotation, by inserting very accurately machined plugs of several sizes between bearings in the fixed and movable parts of the gauges. Microscopes with a graduated field and a movable cross hair for measuring accurately the small deflections of the model are provided.

As an example of practice, let it be required to obtain the influence lines for the horizontal reaction at the base of the first column of a three-column bent. The base of the first column is moved horizontally through a known distance by means of the gauge. All other column bases remain in their normal posi-

Fig. 7. View of Beggs Apparatus Showing Application of Apparatus to Model for
Five-column Catenary Structure

By Maxwell's theorem of reciprocal deflections, this relation is that of reaction to load. If the deflection ratios are plotted, and a smooth curve drawn for each column, the result is a set of influence lines for the reactions at the bases of the columns.

The first step, then, in the mechanical solution is to cut a small-scale model of the structure under consideration from a thin sheet of high-grade cardboard (Fig. 7). To insure the same relative stiffness in the members of the model as in the steel structure which it represents, the widths of the several members are cut to vary as the cube root of the moment of inertia of the corresponding members of the structure. Only the reactions resulting from vertical loads, curve pull, and cross-track wind are determined by means of the model. The effect of wind parallel to the track can be taken care of by a simple analysis. The scale of the model is such that the total length of those representing five and six spans does not exceed 72 in.

When the model is finished it is laid flat on a sheet of glass and "floated" on small steel balls. A deformeter gauge is screwed to the table top at the foot of every column. The movable half of the gauge is fastened to

tions. The vertical displacement of the two truss spans and the horizontal displacement of the three columns is measured at a number of points along the center lines of those members, and tabulated. These readings are divided by the known movement of the base of the first column and the results plotted. The required influence line can be drawn as a smooth curve through those points. Confusion is avoided by plotting the curves for the columns separately from those of the trusses.

When a complete set of influence lines for reaction is prepared, the computation of the maximum moments and shears in the structure, due to any system of loads, becomes simply a matter of statics. If the sections used in the original design are shown to be over stressed, it is, of course, necessary to change them by using heavier angles. Obviously, material change of section destroys the original ratios of stiffness of members and invalidates all the influence lines based on the model. Large changes are not common and an attempt is made always to maintain approximately the same relative moments of inertia in making a revision.

The results obtained with the Beggs apparatus have been checked repeatedly by statics and found to be correct in that respect.

---

[1] Proceedings of the American Concrete Institute, Feb., 1922.

Foundations for Catenary Structures

While vertical loads on foundations are comparatively small, high transverse values result from the assumed wind loading and curve pull. In the single columns with brackets for two tracks, the maximum load is across track; for bridge structures it is usually parallel to the track.

Shallow rectangular side-bearing, or gravity-type, foundations are used. Loads are such that for two-track bracket construction the gravity foundations have a length of 12 ft. at right angles to the track and contain about $7\frac{1}{2}$ cu. yd. An equivalent side-bearing foundation contains about the same yardage

South Chicago branch vary from one to three tracks crossing two of the railroad tracks.

Various methods were studied to handle this situation, all being based on the fact that the surface line crossings must be energized to 600 volts at all times and insulated from 1500 volts.

The details of the final arrangement are shown clearly in Fig. 8.

As will be noted, the surface lines cross in a channel section to insure continuous contact with the trolley wheel, while the railroad company's contact wire and auxiliary messenger are sectionalized with a special wood-stick insulator for the three wires 12 ft.

Fig. 8.   Intersection of Two 600-volt Street Railway Lines with Two 1500-volt Catenary Systems.
The Street Railway Circuit is Continuous Over the Crossing.   The Catenary
Contacts and Auxiliary only are Sectionalized

and has a bearing area of about 65 sq. ft. The maximum working earth pressures were taken at 5000 lb. per sq. ft. The gravity type was preferred generally where track spacing permitted the installation without shoring the tracks. For bridge structures, the gravity-type foundation was used, with the 12-ft. dimension along track.

A concrete mix of 1:2:4 was used for caps of foundations; the body of large sections was made of $1:2\frac{1}{2}:5$ mix.

Trolley Crossings

On both branches, the Blue Island and South Chicago, there are grade crossings with the Chicago Surface Lines; there being six such crossings on the South Chicago branch and one on the Blue Island. The latter is a two-track intersection with a single-track line of the railroad company, while those on the

on either side. Over this dead section the main messenger, which is continuous, is covered with heavy rubber hose so that the trolley pole will not come in contact with the 1500 volts should it come out of the channel. The trough through which the channel passes is set at an angle with the path of the pantograph so that the pantograph will not rise into the trough. Skids are provided to carry the pantograph in the same plane as the underside of the trough, and an additional approach for the pantograph is built between the wood section insulator and the trough to deflect the pantograph to the plane of the skids. Between the two troughs the pantograph is carried on two sections of T-bar discernible in the photograph. The weight of this crossing equipment is not carried on the messenger but is carried by steel poles set for this purpose.

Methods of Constructing Overhead Equipment of Illinois Central Railroad

Special Problems Raised by Working Conditions—Equipment Built to Overcome Them—Method of Erecting Transmission Line—Rapid Work Facilitated by Ingenuity of Contractor—Stringing Signal Control and Telephone Cable

By S. R. NEGLEY

Assistant Engineer, Chicago Terminal Improvement

S. R. NEGLEY

DURING the construction of the catenary and power distribution systems of the Illinois Central, several ingenious and labor-saving methods were developed and used to great advantage. Throughout the construction period the railroad company was operating more than four hundred trains daily over the tracks being electrified, and of necessity could give up the tracks for construction purposes for only a limited amount of time. It was necessary therefore to devise methods of erection in which the tracks could be released for service at the end of the work period each day and have all construction in the clear so as to be of no hazard to train operation. All stringing of wire was done with this in view and a minimum of train delays occurred.

Erection Equipment

The erection equipment as used in the construction consisted of eight permanent tower cars, three reel cars for main and auxiliary messenger and contact wire, two light reel cars for transmission wire, four tool cars and one locomotive crane.

The details of the tower cars are plainly shown in Fig. 1. The platforms were adjustable having a minimum height of 15 ft. 8 in. and a maximum of 19 ft. 8 in. The platforms were raised and lowered by means of a "crab" mounted in the center of the car on the floor of the flat car proper. The hand rail was hinged so that it could be let down when the car was not in use. For night construction, the towers were wired and projectors placed so that they illuminated the tops of the cars and the work. Lighting current was provided by a gasoline engine-driven generator located in the tool car.

The reel car used for stringing the main messenger, auxiliary messenger and contacts was so constructed that it held six reels; the rack or reel cradle extended as a unit the full length of the car. Incorporated with the rack was the brake rigging.

The reel axles were square, except bearings, and braking was done by means of a brake band with hand-wheel adjustment, a square hole arbor plate having been specified for all catenary material reel heads to take this square axle.

The reel cars used for stringing the No. 1 triple-braid weatherproof wire were lighter in construction than those used for the catenary materials and differed in other respects. The reel rack in this case contained space for 12 reels, and the reel axles were round. Braking was accomplished by turnbuckle adjustment on a spring plate applied to the edge of the reel head.

The tool cars contained space for small fittings, work benches, tools and small erection equipment. These cars were reconstructed box cars, and on one end was mounted a set of rollers to take the transmission line wires from the reel car and also a large roller to carry the messenger and auxiliary messenger and contacts when stringing.

Transmission Line Erection

The 4000/2300-volt distribution and signal circuits were composed of No. 1 hard-drawn solid copper with triple-braid weatherproofing.

For the most part, the catenary supporting columns were so located that a track was available adjacent to the column for stringing purposes, and in such cases the wires were strung with the aid of a locomotive crane. A nine-way gang roller was designed and built to be mounted on the cross arm. A train consisting of an engine, reel car, locomotive crane, tool car and tower car was used for this work. All of the 1/0 triple-braid weatherproof wire was ordered in lengths of one mile each. The wire was passed from the reels over the rollers mounted on the end of the tool car and through a system of rollers and guides on the end of the crane boom (Fig. 2). The train was moved along the track adjacent to the column and as the structure was passed the boom was lifted and a lineman placed the wires in position in the rollers. With this outfit a maximum of eight wires were placed in the rollers with one movement of the train and with the minimum number of men. With two reel cars and fair track conditions, sixteen wire miles have been put in the rollers and temporarily sagged in one day, stringing eight wires at one time. A follow-up gang permanently sagged the wires in the rollers, replaced the rollers with insulators and tied them in. No difficulty was encountered in transferring the wires from the top to the bottom arm where necessary.

In that territory in which the cross arm could not be reached with the crane boom, an ingenious method of stringing was devised by the contractor and used to great advantage. A pulling plate (Fig. 3) was designed and built of a steel plate, triangular in shape, approximately thirty-four inches long. Small angles were

the permanent suspension clamp which was to replace the roller after the wire was strung. Insulators, rollers and clamps were hung at the same time.

In order to further facilitate rapid stringing, all main messenger wire had been ordered with the inner end brought out through a hole in the reel head large enough to pass the main messenger splice fitting. A group of linemen were trained under careful supervision in the application of splice fittings, for it was recognized that the value of the fitting depended

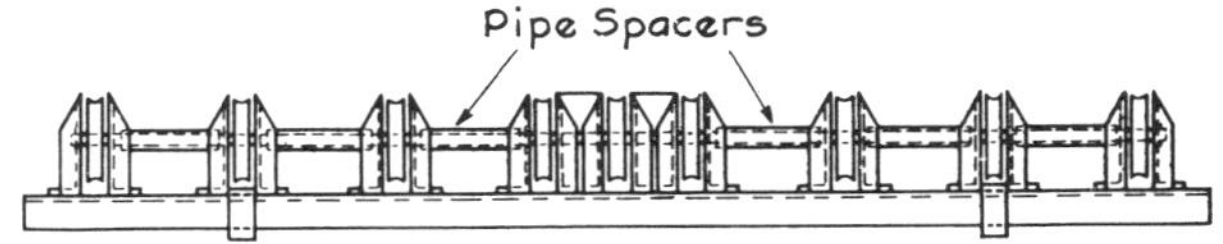

Fig. 2.   Rollers Used in Stringing the Transmission Lines

Fig. 1.   Clipping the Contact Wires and Auxiliary, Showing the Details of the Tower Car.   Note the "crab" for raising the towers mounted in the center of the car

riveted to the underside of this plate having the same distance between angles as the center-to-center distance of the rollers mounted on the cross arm. Holes were drilled along the base for the attaching of six wires. A line was passed over the center roller of the gang mounted on the cross arms and, after anchoring the reel car, the locomotive was attached to the other end of the line and the wires pulled through. In this way it was possible to string approximately six wire miles in one working day. This work was done with a team or truck where it was impossible on account of track conditions to use the work train.

Erection of Catenary System

The stringing of the catenary system was a group of several complete operations.

Previous to stringing the main messenger a small gang of men had placed the suspension insulators in their permanent position over the tracks and attached to them a roller-bearing roller capable of taking the load of the main messenger, which weighs one and one-half pounds per foot. Wired to this assembly was

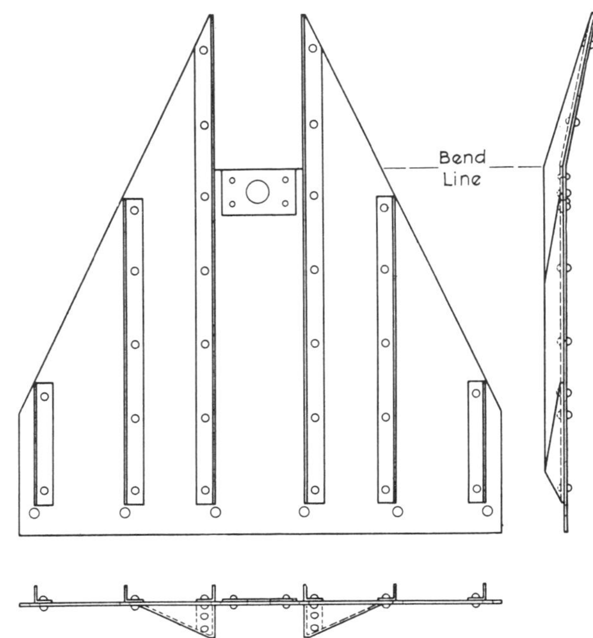

Fig. 3.   Pulling Plate Specially Designed for Stringing the Transmission Lines

primarily upon its application. These splice fittings were put on each end of the reel in the material yard before the wire was loaded on to the reel cars. The stringing of the main messenger was done with the same equipment as the transmission line, except for the heavier reel car as previously described.

A large single roller was placed on the end of the crane boom and the main messenger passed over it. As the train passed each structure the boom was raised and the main messenger placed in the sagging roller attached to the insulator. Enough tension was kept on the messenger by means of the brake to keep it pretty well in the clear when stringing. From one to five miles were strung and sagged in this manner in one working day, returning the track for traffic at the end of that time. Fig. 4 shows the operation in detail.

the one reel of auxiliary covered two continuous reels of contact wire or a total of four contact wire reels.

In order that the contacts and auxiliary messenger could be strung at the same time it was necessary that some form of gang roller be developed in which three wires could be suspended from the hangers and tensioned prior to being clipped. It was advisable also that the rollers be so constructed that the position of the wire in the rollers be as near as possible the same position as when the wire was clipped in. The gang roller was built so that the two contact wires were passed over one pair of rollers on a common shaft while the auxiliary was passed over a roller mounted above the contact wire. These rollers were mounted on a strap which was hooked over the auxiliary messenger clamp on the lower end of the hanger.

Fig. 4.   Stringing the Main Messenger.   Note brake rigging on the heavy type reel car, and the arrangement and use of the train equipment

The hangers were calculated by a graphical method, and previous to their distribution in the field, were assembled on a section of pipe in the order in which they were to be placed in the span. Due to the various lengths of spans the hanger spacing was necessarily variable, the adjustment being made in the center and the ends of each span. It was possible to group these spacings in four groups, *i.e.*, there were only four variations of hanger spacing in any number of span lengths. In order to facilitate placing the hangers on the messenger the contractor devised an extension of this graphical hanger calculation method by making up tapes having four sets of marks for the hanger spaces and also marked for span lengths for setting the tape. The tapes were of sufficient length to be strung alongside the messenger between structures. The lineman who placed the hangers also removed the rollers and placed the messenger in the suspension clamp. The linemen then read their tape setting and spacing from the tag attached to the span of hangers. The tape was clamped between two bridges in accordance with this information, and the linemen rode the messenger, transferring the hangers from the pipe to their proper position on the main messenger.

In order to avoid splices as much as possible the contact wire, and in general the auxiliary messenger, were ordered for one particular section and usually

The auxiliary messenger and two contacts were then run out with a train consisting of an engine, reel car, tool car and four tower cars. The linemen toward the front of the train placed the rollers on every other hanger and those following lifted the three wires in their position. The regular day's run for this work was about ten thousand feet, which included tensioning.

The "clipping in" process or attaching the auxiliary hanger and contact clips was by far the slowest operation, but a train of four tower cars with 14 to 16 men handling clips clipped in as much as 10,000 ft. in one day. The contact wire clips were to be spaced so that the distance between clips was in all cases equal to $\frac{1}{2}$ the distance between hangers. The contractor developed an ingenious method of spacing these clips by the use of a piece of elastic having a hook on each end to attach to the hangers and small markers for the clips. The latter were so placed that the distance between the marks was one-half the length of the tape. This tape being made of elastic, all variations in hanger spacing were automatically taken care of. (Fig. 5). The clipping process was most efficiently performed by working four men to each tower car. It was at this time that all kinks were removed from the wire and the wire greased to prevent formation of scale from steam locomotive exhaust.

Signal Control and Telephone Cable

The signal control cables are supported on the catenary structures south of 80th Street to the end of the line and also on the Blue Island and South Chicago Branches. In general, these cables and messengers were strung in the same manner as the main messenger, though on the south end of the line they were installed without work train service. The ½-in. extra high strength steel supporting messenger was strung out on the ground and then lifted to a position approximately seven feet from the ground and sup-

being pulled at the same time with an equalizer. In sagging a long section of messenger the sag was checked in three places to insure all the slack being pulled out. However, by pulling all wires to 50 per cent more than normal tension and then slacking back, the tension was found to be quite uniform throughout the length of the section.

Practically all of the overhead catenary system was strung by the end of June, 1926, after which all work trains were placed on the special and clean-up work. All wires had been pulled into position as near as

Fig. 5.   View of Clipping Process on Top of the Tower Cars, Showing the Elastic Spacing Tape in Use

Fig. 6.   Stringing the Power Transmission and Signal Circuits. Note the rollers mounted on the cross arm, and on the end of the crane boom

ported by a special clamp attached to the structure at this point. The supporting messenger was then sagged in this position. The control cables were next laid out along the structures and with a gang of men to clip, they were lifted and clipped to the messenger. All that remained was to raise the messenger and cables in position on the structure, which was done with four-inch blocks.

The main messenger and all No. 1 triple-braid weatherproof wires were tensioned by the use of a sag rod or measuring stick. Due to the necessity of obtaining extreme accuracy in the former it was sagged with the aid of a surveyor's level to read the deflection. The contacts and auxiliary were both tensioned with a dynamometer, the two contact wires

possible when they were strung, but all special insulation, pull-off fittings, steady arms, etc., were yet to be installed. This clean-up work required practically five weeks to complete, the majority of the work being in the vicinity of interlocking plants where it was impossible to work on any track but a short length of time between trains.

Construction was started on August 3, 1925, although the force at this time was very small, and it was approximately October first before the construction program assumed any appreciable proportions. The first revenue train was operated July 21, 1926, over the local tracks between Randolph Street and Sixty-seventh Street, and on August 7th, formal opening of all service was made.

The Multiple Unit Cars for Suburban Service on the Illinois Central

Cars Designed After Preliminary Survey of all Existing Types—Incorporate Many Novel Features— Electric and Air Control Equipment Specially Designed and Built—Operation of Equipment—Rigid Tests Given Cars Before Entering Service—School Established for Prospective Motormen

By A. H. WOOLLEN, Equipment Engineer, and A. R. WALKER, Assistant Engineer

Chicago Terminal Improvement

THE general type of steel suburban cars for the Illinois Central suburban service were first designed in 1921. Their construction was the result of data gathered from studies made of suburban cars all over the world, which were applied to the particular conditions of the Illinois Central. The first series of these cars, 20 in number, No. 1301 to 1320, were built in 1921 and their operation watched until 1923, when additional cars were required. As a result of this observation certain modifications of the earlier cars were made to reduce weight and 25 new cars were built, No. 1321 to 1345. The modifications consisted of aluminum alloy roof, aluminum doors

A. R. WALKER

and interior sheathing, and a shortening of the truck wheel base three inches. Electrification of the suburban service was considered in the design of both series of cars. The actual weight of the first cars equipped for electric trailer operation is 94,800 pounds, and of the second series 87,200 pounds, or a saving of 7600 pounds.

The plans for electrification were completed in 1923 to the point where it was necessary to design the rolling stock, and after consideration had been given to train make-up, a unit of one motor car and one trailer car semi-permanently connected for trains, which was decided upon as a basic unit might be composed of from one

Fig. 1.　Eight-car, Four-unit Electric Train on a Suburban

to five of these units. This plan made it possible to use the 45 cars of the first two series as trailers with only minor additions, and to design the new motor cars independently of what had been done before. However, after a thorough study of what was then the latest types of suburban cars as compared to the cars which had been running in steam service, it was decided to continue the general plan of car in the motor car, and all car bodies were made practically alike. Figs. 1, 2, and 3 are general views of the exteriors and interiors of these cars.

Mechanical Description of Cars

The features which immediately command the attention of the riding public to the cars are the spacious platforms, the unusually wide aisles and doors, and the general roomy appearance of the car interior. This interior also has a bright appearance, due to the head-lining being finished practically white, the large size of the windows, and the numerous light fixtures on the lower deck rail. The absence of basket racks and hanging cords is also a notable characteristic. The interior view is shown in the illustration, Fig. 3.

The safety and comfort of passengers, as well as the facilities for handling crowds, were given prime consideration in the design of the equipment.

Prominent among these features are the all-metal construction of the car body, the completely vestibuled platforms and the sliding doors throughout. Ample ventilation is provided by monitor sash ventilators. The electric lights are placed over the seats so that each passenger has ample light for reading. Windows 24 in. by 28 in. are placed opposite each seat, and are designed so as not to obstruct the passenger's vision when raised.

The motor and trailer bodies are alike, with the exception that the motor car underframe is designed to carry the control apparatus and the roof to carry two pantographs, one over each truck center. The body of the car is built entirely of copper-bearing steel. The inside sheathing and the doors, of which there are eleven per car, are made of sheet aluminum. The outside roof sheaths are of aluminum alloy. The inside head-lining is fireproof agasote.

The general dimensions of the car are as follows:

Length overall coupled......................72 ft. 7½ in.
Length over body corner posts..............60 ft. 6½ in.
Length between truck centers...............47 ft. 9 in.
Width overall at eaves.....................9 ft. 11½ in.
Width over trap door nosings...............10 ft. 6 in.
Width over belt rail rivets................9 ft. 9¾ in.
Height from top of rail to top of platform....4 ft. 3⅝ in.
Height from top of rail to top of carline......13 ft. 0 in.
Clear width of end side doors..............4 ft. 0 in.
Clear opening of sliding end doors leading from
    end of platform to car..................4 ft. 0 in.
Clear width of end vestibule door...........2 ft. 2 in.
Spacing of cross seats center to center........2 ft. 9½ in.
Aisle width................................2 ft. 7¼ in.
Total seating capacity.....................84
Weight, Motor car light....................141,200 lb.
Weight, Trailer car light..................87,200 lb.
    (New cars 1926)

The framing conforms to the usual practice for steel car construction. The center sills, side sills and

Branch of the Illinois Central Railroad Out of Chicago

side plates are rolled structural shapes. The side posts and carlines are steel pressings.

Composite floors, insulated with hairfelt, are used throughout. Special care was exercised in providing ample insulation to keep the cars warm

Fig. 2.   Standard Two-car Multiple Unit Train on the Illinois Central, Showing the Motor Car and Trailer

in the winter and cool in the summer. This is accomplished by the application of three-ply Salamander to the sides and roof sheets of the car.

In designing the seating arrangement, particular attention was given to providing ample room between the seats, and ample height of back and seat cushion for the comfort of passengers. No ends are provided on the seats, in order that the passengers may enter and leave quickly and conveniently. The width of the aisle at the seat end is about 31 in., increasing to 36 in. at the edges of the seat backs. There are 34 rattan-covered cross seats and four longitudinal seats, providing a seating capacity for 84 passengers. The standing space in the aisles and vestibules will permit 109 passengers to stand comfortably. Rico hand straps are provided over the longitudinal seats and grab handles on the backs of the cross seats are provided to further the comfort of those passengers who are standing.

At each end of the car there is a vestibule of such depth that side door openings with a clear width of 48 inches can be obtained. These door openings are provided with sliding doors operated by electric motor-driven door engines, with the exception of the first two lots of 45 cars which are operated by electro-pneumatic engines. Control for these doors, placed in the passageway between the cars, is so designed that the trainman can open either the four doors on either side of the unit with one operation, or only the door adjacent to him. The door is provided with a safety edge so that if it meets an obstruction in closing it comes to a standstill and stays in this position until the obstruction is removed. This makes it impossible for a passenger to be caught in the door in such a manner as to cause personal injuries. Provision is also made so that the door can be operated by hand in case the door engine should fail. The door opening between the body of the car

Fig. 3.   Interior View of Motor Car

and the vestibule has a clear opening of 48 inches and is provided with double sliding doors geared so that they operate together. The vestibule end door has an opening of 26 inches. The doors which cover the control mechanism at each end of the unit are so arranged that when they open they form an enclosure 4 ft. by 3 ft. 10 in.   This space forms the cab for the motorman. A folding seat for the motorman is provided in the partition between the car body and the vestibule.

Two trap door steps are provided on the trailer adjacent to the motor car. These steps are for emergency use as high station platforms are used throughout the suburban zone.

Another safety feature is the use of non-shattering glass in the vestibules at each end of the units. This glass may be broken without scattering the fragments.

The trucks, Fig. 4, have cast steel frames with the pedestals cast integral. The wheels are of rolled steel. Clasp brakes are used on both motor and trailer cars. The trucks were assem-

The cars are finished outside in dark olive green with gold lettering and black roof. The interior is dark red to the advertising cards, and has a white, enamel-like finish on the lower decks and in the clerestory.

Fig. 4.   Truck of Motor Car for Multiple Unit Train

Fig. 5.   Control Mechanism in Motorman's Cab

Motors, Control and Auxiliary Equipment

The traction motors on each motor car are four 250 h.p. nominal rated full ventilated series railway motors. There are two motors on each truck connected permanently in series, each motor being geared to one axle. These motors will accelerate a train at 1.5 miles per hour per second and have a balancing speed of 60 miles per hour, although under favorable conditions trains have attained speeds as high as 70 miles per hour. Half of the motors are the General Electric Company Type GE-285A and half are Westinghouse Electric and Manufacturing Company Type 587-D5.

Current is collected from the overhead catenary system by means of pantograph trolleys, two on each motor car. Under normal conditions only one pantograph on each motor car is used, the other being kept for emergency. These pantographs are raised by springs, maintaining a contact pressure of about 20 pounds against the contact wires. They are lowered by means of an air piston which operates on 70 pounds control reservoir pressure. The pantograph is held down by an air-operated latch which may be tripped with a pole from the ground if desired. The air devices are supplied by magnet valves which are controlled by push buttons in each cab. A selector switch in each pantograph circuit determines which pantograph will be used. In this way all active pantographs on one train may be controlled from the driving cab.

The motors are controlled by a pneumatic-cam controller which provides for multiple-unit car control from one cab, with automatic acceleration. The controller unit consists of a bank of contactors operated mechanically by means of a cam shaft which is rotated by an air engine. This engine is controlled electrically by means of magnet valves which are operated by a master controller through a train line from any motorman's cab in the train (Fig. 5).

bled at the car builders' plants, and in the case of the motor cars the motors and gears were also mounted by the car builders.

Accelerating relays (one on each motor car) control the rate of acceleration, and may be set for a predetermined rate. A by-pass feature on the master controller and accelerating relay allows a temporary increase or decrease in the rate of acceleration. The reverser is contained in the controller unit.

Four other pieces of apparatus are auxiliary to the controller.

(1) The line breaker closes the motor circuit initially and is the first to break the circuit when the control is shut off. This device consists of two electro-pneumatic contactors connected in series.

(2) The field control switch, consisting of four cam-operated contactors, automatically taps the fields of the motors to increase speed when the control has reached the full-field parallel position, and the motor current has dropped to a predetermined value. A separate current relay installed with this piece of apparatus controls its operation.

(3) The potential relay closes as soon as the pantograph comes into contact with the overhead wire and drops out if the line potential falls below 800 volts. When the relay is open the controller cannot be operated. This is for protection in case the line voltage drops or is lost altogether. It prevents the restoration of voltage on the motors with resistance out of the circuit.

(4) An aluminum-cell lightning arrester is installed under the car with a suitable choke coil.

All control circuits, lights, and doors are operated on 32 volts direct current which is furnished by a 3½-kw., 1500/32-volt motor-generator set which is installed on each motor car, and operates continuously whenever the pantograph is in contact with the wire. A 300-ampere-hour Edison storage battery floats on the system and acts as a standby in case of failure of the motor-generator set. This battery is located on the trailer car. Diagrams of the 1500-volt and 32-volt circuits are shown in Figs. 6, 7, and 8.

Tomlinson automatic couplers made by the Ohio Brass Company couple the cars together mechanically, electrically, and pneumatically. There are two air-pipe connections for connecting the brake pipe and main reservoir pipe. The control train line is connected through the couplers by brass contacts under spring pressure. Between units 28 contacts are used, all for 32-volt control and auxiliary circuits. Between motor car and trailer 29 contacts are used for 32-volt control and auxiliary circuits and one 1500-volt contact for the heater bus line.

The couplers are equipped for semi-automatic operation between motor car and trailer and for full automatic operation between units. Between units the couplers are operated from either adjacent motorman's cab by push buttons which control magnet valves which operate an air piston to uncouple the cars mechanically, and air-operated drum switches connecting all circuits together. When the cars are uncoupled they open the circuits to the coupler contacts. A cutout cock is connected to each end of the drum switches so that when cars are uncoupled the brake train line and reservoir line are closed.

The brake equipment (Figs. 9 and 10) is the type PS New York Air Brake Company electro-pneumatic brake schedule, the pneumatic portion of which is a standard triple valve with separate emergency valve. The electric control consists of three magnet valves controlled by a drum switch contained in the engineer's brake valve so that all braking operations in all cars of a train are simultaneous. One magnet valve controls the service application, in which air is vented locally on each car from the brake pipe to the brake cylinder and after the triple piston moves, direct to atmosphere; one operates the emergency; and the other provides a holding feature so that when the brake valve is placed in the electric holding position, each triple valve goes into release, but the air is held in the brake cylinder by this magnet valve and may be released in any number of steps or graduations by the engineer's valve, providing a very smooth deceleration. The air brakes are interlocked with the motorman's master controller so that in case of sickness or death of the motorman, the train control will be shut off and the emergency brakes applied as soon as the motorman's hand releases the controller handle. This release feature operates only when the reversing lever is thrown to either the "forward" or "reverse" position. Air is compressed by a 1500-volt air compressor of 35 cu. ft. per minute piston displacement. There is one compressor on each motor car. The compressors are controlled by air-compressor governors which are synchronized by a control wire so that one compressor on a train is not unduly overloaded in case of a leak on that car.

The motorman's starting signal consists of a small green light which is in series with switches on each door on the train so that the light appears as soon as all doors are closed. This operates only when the reversing handle is thrown to the "forward" position. In case the handle is thrown in the "reverse" position, a yellow light appears instead of a green. In case of emergency an electric buzzer is provided which may be operated by a button in each car vestibule. This circuit is fed from the control system and only sounds in the cab actually being used.

Each motor car is provided with a mercury kilowatt-hour meter which measures all power used on the unit except by the heaters. Each motorman's cab is provided with distant meter dial similar to the master meter which is operated electrically from the meter of that unit.

The cars are heated by electric heaters placed under the seats. The heater units in the motor cars were made by the General Electric Company and assembled by the Consolidated Car Heating Company; those in the trailer cars were furnished by the

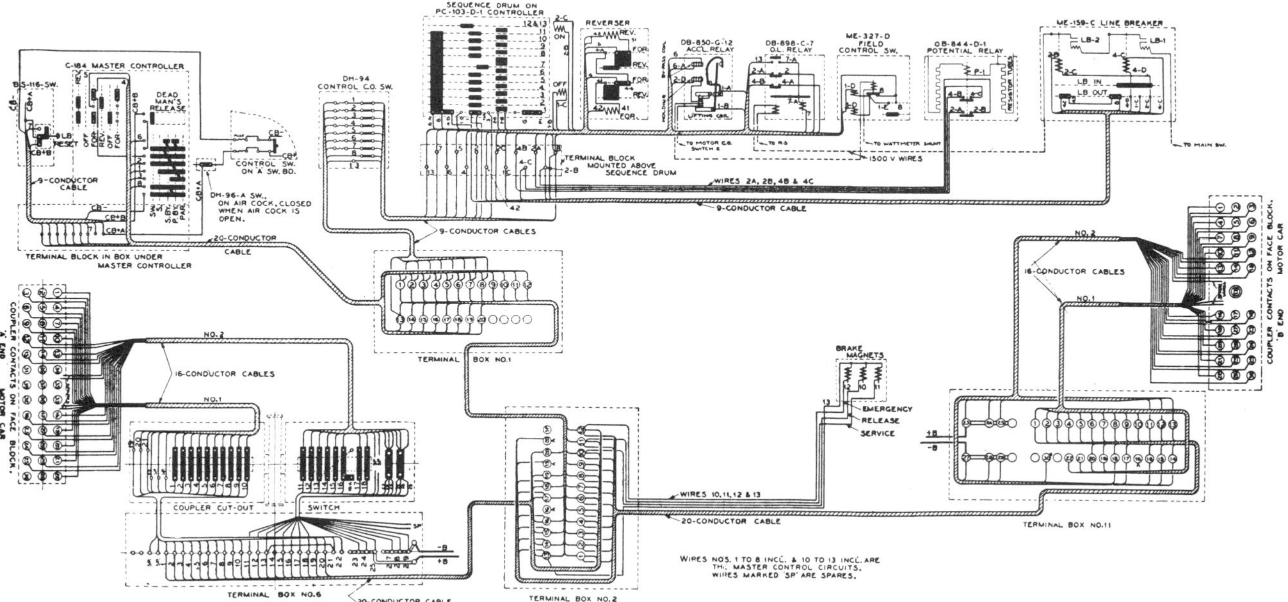

Fig. 6. Master Control Circuits on Motor Car of Multiple Unit Train

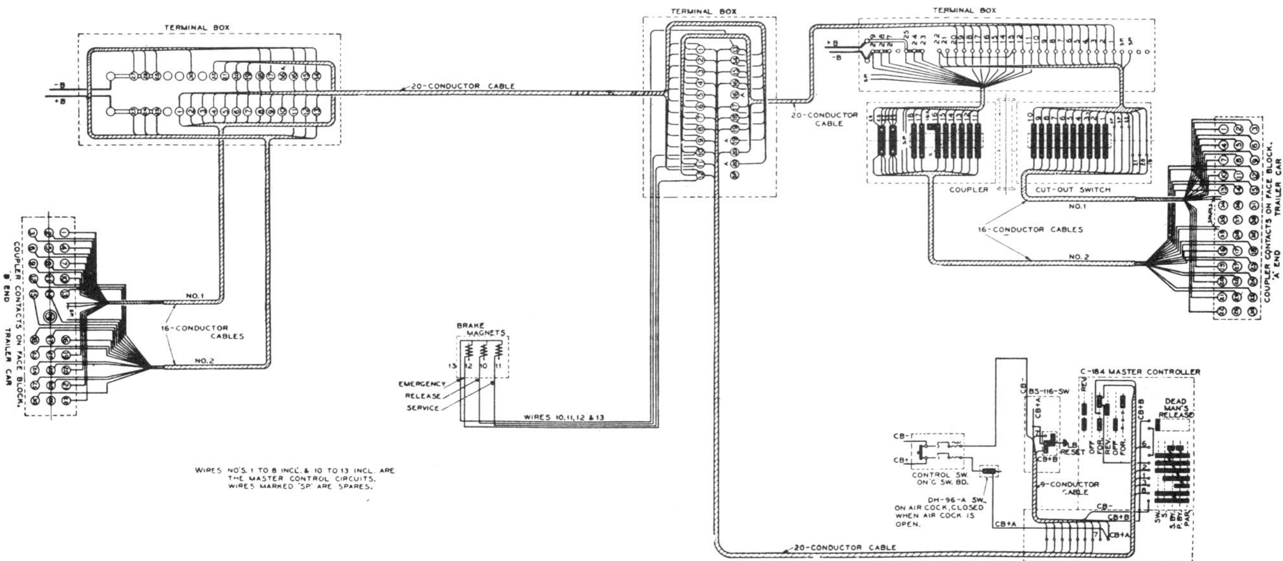

Fig. 7. Master Control Circuits on Trailer Car of Multiple Unit Train

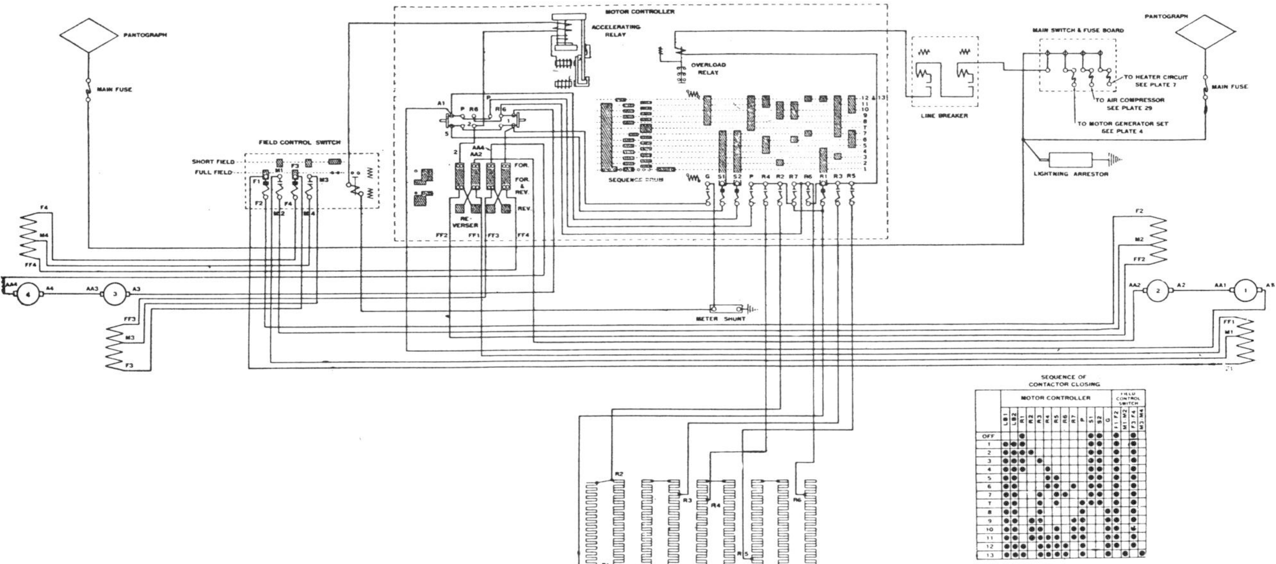

Fig. 8. 1500-volt Circuits on Motor Car

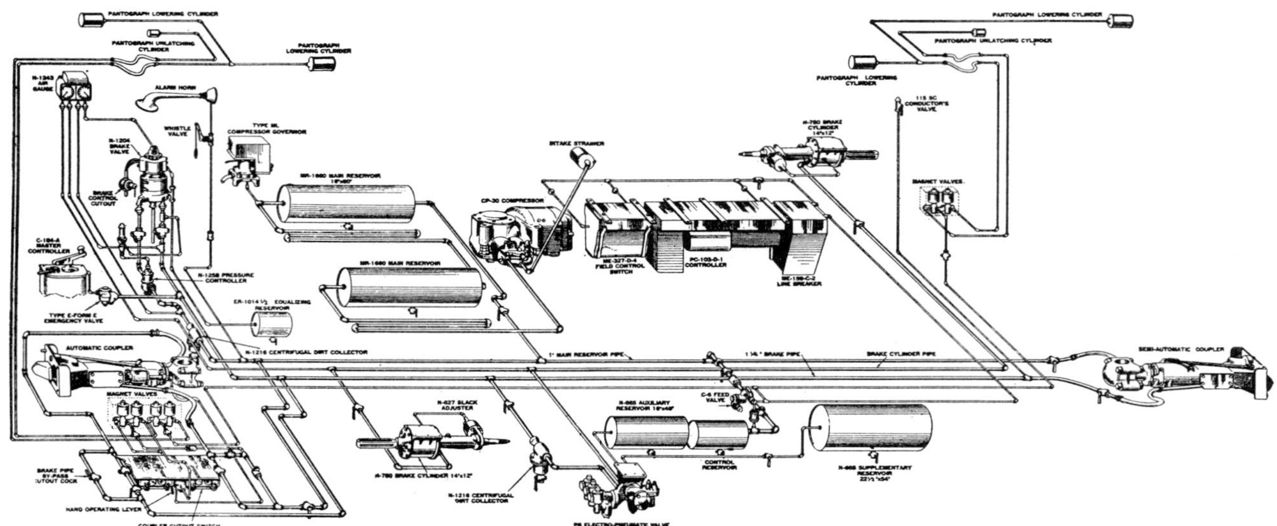

Fig. 9.   Diagram of Brake System Piping on Motor Car

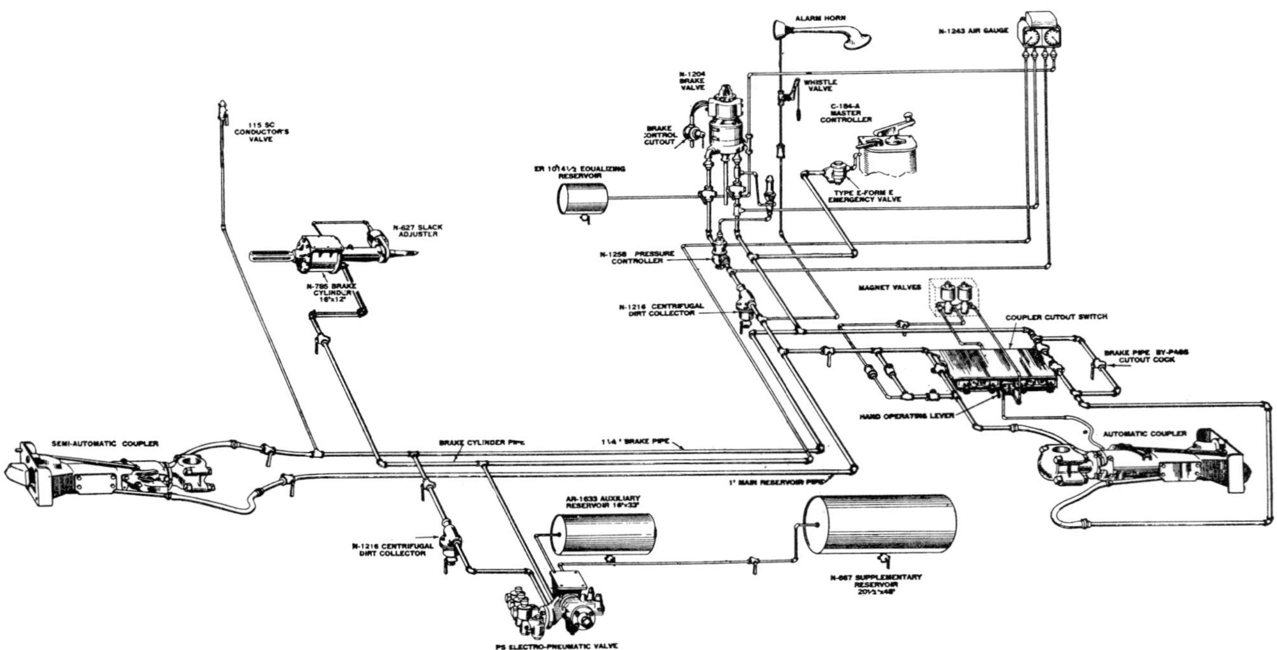

Fig. 10.   Diagram of Brake System Piping on Trailer Car

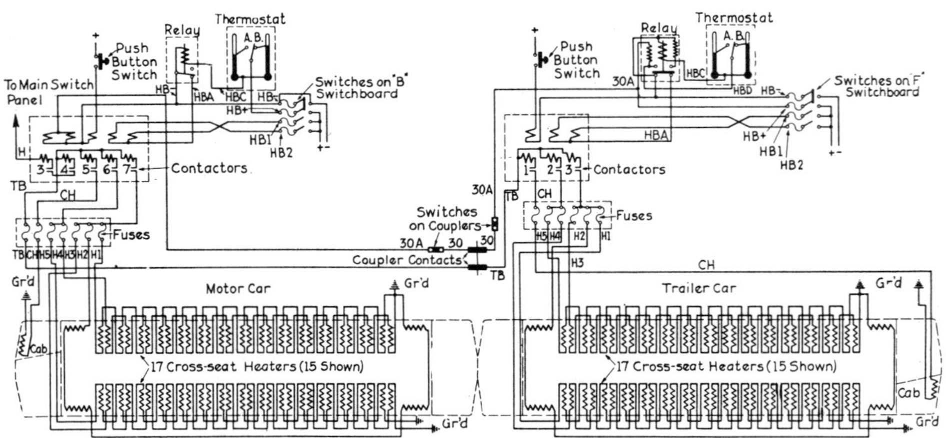

Fig. 11.   Car Heater and Heater Control Circuits for Two-car Multiple Unit Train

Railway Utility Company and contain Chromalox strips. The heater units are of the enclosed type in which the heating element is completely incased so that it is impossible for a passenger to come into contact with a live wire. The heater elements are connected in series for operation on 1500 volts and are controlled by thermostats on each car. Each thermostat has two cutting-out points, 50 degrees and 65 degrees. Current is transmitted to the trailer through the heater bus line which has two magnetic contactors in series with it. The control of these contactors is so interlocked with the couplers that it is

furnished by the General Electric Company. The arrangement of conduit under a car is shown in Fig. 12.

The cars have been inspected, passed and labeled by the Underwriters' Laboratories, Inc., as conforming to the rules and requirements of the National Board of Fire Underwriters.

Inspection and Testing of Electrical Equipment at Factory

The electrical car equipment furnished by the General Electric Company consisted of the control equipment, one-half of the traction motors, the

Fig. 12. Close-up View of Underneath Part of a Car, Showing the Arrangement of the Aluminum Conduit and Conduit Boxes

impossible to uncouple a trailer from a motor car and have the 1500-volt coupler contact alive. The heater and heater control circuits are shown in Fig. 11.

The bus line contactors above mentioned are mounted in a box under the motor car together with five other electro-magnetic contactors, one for the motor-generator, one for the air compressor, two for the car body heaters and one for the cab heater. In a similar box under the trailer are mounted three electro-magnetic contactors, two for the trailer car body heaters and one for the trailer cab heater.

All conduit, junction boxes and fittings are composed of an aluminum alloy, which reduces the weight of the new car approximately 6100 pounds as compared to one equipped with iron conduit and boxes. All wire on the motor cars except the control cable is Kerite. The trailer cars were wired with Okonite. All control cable and jumper cable was

air compressors, one-half of the heaters and the watthour meters. The Westinghouse Electric and Manufacturing Company furnished the balance of the traction motors. When the decision was reached to split the order for the traction motors, the two companies were directed to make the motors interchangeable insofar as truck application and speed curve were concerned. Each company manufactured a sample motor which was completely tested by the Illinois Central engineers in conjunction with the manufacturer's engineers, and the two samples compared by the Illinois Central engineers. The companies came within three per cent of the calculated speed curves and of each other, the motor of the General Electric Company being the faster of the two.

The first production motor of each company was also completely tested, and again they came within 3 per cent of the sample motor curves. Each motor after this was tested for speed, bearings, and high potential. Every fiftieth motor was given a complete test, including core and copper losses, speed curve in both directions, resistance of windings and heat runs. Special tests to determine stability against flashover were also taken. One typical set of control apparatus was given a complete test at the factory, including heat runs on all current-carrying parts and rupturing tests on the line breaker.

The motor-generator set was first built as a sample and completely tested under the same conditions and with the same regulating apparatus and storage batteries as were to be used on the cars, and after the sample set had been approved the first production set and each fiftieth set thereafter was completely tested. These tests included regulation, speed, heat runs, and susceptibility to flashover under normal and excess voltage conditions.

The air compressor being a standard machine, was produced under normal manufacturing conditions, the first and each fiftieth machine being tested for speed, heating, delivery of air, quality of air, and stability of motor against flashover under normal and excess voltage conditions.

The testing of all the apparatus in this manner made certain that the performance of the cars would be close to the calculated and desired performance. It was demonstrated later when the cars were operating that the knowledge gained from the preliminary tests was of inestimable value in finding troubles quickly and correcting them. It also helped when it came to designing the wiring on the cars so that trouble could be quickly isolated and repaired.

Inspection of Multiple Unit Cars

The motor cars were inspected in the Pullman Company shops by two groups of inspectors, one of whom followed the installation of electrical equipment, and the other the construction of the car bodies and trucks. The combined inspection force consisted of about 18 men.

At first the work consisted largely of inspecting and checking the steel work, riveting, etc. Great care was taken in inspecting the fit of the aluminum plates of which the roofs were constructed, and each roof was given a thorough water test to be sure that there were no leaks. As soon as the car bodies were completed they were sand-blasted. This work was inspected by the paint inspector to insure a perfectly smooth surface. The conduit was then installed and was carefully inspected to be sure that it was bent to fit properly before being strapped on, so that there would be no strains which might cause failure later. The ends of the conduits were properly reamed, and all sharp edges were removed. Couplings and elbows were inspected for cracks, and care was taken to see that all were tightly fitted. As the equipment was installed and wire pulled in, it was necessary to watch very closely to make sure that no splices were pulled into the conduit, and that the conduit was properly sponged out.

One inspector was detailed to the truck shop to witness the installation of the motors and the packing and oiling of the bearings.

As the interiors were completed they were given a thorough inspection. It was necessary for each window and each seat to slide easily, and each latch and lock to work smoothly before the car passed inspection. The paint and finish was made perfect on both the inside and the outside before it was accepted.

As soon as the installation of electrical apparatus was completed, the 1500-volt circuits, not including motors, were subjected to a high potential test of 5000 volts alternating current to ground for one minute. This test indicated any wires that had been cut or scraped in pulling them into the conduit. All apparatus was then given a thorough electrical test. Thirty-two volts were impressed on the low-voltage circuits, and air pressure was applied to the reservoirs and the controller was notched up, the pantographs were raised and lowered, the couplers were operated, the doors and door signals were tested and the brake magnet valves operated, and as each piece of apparatus was operated, a voltmeter was applied to the coupler contacts to see that each corresponding contact was respectively energized. As soon as the motor leads were connected, current was passed through the motors and grids and the I R drops were measured at the controller contactors across each bank of resistors and each motor field progressively from ground to determine if all motors were connected properly. Finally the insulation resistance of both the high- and the low-voltage circuits was measured by means of meggers. The 1500-volt insulation resistance was tested with a 2500-volt megger and a resistance of at least four megohms was required. The low-voltage insulation resistance was tested with a 1000-volt megger and it was required to show at least one megohm. Four megohms resistance were required between the high- and low-voltage circuits. In several cases where the insulation resistance was too low it was necessary to dry out the cars in a steam-heated room, which was very effective.

The method of inspection of the trailers at the factory in Hammond, Indiana, was similar to the methods used at Pullman.

Final and Running Tests of Completed Equipment and Instruction of Enginemen as Motormen

As the cars were delivered, they were taken to the Burnside Shops where the motor cars and trailers were connected together. After a final inspection, the units were taken to the test track, a piece of track approximately one and one-half miles long between Burnside and Kensington, which was set aside for breaking in the new cars. On the test track the pantographs were raised, the motor-generators and air compressors started and the pressure controllers and pump governors adjusted. If everything was all right the cars were started and tried in both directions, the necessary adjustments were made and the cars were run until they had made 250 miles or more. They were then turned back into Burnside where all defects not cleared on the track were taken care of. Later, after more track had been released for electric operation, these cars were taken out and run at high speed until they were passed by the inspector as being ready for service as far as bearings, main circuits, brakes, etc., were concerned. The cars were then returned to Burnside where the minor defects were taken care of, and the cars were cleaned and delivered to the yard ready for service.

The enginemen of the Illinois Central were offered the opportunity of going into the new electric service, and when it became apparent that they were all going into it the problem of their instruction arose.

Five engineers were selected as the most promising material for instructors, and these men were sent on a trip, accompanied by a technical engineer thoroughly familiar with the equipment and its operation, to visit railroads operating similar equipment.

In the meantime an instruction room had been built and the equipment installed to illustrate the action of the control, air brake and auxiliary equipment. The actual apparatus was used, but was exposed as much as possible and operated by air and electrical supply as it was expected to function on the car. Three diagram boards were set up, the first being a schematic one, intended to show the control and having small lights at each contactor, and fans to represent motors. This board was so connected that when the master controller was operated the fans revolved and the lights were illuminated as each circuit changed. The second diagram board showed all lighting circuits with actual lamps, including headlight, markers and all body lights. The actual switches used in the cars were set up adjacent to the diagram and operated the lights. The third diagram illustrated the door operation, and lights were used to show which doors were operated from the control stations.

The air brake rack included a motor car equipment complete with artificial train line and complete valve and reservoir equipment.

A typical pantograph, coupler, door engine, motor-generator and air compressor were installed and operated, and such equipment as magnet valves, lightning arresters, auxiliary and main switchboard panels were installed for viewing by the students.

In addition to the instruction room, an instruction book was compiled to assist the men in becoming familiar with the equipment. This included a complete description of all electrical and air equipment, the principles of operation, methods of handling in normal service, and the ways of locating some common troubles, together with photographs and diagrams showing the various pieces of apparatus and all of the electrical circuits.

After their return from the east, the instructors were taken to the car shops where the cars were under construction, and were thoroughly drilled on the operation of the equipment, so that by the time the first cars were delivered they were ready to go ahead with their running practice. As soon as the instructors were thoroughly broken in, the training course was worked out and the men started through.

The entire course was divided into eleven stages. Each stage covered a certain part of the work and required two hours' time. The first five stages were given in the instruction room, and the remaining six on the cars. In order to give everyone a chance to attend classes without losing time from their regular work, classes were conducted in the instruction room during two eight-hour shifts and on the cars for the entire twenty-four hours. The men were assigned to the classes by the traveling engineer, who gave each man an enrollment sheet which was filled out by the instructor for each stage attended. When a man had obtained an instructor's signature for each of the eleven stages, he would be assigned at the earliest opportunity for two days' additional experience running the cars which were being broken in. At the completion of the course each man had to pass a written examination successfully. In order to speed up the work, a complete two-car unit was located for several weeks at the round house where the men tied up. An instructor was stationed with it to answer questions and help the men as much as possible.

Inspection and Repair Shops for Illinois Central Electrification

Plan of Maintenance Routine—Location of Shops Fixed with Reference to Car Movement— Construction and Equipment of Light Inspection Shop—Construction and Equipment of Heavy Inspection Shop

By A. H. WOOLLEN

Equipment Engineer, Chicago Terminal Improvement

THE inspection and repair facilities required for the electric operation of suburban service were designed and built on the basis of a system of light inspection every 1500 miles, heavy inspection every 6000 miles or every fourth light inspection, and overhauling at from one year to eighteen months, estimated to be from 35,000 to 53,000 miles.

Light Inspection Shop

The light inspection of multiple unit cars is accomplished during the off peak day period when approximately 75 per cent of the cars are stored in the vicinity of the downtown terminals. It was estimated that approximately 4½ hours would be required for doing this work, and in order to get over all of the cars every two weeks, or approximately every 1500 miles, a light inspection shop capable of holding 24 cars was designed and built in a location near 18th Street. This shop is long enough to accommodate a complete 6-car train and is four tracks wide. Its general arrangement is shown in Fig. 1.

The shop is constructed of a steel frame of the pre-manufactured building type covered with corrugated galvanized iron sheathing and lined with celotex as a heat insulator. The floor is constructed of concrete, with four concrete pits running the length of the building. The floor is depressed 10 in. and the track laid on bridge timbers laid on top of the concrete pits. The pit design, as well as the general layout of the building is shown in Fig. 2. There is a lean-to on the east side of the building which accommodates a light machine shop, office, wash and locker rooms, toilets, storehouse and heating plant. Each track door consists of a sliding hinge door which is opened manually from the ground. Sufficient pass doors are installed in the main doors to permit entrance and exit without opening the latter.

The building is equipped with a so-called "trolley bug" to enable the cars to be moved in the shop under their own power, and to permit testing of 1500-volt

A. H. WOOLLEN

apparatus on the cars. This device consists of a small car to which is attached a long flexible cable terminating in a suitable hook designed to engage one of the car pantograph horns. It was appreciated that the use of 1500 volts was unwise in a shop unless special provision for the protection of employees was made, and an auxiliary control circuit was installed which is operated by a push-button on the handle of the hook engaging the pantograph. By this means the main trolley rails are energized through a car type line breaker only when the control circuit is energized by the man handling the hook stick. This device has worked very satisfactorily, and it appears that it is going to give good service during a long life. Special graded T-irons were installed in each track door to permit the pantograph to ride in or out of the shop without damage, and subsequent operation has proved this to be a desirable feature. In several instances pantographs were accidently raised as trains were leaving the shop, and in every case the T-iron saved the pantograph from injury. It will be noted in Fig. 2 that inspection platforms are installed the length of the shop to permit ready access to the roof of the cars. These platforms make a handy place to install the trolley bug.

The building is heated by the unit system, drawing air from the floor and passing it over heated pipes to discharge vents halfway up the height of the building. This method was not absolutely satisfactory during the cold weather as the heat tends to pocket in the roof of the building and when the large doors are opened the main floor becomes cold. It is planned to reverse the direction of the air through these heaters, experiment having demonstrated that such a change will cure this condition.

Suitable outlets for compressed air, water, 440-volt, 3-phase, 60-cycle power, and 110-volt, single-phase, 60-cycle lighting circuits are installed at regular intervals throughout the shop.

This shop is of a temporary nature, and at a later date, probably when the new Central Station is built, a permanent light inspection shop will be built at or near the present steam locomotive facilities at 27th Street.

Heavy Inspection Shop

The heavy inspection of multiple unit cars was provided for in connection with annual overhauling facilities at the Burnside Shops by the addition of a new building of a permanent nature, erected in the

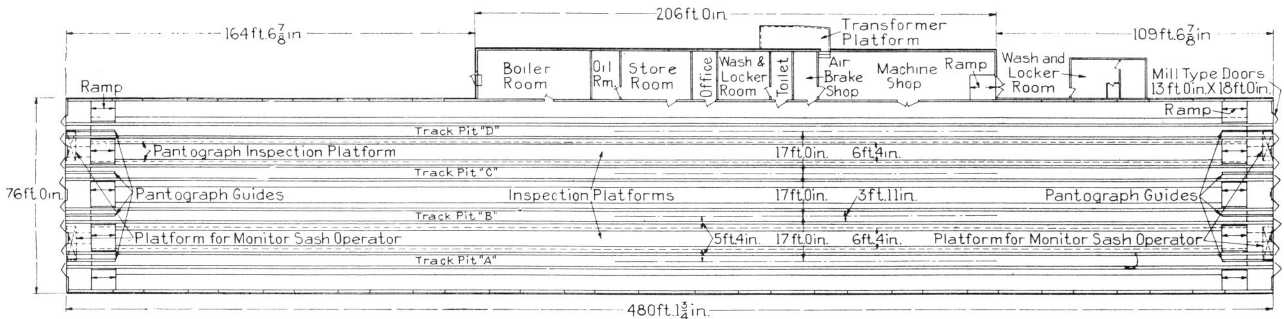

Fig. 1.   Floor Plan of Light Inspection Shop at 18th St.

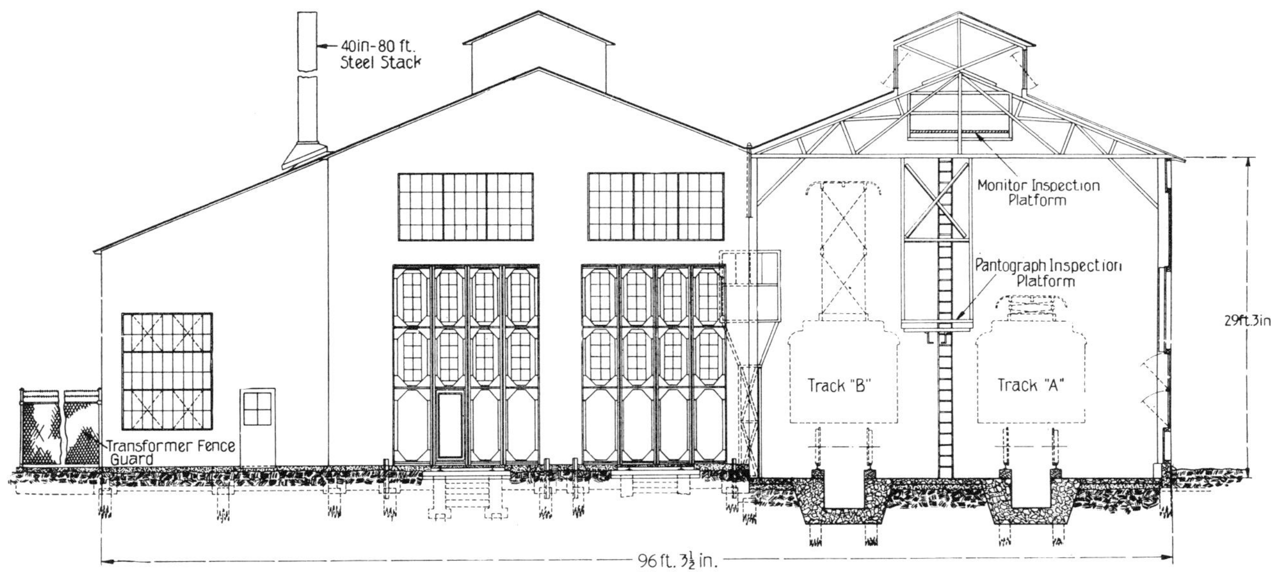

Fig. 2.   Elevation of Light Inspection Shop

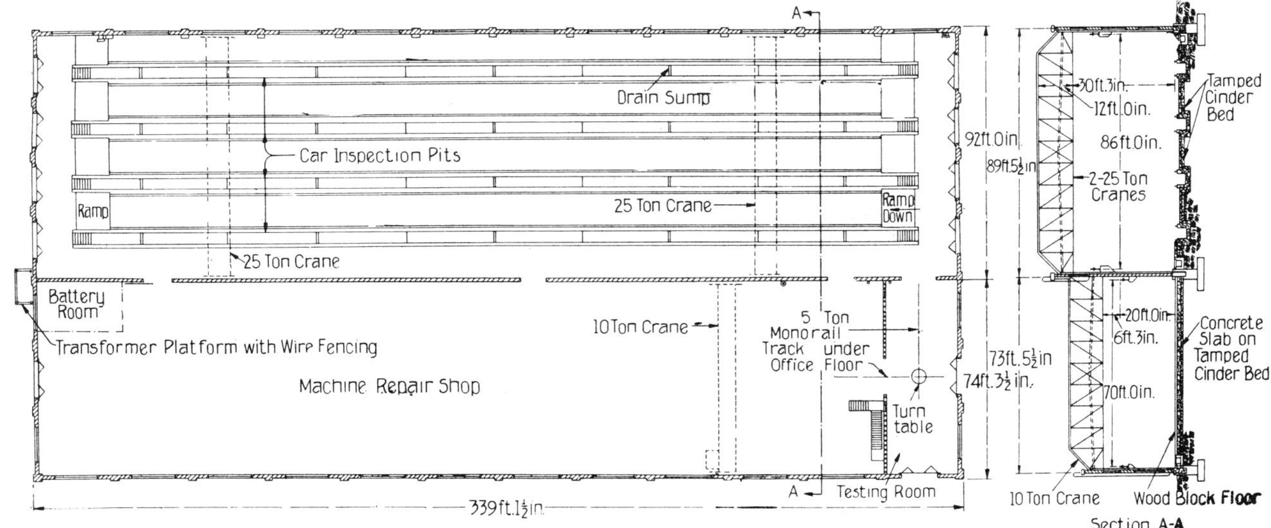

Fig. 3.   Plan and Elevation of Heavy Inspection Shop

Fig. 4. Exterior of Light Inspection Shop

Fig. 6. Exterior of Heavy Inspection Shop

Fig. 5. Interior of Light Inspection Shop

Fig. 7. Interior of Heavy Inspection Shop

Burnside Shop Yard. This building, which consists of an inspection shop having a capacity of 16 cars and a repair shop, is intended, for the present, to take care of all such work as heavy inspection, stripping and assembling of the cars, and repairs to the electrical equipment such as main motors, motor-generators, air compressors, control apparatus, pantographs, etc. Car body work, truck work and wheel work is being taken care of in the regular departments of the Burnside shops for passenger car repairs, and it is the intention to carry this scheme through the first three or four years of operation. At a somewhat later date a stripping shop, assembling shop, truck shop,

auxiliary hoists. A 10-ton, 3-motor crane was installed in the repair shop portion. A special feature of the cranes in the inspection shop consisted of placing the control cages on the trolleys so that they would move with them and enable the operator to see down between the aisles of cars. This has proved an excellent arrangement and has speeded up the work and assisted in the prevention of accidents. The shop is provided with indirect unit heating and with the necessary lighting and power plugs and air and water service. The pit tracks are elevated from the main floor so as to permit access to the underside of the car.

Fig. 8.   Storage Yard at 18th Street

blacksmith shop and wheel shop are planned for addition to the inspection and repair shop unit above mentioned.

It is proposed to cover the heavy inspection of multiple unit cars every two months, the work to be done in approximately 16 hours. Capacity was provided that would enable all of the cars to be inspected every two months and also to allow track and pit space for assembling and stripping. This capacity should be sufficient up to 1935, after which time an extension of the inspection shop, duplicating the unit now used, will be built.

The shop consists of a steel framework with brick walls, concrete floors and four 4-car pits. The arrangement is shown in Fig. 3. A testing room for all apparatus was laid out in one end of the repair shop and office space provided above this testing room for the Maintenance Department having charge of the cars. Provision was made in the electrical repair shop for electrical repairs to passenger car apparatus in regular main line service, and for the maintenance of all storage batteries used on the system. The inspection shop was provided with crane service consisting of two 25-ton, 4-motor electric cranes with 5-ton

Additional Facilities

Additional facilities were necessary in the form of small buildings at each night tie-up point to enable electricians, and air brake men to have a place to keep supplies, have telephone connection with headquarters, and locker space.

The cars are tied up at five points as follows:

83rd Street Yard............................48 cars
South Chicago..............................32 cars

These will be combined at 83rd Street in the near future:

Kensington Coach Yard..................... 32 cars
Blue Island Coach Yard.................... 20 cars
Matteson Coach Yard...................... 12 cars
Van Buren Coach Yard..................... 60 cars

Inspectors inspect the cars as they come in at night and look over air brakes, pantographs, heaters and doors. The shop is equipped so that minor repairs can be made or the lighter apparatus and pantograph wearing strips replaced.

It is hoped that these inspections can be abandoned after a year, when the cars are thoroughly broken in and the troubles due to apparatus design cease. It is believed that routine inspection as planned will take care of the situation.

The Signal System of the Illinois Central Chicago Terminal

Method of Obtaining Signal Power Supply—Location and Grouping of Signal Lights Carefully Planned—Details of the Track Circuit Layout—Design and Operation of the Control System Possesses Interesting Features—Operation of Interlocking Stations

By H. G. MORGAN

Signal Engineer, Illinois Central Railroad

THE improvement of the Chicago Terminal made necessary many changes in the existing signal system. Hall disk signals operated from storage batteries located at each signal bridge had been in service since the time of the World's Fair. These batteries were charged periodically by small motor-generator sets. The track circuits were operated by primary batteries.

Preparatory to the extensive changes in grade and alignment of tracks, color-light signals (Fig. 1) were substituted for the disk signals and the motor-generator sets were replaced by mechanical rectifiers. The signal lamps were operated from temporary power connections from suburban stations or other available alternating-current supply, using a cut-over relay to switch the lamps to the storage battery as a reserve. Storage batteries were used for track circuits where it was convenient to locate them with the other batteries in temporary housings. Polarized track relays were used where line circuits could not be maintained. By these means uninterrupted service was provided through a series of track and signal relocations when no permanent arrangement was possible.

The decision to electrify the terminal at 1500 volts direct current determined the use of 60-cycle alternating current for the operation of the permanent signals. The fundamental requirement of any automatic signal system is that a failure of any sort on account of interruption of power, stray foreign current, broken rail, broken wire, or other defects of apparatus will result in the signals immediately displaying their stop indication. The design of all the apparatus involved has been made with this fundamental requirement in view.

Power Supply

Electrical energy for the operation of the portion of the signal system north of Riverdale is supplied by the Commonwealth Edison Co., from three widely separated generating stations. South of Riverdale

H. G. MORGAN

the power supply is furnished by the Public Service Company of Northern Illinois from two generating stations. This energy is taken from the 12,000-volt, 60-cycle, three-phase underground tie lines at each of the substations, located about six miles apart along the right-of-way, and stepped down by delta-star transformation for three-phase four-wire 4000/2300-volt light and power supply with grounded neutral.

One-to-one insulating transformers are connected to one phase of the light and power buses and serve the signal transmission lines which are in duplicate for the main tracks. On the South Chicago Branch only one single-phase line is provided but one phase of the three-phase light and power line is used for auxiliary service. The transmission wires are No. 1 A.W.G. solid copper, carried on crossarms mounted on the catenary structures, and sectionalized at each substation.

At signal locations, a 2300/110-volt distributing transformer is connected to each transmission line, and the signal load is connected to either transformer through an automatic power switching relay so arranged that the load is normally taken from one set of feeders. By the de-energizing of that set of feeders, or the local transformer, the load cuts over automatically to the duplicate service and also automatically restores to the original source when that line is again energized. A lamp connected in each supply circuit indicates at all times whether the supply lines are alive.

In event of a failure of the power supply through any substation, power is fed from an adjacent substation. This switching is done manually under direction of the Power Supervisor.

The lines are equipped with induction voltage regulators installed in the substations, and the system is adequately protected with electrolytic lightning arresters at each substation. Individual distributing transformers are protected by pellet-type or oxide-film lightning arresters.

The signal power requirements during the first stage of electrification total about 115 kv-a. The one-to-one insulating transformers have a total kv-a. capacity nearly double the normal load to provide for emergency loading of substations.

Signals

With first consideration for the safety of passengers, studies were made of roadway, signal equipment and train-operating characteristics so that signals might be located to provide maximum carrying capacity of the railroad. These elements included profile and alignment of the right-of-way, location of stations and interlocking plants, accelerating and braking rates and the normal and maximum attainable speeds on various grades for all types of equipment to be operated, as well as the visibility of the signals, the simplicity of the scheme of aspects displayed by the signals, and the indications which they convey.

Between Homewood and Richton, existing automatic signal bridges have been retained. North of Homewood the signals are mounted on cages

are burned at twenty per cent under their rated voltage in the daytime and to reduce the intensity of signal lights at night the voltage is reduced one-half by means of relays, controlled from the nearest tower. Current is supplied to the lamps from individual transformers in the signal case, or in a box adjacent to the signal. If one filament burns out, the fact may be detected and the lamp replaced without a failure resulting. These lamps are rebased at the signal

Fig. 1.   Temporary Color-light Signals Used During the Construction Period

repair shop to insure a proper focus without adjustment or realignment when renewing a lamp.

The indications displayed by the signals are red for "stop," meaning that the immediate block is occupied; yellow for "caution," meaning that the second block is occupied; green for "clear," meaning that two or more blocks are unoccupied.

In the automatic signals the three units are arranged in a vertical row with green at the top, yellow in the middle, and red at the bottom. Only one of these lights can be illuminated at one time.

In contrast to the automatic block signals, the home signals at interlocking plants display two or three lights in a vertical row to indicate which route is set up and whether or not the track ahead is occupied. A triangular combination of the units is used where three colors are displayed and a horizontal arrangement for two colors only. The red units are in a vertical row at the left side of each group, the yellow units in a vertical row at the right side of each group, and the green units are at the bottom of the triangular combinations. Thus a yellow or green light displayed by one signal is more distinctive on account of its being slightly out of the

Fig. 2.   Combined Signal and Catenary Bridge Showing Four Automatic Signals, Signal Transformers, Relay Box, Signal Control Cable, and Impedance Bond Between the Rails

suspended from combined signal and catenary structures as shown in Fig. 2. On the South Chicago Branch they are attached to the columns of the catenary structures with suitable platform and ladder arrangement.

The new signals are the three indication Union Style "R" color-light type, equipped with 8⅜-inch doublet lenses and 10-volt, 18-watt, double-filament lamps which are rated at 1500 hours life. The lamps vertical line of the other two red lights. This arrangement, Fig. 3, permits a closer spacing of the three lights, thus preventing the top light from being obscured by the catenary structures and allowing a satisfactory close-up indication from the top light.

Block spacing for high speed has been arranged so that the minimum length of block is, approximately, the maximum braking distance, plus a factor of

Fig. 3. Home Signal Bridge, Showing the Arrangement of Interlocking Signals

safety of fifty per cent. Block spacings at the south end of the terminal are as long as 5000 feet and diminish gradually toward the north as speed and headway are reduced. North of 67th Street block spacings for through passenger and freight tracks average 3100 feet; for express and special suburban tracks 2040 feet; for local suburban tracks 2500 feet. This permits express and special suburban trains to run under clear signals, with $1\frac{1}{4}$ minutes headway; and local suburban trains with three minutes headway. Where local conditions require blocks shorter than braking distance, the caution indication is given by two signals in the rear of a stop signal.

Track Circuits

The limits of a track circuit are established by insulated joints in the rails. All track circuits are a full block long except within interlocking plant limits. Energy is supplied at one end of each track circuit by an air-cooled transformer equipped with taps to permit of fine voltage adjustment. An adjustable reactor or resistor is connected in series between one side of the track transformer and one rail, the object of

which is; first, to establish the proper phase relation in the track relay connected to the rails at the far end of the track circuit; and second, to limit the flow of current and prevent the short-circuiting of the transformer when a train is on the track circuit.

The track relay is of the two-element, two-position, vane type. An aluminum vane is propelled between two cores by the force of currents in two windings, one energized locally, and the other through the track circuit. The major part of the required energy is taken from a local bus and only a small part from the track, therefore, the relay is comparatively economical in its consumption of energy.

Track connections are made through single conductor parkway cables buried two feet below the base of the rail. Beneath the rail a vertical riser of wood trunking brings the wire up to a cross piece of trunking forming the bootleg in which the parkway cable is spliced to No. 9 stranded wire which connects to each side of the rail.

On electrified tracks it is necessary to provide a means of carrying the propulsion current around the insulated joints. An impedance bond with an iron core, having three terminals, one from each end of the coil and one from the middle of the winding, is mounted between ties in the center of the track at each end of a track circuit as shown in Fig. 4. The end terminals are connected to the rails with copper cables of 300,000 cir. mils cross section, by means of lugs welded to the rails. The middle terminal is connected to a similar terminal of the bond in the next track circuit. The coil connected across the track offers an impedance of 0.70 ohm to the 60-cycle signal current; but the direct current used for propulsion, entering both ends of the coil and passing out through the middle

Fig. 4. Double Impedance Bond Layout

terminal to the next impedance bond, does not create any reactance in the coil; the only resistance to the propulsion current, therefore, is ohmic. These bonds have a continuous carrying capacity of 500 amperes with a capacity of 900 amperes for thirty minutes and 1500 amperes for five minutes. An air gap in the iron core permits an unbalancing current of 150 amperes without seriously affecting the impedance of the bond.

Since the first stage of electrification does not include other than the suburban tracks, only those tracks whose rails are required for return are equipped with impedance bonds and rail bonds for the propulsion current. South of 69th Street, this includes only the electrified tracks but north of 69th Street, all tracks are bonded to reduce the drop in potential and prevent the electrolysis of lead-covered cables and water pipes along the right-of-way. Those tracks not used for return of the propulsion current have rails bonded with ordinary galvanized iron signal bond wires.

To avoid the use of a large number of impedance bonds on the short track circuits through interlocking plants one rail only is bonded for the return propulsion current and the other rail is bonded for signal current. On these single-rail track circuits a special relay is used, designed to operate with a resistance in series

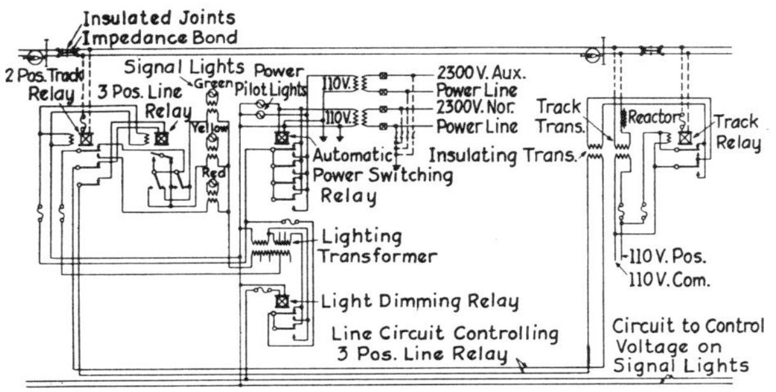

Fig. 5. Diagram of Signal Control Circuits, Showing Duplicate Power Supply Transformers, Relays, and Connections to Signal Lights

with its track winding, and another resistance in series with the secondary of the track transformer to limit the strength of the direct currents which may be forced through its coils due to the propulsion drop in voltage along the return rail.

The polarities of all adjacent track circuits are reversed so that, in case of the failure of an insulated rail joint, the current from the track transformer entering the relay of an adjacent track circuit will reverse the torque in the relay and cause the signal to indicate "stop."

Catenary structures are grounded to alternate rails, except at signal locations, where they are grounded to the neutral connection of the impedance bonds. Cross-bonding of tracks is done between neutral connections of the impedance bonds, at alternate signal locations. Signal and telephone cable messengers are grounded at crossbond locations, and insulated at other points.

Signal Controls

South of 80th Street and on the South Chicago Branch signal control circuits are carried in braided aerial cables, suspended from messengers attached to the catenary structures. Control wires are No. 14 A.W.G. copper, with 4/64-inch wall Kerite insulation. Cables are terminated on standard terminal blocks, in specially designed cast-iron terminal boxes, mounted at the top of the columns which support the catenary

structure. North of 80th Street control circuits are carried in an underground conduit. Braided cables are used and terminated in moisture-proof cast-iron terminal boxes installed in the manholes and handholes. Conductors are No. 14 A.W.G. copper with 5/64-inch wall Kerite insulation.

On account of possible auto-transformer action through the impedance bonds, it is not safe to use a three-position or polarized track relay on electrified roads, therefore a three-position two-element vane-type line relay is used to govern the signal aspect as between the "caution" indication and the "proceed" indication to provide advance information to the approaching motorman. The line circuit passes through the contacts of the track relay and is subject to change in polarity. Fig. 5 shows the connections of the signal control system.

The functioning of the contacts for the control of the signal is as follows: when a train enters the block the track relay is de-energized and the moving member assumes a position by gravity so that a set of front contacts are open and a set of back contacts are closed. The red unit of the signal is then lighted through the back contacts. As soon as the train passes on into the next block the above track relay becomes energized, closing the front contacts and opening the back contacts. This immediately puts out the red signal light and energizes the line relay in one polarity, closing one set of contacts which light the yellow unit of the signal. When the train passes into the third block the polarity of the line circuit is reversed and the moving member of the line relay reverses its position, opening the first set of contacts which puts out the yellow light and closing a second set of contacts which light the green unit of the signal.

Each line relay has the controlled element energized through an insulating transformer which limits the length of each circuit to one block and maintains a high dielectric strength in the circuit. The secondary winding of the insulating transformer has 1800 ohms resistance to produce proper phase displacement in the relay and to provide protection against the effect of crosses or grounds. The system is also immune to induction since all adjacent wires in the signal control cable are parallel and connected together through transformers or relays and any inductive effect upon one line is compensated for by the inductive effect upon the adjacent line. The line relay has also a neutral, or bridging, contact to light the yellow signal unit and avoid a train stop in case of an open line circuit.

The signal control apparatus is housed in wooden relay boxes mounted on the columns of the catenary structures as shown in Fig. 6. Owing to limited clearances between tracks these boxes are high and narrow. They are made of pine covered all over with galvanized iron and are equipped with double doors to keep out dust and snow.

Connections from relay boxes to manholes or handholes are made through five- and seven-conductor parkway cables. The wiring on all signal bridges is carried in galvanized iron conduits, 2½ inch being used for main runs and 1¼ inch for leads to signals. Crouse-Hinds condulets are used at all turns and outlets. Flexible conduit is installed between the rigid conduit and the signal case to permit alignment of the signal to suit the track conditions.

Switches

All hand-thrown switches, which must be lighted at night, are equipped with electric lanterns lighted by a 110-volt, 10-watt lamp. Lighting wires are carried in duplex parkway cable to the nearest catenary structure where they are tapped to conductors in a miscellaneous aerial cable from the nearest signal bridge. The parkway cable terminates in a cast-iron junction box mounted on a concrete riser, and the wires are carried up the switch stand to the lantern in ½-inch double-strip flexible conduit.

Two switch circuit controllers are connected to each facing point switch and one to each trailing switch to shunt the track circuit and set the signal to the "stop" indication, when the switch is thrown from its normal position. The wires leading from the rails to the switch circuit controllers are carried in single-conductor parkway cables.

Interlocking Stations

In connection with track changes incident to electrification, new electric interlocking plants have been built at 51st Street, 67th Street, Homewood and Richton. The existing electric interlocking plant at Kensington has been enlarged. Grade separation has eliminated old interlocking plants at 43d Street, 67th Street, Burnside, Blue Island Junction, Riverdale, Harvey and two at Matteson. A small electro-mechanical plant has been constructed at Burnside to control movements between track No. 1 and Burnside Yard. New interlocking plants will be constructed at 16th Street, Eighth Street and Randolph Street as further terminal development requires.

The most extensive interlocking work was done at 67th Street where the connection to the South Chicago Branch is now made through a tunnel. The original mechanical interlocking plant was first supplanted by a temporary electric interlocking plant, with a temporary tower on the east side of the right-of-way. Two second-hand machines with a total of 112 levers were installed to handle the movements of trains over temporary tracks and switches during the construction of the under-crossing. This in turn was supplanted by a permanet electric plant with a brick tower on the west side of the right-of-way (Fig. 7).

The permanent plant is 3645 feet long and controls 17 switches, 2 single slip ends, 36 double slip ends and 19 movable point frogs. A model 2 improved unit

lever type electric interlocking machine having 176 spaces was installed with 123 working levers. The levers are equipped with circuit controllers, indication magnets, electric locks and vertical locking tappets which are notched to engage horizontal locking bars in such a way that the levers may be operated only in a predetermined order so as to prevent the setting up of conflicting routes or the clearing of opposing signals.

Fig. 6. Relay Box Housing the Control Apparatus for Two Tracks, Including Power Switching Relay, Dimming Relay, Lighting Transformers, and Two Insulating Transformers on the Top Shelf; Line Relay, Track Relay, Track Transformer, and Reactor for each Track on the Lower Shelves

The switches are lined up first and then the signal is cleared, the signal lever locking all the switch levers in the route it governs.

The track circuits and signals are operated by alternating current as described in a preceding paragraph. The signals are controlled through direct-current relays which are operated from the interlocking machine. The switch machines are operated by direct current which is delivered from a 110-volt storage battery charged continuously by a motor-generator.

In addition to the mechanical locking in the machine, routes are controlled, interlocking levers are locked and switches are locked electrically by the presence of a train upon a given track circuit controlling a track relay which in turn interrupts the circuits of such locks, making them effective (Fig. 8).

Another important safety feature is the means provided to check the correspondence of movement between a lever and the switch or signal controlled by it. In the case of switch levers this requirement is met by means of a momentary dynamic current generated by the momentum of the motor of the operated switch which gives the desired indication at the lever end of the circuit when the switch has completed its movement. Signal lever indicating magnets are energized by

Fig. 7. Permanent Interlocking Tower at 67th St., Showing the Electric Interlocking Machine, Clock-work Time Releases, Spot-light Track Diagram, and the Manipulation Charts

110-volt alternating current received through a back contact of the control relay as soon as the signal displays the stop indication.

Each switch is arranged to reverse the polarity of a polarized relay according to whether the switch

Fig. 8. Double Slip Switch Layout, Showing the Electric Switch and the Lock Movements and Fittings

points are in the full normal or full reverse position, and every signal governing train movements over the switch is controlled through the polar contacts of this relay to assure that a route is set up before the signal can be cleared.

The position of trains is indicated to the towerman on a track diagram on which small spot-lights mark the occupied sections of track, both within the plant limits and approaching the plant. As soon as a train reaches the approach circuit the route lined up is locked automatically and can be taken away only by the use of a clock-work time release which requires an elapse of one minute after the home signal has been set against the train. If the train should pass the home signal the route is then locked the full distance ahead through the sectional route locking but the switches are released behind the train as each section is passed. A detector lock circuit for each switch loops through the track relay of the section in which the switch is located to prevent the throwing of the switch under a train. Route and section locking may be released in case of emergency by breaking a seal on a special releasing device which must be restored to normal before the signals can be cleared again. Each signal control circuit is protected against crosses by an individual polarized relay, and the plant is equipped with a ground detector.

The general construction is similar at the other interlocking stations. The plant at Richton controls 36 switches and three derails. This is the southern end of the terminal, and is the end of the six-track and the beginning of the four-track system. The plant is 4050 feet long. The interlocking plant at Homewood governs switches at the south entrance to Markham Yard.

At Kensington the plant governs the junction of the Michigan Central, the Chicago, South Shore and South Bend Railway, and the Blue Island Branch with the main line. This plant is 5350 feet long and includes 27 switches, 17 derails, 8 single slip ends, 10 double slip ends and 14 movable point frogs.

The 51st Street plant includes nine switches for the four-track, six-track suburban connections and the freight connection with the Chicago Junction Railway.

Plans, specifications, and material requisitions for the construction of all the interlocking plants, as well as the automatic signals were prepared by the Illinois Central Signal Department and the work was installed by local electrical contractors under the supervision of the Signal Engineer.